A BANKER'S SECRET

OUR MORTGAGE IS A GREAT INVESTMENT

MARC EISENSON

For Robin, Sharon, and Adam

A Banker's Secret is published by:

GOOD ADVICE PRESS
Box 78
Elizaville, NY 12523

Library of Congress Catalog Card No. 89-2007

Cover design by Avis Kalman

Library of Congress Cataloging-in-Publication Data:
Eisenson, Marc, 1943-
A banker's secret : your mortgage is a great investment / Marc Eisenson.
p. cm.
ISBN 0-943973-05-8 : $9.95
1. Mortgage loans--United States. 2. Interest--Tables.
3. Prepayment of debts--United States. I. Title.
HG2040 . 5 . U6E57 1989
332.1'753--dc19

89-2007
CIP
ISBN # 0-943973-05-8

TABLE OF CONTENTS

PART THREE: PRE-PAYMENT TABLES

PART FOUR: APPENDICES

LIST OF FIGURES

PREFACE

If you're looking at *A Banker's Secret* for the first time, the quantity of charts, tables, and numbers may scare you. Don't panic! By the time you've read the first 5 paragraphs of the INTRODUCTION, you'll realize just how powerful and easy the *Banker's Secret Pre-Payment System* can be. A few more pages, and perhaps you'll want to kick yourself for not having invested in your mortgage all along!

If you have a mortgage -- or virtually any other loan -- you can benefit from our system, starting right now. Savings of $30,000, and more, are not at all unusual. I know this sounds like a "get rich quick" scheme, but I personally GUARANTEE that the *Banker's Secret Pre-Payment System* works. It's been recommended in many well respected financial publications, and we've already helped tens of thousands of families to begin their own money saving programs.

There's no reason to keep your family enslaved in debt for 30 years, while you pay the bank back 3 or 4 times the mortgage money you borrowed. We're going to show you a really easy, painless way for you to build up your net worth, by keeping a lot more of your hard earned money right where it belongs ... in your own pocket.

I truly believe that *A Banker's Secret* is one of those simple, but powerful ideas that really can make a difference in your life. It did in mine.

While I ultimately take either the credit, or blame, for every thing in this book, there are many others who helped make this project a success. Special thanks to: Hekmat Abasi, Nancy Castleman, Harry Lazare, Tom Lococo, Rose Morrison, and Sylvia Smith. I'm forever in their debt ... the only kind of debt I find pleasant to incur.

I hope you'll soon be well on your way to living debt free -- in the usual sense of the word. There's a lot to be said for financial independence!

Marc Eisenson
Elizaville, New York

INTRODUCTION

When you take out a loan, you agree to pay back the amount borrowed plus interest. That's fair. But you've probably never realized just how much that interest can be. For example, on a $75,000, 30 year mortgage, written at 10% interest, the total payback will be almost $237,000. That's nearly $162,000 in interest charges on a $75,000 loan. **More than twice what was borrowed!** Shocking, isn't it?

Well, take heart. If you make small investments in your mortgage -- as little as $25 each month -- you'll save more than $34,000 in interest on that $75,000 example, and you'll reduce the loan's term by over 5 years. Just $100 a month, and you'll end up $78,000 richer ... 12.5 years sooner!

All it takes is an occasional check for slightly more than your usual mortgage payment. Sound easy? It is! But sadly, few homeowners take advantage of the dramatic savings that small *pre-payments*[1] can bring. Myths about bank rules, tax deductions, pre-payment penalties, and the supposed advantages of deficit living keep most borrowers from reaping the dramatic savings small mortgage pre-payments do produce.

That's why we've written *A Banker's Secret*. In the next few pages, we'll show you step-by-step exactly how pre-paying works and why it will save *you* tens of thousands of dollars. If you're anything like the rest of us, you could use that money. So why *give* an extra $34,000 or more to your bank?

Pre-paying is available to most of us, is easy to understand, fun to use, and can be a powerful investment tool, saving you extraordinary sums of money ... while dramatically reducing your term of indebtedness. In fact, the only difficult thing about pre-paying is understanding how such a good idea could have been kept "a banker's secret" for so long.

Whether you've been paying off your home loan for years, are just shopping for your first mortgage, or are refinancing, PART ONE will show you how easy it is to reap the benefits of "pocket change" pre-payments. As Figure #1 makes clear for

---

1. Pre-payment and other mortgage related terms are defined in the appended *Glossary*. A pre-payment is **not** an extra cost, but rather, a payment made in advance of its due date.

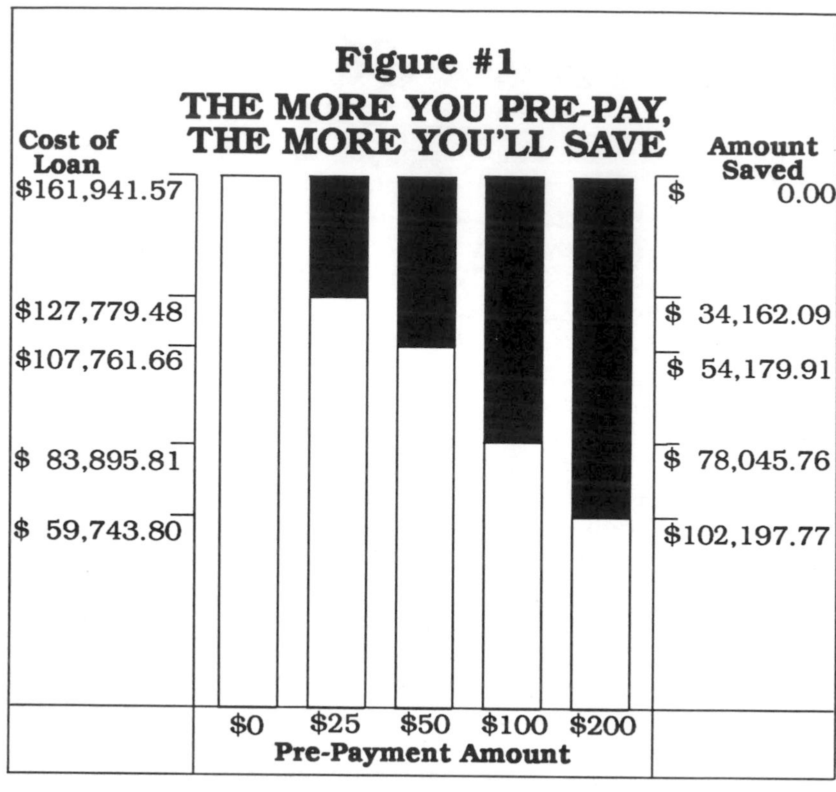

the typical $75,000 loan mentioned above, it really doesn't take large pre-payments to effect great savings. In Figure #1, the white sections indicate the total interest cost of this loan, while the black sections represent the savings in interest that pre-payments ranging from $25 to $200 will produce. For example, pre-pay $200 a month, and you'll reduce your interest cost from $161,941.57 to $59,743.80, leaving you $102,197.77 richer than had you not pre-paid.

In PART TWO, we've tried to answer all the questions you might have -- about taxes, pre-payment penalties, and so on. PART THREE includes 160 tables that will make it easy for you to figure out how much time and money you can save by pre-paying. PART FOUR contains a *Glossary* of mortgage terms, as well as step-by-step instructions for making basic pre-payment calculations. **However, you need not understand math to benefit from pre-paying.**

PART ONE: INSTRUCTIONS

WHY PRE-PAYING SAVES SO MUCH

We'll be using the $75,000 mortgage that we mentioned in the INTRODUCTION as our example throughout this book. We'll show you how making small, frequent pre-payments with pocket change -- that money most of us would *never* invest, notice, or miss -- will save a substantial portion of the nearly $162,000 in interest that this $75,000 loan would normally incur. But first we'll explain why pre-paying works.

Each month, the bank computes the interest due on the *outstanding balance* of your loan. Pre-paying shrinks that balance -- and therefore reduces your interest charge. Once your balance drops, of course, it stays that way. Advance payments stop the bank from collecting compound interest on the amount you pre-pay, not just once, but month after month ... year after year.

In short, pre-paying saves you the compound interest that you will never have to pay. **By pre-paying, you invest nothing extra to save thousands. Pre-payments are not additional costs. They are simply small amounts paid sooner.**

PRE-PAYMENT SCHEDULES

Every month, or whenever you are expected to make a payment to your lender (for convenience we'll assume all borrowers are homeowners and all lenders are banks), the bank's computer calculates the amount of interest you owe (for having used its money during the previous month), and subtracts that interest from the amount of your check. The difference is credited towards the outstanding balance of your loan. To make it easy to keep track of how much interest you are being charged and how much of each payment is being credited towards the principal of your loan, it is necessary to use an appropriate *prepayment schedule.* These computer printed charts, often referred to as *amortization* schedules, separate out the interest and principal components of each monthly payment, along with the balance remaining after each payment has been made.

Samples of the various styles of schedules we individually prepare for our clients appear throughout this book. We designed them to make it easy to keep a running tally of your savings and to make sure that your bank is properly crediting your pre-payments. Soon you'll learn which schedule will best suit your personal needs.

YOUR MORTGAGE IS A GREAT INVESTMENT

Figure #2 is a partial pre-payment schedule showing the first and last 5 payments for our sample loan. By referring to it as you read the next few paragraphs, you'll quickly see just how powerful an investment your mortgage can be. Notice that even though each monthly payment (except the last) remains constant at $658.18 (interest + principal always = $658.18), each successive interest payment gets slightly smaller, while its affiliated principal payment increases by that same small amount.

When each payment is made, the balance of the loan gets reduced by the amount of the principal portion only, not by the amount of the total monthly payment. Naturally, the actual numbers for your loan will be different, but the concept remains true for virtually all loans.

If the sample loan shown in Figure #2 were your mortgage, you would be expected to pay $658.18 every month for 30 years. You could not pay less, or skip any payments without risking a *foreclosure*. But, you could pay more.

Making early principal payments -- pre-paying -- in the amounts shown under the principal column on your pre-payment schedule, will save you the corresponding interest payments.

Pre-payments can begin at any time during the life of your loan, not just at its inception or during its early years. However, for illustrative purposes, let's assume that you are about to mail in mortgage payment #1. If you add $33.46 (principal payment #2) to the $658.18 which is due every month, and mail in a single check for $691.64, the bank will properly credit your pre-pay-

Figure #2
IRREGULAR MONTHLY PRE-PAYMENT SCHEDULE

Loan Amount:	75,000.00
Interest Rate:	10.00 %
Loan Term:	360 Months
Periodic Payment:	658.18 Per Month
Total Interest, If Not Pre-Paid:	161,941.57
Total Principal:	75,000.00
Total Cash Outlay:	236,941.57

Payment Number	Date Paid	Interest Portion	Interest Saved	Principal Portion	Amount Paid	Balance Remaining
1	....	625.00	....	33.18	....	74,966.82
2	....	624.72	....	33.46	....	74,933.36
3	....	624.44	....	33.74	....	74,899.62
4	....	624.16	....	34.02	....	74,865.60
5	....	623.88	....	34.30	....	74,831.30
356	....	26.73	....	631.45	....	2,575.65
357	....	21.46	....	636.72	....	1,938.93
358	....	16.16	....	642.02	....	1,296.91
359	....	10.81	....	647.37	....	649.54
360	....	5.41	....	649.54	....	0.00

ment of $33.46 and you'll save interest payment #2, $624.72. You will *never* pay that $624.72.

Next month, when you mail in your check for $658.18, it will be credited as if it were payment #3, since the principal portion of payment #2 will have already been credited, and the interest payment which the bank's computer will now show as due, is the interest amount shown for payment #3.

Now for the bonus: Not only will that $33.46 save you $624.72, but it will also reduce the term of your loan by 1 month. That's pre-paying in a nutshell.

Now let's assume you recently bought your house, had the $658.18 that's due for payment #1, and could afford to send some extra money. A little over $100, $101.22 to be exact, would be enough to pre-pay principal payments #2, #3, and #4 ($33.46 + $33.74 + $34.02), which would ultimately save you $1,873.32 in interest payments -- #2, #3, and #4 ($624.72 + $624.44 + $624.16) -- making the house yours 3 months sooner. **Where else, but in your mortgage, can you get such safe, high, guaranteed returns on such tiny investments?**

IRREGULAR PRE-PAYMENTS

You can generally pre-pay at any time and in any amount. Because your ability to pre-pay may vary from month to month and from year to year, you may choose to make *Irregular* pre-payments, with the actual amount varying each month to match the principal column on your pre-payment schedule. But *Regular* pre-payments of, say $25, $50, or $100 a month work also and, for many people, are easier to manage.

Once you've read the next few sections, you'll be ready to select the pre-payment plan that's best for you. By obtaining the correct type of pre-payment schedule for your needs ... *Regular* or *Irregular* ... you'll be able to track your savings to the penny. Please refer to Figure #3, a partial pre-payment schedule, which illustrates a simple method for keeping records when making *Irregular* pre-payments.

Let's assume that your first payment comes due on October 1, and you make one pre-payment. Your check would be for $691.64 ($658.18 + 33.46 = $691.64). Enter that on your chart as we did on Figure #3. Then, you make two pre-payments in November, but in December you make none. Figure #3 shows what your schedule would look like after making December's payment. By speeding up your principal payments a mere $101.78 ($33.46 pre-paid in October and $34.02 + $34.30 pre-paid in November), you would reduce the loan's term by 3 months, while saving $1,872.76 ($624.72 + $624.16 + $623.88) in interest.

When January 1 arrives, you will again owe $658.18, now composed of a $623.31 interest payment and a $34.87 principal payment. You can add extra principal payments to your check if you want, or just mail in the $658.18. The choice is yours! If you add principal payment #8 ($35.16) to the $658.18, and mail in a check for $693.34, you will save another $623.02 (interest payment #8). Adding principal payments #9, #10, and up will

Figure #3
IRREGULAR MONTHLY PRE-PAYMENT SCHEDULE: RECORD KEEPING

Loan Amount:	75,000.00
Interest Rate:	10.00 %
Loan Term:	360 Months
Periodic Payment:	658.18 Per Month
Total Interest, If Not Pre-Paid:	161,941.57
Total Principal:	75,000.00
Total Cash Outlay:	236,941.57

Payment Number	Date Paid	Interest Portion	Interest Saved	Principal Portion	Amount Paid	Balance Remaining
1	....	625.00	....	33.18	....	~~74,966.82~~
2	Oct. 1	~~624.72~~	624.72	33.46	691.64	74,933.36
3	....	624.44	....	33.74	....	~~74,899.62~~
4	....	~~624.16~~	624.16	34.02	....	~~74,865.60~~
5	Nov. 1.	~~623.88~~	623.88	34.30	726.50	74,831.30
6	Dec. 1.	623.59	....	34.59	658.18	74,796.71
7	....	623.31	....	34.87	....	74,761.84
8	....	623.02	....	35.16	....	74,726.68
9	....	622.72	....	35.46	....	74,691.22
10	....	622.43	....	35.75	....	74,655.47

speed you to debt-free ownership even faster, and save additional -- substantial -- dollars.

Your total cost? Nothing! Pre-payments are not additional costs. They are advance ... or pre ... payments that would have to be paid shortly in any event. By routinely advancing a few dollars whenever you can, you'll ultimately save a small fortune in interest without having spent one cent extra.

REGULAR PRE-PAYMENTS

Making *Regular* pre-payments is simpler than making *Irregular* ones. Just send in the same advance each month (for example, $25, $50, etc.).

Figure #4
REGULAR MONTHLY PRE-PAYMENT SCHEDULE

Loan Amount:	75,000.00
Interest Rate:	10.00 %
Actual Term:	297 Months
Base Payment:	658.18 Per Month
Regular Pre-Payment:	25.00 Per Month
Total Payment:	683.18 Per Month
Total Interest, If Not Pre-Paid:	161,941.57
Total Interest, If Pre-Paid:	127,779.48
Total Outlay (Not Pre-Paid):	236,941.57
Total Outlay (Pre-Paid):	202,779.48
Time Saved By Pre-Payment:	63 Months
Interest Saved By Pre-Payment:	34,162.09

Payment Number	Date Paid	Interest Portion	Interest Saved	Principal Portion	Amount Paid	Balance Remaining
①	Oct. 1	625.00	....	58.18	683.18	74,941.82
②	Nov. 1	624.52	....	58.66	683.18	74,883.16
③	Dec. 1	624.03	....	59.15	683.18	74,824.01
4	....	623.53	....	59.65 }	....	~~74,764.36~~
⑤	Jan. 1	~~623.04~~	623.04	60.14 }	743.32	74,704.22
6	....	622.54	....	60.64	....	74,643.58

Figure #4 shows payments #1-6 for our sample loan. The Summary Section tells you that a *Regular* pre-payment of $25 per month will save you 63 months off the life of your loan, plus $34,162.09.

Our *Regular* Schedules make it easy for you to save even more, whenever you can. For example, Figure #4 shows how an additional pre-payment of $60.14 (principal portion #5), enclosed with payment #4, will save $623.04 more than the $34,162.09 that the *Regular* pre-payment of $25 per month will save.

Important note: If you want to make *Regular* pre-payments, and your loan is not brand new, make certain to obtain

Figure #5

10.00% TO 10.50% **30 YEAR** **10.00% TO 10.50%**

PRE-PAYMENT SAVINGS TABLE

LOAN AMOUNT	PRE-PMT	10.00%		10.25%		10.50%	
		DOLLARS	MOS	DOLLARS	MOS	DOLLARS	MOS
65,000	200	92,608	213	95,937	214	99,289	215
75,000	25	34,162	63	35,943	64	37,787	65
	50	54,180	101	56,687	103	59,263	104
	100	78,046	150	81,228	151	84,470	153
	200	102,198	202	105,930	204	109,712	205
85,000	25	35,286	57	37,163	58	39,112	59

a pre-payment schedule that starts with your current balance, or your records will not be accurate.

DECIDE ON YOUR SAVINGS IN ADVANCE

Figure #5 is an excerpt from one of the Pre-Payment Savings Tables in PART THREE of this book. It documents how much time and money will be saved on sample 30 year loans, at interest rates of 10 to 10.50%, for amounts ranging from $65,000 through $85,000. For example, it shows that pre-paying our sample $75,000 loan by $100 a month would save $78,046, while it cuts the loan's term by 12.5 years (150 months). By pre-paying, you can save more than you borrowed!

If you want to get a quick sense of what $25 to $200 a month can save you, just find the Pre-Payment Savings Table that comes closest to your loan figures. Similarly, if you're looking for a nest egg of a particular size, one of our Pre-Payment Savings Tables can help you approximate how much of an advance you'll need to make it happen. (For exact figures, you'll

Figure #6

10.00% 10.00%

DEBT REDUCTION TABLE

TO REDUCE A 30 YEAR LOAN TO:

LOAN AMOUNT	25 YEARS		20 YEARS		15 YEARS	
	PRE-PAY	SAVE	PRE-PAY	SAVE	PRE-PAY	SAVE
30,000	9.34	12,988	26.23	25,282	59.11	36,735
35,000	10.89	15,147	30.60	29,496	68.96	42,858
45,000	14.01	19,491	39.35	37,939	88.67	55,120
55,000	17.12	23,818	48.10	46,370	108.37	67,364
65,000	20.23	28,144	56.84	54,796	128.07	79,609
75,000	23.35	32,488	65.59	63,239	147.78	91,871
85,000	26.46	36,815	74.33	71,666	167.48	104,116
100,000	31.13	43,309	87.45	84,308	197.03	122,481
120,000	37.36	51,980	104.94	101,179	236.44	146,989

want to use our *Banker's Secret Software* or have us run an appropriate *Regular* pre-payment schedule for you.)

DECIDE WHEN YOU'LL BE DEBT- FREE

The Debt Reduction Tables in PART THREE make it easy to find out exactly how much of a *Regular* pre-payment you'll need to retire a 30 year loan in 15, 20, or 25 years. We've also included tables for 15 year loans, which show how much is required to reduce their terms by 2.5, 5, or 7.5 years. In both cases, we show how much money you'll save as well.

Figure #6 is an excerpt from the Debt Reduction Table for 10%, 30 year loans. It shows how simple it is to find out what pre-payment will take 10 years, for example, off the term of our $75,000 sample loan: An advance of $65.59 a month will pay this loan off a decade early, saving $63,239. Curious about your mortgage? Just turn to the Debt Reduction Tables.

Figure #7
IRREGULAR MONTHLY PRE-PAYMENT SCHEDULE: YEAR 10

Loan Amount:	75,000.00
Interest Rate:	10.00 %
Loan Term:	360 Months
Periodic Payment:	658.18 Per Month
Total Interest, If Not Pre-Paid:	161,941.57
Total Principal:	75,000.00
Total Cash Outlay:	236,941.57

Payment Number	Date Paid	Interest Portion	Interest Saved	Principal Portion	Amount Paid	Balance Remaining
120	....	569.10	....	89.08	....	68,203.24
121	....	568.36	....	89.82	....	68,113.42
122	....	567.61	....	90.57	....	68,022.85
123	....	566.86	....	91.32	....	67,931.53
124	....	566.10	....	92.08	....	67,839.45
125	....	565.33	....	92.85	....	67,746.60

START PRE-PAYING NOW

As we've said, you can begin pre-paying at any time. However, **the sooner you begin, the greater your savings will be.** That's because interest payments are highest and principal payments are lowest at the inception of the loan. Later on, the savings will still be substantial, although smaller.

Under the terms of a conventional mortgage, the loan's balance is reduced very slowly and the monthly interest payments remain high for many years. **Small pre-payments result in large savings well into the life of the loan**. To prove it, let's look at a portion of the schedule for our sample mortgage -- ten years down the road. We'll assume that no pre-payments have been made. (See Figure #7.)

If an additional principal payment of $90.57 is mailed in with payment #121 (for a total of $658.18 + $90.57 = $748.75), you will save $567.61 (interest payment #122), and retire the loan one month earlier. The following month's payment would be

#123, not payment #122. Even during year 23 (not shown), when the principal and interest components of our example's monthly payments will finally begin to approach each other, deferred savings of 100% will result from pre-paying the next month's principal.

Note from Figure #7 that even after 120 payments of $658.18 each have been made, totalling $78,981.60 (120 x $658.18), the balance due on this loan has only been reduced by $6,796.76 ($75,000 - $68,203.24). The remaining $72,184.84 ($78,981.60 - $6,796.76), all would have gone towards interest -- almost as much as was borrowed in the first place! That's a big chunk of money out of your pocket, no matter what tax bracket you're in. (More on taxes, later.)

TOWARDS THE END

The last few payments are predominantly principal payments. By the time you get to the end, very large pre-payments will only save small amounts of interest, although the guaranteed return remains just as high as always (10% in our example). By now, you'll probably have saved tens of thousands of dollars, and your home will soon be yours, free and clear, years earlier than you ever thought possible.

When you make that long awaited last payment, request a "*Letter of Satisfaction*" from your lender. When filed with your county clerk or registrar of deeds, this piece of paper will tell the world that you now own your home, free and clear.

If you've been carrying a mortgage insurance policy, it no longer serves the purpose for which you bought it. In fact, if you've been pre-paying, that policy has probably been excessive for quite some time. Keep track both of your principal balance and the declining value of your insurance as you pre-pay. The time may come when you want to cancel your mortgage insurance policy or obtain a more suitable one.

GETTING STARTED

If, as we expect, pre-paying seems like a good idea to you, get a pre-payment schedule for your loan, and begin! **No matter what type of loan you have, whether it's a fixed rate, adjus-**

table, or bi-weekly, the more you pre-pay and the sooner you begin, the sooner your home will be debt-free and the more you will save. We know you'll get a lot of pleasure out of watching those savings mount up, and you'll be glad to have all that extra money when the time comes to finance college, retire, or do whatever else it is you may want!

As a courtesy before you begin, you might want to tell one of your bank's officers that you plan to pre-pay. The odds are good that your banker will be pleased to help you begin your pre-payment program. However, if he or she has a problem with this idea, or if your mortgage agreement has a pre-payment penalty, see the relevant question(s) in PART TWO of this book.

In most cases, all you'll have to do is add your pre-payment to your normal monthly payment and mail in one check; the bank's computer will automatically credit your pre-payment correctly. But your bank might prefer a separate check for the pre-payment. Just ask. In any event, you can include a note such as the following: "Please credit the additional $______ principal payment I've enclosed to the outstanding balance of my loan."

Important Note: When making your payments, don't forget to include the required amounts for real estate taxes, other escrow accounts, and/or life insurance premiums. However, those figures should *not* appear on your pre-payment schedule because they're not part of what you borrowed and therefore you don't have to pay interest on them. **Make certain to deduct all taxes and insurance from your required payment whenever you have a schedule personalized**.

In studying Figure #2, you may have noticed that the last payment was a little different than the rest. That's because fractional cents can't be paid and the numbers on the schedule have been rounded off accordingly. By the same token, don't be surprised if your figures seem to be slightly different from your bank's. While we use the industry standard for our calculations, other computers occasionally round off differently. If necessary, talk to your banker and agree to follow the same schedule.

In the following section, we hope to answer any remaining questions you may have about pre-paying.

PART TWO: QUESTIONS ANSWERED

CAN ALL LOANS BE PRE-PAID?

Virtually all loans can be pre-paid. The major exception is what the finance industry refers to as "Rule of 78's Method" or "Sum of the Digits" loans. In the past, they were used to finance such purchases as cars and boats. Because they front load interest costs, these loans are unfair to consumers. Fortunately, many states have outlawed "Rule of 78" loans.

In almost every other case, the pre-payment technique for home equity, car, boat, motorcycle, mobile home, RV, home improvement, and student loans, as well as credit card purchases ... **any loans at all** ... remains exactly the same as for home mortgages. **The larger the loan, the higher the interest rate, and the longer the term, the more you'll save with each pre-payment.**

Given the high interest charged on outstanding credit card and debit card balances, pre-paying will be especially effective when you owe money to MasterCard, Visa, etc.

HOW DOES PRE-PAYING AFFECT MY HOME EQUITY ?

Every time you pre-pay on your mortgage, you increase your home equity. This increase in equity is an increase in your net worth. Like a savings account or pension plan, it represents real wealth ... wealth that can put a child through college, help finance your retirement, buy you a more expensive home, or serve as collateral for a home equity loan.

With bankers (and brokers) competing heavily to write home equity loans, these *second mortgages* have recently become very accessible. Their interest rates appear to be relatively low, their interest costs are tax deductible (within wide limits), and careful shopping can keep closing costs down. Most important, they make the equity in your home extremely "liquid." In many cases, once you have a home equity line of credit, you can access it by simply writing a check or producing a credit card. But please be careful.

Home equity loans can be dangerous. They can cost two or three times their apparent interest rate when used for small, sporadic purchases. But more to the point, home equity loans are *mortgages*. They represent a *lien* on your home. By abusing their credit lines, some borrowers are putting their homes in jeopardy for frivolous reasons. If you now have, or do get a home equity loan, try to pre-pay it.

HOW DO I GET A PRE-PAYMENT SCHEDULE?

To keep track of your pre-payments, interest savings, and the speed with which your loan is decreasing, you will want a pre-payment schedule personalized for your loan. The faster you get yours, the faster you'll begin saving.

The first thing you'll need to decide is whether you want a *Regular* or an *Irregular* schedule. If you hate to balance your checkbook or just want the absolutely easiest pre-payment system, we recommend that you use a *Regular* schedule.

If you don't mind a little addition and subtraction, an *Irregular* schedule will give you the most flexibility. And if you're very good at math, and want to bother, you can follow the instructions given in Appendix #2, and calculate your own schedule.

If you have access to an IBM® compatible computer, you might want to consider the *Banker's Secret Software*, which will make all of the calculations and let you produce all of the pre-payment schedules you'll want -- as your needs, interest rates, and finances vary over the years. Our software is a user friendly version of the program we use to run schedules for thousands of families.

There's an Order Form in the back of this book that you can use to obtain either your pre-payment schedule or your software. Before you order a pre-payment schedule, please be sure to verify all of your figures. Then fill out the Data Sheet -- remembering that the schedule we run for you can only be as accurate as the information you provide. If you are at all unsure of your interest rate, current balance, or monthly payment (without taxes and/or insurance), please contact your lender before placing your order.

HOW ABOUT ADJUSTABLE MORTGAGES?

Fixed interest, *self-amortizing* mortgages, like our sample loan, once financed most homes. They called for equal monthly payments at pre-determined interest rates, until the entire debt was repaid. While still popular, other types of mortgages are now available as well. These new financing concepts are only modifications of the self-amortizing loan. Some are written for short periods of time, while others incorporate adjustable interest rates, shorter premium periods, or graduated payments.

In general, all of these loans can be pre-paid. However some of the details may be different from those we've discussed. For example, if you have an adjustable rate loan, and if you want to track your pre-payment savings to the penny, you'll need a new pre-payment schedule whenever your interest rate changes. But no matter what type of loan you may have, the basic pre-payment concept remains the same: **Pay a little in advance and save a lot at the end.**

SHOULD I GET A FIXED RATE OR AN ADJUSTABLE LOAN?

The choice between fixed rate and adjustable loans is not always clear. Generally, an adjustable rate loan will be written at a lower rate than competitive fixed rate loans. If a move within the next few years is likely, adjustable rate loans may make the most sense. For example, if you expect to live in your house for 4 years and can either obtain a 10% fixed interest loan or an 8% adjustable, with 0.5% increases allowed every 6 months, the worst that could happen with the adjustable is that it could increase to 11.5% by the time you moved. Its *average*

Figure #8

10.00% 10.00%

MONTHLY LOAN PAYMENT TABLE

DOLLARS REQUIRED TO AMORTIZE A LOAN

LOAN AMOUNT	TERM OF LOAN IN YEARS 1	3	5	15	20	30
10,000	879.16	322.68	212.48	107.47	96.51	87.76
15,000	1,318.74	484.01	318.71	161.20	144.76	131.64
20,000	1,758.32	645.35	424.95	214.93	193.01	175.52
25,000	2,197.90	806.68	531.18	268.66	241.26	219.40
30,000	2,637.48	968.02	637.42	322.39	289.51	263.28
35,000	3,077.06	1,129.36	743.65	376.12	337.76	307.16
45,000	3,956.22	1,452.03	956.12	483.58	434.26	394.91
55,000	4,835.38	1,774.70	1,168.59	591.04	530.77	482.67
65,000	5,714.54	2,097.37	1,381.06	698.50	627.27	570.43
75,000	6,593.70	2,420.04	1,593.53	805.96	723.77	658.18
85,000	7,472.86	2,742.72	1,806.00	913.42	820.27	745.94

cost under the worst case would be just under 10%, or less than the fixed rate loan.

But, if you stayed another year and the rate rose above 12%, the average cost would go above that of the 10% fixed rate loan. (In fact, the interest due on higher balances early in the loan would have been charged at the lower rate, so ... actually ... it would take somewhat longer for the cost under the adjustable rate loan to equal that of the fixed rate loan.) For longer terms, where the cap could allow for a fairly high average interest rate, adjustables clearly become more of a gamble. However, if interest rates hold or drop, the adjustable again becomes the best bet.

With an adjustable rate loan, you can profit by repaying it from the start as if it were the higher cost fixed rate loan. While its interest rate is at 8%, for example, pay like it was a 10% loan. (You can look up the monthly payment for any loan you are considering in the appropriate Monthly Loan Payment Table in PART THREE of this book.[2] See Figure #8 for a sample.)

By making payments at the 10% rate, you'll be automatically building in a pre-payment. Then, if the interest rate climbs, as it is likely to do, your monthly payment will stay constant (at 10% in this case) for at least two years. During those two years of rising interest rates, you'll make progressively smaller pre-payments, but your savings and net worth will both continue to grow. And of course, you can always increase the size of your pre-payments as time goes on.

WHAT ABOUT BI-WEEKLY AND "PSEUDO BI-WEEKLY" LOANS?

Bi-weeklies began in Canada and are now being offered by a relatively small number of banks in the United States. They save interest costs by building in a pre-payment. Instead of 12 monthly payments, the bi-weeklies require one half of a normal loan's monthly payment every 2 weeks (or 26 payments per year). Since 26 yearly payments are the equivalent of 13 monthly payments, under a bi-weekly plan you pre-pay 1 month's mortgage payment per year.

To participate in the program, you have to get a new mortgage (which means extra trouble and expense if you have an existing loan). In addition, you may have to pay a higher interest rate and/or higher closing costs than competitive lenders are offering on traditional loans. You'll also be expected to open a "Transaction" account from which your bank will *automatically* deduct your required payment every 2 weeks.

If you already have a bi-weekly loan or do decide to get one, by all means remember that it, too, can be pre-paid. Figure #9 (on the following page) shows the effects of a *Regular* pre-payment of $25 every two weeks on our $75,000 loan, this time set up as a bi-weekly. Note that the $23,855.69 in savings shown on Figure #9, is on top of the interest that would be saved, over the cost of a 30 year loan, because it's a true bi-weekly.

---

2. If your exact loan figure does not appear on a Monthly Loan Payment Table, turn to the Mortgage Factor Tables section of PART THREE, where you can calculate the monthly payment for any loan, written at virtually any interest rate.

Figure #9
REGULAR BI-WEEKLY PRE-PAYMENT SCHEDULE

Loan Amount:	75,000.00	
Interest Rate:	10.00 %	
Actual Term:	440	2 Week Periods
Base Payment:	329.09	Per Period
Regular Pre-Payment:	25.00	Per Period
Total Periodic Payment:	354.09	Per Period
Total Interest, If Not Pre-Paid:	104,330.54	
Total Interest, If Pre-Paid:	80,474.85	
Total Outlay (Not Pre-Paid):	179,330.54	
Total Outlay (Pre-Paid):	155,474.85	
Time Saved By Pre-Payment:	105	Payments
Interest Saved By Pre-Payment:	23,855.69	

Payment Number	Date Paid	Interest Portion	Interest Saved	Principal Portion	Amount Paid	Balance Remaining
1	....	288.46	....	65.63	....	74,934.37
2	....	288.21	....	65.88	....	74,868.49
3	....	287.96	....	66.13	....	74,802.36
4	....	287.70	....	66.39	....	74,735.97
5	....	287.45	....	66.64	....	74,669.33

If you're thinking about having someone convert your existing loan into a bi-weekly one -- creating a "pseudo bi-weekly" -- we urge you to consider the matter carefully before you sign on the dotted line. Remember you can't benefit from paying on a bi-weekly basis unless your bank credits your payment every two weeks. Most don't and won't! Those who claim to convert your loan to a bi-weekly can't do anything that you can't do much better yourself. But they'll charge you hundreds, often thousands of dollars for a service you really don't need!

Here's how a "pseudo bi-weeky" generally works: Your current monthly payment is divided by 2. That new payment is automatically deducted from your checking account every 2 weeks. However, it will *not* then be credited to your loan. In-

10.00% **Figure #10** 10.00%

BI-WEEKLY PAYMENT TABLE

TYPICAL 30 YEAR LOAN COMPARED TO A BI-WEEKLY

LOAN AMOUNT	MONTHLY PAYMENT	TOTAL INTEREST	BI-WEEKLY PAYMENT	INTEREST SAVED	YRS/WKS SAVED
30,000	263.28	64,761.40	131.64	23,034.20	9/02
35,000	307.16	75,556.32	153.58	26,874.76	9/02
45,000	394.91	97,161.06	197.46	34,570.24	9/02
55,000	482.67	118,748.77	241.34	42,249.36	9/02
65,000	570.43	140,336.06	285.22	49,926.93	9/02
75,000	658.18	161,941.57	329.09	57,611.03	9/02
85,000	745.94	183,529.16	372.97	65,289.44	9/02
100,000	877.58	215,909.34	438.79	76,805.96	9/02
120,000	1,053.09	259,102.77	526.55	92,180.97	9/02

stead, it'll be put into a trust account, not under your control and probably not even in your bank. Every month, a check in the amount of your required payment will be sent to your bank. Then, every 6 months, a pre-payment of half your monthly payment will be sent in.

For greater savings than you can get from a "pseudo bi-weekly:" Divide your current mortgage payment by twelve, and send in that pre-payment amount with each month's check. For our $75,000 loan, that would mean a *Regular* pre-payment of $54.85 ($658.18 ÷ 12) -- or, a monthly check of $713.03 ($658.18 + $54.85) -- for a total savings of $57,210.71, plus 8 years and 11 months.

If you're considering a bi-weekly loan, you may want to consult the Bi-weekly Payment Tables in PART THREE, which compare the total interest costs of self-amortizing, 30 year loans which have not been pre-paid at all, to the costs of a real bi-weekly. Figure #10 is an excerpt from the table for our 10%, $75,000 loan. As you can see, the real bi-weekly would reduce the cost of our $75,000 loan by more than $57,000!

WHAT ABOUT GPM'S, 15 YEAR, AND OTHER INTEREST SAVING LOANS?

Like bi-weekly mortgages, graduated payment mortgages (GPM's), 15 year mortgages, and other interest saving loans are generally less flexible pre-payment plans which are available only to new borrowers. The directions we've already given you are applicable to all loans ... old or new, fixed rate, adjustable, graduated, balloon, monthly or bi-weekly.

Graduated Payment Mortgages (GPM's) are home loans whose principal component becomes larger on each anniversary of the mortgage. For example, the first year's payment may be based on a 30 year self-amortizing loan. Every year thereafter, the monthly payment will increase by a few percent, with the extra money going towards principal. All borrowers can pre-pay in this fashion whether they have a GPM or not.

To entice younger purchasers to become homeowners, some GPM's begin by requiring payments that do not even cover the interest costs. That interest deficit gets added to the outstanding balance (technically this is *negative amortization*), resulting in an ever increasing level of debt. Watch out!

Fifteen year loans may seem like a new invention, but they've always been available. By calling for somewhat higher monthly payments, they retire loans faster than 30 year mortgages would, and therefore save interest costs. By increasing your monthly mortgage payment on a 20 or 30 year loan, you can create your own 15 year (or shorter) loan without strapping yourself, by contract, to the higher payment. To see how easy it would be for you to dramatically cut your loan's term and costs, just find the correct Debt Reduction Table for your loan in PART THREE.

As always, the more you pre-pay, the sooner your loan will be paid off, and the more you'll save. With the *Banker's Secret Pre-Payment System* you can have all of the benefits of most specialty loans ... plus a few extras. You decide how much to pre-pay and when to do it. Your savings will be dramatic even if you can't pre-pay every month. And if your cash flow should take a sudden jump, you can pre-pay faster -- and save more -- than you could with a rigidly scheduled bank or other commercially available, profit-making plan.

HOW WILL PRE-PAYING AFFECT MY TAX DEDUCTIONS?

The interest paid on a mortgage is one of the last remaining tax deductible expenses, so it may seem like you would be giving up something important if you pre-paid. That's just not so! You always come out further ahead by avoiding an expense rather than by incurring one ... no matter what your tax bracket. But let's take on the tax question directly.

Look at our $75,000 example again. If you don't pre-pay, your first year's interest payments will total $7,481.24. If you pre-pay $25 per month, your tax deductible interest cost for the year would be reduced a miniscule $14.12, to $7,467.12. Your deferred savings however, would be more than $5,000.

Pre-paying reduces the total number of interest payments you'll make, and therefore, your total interest costs. *But*, your monthly interest costs decrease very slowly. Until you've paid off your mortgage, you will continue to make interest payments of only a little bit less each month than had you not pre-paid. As the years go by, the tax savings will go down, but the interest saved will have gone way up. And you'll have plenty of time before that wonderful day when all mortgage payments stop, to create new tax shelters.

As a tax bonus, the earnings on pre-payments -- the build-up of equity in your home -- are typically tax deferred at least until the family's very last home has been sold. In some cases, your equity build-up will never be taxed. Pre-paying a mortgage is a great, tax deferred investment program for every homeowner.

IS IT IN THE BANK'S INTEREST FOR ME TO PRE-PAY?

In the past few years, more and more banks have opted to make the bulk of their loan profits up front. Application fees, points, and other closing costs go directly -- and quickly -- to the bank. Then, many banks sell mortgages on the *secondary mortgage market*, for additional profits. In this situation, your bank neither profits from, nor loses, by your pre-payment.

If your bank does hold its loans, the more it receives in pre-payments, the more money it will have available to use for new loans -- which again, is where the bank's extra up-front profits come in. After all, banks don't care whether they earn their interest on your $25 pre-payment from you or from their next borrower. The interest is the same. But the more loans they write, the more closing costs they can collect, and the more they can sell on the secondary mortgage market.

Then there's the question of community relations. Any banker who actually helps you save money will likely have your respect and business forever!

WHAT IF MY BANKER SAYS "NO!"?

You should first verify that your loan has no pre-payment restrictions (restrictions ... not penalties). If there are no restrictions in your mortgage agreement, but your banker is still unwilling to let you pre-pay, you might want to contact your state's Superintendent (or Commissioner) of Banking for an opinion about whether you can pre-pay or not.

In many states, you automatically have the right to pre-pay. And even where homeowners don't have this presumptive right, most people have no trouble making pre-payments -- even when the bank officer at the front desk says, "No!"

In the very few cases where we've been consulted about an uncooperative bank officer, we have suggested simply mailing in one check, which includes both the pre-payment amount and the monthly payment. In every case, the bank's bookkeeping department has punched into the computer, and correctly credited, both the monthly payment and the pre-payment.

To verify that your pre-payments are being properly credited, wait a few days, and then call the bank to ask for your current loan balance. Check this figure against your own pre-payment schedule. The two should agree, and probably will. If they don't, bring your schedule to one of your bank's loan officers, and discuss the discrepancy.

WHAT IF I PLAN ON MOVING SOON?

While you pre-pay, you are taking advantage of a safe, reliable, guaranteed way to earn generally higher-than-market rates -- on even the smallest of investments. And as a bonus, those interest earnings are tax deferred in an even more accessible, reliable, and beneficial fashion than most pension plans. At the same time, the continuously compounded pre-payments increase your home equity.

When you move, those extra few thousand dollars you've built up in your existing home's equity can be applied towards the down payment on your next home. That extra down payment will then lower the required monthly payment on your new mortgage, which means that you will be able to afford either a more expensive property or a larger pre-payment, or both!

While typical homeowners do move every 5 to 7 years, they generally move from one mortgaged home to another, creating a sort of "*serial*," variable rate (and payment) mortgage, unique to themselves. If the equity increases earned through pre-payments continue to be plowed back from loan to loan, and pre-payments are kept up, the ultimate result will be an early escape from mortgage debt, your home free and clear, and years of mortgage payments you'll never have to make. You'll save tens of thousands of dollars which will be yours to do with as you please ... finance college, set up a retirement fund, travel ... .

WHAT ABOUT PRE-PAYMENT PENALTIES?

Although not nearly as common as you may have been led to believe, some mortgage agreements do penalize pre-payments. Should yours have a pre-payment penalty clause, you'll be relieved to know that, at worst, its effect on your savings will be minimal.

In those few cases where penalties exist, they are generally imposed *only* during the first year of the loan, in order to discourage early repayment of the entire debt. Pre-payment penalties usually cannot be imposed on FHA or VA guaranteed loans, or in an ever increasing number of states. Even where they can be imposed, they rarely are. The reason is simple: The penalties on the modest pre-payments we've been discussing are so small, it would cost the lender far more than the fee collected just to do the additional bookkeeping and billing required!

Referring back to our $75,000 example, let's assume that a 5% pre-payment penalty could be charged. (In fact, pre-payment penalties are likely to be much less.) If you were to pre-pay principal payment #2, $33.46, the penalty would be 5% of that $33.46, or $1.67. The interest saved would be $624.72 (interest payment #2), which is a substantial return on a $1.67 charge. Remember, the $33.46 is not an added cost. It would have been due the following month, anyway.

WHEN SHOULD I PRE-PAY AND WHEN SHOULD I REFINANCE?

Interest rates are cyclical. They go up, and they go back down. They always have and probably always will. If you have a fixed rate loan, it may make sense to refinance when interest rates drop about 2 points below your current mortgage level.

The longer you expect to be living in your house, the more likely it is that refinancing will pay. If you have an adjustable rate mortgage, or plan on moving in the near future, it is less likely that refinancing will prove worthwhile. Check the total costs over the expected life of the loan, both for refinancing and for sticking with your present agreement. Go for the less expensive alternative.

Figure #11 shows you how combining pre-paying with refinancing can more than triple your savings. Let's say that you borrowed $75,000, 5 years ago, when interest rates were 15%, and you're now considering refinancing at 10%. If you were to stick with your old 15% loan and pre-pay $100 per month, you would save $103,552, or more than twice the $47,556 that refinancing would save! Combining the two methods would increase your interest savings another $57,986 to $161,538. Hard to believe? Perhaps that's why the power of pre-paying has been "a banker's secret" all these years!

And don't forget that refinancing, alone, will likely re-extend the time you'll spend in debt, whereas pre-paying will get you out of debt, sooner. **Again, whether or not you decide to refinance, you should pre-pay! The more you pre-pay and the sooner you begin, the more you'll save.**

Figure #11
THE BANKER'S SECRET REFINANCING PLAN

Original Loan:	75,000.00
Interest Rate:	15.00 %
Loan Term:	30 Years
Monthly Payment:	948.34

Refinanced After 5 Years:

Balance Remaining:	74,040
New Loan Amount:	75,000[1]
New Interest Rate:	10 %
New Term:	30 Years
New Monthly Payment:	658.18

Refinancing Option	Interest Rate(%)	Loan Amount	Cost/ Month	Term Left	Cost[2] to Term	Interest Savings
Pay as Agreed	15	74,040	948	25 yrs	284,500	0
Refinance	10	75,000	658	30 yrs	236,944	47,556
Pre-pay $100/Mo	15	74,040	1,048	14y/5m	180,948	103,552
Refinance/Pre-pay	10	75,000	948	10y/10m	122,962	161,538

Notes:

1. For simplicity we took out a $75,000 loan, rounded our figures to the nearest dollar, and are disregarding any of the closing costs above the $960 (75,000 - 74,040), which might have had to be paid when the loan was refinanced. (We're assuming additional cash was laid out for these costs.)

2. These figures do not include the $56,900 paid during the first 5 years of the mortgage , of which $55,940 was interest and only $960 was credited towards the loan's balance.

WHAT SHOULD I DO IF I'VE JUST REFINANCED?

If you are about to refinance, or recently have, we recommend that you get a pre-payment schedule with your old payment built in. (We call these schedules our *Refinancer's Specials.*)

Figure #12
REFINANCER'S SPECIAL

Loan Amount:	75,000.00
Interest Rate:	10.00 %
Actual Term:	130 Months
Base Payment:	658.18 Per Month
Regular Pre-Payment:	290.16 Per Month
Total Periodic Payment:	948.34 Per Month
Total Interest, If Not Pre-Paid:	161,941.57
Total Interest, If Pre-Paid:	47,961.03
Total Outlay (Not Pre-Paid):	236,941.57
Total Outlay (Pre-Paid):	122,961.03
Time Saved By Pre-Payment:	230 Months
Interest Saved By Pre-Payment:	113,980.54

Payment Number	Date Paid	Interest Portion	Interest Saved	Principal Portion	Amount Paid	Balance Remaining
1	....	625.00	....	323.34	....	74,676.66
2	....	622.31	....	326.03	....	74,350.63
3	....	619.59	....	328.75	....	74,021.88
4	....	616.85	....	331.49	....	73,690.39
5	....	614.09	....	334.25	....	73,356.14
126	....	35.96	....	912.38	....	3,403.01
127	....	28.36	....	919.98	....	2,483.03
128	....	20.69	....	927.65	....	1,555.38
129	....	12.96	....	935.38	....	620.00
130	....	5.17	....	620.00	....	0.00

The basic idea is that since you could already afford your original monthly payment, continuing to pay that amount every month shouldn't present any significant hardship ... and the savings it will buy you are almost unbelievable! Who wouldn't like to retire with more than $160,000 of extra net worth? (The $47,556 saved by refinancing is added to the $113,981 saved by pre-paying.)

Figure #12 is a *Refinancer's Special* for our refinanced loan. It shows the monthly payment at the old figure of $948.34 (which was due every month on the $75,000, 15% loan). Note that this is a *Regular* Monthly Pre-Payment Schedule with a $290.16 pre-payment built in ($948.34 - $290.16 = $658.18). Should you find yourself able to make additional pre-payments, you could use this schedule exactly as we explained for an *Irregular* Monthly Pre-Payment Schedule. (You may have noticed a discrepancy between Figures #11 and #12. That's because the calculations in Figure #11 begin 5 years after the original loan was taken out, and were rounded off to the nearest dollar.)

WILL *REGULAR* OR *IRREGULAR* PRE-PAYMENTS SAVE ME MORE?

It turns out that *Regular* pre-payments can save more than *Irregular* ones. For example, let's say you want to pay off the $75,000 loan in 15 years instead of 30. You could send in:

A) A *Regular* pre-payment of $147.78 every month, or

B) The next month's principal with each mortgage check.

Both would cut the loan's term in half. But, the $147.78 every month will save you $91,871.21, while the *Irregular* method will save you only $80,815.20. Why? Because under the *Regular* approach, you would be making much larger pre-payments early in the life of the loan, when interest costs, and therefore your potential savings, are highest.

WHAT ABOUT PRE-PAID COLLEGE PLANS?

There are three main types of pre-paid college tuition plans: Those set up by individual colleges or universities; those set up by states; and those set up by private institutions. Most of them have serious flaws. Some will heavily penalize you if, a decade and a half from now, your child chooses another school ... transfers ... moves to another state ... decides not to go to college ... or isn't accepted for admission. By limiting a student's future choices, school-sponsored and, to a lesser extent, state plans, increase the likelihood of school/student mismatches.

As if that weren't bad enough, many plans require large initial deposits, when most parents can least afford them. But, perhaps worst of all, some of the pre-paid college tuition plans are almost certain to pay less -- while charging higher management costs -- than virtually every other investment possibility open to middle income parents.

Yet some colleges already cost $20,000 a year. What's a parent to do? Consider other options, like mutual funds, CDs, and annuities. And if you have a mortgage, set up a "do-it-yourself" pre-paid college tuition plan, as we describe below. You'll have the most available money and the greatest number of choices -- in the shortest possible time. And if your child should get a full scholarship, the money ... all of it ... will remain yours to do with as you please!

HOW CAN I USE MY MORTGAGE TO CREATE A COLLEGE TUITION PLAN?

Pre-pay as much as you can on your mortgage every month, and once your loan's been retired, put that same monthly amount into a savings account, CD, or other secure investment.

Let's say you have the sample $75,000 mortgage, and two children to put through college. If you send in about $860 a month, building in a $200 pre-payment, you'll save over $100,000 in interest costs (see Figure #5), and own your home, free and clear, almost 17 years early. That $860 a month then becomes "found money" that you can use for any purpose, including college tuition. This fairly substantial increase in your home equity, plus the extra $860 every month, will put your children through *any* college!

If you can't afford $200 a month, perhaps you could come up with a $25 per month pre-payment. If our sample loan was your mortgage, that $34,000 increase in your net worth would really help to foot the bill, especially since most college students use a mix of cash and loans to finance their educations.

By the way, after graduation, pre-paying a student loan is an excellent way to begin benefitting from this important investment strategy. After all, many a young doctor, lawyer, or dentist is $50,000 to $100,000 in debt on the day their shingle is first hung out.

WHAT ABOUT LOW INTEREST LOANS?

If your mortgage was written when rates were lower, you may be tempted to invest those pre-payment dollars where they will return more than the guaranteed savings we've documented. Before deciding, remember that it's always difficult to get high returns on small investments, and the pre-payments we've been talking about involve very small amounts ... spare change ... that few of us would ever invest, notice, or miss. Yet pre-paying as little as $25 a month on a mortgage will save thousands ... even tens of thousands of dollars.

But pre-paying will do more than just save you money. It will increase your home equity and speed up the day when your property will be freed of its mortgage lien, thereby reducing the danger of *foreclosure*. Pre-paying is a powerful, painless, long-term savings device, even on low interest loans.

WHAT IF I MISS A PAYMENT?

Whether you pre-pay or not, you are generally obliged to make the payment stipulated in your mortgage agreement every month without fail. Not doing so could lead to a foreclosure. Therefore, we suggest that you pre-pay using spare change. Never strap yourself by pre-paying so much in any month that you will be unable to meet your normal expenses ... or cope with unexpected emergencies.

WHAT ABOUT INFLATION?

For many people, "real income" -- the ability to purchase goods and services -- has gone down over the years, even though apparent income has increased. While inflation does make dollars less valuable, it also makes them harder to obtain. By paying off your home quickly, you help secure it from future bad times while saving thousands of dollars. Whether inflation becomes rampant or not, pre-paying can help make sure your house will be yours to keep no matter what the economy does.

OK, WHAT'S THE CATCH?

The simple truth is that there is none! Small pre-payments save you money and time, build up your personal net worth, and free you from debt. Pre-paying works on almost all loans, no matter what!

PART THREE: PRE-PAYMENT TABLES

OVERVIEW

While our Monthly Loan Payment Tables are similar to the charts that bankers and brokers have been using for years, our Pre-Payment Savings Tables, Debt Reduction Tables, Mortgage Factor Tables, and Bi-Weekly Payment Tables are not available anywhere else. All of our tables are easy to use, and in conjunction with the rest of the *Banker's Secret Pre-Payment System*, will guide you towards dramatic savings on your home mortgage. There are three basic ways you can use these tables.

A) To determine, at a glance, the savings possible by pre-paying virtually any loan the *Banker's Secret* way.

B) To find the monthly payment required to pay off a loan.

C) To find the bi-weekly payment required to pay off a loan.

As you now know, a $25 per month pre-payment on a 10%, $75,000, 30 year loan, will save $34,162 and reduce that loan's term by 63 months. Look up your loan in the Pre-Payment Savings Tables section (the first grouping of tables that you'll come to), and see what a $25 a month pre-payment can do for you!

While great care was taken in compiling these tables, complete accuracy cannot be guaranteed. We therefore recommend that you use these figures as a guide.

If you love math, Appendix #2 will teach you how to make most pre-payment calculations. If math is not for you, or you want exact figures, our *Banker's Secret Software* computes all the figures presented in this book, and will also happily generate an unlimited number of *Regular* or *Irregular* pre-payment schedules.

If you don't have access to a computer, a *Regular* pre-payment schedule will show you exactly how much time and money you'll save when making the same pre-payments with every mortgage check. Our *Irregular* schedules let you pre-pay whenever you can afford to, and therefore, provide the most flexible pre-payment option. Either one will let you verify your bank's statements.

Pre-paying is a fast, easy, sensible way to pay off your home mortgage (and virtually every other kind of loan), while earning a very respectable, tax deferred interest rate ... on "pocket change" sized investments. Isn't it just amazing that this powerful financial tool has been kept "a banker's secret" for so long?

LOCATING THE TABLES YOU NEED

There are five sets of tables in PART THREE, each highlighted by a *Tab*, and each containing its own complete, step-by-step instructions. On the following page, we've provided a brief description of each section and shown you what the *Tabs* look like. Although they have intentionally been designed not to bleed off the edge of the page, you can use them to quickly find the section of tables you want. Just fan the pages of the book and you'll see how each section is clearly marked by its *Tab*.

Section 1. THE PRE-PAYMENT SAVINGS TABLES are designed to give you a good idea of the savings possible when making *Regular* pre-payments -- from $25 to $200 a month -- on loans from $10,000 to $200,000. Both 15 and 30 year loans are tabulated -- at interest rates ranging from 7.00% to 14.75%.

Section 2. THE DEBT REDUCTION TABLES are perfect for gaining a quick sense of what size pre-payment would be required to pay off your 30 year loan 5,10, or 15 years early, or your 15 year loan 2.5, 5, or 7.5 years prematurely. Again, we take you from 7.00% to 14.75%, but this set of tables covers loans from $50 all the way up through $550,000.

Section 3. THE MONTHLY LOAN PAYMENT TABLES allow you to read the monthly payments required to pay off a series of loans, ranging from $50 to $550,000 written for 1, 3, 5, 15, 20, and 30 years. These tables are also set up by interest rate, starting with 7.00% and going up, in 0.25% increments, to 14.75%.

Section 4. THE BI-WEEKLY PAYMENT TABLES compare the costs of monthly and bi-weekly loans. They show the time and money bi-weekly payments will save. But, remember: A bi-weekly only works when your lender actually credits your payments on a bi-weekly basis, and pre-paying on a monthly loan can save you just as much. Beware of "pseudo bi-weeklies" (see PART TWO).

Section 5. THE MORTGAGE FACTOR TABLES, plus a one-step calculation, let you determine the monthly payment required to pay off virtually any mortgage -- written for 1, 2, 3, 4, 5, 7.5, 10, 12.5, 15, 20, 25, or 30 years -- at interest rates from 7.000% to 14.975%.

PRE-PAYMENT SAVINGS TABLE

LOAN AMOUNT	PRE-PMT.	10.00%		10.25%		10.50%		10.75%	
		DOLLARS	MOS	DOLLARS	MOS	DOLLARS	MOS	DOLLARS	MOS
10,000	25	13,335	198	13,813	198	14,318	200	14,830	201
	50	16,172	248	16,707	248	17,270	249	17,838	249
	100	18,314	289	18,892	289	19,497	289	20,108	290
	200	19,732	318	20,340	318	20,975	318	21,614	319
25,000	25	22,617	129	23,594	130	24,586	132	25,593	133
	50	30,786	181	31,965	182	33,156	183	34,355	184
	100	38,313	232	39,650	233	40,996	234	42,346	234
	200	44,266	277	45,723	277	47,186	277	48,651	278
50,000	25	30,161	84	31,627	85	33,154	87	34,704	88
	50	45,248	129	47,186	130	49,188	132	51,202	133
	100	61,589	181	63,929	182	66,330	183	68,730	184
	200	76,644	232	79,300	233	82,011	234	84,714	235
65,000	25	32,802	70	34,478	71	36,202	72	37,993	74
	50	51,031	111	53,339	112	55,691	114	58,114	115
	100	72,043	161	74,918	162	77,826	163	80,798	165
	200	92,608	213	95,937	214	99,289	215	102,695	216
75,000	25	34,162	63	35,943	64	37,787	65	39,694	67
	50	54,180	101	56,687	103	59,263	104	61,899	106
	100	78,046	150	81,228	151	84,470	153	87,765	154
	200	102,198	202	105,930	204	109,712	205	113,534	206
85,000	25	35,286	57	37,163	58	39,112	59	41,132	61
	50	56,887	94	59,584	95	62,361	97	65,210	98
	100	83,409	141	86,892	142	90,447	144	94,068	145
	200	111,051	193	115,185	194	119,380	195	123,626	196
100,000	25	36,657	50	38,652	51	40,732	52	42,882	54
	50	60,322	84	63,265	85	66,307	87	69,421	88
	100	90,496	129	94,388	130	98,375	132	102,423	133
	200	123,176	181	127,875	182	132,658	183	137,482	184
125,000	25	38,379	42	40,528	43	42,767	44	45,099	45
	50	64,848	72	68,136	73	71,531	75	75,035	76
	100	100,347	113	104,846	115	109,448	116	114,158	118
	200	140,883	164	146,459	165	152,123	166	157,876	168
150,000	25	39,633	36	41,896	37	44,269	38	46,737	39
	50	68,325	63	71,884	64	75,585	65	79,401	67
	100	108,359	101	113,373	103	118,539	104	123,816	106
	200	156,091	150	162,456	151	168,957	153	175,552	154
175,000	25	40,587	31	42,948	32	45,413	33	47,994	34
	50	71,078	56	74,877	57	78,814	58	82,901	59
	100	115,013	92	120,503	93	126,137	95	131,930	96
	200	169,330	139	176,446	140	183,692	141	191,078	143
200,000	25	41,343	28	43,776	29	46,327	29	48,992	30
	50	73,323	50	77,313	51	81,466	52	85,771	54
	100	120,655	84	126,543	85	132,616	87	138,856	88
	200	181,007	129	188,792	130	196,752	132	204,861	133

PRE-PAYMENT SAVINGS TABLES

INSTRUCTIONS

In PARTS ONE and TWO of *A Banker's Secret*, we provide complete instuctions for how you can painlessly achieve dramatic savings on virtually every loan you now have or may ever get ... simply by making "pocket change" pre-payments. The larger the loan, and the longer its term, the more you'll save by pre-paying.

The tables we present on the following sixteen pages will give you a quick and accurate sense of just how impressive those savings can be. (All savings figures have been rounded off to the nearest dollar.)

Here's how to proceed: Let's say you have our sample $75,000 loan, which was written at 10.00% for 30 years, and you want to see what a *Regular* monthly pre-payment of $25 will save you.

- Turn to the **30 Year Pre-Payment Savings Table** for 10.00% to 10.75% loans. (It's reproduced on the preceding page for your convenience.)
- Follow the *Loan Amount* column down to $75,000.
- In the Pre-Payment (*Pre-Pmt*) column, you'll see four choices: $25, $50, $100, and $200. Follow the $25 per month pre-payment row to the right until it intersects with the 10.00% column.
- You'll see that a monthly pre-payment of $25 will save $34,162 in interest costs over the life of this loan, while reducing the mortgage's term by 63 months.

If you follow the $200 pre-payment row for the same loan, you'll find a $102,198 savings ... far more than the amount borrowed ... and 202 months worth of payments subtracted from the loan's term (a 16 year, 10 month reduction).

For loan amounts that do not appear on the table, you can get a good sense of the magnitude of your savings by comparing the two nearest listed values. For example, let's say you have a $90,000 loan, at 10% for 30 years, and you plan to pre-pay $50 a month. The nearest loans listed are $85,000 and $100,000, which indicate savings of $56,887 and $60,322, respectively. Your anticipated savings will be somewhere between $57,000 and $60,000.

PRE-PAYMENT SAVINGS TABLE

LOAN AMOUNT	PRE-PMT.	7.00%		7.25%		7.50%		7.75%	
		DOLLARS	MOS	DOLLARS	MOS	DOLLARS	MOS	DOLLARS	MOS
10,000	25	7,984	185	8,392	186	8,799	187	9,218	188
	50	10,032	240	10,513	241	10,990	241	11,478	242
	100	11,596	285	12,129	286	12,657	286	13,196	286
	200	12,624	317	13,191	317	13,753	317	14,326	317
25,000	25	12,624	113	13,339	114	14,074	115	14,831	116
	50	18,171	167	19,112	168	20,074	169	21,056	170
	100	23,557	223	24,691	224	25,844	225	27,015	225
	200	27,900	272	29,180	273	30,477	273	31,790	273
50,000	25	15,824	69	16,801	70	17,813	71	18,863	72
	50	25,249	113	26,683	114	28,154	115	29,669	116
	100	36,342	167	38,231	168	40,156	169	42,122	170
	200	47,114	223	49,390	224	51,697	225	54,040	225
65,000	25	16,837	56	17,902	57	19,013	58	20,168	59
	50	27,824	94	29,451	96	31,137	97	32,874	98
	100	41,689	145	43,920	147	46,211	148	48,554	149
	200	56,175	202	58,948	203	61,778	204	64,653	205
75,000	25	17,334	50	18,444	51	19,603	52	20,814	53
	50	29,158	85	30,894	87	32,690	88	34,554	89
	100	44,636	134	47,068	135	49,566	137	52,135	138
	200	61,466	190	64,546	191	67,686	192	70,894	193
85,000	25	17,736	45	18,887	46	20,086	46	21,338	47
	50	30,277	78	32,109	79	34,003	80	35,967	81
	100	47,208	125	49,826	126	52,512	127	55,273	128
	200	66,266	180	69,639	181	73,072	182	76,577	183
100,000	25	18,212	39	19,410	40	20,661	40	21,968	41
	50	31,651	69	33,602	70	35,626	71	37,725	72
	100	50,503	113	53,365	114	56,309	115	59,338	116
	200	72,690	167	76,462	168	80,312	169	84,243	170
125,000	25	18,792	32	20,044	33	21,360	33	22,736	34
	50	33,390	58	35,491	59	37,685	60	39,964	61
	100	54,899	97	58,094	98	61,401	99	64,807	101
	200	81,768	149	86,120	150	90,589	151	95,155	152
150,000	25	19,200	27	20,495	28	21,854	28	23,282	29
	50	34,667	50	36,890	51	39,209	52	41,630	53
	100	58,318	85	61,792	87	65,386	88	69,108	89
	200	89,271	134	94,142	135	99,139	137	104,270	138
175,000	25	19,506	23	20,831	24	22,226	25	23,689	25
	50	35,651	44	37,968	44	40,388	45	42,914	46
	100	61,061	76	64,765	77	68,605	79	72,582	80
	200	95,602	122	100,922	124	106,391	125	112,008	126
200,000	25	19,739	21	21,091	21	22,514	22	24,006	22
	50	36,428	39	38,820	40	41,325	40	43,940	41
	100	63,306	69	67,204	70	71,256	71	75,455	72
	200	101,011	113	106,729	114	112,624	115	118,682	116

PRE-PAYMENT SAVINGS TABLE

LOAN AMOUNT	PRE-PMT.	8.00%		8.25%		8.50%		8.75%	
		DOLLARS	MOS	DOLLARS	MOS	DOLLARS	MOS	DOLLARS	MOS
10,000	25	9,649	189	10,085	190	10,521	191	10,969	192
	50	11,979	242	12,481	243	12,984	244	13,497	244
	100	13,747	286	14,299	287	14,850	287	15,411	287
	200	14,911	317	15,496	317	16,079	317	16,672	318
25,000	25	15,608	118	16,414	119	17,237	120	18,078	122
	50	22,058	171	23,087	172	24,132	173	25,191	175
	100	28,202	226	29,415	227	30,641	228	31,877	228
	200	33,116	274	34,468	274	35,829	274	37,198	275
50,000	25	19,951	73	21,080	75	22,252	76	23,458	77
	50	31,225	118	32,826	119	34,474	120	36,155	122
	100	44,126	171	46,173	172	48,264	173	50,382	175
	200	56,415	226	58,830	227	61,282	228	63,755	228
65,000	25	21,369	60	22,616	61	23,915	62	25,266	63
	50	34,665	99	36,510	101	38,414	102	40,376	103
	100	50,950	150	53,398	151	55,904	153	58,465	154
	200	67,575	206	70,543	207	73,562	207	76,629	208
75,000	25	22,073	54	23,388	55	24,752	56	26,172	57
	50	36,473	90	38,462	92	40,508	93	42,620	94
	100	54,758	139	57,454	140	60,204	142	63,021	143
	200	74,148	194	77,471	195	80,838	196	84,264	197
85,000	25	22,650	48	24,014	49	25,436	50	26,918	51
	50	38,008	83	40,110	84	42,286	85	44,534	87
	100	58,116	130	61,022	131	64,004	132	67,058	134
	200	80,160	184	83,798	185	87,503	186	91,272	187
100,000	25	23,337	42	24,766	43	26,257	44	27,814	45
	50	39,906	73	42,166	75	44,503	76	46,924	77
	100	62,456	118	65,660	119	68,947	120	72,321	122
	200	88,260	171	92,356	172	96,527	173	100,777	175
125,000	25	24,177	35	25,687	35	27,267	36	28,921	37
	50	42,334	62	44,798	63	47,358	64	50,018	65
	100	68,320	102	71,940	103	75,669	105	79,510	106
	200	99,828	153	104,604	155	109,483	156	114,469	157
150,000	25	24,779	30	26,348	30	27,990	31	29,715	32
	50	44,149	54	46,775	55	49,503	56	52,345	57
	100	72,952	90	76,924	92	81,014	93	85,241	94
	200	109,523	139	114,908	140	120,407	142	126,042	143
175,000	25	25,228	26	26,844	26	28,538	27	30,317	28
	50	45,554	47	48,307	48	51,178	49	54,171	50
	100	76,706	81	80,971	82	85,384	83	89,941	85
	200	117,784	127	123,705	129	129,777	130	135,998	131
200,000	25	25,579	23	27,227	23	28,962	24	30,783	24
	50	46,677	42	49,533	43	52,519	44	55,632	45
	100	79,817	73	84,332	75	89,014	76	93,856	77
	200	124,920	118	131,321	119	137,904	120	144,651	122

PRE-PAYMENT SAVINGS TABLE

LOAN AMOUNT	PRE-PMT.	9.00%		9.25%		9.50%		9.75%	
		DOLLARS	MOS	DOLLARS	MOS	DOLLARS	MOS	DOLLARS	MOS
10,000	25	11,428	193	11,900	194	12,368	195	12,847	196
	50	14,021	245	14,555	246	15,085	246	15,624	247
	100	15,982	287	16,563	288	17,138	288	17,722	288
	200	17,275	318	17,888	318	18,494	318	19,109	318
25,000	25	18,943	123	19,835	125	20,737	126	21,674	127
	50	26,273	176	27,380	177	28,493	178	29,639	179
	100	33,135	229	34,413	230	35,693	231	37,005	231
	200	38,587	275	39,994	276	41,400	276	42,837	276
50,000	25	24,713	78	26,014	80	27,352	81	28,736	83
	50	37,887	123	39,669	125	41,485	126	43,347	127
	100	52,548	176	54,759	177	56,999	178	59,277	179
	200	66,270	229	68,824	230	71,401	231	74,010	231
65,000	25	26,667	65	28,123	66	29,627	67	31,184	68
	50	42,394	105	44,473	106	46,600	108	48,783	109
	100	61,078	155	63,748	157	66,460	158	69,222	159
	200	79,739	209	82,899	210	86,092	211	89,324	212
75,000	25	27,653	58	29,187	59	30,781	60	32,442	61
	50	44,802	96	47,044	97	49,350	98	51,732	100
	100	65,904	144	68,845	146	71,843	147	74,916	149
	200	87,748	198	91,281	199	94,860	200	98,506	201
85,000	25	28,464	52	30,069	53	31,743	55	33,476	56
	50	46,858	88	49,250	89	51,722	91	54,260	92
	100	70,188	135	73,383	136	76,656	138	79,990	139
	200	95,110	189	98,999	190	102,959	191	106,967	192
100,000	25	29,441	46	31,137	47	32,902	48	34,743	49
	50	49,434	78	52,028	80	54,704	81	57,471	83
	100	75,785	123	79,339	125	82,971	126	86,694	127
	200	105,108	176	109,518	177	113,997	178	118,554	179
125,000	25	30,652	38	32,458	39	34,348	40	36,318	41
	50	52,779	67	55,636	68	58,603	69	61,670	70
	100	83,461	108	87,514	109	91,685	110	95,957	112
	200	119,558	158	124,738	160	130,026	161	135,402	162
150,000	25	31,521	32	33,413	33	35,393	34	37,464	35
	50	55,304	58	58,377	59	61,569	60	64,883	61
	100	89,602	96	94,090	97	98,711	98	103,464	100
	200	131,807	144	137,691	146	143,699	147	149,831	149
175,000	25	32,183	28	34,137	29	36,190	30	38,337	30
	50	57,290	51	60,533	52	63,914	53	67,425	54
	100	94,652	86	99,509	88	104,526	89	109,690	90
	200	142,372	133	148,885	134	155,559	136	162,367	137
200,000	25	32,696	25	34,704	26	36,815	26	39,026	27
	50	58,885	46	62,273	47	65,812	48	69,495	49
	100	98,874	78	104,054	80	109,418	81	114,954	83
	200	151,581	123	158,676	125	165,955	126	173,402	127

PRE-PAYMENT SAVINGS TABLE

LOAN AMOUNT	PRE-PMT.	10.00%		10.25%		10.50%		10.75%	
		DOLLARS	MOS	DOLLARS	MOS	DOLLARS	MOS	DOLLARS	MOS
10,000	25	13,335	198	13,813	198	14,318	200	14,830	201
	50	16,172	248	16,707	248	17,270	249	17,838	249
	100	18,314	289	18,892	289	19,497	289	20,108	290
	200	19,732	318	20,340	318	20,975	318	21,614	319
25,000	25	22,617	129	23,594	130	24,586	132	25,593	133
	50	30,786	181	31,965	182	33,156	183	34,355	184
	100	38,313	232	39,650	233	40,996	234	42,346	234
	200	44,266	277	45,723	277	47,186	277	48,651	278
50,000	25	30,161	84	31,627	85	33,154	87	34,704	88
	50	45,248	129	47,186	130	49,188	132	51,202	133
	100	61,589	181	63,929	182	66,330	183	68,730	184
	200	76,644	232	79,300	233	82,011	234	84,714	235
65,000	25	32,802	70	34,478	71	36,202	72	37,993	74
	50	51,031	111	53,339	112	55,691	114	58,114	115
	100	72,043	161	74,918	162	77,826	163	80,798	165
	200	92,608	213	95,937	214	99,289	215	102,695	216
75,000	25	34,162	63	35,943	64	37,787	65	39,694	67
	50	54,180	101	56,687	103	59,263	104	61,899	106
	100	78,046	150	81,228	151	84,470	153	87,765	154
	200	102,198	202	105,930	204	109,712	205	113,534	206
85,000	25	35,286	57	37,163	58	39,112	59	41,132	61
	50	56,887	94	59,584	95	62,361	97	65,210	98
	100	83,409	141	86,892	142	90,447	144	94,068	145
	200	111,051	193	115,185	194	119,380	195	123,626	196
100,000	25	36,657	50	38,652	51	40,732	52	42,882	54
	50	60,322	84	63,265	85	66,307	87	69,421	88
	100	90,496	129	94,388	130	98,375	132	102,423	133
	200	123,176	181	127,875	182	132,658	183	137,482	184
125,000	25	38,379	42	40,528	43	42,767	44	45,099	45
	50	64,848	72	68,136	73	71,531	75	75,035	76
	100	100,347	113	104,846	115	109,448	116	114,158	118
	200	140,883	164	146,459	165	152,123	166	157,876	168
150,000	25	39,633	36	41,896	37	44,269	38	46,737	39
	50	68,325	63	71,884	64	75,585	65	79,401	67
	100	108,359	101	113,373	103	118,539	104	123,816	106
	200	156,091	150	162,456	151	168,957	153	175,552	154
175,000	25	40,587	31	42,948	32	45,413	33	47,994	34
	50	71,078	56	74,877	57	78,814	58	82,901	59
	100	115,013	92	120,503	93	126,137	95	131,930	96
	200	169,330	139	176,446	140	183,692	141	191,078	143
200,000	25	41,343	28	43,776	29	46,327	29	48,992	30
	50	73,323	50	77,313	51	81,466	52	85,771	54
	100	120,655	84	126,543	85	132,616	87	138,856	88
	200	181,007	129	188,792	130	196,752	132	204,861	133

11.00% TO 11.75% **30 YEAR** **11.00% TO 11.75%**

PRE-PAYMENT SAVINGS TABLE

LOAN AMOUNT	PRE-PMT.	11.00%		11.25%		11.50%		11.75%	
		DOLLARS	MOS	DOLLARS	MOS	DOLLARS	MOS	DOLLARS	MOS
10,000	25	15,329	202	15,854	203	16,384	204	16,892	205
	50	18,390	250	18,969	251	19,551	251	20,109	252
	100	20,700	290	21,320	290	21,941	291	22,537	291
	200	22,236	319	22,884	319	23,533	319	24,157	319
25,000	25	26,627	135	27,692	136	28,760	138	29,854	140
	50	35,581	185	36,833	187	38,084	188	39,356	189
	100	43,719	235	45,117	236	46,508	237	47,917	238
	200	50,136	278	51,645	279	53,144	279	54,659	279
50,000	25	36,311	90	37,961	91	39,666	93	41,408	95
	50	53,274	135	55,382	137	57,543	138	59,733	140
	100	71,185	186	73,665	187	76,193	188	78,740	189
	200	87,463	235	90,233	236	93,043	237	95,864	238
65,000	25	39,834	75	41,753	77	43,717	78	45,737	80
	50	60,580	117	63,129	119	65,713	120	68,348	122
	100	83,805	166	86,887	168	89,992	169	93,136	170
	200	106,126	217	109,624	218	113,134	219	116,672	220
75,000	25	41,673	68	43,723	69	45,838	71	48,019	72
	50	64,613	108	67,395	109	70,242	111	73,148	112
	100	91,129	156	94,552	157	98,030	159	101,553	160
	200	117,414	207	121,342	208	125,313	209	129,316	210
85,000	25	43,219	62	45,382	63	47,633	65	49,953	66
	50	68,129	100	71,125	101	74,213	103	77,369	105
	100	97,747	147	101,491	148	105,322	150	109,204	151
	200	127,916	198	132,259	199	136,676	200	141,130	201
100,000	25	45,121	55	47,442	56	49,852	57	52,359	59
	50	72,638	90	75,940	91	79,333	93	82,835	95
	100	106,567	135	110,786	137	115,087	138	119,488	140
	200	142,391	186	147,355	187	152,388	188	157,505	189
125,000	25	47,531	46	50,066	47	52,697	48	55,431	50
	50	78,658	77	82,396	79	86,241	80	90,199	82
	100	118,983	120	123,917	121	128,948	123	134,083	124
	200	163,728	169	169,672	170	175,689	172	181,791	173
150,000	25	49,318	40	52,010	41	54,820	42	57,742	43
	50	83,359	68	87,448	69	91,679	71	96,039	72
	100	129,242	108	134,791	109	140,486	111	146,298	112
	200	182,278	156	189,106	157	196,062	159	203,105	160
175,000	25	50,695	35	53,517	36	56,458	37	59,539	38
	50	87,141	61	91,534	62	96,071	63	100,781	65
	100	137,887	98	144,002	100	150,255	101	156,691	103
	200	198,617	144	206,285	146	214,074	147	222,022	149
200,000	25	51,791	31	54,711	32	57,772	33	60,976	34
	50	90,252	55	94,894	56	99,716	57	104,717	59
	100	145,289	90	151,894	91	158,683	93	165,668	95
	200	213,151	135	221,591	137	230,195	138	238,975	140

PRE-PAYMENT SAVINGS TABLE

LOAN AMOUNT	PRE-PMT.	12.00%		12.25%		12.50%		12.75%	
		DOLLARS	MOS	DOLLARS	MOS	DOLLARS	MOS	DOLLARS	MOS
10,000	25	17,424	206	17,990	207	18,523	208	19,083	210
	50	20,689	252	21,305	253	21,884	254	22,490	255
	100	23,156	291	23,809	292	24,424	292	25,067	292
	200	24,803	319	25,484	319	26,126	319	26,795	320
25,000	25	30,970	141	32,105	143	33,257	144	34,424	146
	50	40,647	190	41,952	192	43,270	193	44,598	194
	100	49,343	238	50,778	239	52,223	240	53,675	241
	200	56,187	280	57,725	280	59,269	281	60,817	281
50,000	25	43,199	96	45,036	98	46,917	100	48,830	101
	50	61,965	141	64,238	143	66,546	144	68,878	146
	100	81,322	190	83,936	192	86,574	193	89,229	194
	200	98,714	238	101,590	239	104,482	240	107,384	241
65,000	25	47,824	81	49,954	83	52,170	85	54,418	86
	50	71,046	123	73,779	125	76,595	127	79,429	128
	100	96,335	172	99,554	173	102,849	174	106,146	176
	200	120,255	221	123,848	222	127,508	223	131,158	224
75,000	25	50,273	74	52,579	75	54,968	77	57,441	79
	50	76,126	114	79,146	116	82,247	117	85,427	119
	100	105,138	161	108,747	163	112,430	164	116,181	166
	200	133,370	211	137,435	212	141,562	213	145,746	214
85,000	25	52,335	68	54,813	69	57,379	71	60,012	72
	50	80,579	106	83,886	108	87,281	109	90,730	111
	100	113,128	153	117,136	154	121,222	156	125,346	157
	200	145,609	202	150,161	203	154,777	204	159,417	205
100,000	25	54,936	60	57,618	62	60,388	63	63,242	64
	50	86,398	96	90,070	98	93,830	100	97,664	101
	100	123,931	141	128,474	143	133,088	144	137,759	146
	200	162,645	190	167,868	192	173,146	193	178,461	194
125,000	25	58,278	51	61,221	52	64,285	53	67,467	55
	50	94,284	84	98,464	85	102,773	87	107,209	88
	100	139,333	126	144,665	128	150,112	129	155,670	131
	200	187,992	174	194,246	176	200,598	177	207,041	179
150,000	25	60,791	44	63,956	45	67,254	46	70,682	48
	50	100,545	74	105,178	75	109,957	77	114,882	79
	100	152,251	114	158,316	116	164,522	117	170,853	119
	200	210,276	161	217,524	163	224,892	164	232,362	166
175,000	25	62,741	39	66,092	40	69,569	41	73,200	42
	50	105,635	66	110,666	68	115,837	69	121,186	71
	100	163,261	104	170,007	106	176,876	108	183,918	109
	200	230,076	151	238,284	152	246,582	154	255,025	155
200,000	25	64,316	35	67,805	36	71,451	37	75,250	38
	50	109,887	60	115,238	62	120,778	63	126,504	64
	100	172,814	96	180,142	98	187,662	100	195,354	101
	200	247,884	141	256,949	143	266,179	144	275,549	146

PRE-PAYMENT SAVINGS TABLE

LOAN AMOUNT	PRE-PMT.	13.00%		13.25%		13.50%		13.75%	
		DOLLARS	MOS	DOLLARS	MOS	DOLLARS	MOS	DOLLARS	MOS
10,000	25	19,640	211	20,189	212	20,726	212	21,296	214
	50	23,092	255	23,684	256	24,263	256	24,874	257
	100	25,704	292	26,330	293	26,942	293	27,586	293
	200	27,458	320	28,110	320	28,748	320	29,416	320
25,000	25	35,633	148	36,815	149	38,040	151	39,298	152
	50	45,966	195	47,300	196	48,671	198	50,076	199
	100	55,164	242	56,614	242	58,100	243	59,616	244
	200	62,403	282	63,944	282	65,521	282	67,127	283
50,000	25	50,808	103	52,808	105	54,861	106	56,956	108
	50	71,269	148	73,670	149	76,115	151	78,596	152
	100	91,935	195	94,641	197	97,381	198	100,150	199
	200	110,331	242	113,271	242	116,240	243	119,230	244
65,000	25	56,762	88	59,127	90	61,582	91	64,068	93
	50	82,359	130	85,290	132	88,310	133	91,344	135
	100	109,534	177	112,904	179	116,356	180	119,807	181
	200	134,893	225	138,597	226	142,376	226	146,142	227
75,000	25	59,969	80	62,544	82	65,235	83	67,957	85
	50	88,651	121	91,907	122	95,279	124	98,664	126
	100	119,959	167	123,751	169	127,655	170	131,550	172
	200	149,945	215	154,142	216	158,445	217	162,724	218
85,000	25	62,725	74	65,511	75	68,364	77	71,332	79
	50	94,254	113	97,841	115	101,481	116	105,232	118
	100	129,530	159	133,757	160	138,024	162	142,390	163
	200	164,101	207	168,814	208	173,549	209	178,375	210
100,000	25	66,209	66	69,241	67	72,377	69	75,616	71
	50	101,615	103	105,616	105	109,718	106	113,912	108
	100	142,538	148	147,338	149	152,227	151	157,190	152
	200	183,869	195	189,280	197	194,761	198	200,300	199
125,000	25	70,757	56	74,157	58	77,670	59	81,296	60
	50	111,750	90	116,396	92	121,156	93	126,014	95
	100	161,320	133	167,049	134	172,872	136	178,776	137
	200	213,549	180	220,115	181	226,753	183	233,442	184
150,000	25	74,237	49	77,908	50	81,755	52	85,715	53
	50	119,939	80	125,111	82	130,474	83	135,947	85
	100	177,303	121	183,844	122	190,562	124	197,368	126
	200	239,920	167	247,536	169	255,312	170	263,146	172
175,000	25	76,986	43	80,906	45	84,981	46	89,228	47
	50	126,710	72	132,371	74	138,206	76	144,223	77
	100	191,122	111	198,443	113	205,919	114	213,560	116
	200	263,605	157	272,262	158	281,044	160	289,967	161
200,000	25	79,214	39	83,338	40	87,629	41	92,102	42
	50	132,414	66	138,509	68	144,783	69	151,262	71
	100	203,226	103	211,265	105	219,472	106	227,859	108
	200	285,071	148	294,714	149	304,496	151	314,423	152

PRE-PAYMENT SAVINGS TABLE

LOAN AMOUNT	PRE-PMT.	14.00%		14.25%		14.50%		14.75%	
		DOLLARS	MOS	DOLLARS	MOS	DOLLARS	MOS	DOLLARS	MOS
10,000	25	21,897	215	22,480	216	23,044	217	23,642	218
	50	25,515	258	26,138	258	26,739	259	27,375	260
	100	28,260	294	28,915	294	29,547	294	30,214	294
	200	30,116	320	30,795	320	31,451	320	32,142	320
25,000	25	40,553	154	41,797	155	43,115	157	44,421	158
	50	51,470	200	52,847	201	54,300	203	55,732	204
	100	61,117	245	62,599	245	64,154	246	65,685	247
	200	68,715	283	70,281	283	71,920	284	73,533	284
50,000	25	59,091	110	61,261	111	63,503	113	65,757	115
	50	81,106	154	83,639	155	86,240	157	88,841	158
	100	102,940	200	105,744	201	108,609	203	111,463	204
	200	122,235	245	125,248	245	128,317	246	131,369	247
65,000	25	66,639	95	69,257	96	71,906	98	74,673	100
	50	94,456	137	97,603	138	100,764	140	104,040	142
	100	123,327	183	126,866	184	130,408	185	134,059	187
	200	149,968	228	153,806	229	157,635	230	161,566	231
75,000	25	70,762	87	73,643	89	76,589	90	79,600	92
	50	102,123	127	105,644	129	109,221	131	112,849	133
	100	135,506	173	139,514	174	143,561	176	147,644	177
	200	167,054	219	171,423	220	175,823	221	180,246	222
85,000	25	74,345	80	77,464	82	80,646	84	83,920	85
	50	109,014	120	112,894	121	116,816	123	120,821	125
	100	146,765	165	151,225	166	155,711	168	160,264	169
	200	183,193	211	188,085	212	192,988	213	197,947	214
100,000	25	78,946	72	82,387	74	85,906	75	89,517	77
	50	118,184	110	122,565	112	127,001	113	131,518	115
	100	162,213	154	167,327	155	172,473	157	177,685	158
	200	205,881	200	211,539	201	217,212	203	222,929	204
125,000	25	85,074	62	88,946	63	92,925	65	97,036	67
	50	131,034	97	136,130	99	141,320	100	146,628	102
	100	184,823	139	190,917	141	197,083	142	203,344	144
	200	240,263	185	247,103	187	253,987	188	260,949	189
150,000	25	89,818	54	94,040	56	98,440	57	102,964	59
	50	141,558	87	147,282	89	153,183	90	159,196	92
	100	204,288	127	211,286	129	218,448	131	225,694	133
	200	271,058	173	279,026	174	287,128	176	295,284	177
175,000	25	93,620	48	98,168	50	102,884	51	107,772	53
	50	150,386	79	156,711	80	163,199	82	169,854	84
	100	221,320	118	229,214	120	237,253	121	245,424	123
	200	298,968	163	308,067	164	317,282	166	326,593	167
200,000	25	96,737	44	101,562	45	106,561	46	111,750	48
	50	157,916	72	164,772	74	171,808	75	179,031	77
	100	236,404	110	245,129	112	253,997	113	263,032	115
	200	324,466	154	334,653	155	344,943	157	355,367	158

PRE-PAYMENT SAVINGS TABLE

LOAN AMOUNT	PRE-PMT.	7.00%		7.25%		7.50%		7.75%	
		DOLLARS	MOS	DOLLARS	MOS	DOLLARS	MOS	DOLLARS	MOS
10,000	25	2,179	58	2,280	58	2,382	58	2,487	58
	50	3,201	87	3,344	87	3,488	87	3,635	87
	100	4,196	116	4,377	116	4,559	117	4,745	117
	200	4,980	141	5,190	141	5,401	141	5,615	141
25,000	25	2,791	29	2,926	29	3,064	29	3,206	29
	50	4,700	49	4,920	50	5,144	50	5,373	50
	100	7,161	77	7,483	77	7,811	77	8,144	77
	200	9,732	107	10,155	107	10,583	107	11,017	108
50,000	25	3,083	15	3,236	16	3,392	16	3,553	16
	50	5,582	29	5,852	29	6,129	29	6,411	29
	100	9,400	49	9,841	50	10,290	50	10,747	50
	200	14,321	77	14,967	77	15,623	77	16,289	77
65,000	25	3,160	12	3,317	12	3,479	12	3,644	12
	50	5,837	23	6,122	23	6,415	23	6,713	23
	100	10,138	41	10,619	41	11,111	41	11,612	41
	200	16,085	66	16,821	66	17,570	66	18,331	66
75,000	25	3,195	11	3,355	11	3,519	11	3,686	11
	50	5,958	20	6,251	20	6,551	20	6,857	20
	100	10,505	36	11,008	36	11,521	37	12,044	37
	200	17,019	60	17,805	60	18,604	60	19,416	61
85,000	25	3,223	9	3,384	9	3,550	9	3,720	9
	50	6,054	18	6,353	18	6,658	18	6,972	18
	100	10,805	33	11,325	33	11,856	33	12,398	33
	200	17,813	55	18,641	55	19,482	56	20,340	56
100,000	25	3,254	8	3,417	8	3,585	8	3,757	8
	50	6,167	15	6,472	16	6,785	16	7,105	16
	100	11,165	29	11,705	29	12,258	29	12,823	29
	200	18,801	49	19,682	50	20,579	50	21,494	50
125,000	25	3,291	6	3,457	6	3,627	6	3,801	6
	50	6,299	13	6,613	13	6,934	13	7,263	13
	100	11,603	24	12,170	24	12,750	24	13,343	24
	200	20,065	42	21,017	42	21,987	42	22,977	42
150,000	25	3,315	5	3,483	5	3,655	5	3,831	5
	50	6,391	11	6,710	11	7,037	11	7,373	11
	100	11,916	20	12,502	20	13,101	20	13,715	20
	200	21,011	36	22,016	36	23,042	37	24,089	37
175,000	25	3,334	4	3,503	4	3,676	4	3,853	4
	50	6,457	9	6,780	9	7,112	9	7,453	9
	100	12,151	18	12,751	18	13,365	18	13,993	18
	200	21,744	32	22,791	32	23,861	32	24,955	32
200,000	25	3,347	4	3,516	4	3,690	4	3,868	4
	50	6,508	8	6,835	8	7,170	8	7,514	8
	100	12,334	15	12,944	16	13,570	16	14,210	16
	200	22,330	29	23,411	29	24,516	29	25,646	29

 8.00% TO 8.75%

PRE-PAYMENT SAVINGS TABLE

LOAN AMOUNT	PRE-PMT.	8.00%		8.25%		8.50%		8.75%	
		DOLLARS	MOS	DOLLARS	MOS	DOLLARS	MOS	DOLLARS	MOS
10,000	25	2,593	58	2,701	59	2,811	59	2,923	59
	50	3,784	87	3,934	87	4,087	88	4,242	88
	100	4,932	117	5,120	117	5,311	117	5,505	117
	200	5,831	141	6,048	141	6,268	141	6,490	141
25,000	25	3,350	29	3,497	29	3,648	30	3,801	30
	50	5,606	50	5,843	50	6,085	50	6,330	51
	100	8,481	78	8,824	78	9,172	78	9,525	78
	200	11,455	108	11,899	108	12,348	108	12,802	108
50,000	25	3,717	16	3,884	16	4,057	16	4,233	16
	50	6,700	29	6,995	29	7,296	30	7,603	30
	100	11,213	50	11,686	50	12,171	50	12,662	51
	200	16,964	78	17,649	78	18,346	78	19,051	78
65,000	25	3,814	12	3,987	12	4,165	13	4,347	13
	50	7,019	23	7,331	23	7,651	24	7,977	24
	100	12,123	41	12,644	41	13,175	42	13,716	42
	200	19,103	67	19,888	67	20,686	67	21,497	67
75,000	25	3,858	11	4,034	11	4,215	11	4,400	11
	50	7,171	21	7,492	21	7,820	21	8,156	21
	100	12,579	37	13,123	37	13,680	37	14,248	37
	200	20,243	61	21,083	61	21,937	61	22,807	61
85,000	25	3,894	10	4,072	10	4,255	10	4,442	10
	50	7,292	18	7,620	19	7,956	19	8,299	19
	100	12,952	33	13,517	34	14,094	34	14,682	34
	200	21,212	56	22,101	56	23,005	56	23,923	57
100,000	25	3,933	8	4,114	8	4,299	8	4,490	8
	50	7,433	16	7,769	16	8,113	16	8,466	16
	100	13,400	29	13,990	29	14,593	30	15,207	30
	200	22,425	50	23,374	50	24,341	50	25,324	51
125,000	25	3,980	6	4,164	7	4,353	7	4,545	7
	50	7,601	13	7,946	13	8,301	13	8,663	13
	100	13,949	24	14,569	24	15,203	24	15,851	25
	200	23,987	43	25,015	43	26,063	43	27,131	43
150,000	25	4,012	5	4,197	5	4,388	5	4,583	5
	50	7,717	11	8,069	11	8,430	11	8,801	11
	100	14,343	21	14,984	21	15,641	21	16,312	21
	200	25,157	37	26,247	37	27,360	37	28,495	37
175,000	25	4,035	5	4,222	5	4,414	5	4,610	5
	50	7,802	9	8,160	9	8,527	9	8,903	9
	100	14,637	18	15,295	18	15,970	18	16,660	18
	200	26,070	33	27,208	33	28,371	33	29,559	33
200,000	25	4,051	4	4,239	4	4,432	4	4,630	4
	50	7,867	8	8,228	8	8,599	8	8,980	8
	100	14,867	16	15,538	16	16,227	16	16,931	16
	200	26,800	29	27,980	29	29,185	30	30,414	30

9.00% TO 9.75% **15 YEAR** 9.00% TO 9.75%

PRE-PAYMENT SAVINGS TABLE

LOAN AMOUNT	PRE-PMT.	9.00%		9.25%		9.50%		9.75%	
		DOLLARS	MOS	DOLLARS	MOS	DOLLARS	MOS	DOLLARS	MOS
10,000	25	3,037	59	3,153	59	3,269	60	3,389	60
	50	4,399	88	4,558	88	4,718	88	4,882	89
	100	5,700	117	5,898	117	6,096	117	6,298	117
	200	6,714	141	6,941	141	7,167	141	7,398	141
25,000	25	3,958	30	4,119	30	4,283	30	4,450	30
	50	6,581	51	6,836	51	7,095	51	7,358	51
	100	9,883	78	10,247	79	10,615	79	10,987	79
	200	13,263	108	13,728	108	14,198	108	14,672	109
50,000	25	4,413	16	4,598	16	4,787	16	4,981	17
	50	7,917	30	8,238	30	8,566	30	8,900	30
	100	13,162	51	13,672	51	14,190	51	14,718	51
	200	19,767	78	20,494	79	21,229	79	21,975	79
65,000	25	4,534	13	4,726	13	4,921	13	5,122	13
	50	8,311	24	8,653	24	9,001	24	9,359	24
	100	14,269	42	14,832	42	15,405	42	15,990	43
	200	22,322	67	23,158	68	24,007	68	24,870	68
75,000	25	4,590	11	4,785	11	4,985	11	5,189	11
	50	8,500	21	8,851	21	9,212	21	9,579	21
	100	14,827	38	15,416	38	16,019	38	16,632	38
	200	23,690	62	24,586	62	25,499	62	26,425	62
85,000	25	4,634	10	4,831	10	5,033	10	5,240	10
	50	8,650	19	9,010	19	9,378	19	9,755	19
	100	15,284	34	15,897	34	16,523	34	17,162	35
	200	24,858	57	25,809	57	26,775	57	27,760	57
100,000	25	4,685	8	4,885	8	5,090	8	5,301	9
	50	8,827	16	9,196	16	9,575	16	9,961	17
	100	15,835	30	16,476	30	17,131	30	17,801	30
	200	26,325	51	27,343	51	28,381	51	29,437	51
125,000	25	4,743	7	4,947	7	5,155	7	5,369	7
	50	9,035	13	9,416	13	9,807	13	10,207	13
	100	16,513	25	17,189	25	17,881	25	18,589	25
	200	28,221	43	29,331	43	30,462	44	31,614	44
150,000	25	4,784	6	4,990	6	5,200	6	5,416	6
	50	9,180	11	9,570	11	9,969	11	10,378	11
	100	17,000	21	17,703	21	18,423	21	19,159	21
	200	29,653	38	30,833	38	32,037	38	33,265	38
175,000	25	4,812	5	5,019	5	5,232	5	5,450	5
	50	9,289	10	9,683	10	10,088	10	10,503	10
	100	17,367	18	18,091	18	18,830	19	19,587	19
	200	30,771	33	32,010	33	33,271	34	34,559	34
200,000	25	4,833	4	5,042	4	5,256	4	5,476	4
	50	9,370	8	9,770	8	10,181	8	10,601	9
	100	17,653	16	18,392	16	19,150	16	19,924	17
	200	31,670	30	32,953	30	34,264	30	35,603	30

PRE-PAYMENT SAVINGS TABLE

LOAN AMOUNT	PRE-PMT.	10.00% DOLLARS	10.00% MOS	10.25% DOLLARS	10.25% MOS	10.50% DOLLARS	10.50% MOS	10.75% DOLLARS	10.75% MOS
10,000	25	3,510	60	3,634	60	3,760	60	3,886	61
	50	5,046	89	5,214	89	5,385	89	5,555	89
	100	6,501	118	6,707	118	6,915	118	7,124	118
	200	7,628	141	7,863	141	8,100	142	8,336	142
25,000	25	4,621	31	4,795	31	4,973	31	5,155	31
	50	7,627	52	7,900	52	8,179	52	8,461	52
	100	11,365	79	11,750	79	12,139	80	12,533	80
	200	15,152	109	15,639	109	16,129	109	16,624	109
50,000	25	5,179	17	5,381	17	5,589	17	5,802	17
	50	9,242	31	9,590	31	9,947	31	10,310	31
	100	15,255	52	15,801	52	16,357	52	16,922	52
	200	22,733	79	23,500	79	24,279	80	25,065	80
65,000	25	5,328	13	5,539	13	5,756	13	5,977	13
	50	9,724	25	10,097	25	10,477	25	10,867	25
	100	16,585	43	17,192	43	17,810	43	18,440	43
	200	25,745	68	26,635	68	27,536	69	28,451	69
75,000	25	5,399	11	5,613	12	5,833	12	6,058	12
	50	9,955	22	10,339	22	10,733	22	11,135	22
	100	17,259	38	17,896	39	18,547	39	19,210	39
	200	27,368	62	28,323	63	29,295	63	30,280	63
85,000	25	5,453	10	5,671	10	5,894	10	6,123	10
	50	10,140	19	10,536	20	10,939	20	11,351	20
	100	17,813	35	18,478	35	19,157	35	19,848	35
	200	28,758	58	29,774	58	30,807	58	31,855	58
100,000	25	5,516	9	5,737	9	5,964	9	6,196	9
	50	10,358	17	10,763	17	11,179	17	11,604	17
	100	18,485	31	19,181	31	19,894	31	20,620	31
	200	30,511	52	31,602	52	32,715	52	33,846	52
125,000	25	5,588	7	5,813	7	6,045	7	6,282	7
	50	10,617	14	11,036	14	11,466	14	11,906	14
	100	19,313	25	20,053	26	20,807	26	21,578	26
	200	32,788	44	33,985	44	35,204	45	36,442	45
150,000	25	5,638	6	5,866	6	6,100	6	6,340	6
	50	10,797	11	11,227	12	11,667	12	12,117	12
	100	19,911	22	20,680	22	21,466	22	22,271	22
	200	34,518	38	35,794	39	37,095	39	38,420	39
175,000	25	5,674	5	5,904	5	6,140	5	6,383	5
	50	10,929	10	11,366	10	11,814	10	12,272	10
	100	20,362	19	21,155	19	21,966	19	22,797	19
	200	35,874	34	37,215	34	38,586	34	39,981	35
200,000	25	5,701	4	5,933	4	6,171	4	6,416	4
	50	11,032	9	11,474	9	11,927	9	12,392	9
	100	20,715	17	21,527	17	22,357	17	23,208	17
	200	36,969	31	38,363	31	39,787	31	41,241	31

11.00% TO 11.75% **15 YEAR** **11.00% TO 11.75%**

PRE-PAYMENT SAVINGS TABLE

LOAN AMOUNT	PRE-PMT.	11.00%		11.25%		11.50%		11.75%	
		DOLLARS	MOS	DOLLARS	MOS	DOLLARS	MOS	DOLLARS	MOS
10,000	25	4,016	61	4,147	61	4,281	61	4,415	62
	50	5,730	90	5,904	90	6,083	90	6,261	90
	100	7,336	118	7,548	118	7,765	118	7,981	118
	200	8,577	142	8,816	142	9,061	142	9,304	142
25,000	25	5,341	31	5,530	32	5,723	32	5,920	32
	50	8,749	53	9,040	53	9,337	53	9,639	53
	100	12,932	80	13,336	80	13,746	80	14,159	81
	200	17,126	109	17,631	109	18,142	110	18,656	110
50,000	25	6,020	17	6,242	17	6,471	18	6,703	18
	50	10,681	31	11,059	32	11,446	32	11,839	32
	100	17,498	53	18,080	53	18,675	53	19,279	53
	200	25,865	80	26,672	80	27,492	80	28,321	81
65,000	25	6,204	14	6,436	14	6,674	14	6,917	14
	50	11,265	25	11,672	25	12,088	26	12,511	26
	100	19,081	44	19,733	44	20,397	44	21,075	44
	200	29,379	69	30,321	69	31,276	70	32,244	70
75,000	25	6,290	12	6,526	12	6,768	12	7,018	12
	50	11,547	22	11,968	22	12,398	23	12,837	23
	100	19,886	39	20,576	40	21,276	40	21,992	40
	200	31,283	63	32,299	64	33,329	64	34,378	64
85,000	25	6,358	10	6,598	11	6,844	11	7,096	11
	50	11,773	20	12,205	20	12,647	20	13,099	20
	100	20,553	36	21,272	36	22,004	36	22,753	36
	200	32,922	59	34,003	59	35,102	59	36,220	59
100,000	25	6,434	9	6,679	9	6,930	9	7,187	9
	50	12,039	17	12,485	17	12,942	18	13,408	18
	100	21,363	31	22,120	32	22,893	32	23,680	32
	200	34,995	53	36,163	53	37,352	53	38,559	53
125,000	25	6,525	7	6,774	7	7,031	7	7,294	7
	50	12,357	14	12,819	14	13,293	14	13,778	14
	100	22,366	26	23,171	26	23,996	26	24,836	27
	200	37,704	45	38,989	45	40,300	45	41,630	46
150,000	25	6,587	6	6,839	6	7,099	6	7,365	6
	50	12,579	12	13,053	12	13,538	12	14,036	12
	100	23,094	22	23,937	22	24,796	23	25,675	23
	200	39,773	39	41,152	40	42,554	40	43,983	40
175,000	25	6,631	5	6,886	5	7,149	5	7,418	5
	50	12,743	10	13,226	10	13,721	10	14,229	10
	100	23,647	19	24,516	20	25,404	20	26,313	20
	200	41,404	35	42,856	35	44,338	35	45,851	36
200,000	25	6,666	4	6,924	4	7,189	4	7,461	4
	50	12,869	9	13,358	9	13,860	9	14,374	9
	100	24,079	17	24,971	17	25,884	18	26,816	18
	200	42,725	31	44,242	32	45,785	32	47,360	32

PRE-PAYMENT SAVINGS TABLE

LOAN AMOUNT	PRE-PMT.	12.00%		12.25%		12.50%		12.75%	
		DOLLARS	MOS	DOLLARS	MOS	DOLLARS	MOS	DOLLARS	MOS
10,000	25	4,553	62	4,693	62	4,833	62	4,977	63
	50	6,444	90	6,628	91	6,812	91	7,000	91
	100	8,201	119	8,423	119	8,643	119	8,868	119
	200	9,552	142	9,801	142	10,049	142	10,301	142
25,000	25	6,120	32	6,326	32	6,534	33	6,748	33
	50	9,945	54	10,258	54	10,574	54	10,897	54
	100	14,579	81	15,005	81	15,434	81	15,872	82
	200	19,176	110	19,702	110	20,231	110	20,769	110
50,000	25	6,942	18	7,187	18	7,436	18	7,693	18
	50	12,242	32	12,653	32	13,070	33	13,498	33
	100	19,893	54	20,517	54	21,149	54	21,795	54
	200	29,160	81	30,012	81	30,871	81	31,744	82
65,000	25	7,168	14	7,423	14	7,685	14	7,954	14
	50	12,945	26	13,387	26	13,841	26	14,303	27
	100	21,764	45	22,463	45	23,177	45	23,903	45
	200	33,226	70	34,221	70	35,231	71	36,252	71
75,000	25	7,273	12	7,534	12	7,802	12	8,076	13
	50	13,286	23	13,746	23	14,215	23	14,696	24
	100	22,720	40	23,462	40	24,217	41	24,987	41
	200	35,441	64	36,518	65	37,610	65	38,721	65
85,000	25	7,355	11	7,621	11	7,893	11	8,172	11
	50	13,561	21	14,034	21	14,517	21	15,011	21
	100	23,515	37	24,292	37	25,083	37	25,890	37
	200	37,354	60	38,505	60	39,674	60	40,860	60
100,000	25	7,452	9	7,722	9	8,000	9	8,285	10
	50	13,885	18	14,374	18	14,873	18	15,386	18
	100	24,485	32	25,306	32	26,142	33	26,995	33
	200	39,788	54	41,035	54	42,301	54	43,591	54
125,000	25	7,563	7	7,840	7	8,124	8	8,414	8
	50	14,275	15	14,782	15	15,302	15	15,835	15
	100	25,692	27	26,569	27	27,465	27	28,380	27
	200	42,984	46	44,363	46	45,768	46	47,194	47
150,000	25	7,639	6	7,920	6	8,208	6	8,504	6
	50	14,545	12	15,069	12	15,604	12	16,153	13
	100	26,572	23	27,492	23	28,431	23	29,392	24
	200	45,440	40	46,927	40	48,435	41	49,974	41
175,000	25	7,695	5	7,979	5	8,270	5	8,570	5
	50	14,749	11	15,281	11	15,826	11	16,386	11
	100	27,243	20	28,194	20	29,169	20	30,164	21
	200	47,388	36	48,956	36	50,557	36	52,189	36
200,000	25	7,739	5	8,024	5	8,317	5	8,618	5
	50	14,902	9	15,445	9	16,000	9	16,569	10
	100	27,770	18	28,748	18	29,747	18	30,772	18
	200	48,970	32	50,613	32	52,285	33	53,991	33

PRE-PAYMENT SAVINGS TABLE

LOAN AMOUNT	PRE-PMT.	13.00%		13.25%		13.50%		13.75%	
		DOLLARS	MOS	DOLLARS	MOS	DOLLARS	MOS	DOLLARS	MOS
10,000	25	5,123	63	5,270	63	5,420	64	5,573	64
	50	7,190	91	7,382	91	7,575	92	7,773	92
	100	9,096	119	9,324	119	9,554	119	9,789	120
	200	10,556	142	10,811	142	11,067	142	11,329	142
25,000	25	6,965	33	7,188	33	7,415	34	7,645	34
	50	11,222	55	11,555	55	11,894	55	12,236	56
	100	16,310	82	16,756	82	17,210	82	17,665	83
	200	21,306	110	21,852	111	22,403	111	22,956	111
50,000	25	7,954	18	8,223	19	8,496	19	8,776	19
	50	13,932	33	14,377	33	14,830	34	15,289	34
	100	22,447	55	23,113	55	23,787	55	24,471	56
	200	32,623	82	33,516	82	34,419	82	35,329	83
65,000	25	8,229	15	8,510	15	8,797	15	9,092	15
	50	14,774	27	15,256	27	15,748	27	16,250	27
	100	24,641	46	25,392	46	26,155	46	26,931	47
	200	37,289	71	38,340	71	39,402	72	40,476	72
75,000	25	8,356	13	8,644	13	8,939	13	9,241	13
	50	15,185	24	15,685	24	16,198	24	16,720	24
	100	25,770	41	26,568	41	27,380	42	28,204	42
	200	39,845	66	40,984	66	42,142	66	43,312	66
85,000	25	8,458	11	8,752	11	9,052	12	9,360	12
	50	15,517	21	16,034	21	16,561	22	17,101	22
	100	26,713	38	27,550	38	28,402	38	29,272	38
	200	42,064	61	43,285	61	44,523	61	45,783	62
100,000	25	8,575	10	8,875	10	9,181	10	9,495	10
	50	15,910	18	16,446	19	16,993	19	17,553	19
	100	27,865	33	28,754	33	29,660	34	30,581	34
	200	44,897	55	46,225	55	47,575	55	48,945	56
125,000	25	8,713	8	9,018	8	9,333	8	9,655	8
	50	16,381	15	16,940	15	17,513	15	18,100	16
	100	29,312	28	30,263	28	31,237	28	32,229	28
	200	48,644	47	50,120	47	51,623	48	53,146	48
150,000	25	8,808	6	9,120	6	9,439	7	9,765	7
	50	16,714	13	17,289	13	17,879	13	18,482	13
	100	30,371	24	31,372	24	32,396	24	33,441	24
	200	51,541	41	53,138	41	54,760	42	56,410	42
175,000	25	8,877	5	9,192	6	9,515	6	9,846	6
	50	16,959	11	17,548	11	18,151	11	18,770	11
	100	31,179	21	32,219	21	33,283	21	34,372	21
	200	53,849	37	55,541	37	57,267	37	59,027	37
200,000	25	8,927	5	9,244	5	9,571	5	9,905	5
	50	17,152	10	17,749	10	18,361	10	18,990	10
	100	31,820	18	32,891	19	33,986	19	35,105	19
	200	55,732	33	57,508	33	59,319	34	61,162	34

PRE-PAYMENT SAVINGS TABLE

LOAN AMOUNT	PRE-PMT.	14.00%		14.25%		14.50%		14.75%	
		DOLLARS	MOS	DOLLARS	MOS	DOLLARS	MOS	DOLLARS	MOS
10,000	25	5,726	64	5,883	64	6,039	65	6,199	65
	50	7,970	92	8,171	92	8,370	93	8,574	93
	100	10,021	120	10,258	120	10,493	120	10,732	120
	200	11,588	142	11,851	142	12,112	142	12,377	142
25,000	25	7,880	34	8,119	34	8,363	35	8,612	35
	50	12,583	56	12,935	56	13,293	56	13,656	57
	100	18,125	83	18,592	83	19,064	83	19,540	84
	200	23,514	111	24,078	111	24,646	112	25,219	112
50,000	25	9,062	19	9,357	19	9,656	20	9,962	20
	50	15,759	34	16,240	34	16,727	35	17,224	35
	100	25,165	56	25,873	56	26,587	56	27,312	57
	200	36,250	83	37,187	83	38,127	83	39,080	84
65,000	25	9,394	15	9,704	15	10,021	15	10,345	16
	50	16,762	28	17,285	28	17,819	28	18,364	28
	100	27,720	47	28,523	47	29,340	47	30,168	48
	200	41,567	72	42,674	73	43,790	73	44,921	73
75,000	25	9,551	13	9,868	13	10,194	14	10,526	14
	50	17,255	25	17,800	25	18,356	25	18,926	25
	100	29,046	42	29,901	43	30,771	43	31,657	43
	200	44,500	67	45,702	67	46,922	67	48,159	68
85,000	25	9,674	12	9,997	12	10,329	12	10,668	12
	50	17,652	22	18,216	22	18,794	22	19,383	23
	100	30,155	39	31,056	39	31,973	39	32,909	39
	200	47,054	62	48,347	62	49,660	62	50,988	63
100,000	25	9,817	10	10,148	10	10,487	10	10,835	10
	50	18,125	19	18,713	19	19,313	20	19,925	20
	100	31,519	34	32,481	34	33,455	35	34,450	35
	200	50,332	56	51,746	56	53,177	56	54,629	57
125,000	25	9,985	8	10,324	8	10,673	8	11,031	8
	50	18,698	16	19,312	16	19,940	16	20,584	16
	100	33,243	29	34,275	29	35,329	29	36,407	29
	200	54,697	48	56,275	48	57,875	49	59,503	49
150,000	25	10,101	7	10,447	7	10,800	7	11,164	7
	50	19,102	13	19,738	13	20,387	14	21,052	14
	100	34,511	25	35,601	25	36,712	25	37,852	25
	200	58,092	42	59,806	43	61,541	43	63,313	43
175,000	25	10,187	6	10,535	6	10,894	6	11,262	6
	50	19,405	11	20,054	12	20,718	12	21,398	12
	100	35,486	22	36,619	22	37,779	22	38,964	22
	200	60,813	38	62,634	38	64,491	38	66,380	39
200,000	25	10,249	5	10,602	5	10,965	5	11,338	5
	50	19,635	10	20,296	10	20,975	10	21,671	10
	100	36,252	19	37,426	19	38,627	20	39,852	20
	200	63,041	34	64,961	34	66,913	35	68,901	35

10.00% 10.00%

DEBT REDUCTION TABLE

TO REDUCE A 30 YEAR LOAN TO:

LOAN AMOUNT	25 YEARS		20 YEARS		15 YEARS	
	PRE-PAY	SAVE	PRE-PAY	SAVE	PRE-PAY	SAVE
50	0.02	25	0.05	44	0.10	60
100	0.03	40	0.09	82	0.20	119
200	0.06	81	0.18	165	0.39	236
300	0.09	120	0.26	242	0.59	355
400	0.12	161	0.35	325	0.78	473
500	0.16	220	0.44	420	0.99	610
600	0.19	260	0.53	502	1.18	727
700	0.22	298	0.61	579	1.38	845
800	0.24	329	0.70	662	1.57	963
900	0.28	388	0.79	758	1.78	1,101
1,000	0.31	428	0.88	840	1.97	1,218
2,000	0.62	856	1.75	1,675	3.94	2,436
3,000	0.94	1,305	2.63	2,530	5.91	3,671
4,000	1.24	1,720	3.50	3,363	7.88	4,887
5,000	1.56	2,168	4.38	4,218	9.86	6,125
6,000	1.87	2,596	5.25	5,053	11.82	7,340
7,000	2.17	3,014	6.12	5,888	13.79	8,558
8,000	2.49	3,461	7.00	6,742	15.76	9,792
9,000	2.80	3,890	7.87	7,578	17.73	11,011
10,000	3.12	4,337	8.75	8,431	19.71	12,247
15,000	4.67	6,494	13.12	12,644	29.56	18,368
20,000	6.23	8,662	17.49	16,856	39.41	24,490
25,000	7.78	10,821	21.86	21,070	49.26	30,613
30,000	9.34	12,988	26.23	25,282	59.11	36,735
35,000	10.89	15,147	30.60	29,496	68.96	42,858
45,000	14.01	19,491	39.35	37,939	88.67	55,120
55,000	17.12	23,818	48.10	46,370	108.37	67,364
65,000	20.23	28,144	56.84	54,796	128.07	79,609
75,000	23.35	32,488	65.59	63,239	147.78	91,871
85,000	26.46	36,815	74.33	71,666	167.48	104,116
100,000	31.13	43,309	87.45	84,308	197.03	122,481
120,000	37.36	51,980	104.94	101,179	236.44	146,989
140,000	43.58	60,631	122.43	118,035	275.84	171,477
160,000	49.81	69,303	139.92	134,905	315.25	195,985
180,000	56.04	77,974	157.41	151,775	354.66	220,491
200,000	62.26	86,627	174.90	168,631	394.07	244,983
225,000	70.04	97,456	196.76	189,715	443.33	275,613
250,000	77.83	108,295	218.63	210,802	492.59	306,241
275,000	85.60	119,106	240.48	231,867	541.84	336,853
300,000	93.39	129,945	262.35	252,954	591.10	367,482
350,000	108.95	151,594	306.07	295,106	689.61	428,722
400,000	124.52	173,262	349.80	337,277	788.14	489,982
450,000	140.08	194,911	393.52	379,428	886.65	551,222
500,000	155.65	216,581	437.25	421,600	985.17	612,482
550,000	171.21	238,229	480.97	463,751	1,083.68	673,721

DEBT REDUCTION TABLES

INSTRUCTIONS

It's reasonable to wonder, "How much would I have to add to my monthly payment to pay off my 30 year loan in 20 years? My 15 year loan in 7.5 years?" These questions are immediately answered by referring to our exclusive Debt Reduction Tables.

Here's how to proceed: Let's say you wanted to pay off your $75,000, 10%, 30 year loan in half the time ... 15 years.

- Turn to the 30 year, 10% table. (Reproduced on the preceding page for your convenience.)
- Look down the left hand (*Loan Amount*) column until you see $75,000.
- Read across to the right, until you are under the *15 Years/Pre-Pay* column.
- You'll find that by adding a monthly pre-payment of $147.78 to your regular monthly payment ($658.18 in this case), you'll reduce the term of your loan down from its contractual term of 30 years to a money saving 15 years.
- Continue reading across to the right until you are looking under the next (*Save*) column.
- You'll see that your monthly pre-payment of $147.78 will save you $91,871.

To find the correct table, simply thumb through this section to find the one with both the interest rate and term that most closely matches your loan. Because most homeowners have 30 year loans, the 30 year tables come before the 15 year ones.

If you're not certain what your monthly payment is, you can look it up on the Monthly Loan Payment Tables, which follow this Debt Reduction Tables section.

And remember: No applications, fees, permission, or refinancing of any sort are necessary to immediately take advantage of your personal, self-managed, mortgage investment program. Just decide when you want your loan to be paid off, and pre-pay the necessary amount every month. That will reduce both the term and the overall cost of your loan.

7.00% 7.00%

DEBT REDUCTION TABLE

TO REDUCE A 30 YEAR LOAN TO:

LOAN AMOUNT	25 YEARS		20 YEARS		15 YEARS	
	PRE-PAY	SAVE	PRE-PAY	SAVE	PRE-PAY	SAVE
50	0.02	11	0.05	22	0.11	33
100	0.04	25	0.11	51	0.23	74
200	0.08	51	0.22	102	0.46	148
300	0.13	84	0.33	158	0.70	230
400	0.16	104	0.44	209	0.93	304
500	0.21	137	0.55	265	1.17	386
600	0.25	162	0.66	316	1.40	460
700	0.29	191	0.77	373	1.64	543
800	0.33	217	0.88	423	1.87	617
900	0.38	250	0.99	480	2.10	697
1,000	0.41	270	1.10	530	2.33	771
2,000	0.83	549	2.20	1,067	4.67	1,552
3,000	1.25	827	3.30	1,602	7.01	2,331
4,000	1.66	1,097	4.40	2,133	9.34	3,103
5,000	2.07	1,370	5.50	2,669	11.68	3,883
6,000	2.49	1,649	6.60	3,205	14.01	4,662
7,000	2.90	1,919	7.70	3,736	16.34	5,433
8,000	3.32	2,197	8.80	4,271	18.68	6,213
9,000	3.74	2,475	9.90	4,808	21.02	6,993
10,000	4.14	2,740	10.99	5,335	23.35	7,765
15,000	6.22	4,119	16.50	8,013	35.03	11,655
20,000	8.29	5,489	21.99	10,680	46.70	15,537
25,000	10.37	6,868	27.50	13,357	58.38	19,426
30,000	12.44	8,238	32.99	16,024	70.05	23,309
35,000	14.52	9,617	38.50	18,701	81.73	27,198
45,000	18.67	12,365	49.50	24,045	105.09	34,971
55,000	22.81	15,109	60.50	29,389	128.44	42,743
65,000	26.96	17,858	71.50	34,733	151.79	50,516
75,000	31.11	20,606	82.50	40,077	175.15	58,288
85,000	35.26	23,356	93.50	45,421	198.50	66,061
100,000	41.47	27,469	109.99	53,431	233.52	77,713
120,000	49.77	32,967	131.99	64,119	280.23	93,259
140,000	58.07	38,464	153.99	74,807	326.93	108,802
160,000	66.36	43,957	175.99	85,495	373.64	124,347
180,000	74.66	49,454	197.99	96,183	420.35	139,892
200,000	82.95	54,946	219.99	106,870	467.05	155,435
225,000	93.32	61,815	247.49	120,228	525.43	174,862
250,000	103.69	68,686	274.99	133,590	583.82	194,298
275,000	114.06	75,553	302.49	146,947	642.19	213,722
300,000	124.43	82,424	329.99	160,310	700.58	233,158
350,000	145.17	96,163	384.99	187,029	817.34	272,018
400,000	165.91	109,903	439.99	213,750	934.11	310,881
450,000	186.64	123,632	494.98	240,461	1,050.86	349,732
500,000	207.38	137,372	549.98	267,181	1,167.63	388,594
550,000	228.12	151,110	604.98	293,900	1,284.39	427,454

7.25% 7.25%

DEBT REDUCTION TABLE

TO REDUCE A 30 YEAR LOAN TO:

LOAN AMOUNT	25 YEARS		20 YEARS		15 YEARS	
	PRE-PAY	SAVE	PRE-PAY	SAVE	PRE-PAY	SAVE
50	0.02	11	0.05	22	0.11	34
100	0.04	26	0.11	52	0.23	75
200	0.08	55	0.22	110	0.46	158
300	0.12	84	0.33	167	0.69	241
400	0.17	119	0.44	225	0.93	325
500	0.20	139	0.54	274	1.15	399
600	0.24	168	0.65	331	1.38	482
700	0.28	197	0.76	389	1.62	566
800	0.33	232	0.87	447	1.85	649
900	0.37	261	0.98	505	2.08	732
1,000	0.40	281	1.08	553	2.30	805
2,000	0.81	571	2.16	1,113	4.61	1,620
3,000	1.22	861	3.25	1,675	6.92	2,434
4,000	1.63	1,151	4.33	2,234	9.23	3,248
5,000	2.04	1,442	5.41	2,794	11.54	4,063
6,000	2.43	1,717	6.49	3,347	13.84	4,869
7,000	2.84	2,006	7.57	3,907	16.15	5,683
8,000	3.25	2,297	8.66	4,469	18.45	6,497
9,000	3.66	2,587	9.74	5,028	20.76	7,310
10,000	4.07	2,877	10.82	5,587	23.07	8,125
15,000	6.10	4,313	16.23	8,382	34.60	12,187
20,000	8.13	5,748	21.64	11,176	46.14	16,250
25,000	10.16	7,185	27.05	13,970	57.67	20,313
30,000	12.19	8,621	32.46	16,764	69.20	24,374
35,000	14.22	10,056	37.87	19,557	80.74	28,437
45,000	18.29	12,936	48.69	25,151	103.81	36,570
55,000	22.35	15,809	59.51	30,740	126.88	44,696
65,000	26.41	18,680	70.33	36,327	149.95	52,821
75,000	30.47	21,552	81.15	41,915	173.01	60,945
85,000	34.54	24,432	91.97	47,509	196.09	69,079
100,000	40.63	28,740	108.20	55,891	230.69	81,266
120,000	48.75	34,483	129.84	67,067	276.82	97,514
140,000	56.88	40,235	151.48	78,249	322.96	113,773
160,000	65.01	45,983	173.12	89,424	369.10	130,023
180,000	73.14	51,736	194.76	100,606	415.24	146,281
200,000	81.26	57,479	216.40	111,782	461.37	162,530
225,000	91.42	64,668	243.45	125,758	519.05	182,852
250,000	101.57	71,847	270.49	139,725	576.71	203,163
275,000	111.73	79,035	297.55	153,703	634.39	223,484
300,000	121.90	86,228	324.60	167,679	692.06	243,803
350,000	142.21	100,595	378.70	195,624	807.41	284,437
400,000	162.52	114,962	432.80	223,570	922.75	325,069
450,000	182.84	129,335	486.90	251,516	1,038.09	365,702
500,000	203.15	143,702	540.99	279,458	1,153.43	406,334
550,000	223.47	158,079	595.10	307,413	1,268.78	446,975

DEBT REDUCTION TABLE

TO REDUCE A 30 YEAR LOAN TO:

LOAN AMOUNT	25 YEARS		20 YEARS		15 YEARS	
	PRE-PAY	SAVE	PRE-PAY	SAVE	PRE-PAY	SAVE
50	0.02	15	0.06	31	0.12	43
100	0.04	30	0.11	59	0.23	85
200	0.08	60	0.22	118	0.46	169
300	0.12	90	0.32	174	0.69	254
400	0.16	119	0.43	233	0.91	337
500	0.20	150	0.53	289	1.14	421
600	0.24	179	0.64	348	1.37	506
700	0.28	209	0.74	403	1.59	589
800	0.32	238	0.85	462	1.82	673
900	0.36	269	0.96	522	2.05	758
1,000	0.39	293	1.06	578	2.28	843
2,000	0.79	594	2.13	1,164	4.56	1,692
3,000	1.19	898	3.19	1,749	6.84	2,544
4,000	1.59	1,200	4.26	2,336	9.12	3,394
5,000	1.98	1,492	5.31	2,909	11.39	4,235
6,000	2.38	1,794	6.38	3,497	13.67	5,085
7,000	2.78	2,097	7.45	4,084	15.95	5,936
8,000	3.18	2,399	8.51	4,668	18.23	6,787
9,000	3.58	2,702	9.58	5,255	20.51	7,638
10,000	3.97	2,994	10.63	5,829	22.78	8,478
15,000	5.96	4,496	15.95	8,749	34.17	12,722
20,000	7.95	5,998	21.27	11,668	45.56	16,965
25,000	9.94	7,500	26.59	14,588	56.95	21,209
30,000	11.93	9,002	31.91	17,508	68.34	25,452
35,000	13.92	10,504	37.23	20,427	79.73	29,695
45,000	17.90	13,508	47.87	26,266	102.51	38,182
55,000	21.88	16,512	58.51	32,105	125.29	46,669
65,000	25.86	19,516	69.15	37,944	148.07	55,155
75,000	29.83	22,510	79.78	43,774	170.84	63,652
85,000	33.81	25,514	90.42	49,613	193.63	72,121
100,000	39.78	30,020	106.38	58,372	227.80	84,851
120,000	47.73	36,022	127.66	70,050	273.36	101,824
140,000	55.68	42,020	148.93	81,719	318.91	118,788
160,000	63.64	48,028	170.20	93,394	364.47	135,762
180,000	71.60	54,035	191.48	105,071	410.04	152,736
200,000	79.56	60,043	212.76	116,750	455.60	169,710
225,000	89.50	67,543	239.35	131,338	512.54	190,917
250,000	99.44	75,047	265.95	145,936	569.50	212,136
275,000	109.39	82,557	292.55	160,533	626.45	233,352
300,000	119.33	90,057	319.13	175,119	683.39	254,559
350,000	139.21	105,061	372.32	204,304	797.29	296,984
400,000	159.11	120,081	425.52	233,500	911.19	339,418
450,000	179.00	135,090	478.70	262,682	1,025.09	381,843
500,000	198.88	150,094	531.89	291,868	1,138.99	424,269
550,000	218.78	165,114	585.09	321,063	1,252.89	466,702

DEBT REDUCTION TABLE

TO REDUCE A 30 YEAR LOAN TO:

LOAN AMOUNT	25 YEARS		20 YEARS		15 YEARS	
	PRE-PAY	SAVE	PRE-PAY	SAVE	PRE-PAY	SAVE
50	0.02	15	0.06	32	0.12	44
100	0.04	30	0.11	60	0.23	86
200	0.08	61	0.21	117	0.45	171
300	0.12	96	0.32	184	0.68	266
400	0.16	126	0.42	241	0.90	350
500	0.19	150	0.52	298	1.12	435
600	0.24	191	0.63	365	1.35	530
700	0.27	215	0.73	422	1.57	614
800	0.31	246	0.83	479	1.80	700
900	0.35	281	0.94	546	2.03	795
1,000	0.39	312	1.04	603	2.25	880
2,000	0.78	627	2.09	1,216	4.50	1,768
3,000	1.16	931	3.13	1,819	6.74	2,647
4,000	1.56	1,253	4.18	2,432	9.00	3,537
5,000	1.94	1,558	5.22	3,035	11.24	4,415
6,000	2.33	1,873	6.27	3,649	13.49	5,304
7,000	2.73	2,195	7.32	4,262	15.74	6,193
8,000	3.11	2,500	8.36	4,864	17.99	7,072
9,000	3.50	2,815	9.41	5,478	20.24	7,961
10,000	3.89	3,126	10.45	6,081	22.48	8,839
15,000	5.83	4,688	15.68	9,126	33.73	13,265
20,000	7.78	6,256	20.90	12,168	44.97	17,609
25,000	9.73	7,825	26.13	15,214	56.21	22,113
30,000	11.67	9,388	31.36	18,260	67.46	26,538
35,000	13.62	10,956	36.59	21,305	78.70	30,962
45,000	17.51	14,086	47.04	27,393	101.19	39,811
55,000	21.41	17,223	57.50	33,484	123.68	48,662
65,000	25.30	20,354	67.95	39,572	146.16	57,510
75,000	29.19	23,483	78.41	45,663	168.65	66,359
85,000	33.07	26,604	88.85	51,739	191.13	75,198
100,000	38.91	31,302	104.53	60,873	224.86	88,471
120,000	46.70	37,569	125.44	73,052	269.84	106,170
140,000	54.49	43,837	146.35	85,231	314.81	123,868
160,000	62.27	50,097	167.26	97,409	359.79	141,567
180,000	70.05	56,354	188.16	109,578	404.75	159,254
200,000	77.83	62,615	209.07	121,756	449.73	176,953
225,000	87.56	70,445	235.21	136,981	505.95	199,076
250,000	97.29	78,269	261.34	152,195	562.15	221,187
275,000	107.02	86,099	287.47	167,416	618.37	243,311
300,000	116.75	93,928	313.61	182,640	674.59	265,433
350,000	136.21	109,583	365.87	213,075	787.02	309,669
400,000	155.67	125,241	418.15	243,524	899.46	353,915
450,000	175.12	140,889	470.41	273,959	1,011.89	398,151
500,000	194.58	156,543	522.68	304,396	1,124.31	442,385
550,000	214.04	172,202	574.95	334,842	1,236.75	486,631

8.00% 8.00%

DEBT REDUCTION TABLE

TO REDUCE A 30 YEAR LOAN TO:

LOAN AMOUNT	25 YEARS		20 YEARS		15 YEARS	
	PRE-PAY	SAVE	PRE-PAY	SAVE	PRE-PAY	SAVE
50	0.02	16	0.06	29	0.12	43
100	0.04	31	0.11	58	0.23	86
200	0.08	66	0.21	126	0.45	183
300	0.11	92	0.31	181	0.67	268
400	0.15	127	0.42	250	0.89	364
500	0.19	162	0.52	319	1.11	460
600	0.23	193	0.62	372	1.34	545
700	0.27	229	0.72	442	1.56	641
800	0.30	253	0.83	499	1.78	727
900	0.34	289	0.93	564	2.00	824
1,000	0.38	325	1.03	634	2.22	919
2,000	0.76	649	2.06	1,263	4.44	1,839
3,000	1.14	974	3.09	1,897	6.66	2,756
4,000	1.52	1,298	4.11	2,526	8.88	3,675
5,000	1.91	1,635	5.14	3,171	11.10	4,606
6,000	2.28	1,953	6.17	3,801	13.32	5,524
7,000	2.66	2,277	7.19	4,435	15.54	6,443
8,000	3.04	2,602	8.22	5,064	17.76	7,363
9,000	3.43	2,938	9.24	5,706	19.97	8,292
10,000	3.81	3,263	10.27	6,339	22.19	9,211
15,000	5.71	4,890	15.41	9,507	33.29	13,815
20,000	7.61	6,518	20.54	12,674	44.38	18,421
25,000	9.51	8,146	25.67	15,845	55.48	23,025
30,000	11.42	9,786	30.81	19,025	66.57	27,642
35,000	13.32	11,414	35.94	22,193	77.67	32,246
45,000	17.12	14,671	46.21	28,529	99.85	41,457
55,000	20.92	17,926	56.48	34,868	122.04	50,666
65,000	24.74	21,199	66.74	41,214	144.23	59,887
75,000	28.54	24,456	77.01	47,554	166.42	69,097
85,000	32.35	27,723	87.28	53,900	188.61	78,318
100,000	38.05	32,607	102.68	63,407	221.89	92,133
120,000	45.66	39,130	123.22	76,090	266.27	110,564
140,000	53.27	45,649	143.75	88,765	310.65	128,984
160,000	60.88	52,172	164.29	101,450	355.03	147,414
180,000	68.49	58,695	184.82	114,136	399.40	165,845
200,000	76.11	65,225	205.36	126,822	443.78	184,276
225,000	85.61	73,365	231.02	142,664	499.25	207,299
250,000	95.13	81,522	256.69	158,517	554.72	230,336
275,000	104.64	89,674	282.36	174,371	610.20	253,372
300,000	114.15	97,825	308.03	190,225	665.67	276,407
350,000	133.18	114,134	359.37	221,933	776.61	322,479
400,000	152.21	130,443	410.71	253,640	887.56	368,550
450,000	171.23	146,741	462.04	285,336	998.50	414,611
500,000	190.26	163,050	513.38	317,044	1109.44	460,684
550,000	209.28	179,352	564.72	348,751	1220.39	506,754

8.25% 8.25%

DEBT REDUCTION TABLE

TO REDUCE A 30 YEAR LOAN TO:

LOAN AMOUNT	25 YEARS		20 YEARS		15 YEARS	
	PRE-PAY	SAVE	PRE-PAY	SAVE	PRE-PAY	SAVE
50	0.02	16	0.05	29	0.11	44
100	0.03	25	0.10	59	0.22	88
200	0.07	61	0.20	125	0.44	185
300	0.11	98	0.30	192	0.66	282
400	0.15	134	0.40	259	0.88	379
500	0.19	171	0.51	329	1.10	476
600	0.23	207	0.61	396	1.32	574
700	0.26	237	0.71	463	1.54	671
800	0.29	262	0.80	517	1.75	757
900	0.33	298	0.90	584	1.97	854
1,000	0.37	334	1.01	654	2.19	951
2,000	0.74	673	2.02	1,317	4.38	1,912
3,000	1.12	1,020	3.03	1,979	6.57	2,873
4,000	1.48	1,347	4.03	2,629	8.75	3,822
5,000	1.86	1,693	5.04	3,292	10.94	4,784
6,000	2.23	2,033	6.05	3,955	13.13	5,745
7,000	2.61	2,379	7.06	4,618	15.32	6,707
8,000	2.97	2,706	8.06	5,268	17.51	7,658
9,000	3.35	3,052	9.07	5,931	19.70	8,619
10,000	3.72	3,392	10.08	6,593	21.89	9,580
15,000	5.58	5,090	15.12	9,895	32.84	14,376
20,000	7.44	6,783	20.16	13,187	43.77	19,158
25,000	9.30	8,482	25.20	16,488	54.72	23,955
30,000	11.16	10,180	30.24	19,788	65.67	28,750
35,000	13.01	11,866	35.28	23,081	76.60	33,533
45,000	16.74	15,270	45.36	29,683	98.50	43,126
55,000	20.45	18,654	55.44	36,275	120.38	52,703
65,000	24.17	22,046	65.52	42,869	142.27	62,283
75,000	27.89	25,443	75.60	49,471	164.16	71,874
85,000	31.61	28,834	85.68	56,064	186.04	81,453
100,000	37.19	33,924	100.80	65,957	218.88	95,828
120,000	44.63	40,712	120.96	79,152	262.65	114,997
140,000	52.06	47,488	141.12	92,339	306.42	134,155
160,000	59.50	54,276	161.28	105,534	350.20	153,326
180,000	66.94	61,064	181.44	118,729	393.98	172,496
200,000	74.37	67,841	201.60	131,916	437.75	191,655
225,000	83.67	76,327	226.80	148,411	492.47	215,620
250,000	92.96	84,801	252.00	164,898	547.19	239,574
275,000	102.25	93,276	277.20	181,386	601.90	263,527
300,000	111.56	101,769	302.40	197,881	656.63	287,493
350,000	130.14	118,718	352.79	230,852	766.06	335,401
400,000	148.74	135,686	403.20	263,839	875.50	383,320
450,000	167.33	152,647	453.60	296,822	984.94	431,239
500,000	185.92	169,602	503.99	329,793	1,094.37	479,147
550,000	204.51	186,564	554.40	362,780	1,203.81	527,066

8.50% 8.50%

DEBT REDUCTION TABLE

TO REDUCE A 30 YEAR LOAN TO:

LOAN AMOUNT	25 YEARS		20 YEARS		15 YEARS	
	PRE-PAY	SAVE	PRE-PAY	SAVE	PRE-PAY	SAVE
50	0.02	16	0.05	30	0.11	45
100	0.04	37	0.10	68	0.22	99
200	0.08	74	0.20	136	0.43	196
300	0.11	105	0.30	204	0.65	296
400	0.15	142	0.40	272	0.86	393
500	0.18	172	0.49	336	1.08	492
600	0.22	209	0.59	404	1.29	589
700	0.25	240	0.69	473	1.51	689
800	0.29	277	0.79	540	1.72	786
900	0.32	307	0.89	608	1.94	885
1,000	0.37	357	0.99	685	2.16	995
2,000	0.73	707	1.98	1,370	4.32	1,990
3,000	1.09	1,056	2.97	2,054	6.48	2,984
4,000	1.45	1,406	3.96	2,739	8.63	3,978
5,000	1.82	1,763	4.95	3,424	10.79	4,972
6,000	2.18	2,112	5.93	4,105	12.95	5,968
7,000	2.54	2,462	6.92	4,790	15.11	6,963
8,000	2.90	2,811	7.91	5,475	17.26	7,955
9,000	3.27	3,168	8.90	6,159	19.42	8,950
10,000	3.63	3,519	9.89	6,845	21.58	9,946
15,000	5.45	5,287	14.84	10,278	32.38	14,931
20,000	7.26	7,042	19.78	13,699	43.16	19,902
25,000	9.08	8,810	24.73	17,132	53.96	24,888
30,000	10.89	10,566	29.67	20,553	64.75	29,861
35,000	12.71	12,334	34.62	23,987	75.54	34,845
45,000	16.34	15,853	44.51	30,832	97.12	44,790
55,000	19.97	19,376	54.40	37,685	118.70	54,746
65,000	23.60	22,900	64.29	44,539	140.29	64,705
75,000	27.24	26,431	74.18	51,394	161.87	74,662
85,000	30.87	29,956	84.07	58,248	183.45	84,618
100,000	36.31	35,234	98.91	68,525	215.82	99,547
120,000	43.58	42,289	118.69	82,234	258.99	119,463
140,000	50.84	49,338	138.48	95,945	302.16	139,378
160,000	58.10	56,379	158.25	109,640	345.32	159,280
180,000	65.36	63,427	178.04	123,352	388.49	179,194
200,000	72.63	70,482	197.82	137,060	431.65	199,108
225,000	81.71	79,292	222.55	154,192	485.61	223,995
250,000	90.78	88,095	247.27	171,321	539.56	248,881
275,000	99.86	96,907	272.00	188,454	593.52	273,770
300,000	108.94	105,716	296.72	205,581	647.47	298,655
350,000	127.10	123,343	346.19	239,859	755.39	348,442
400,000	145.25	140,956	395.64	274,120	863.30	398,215
450,000	163.41	158,577	445.09	308,380	971.21	447,989
500,000	181.57	176,203	494.55	342,655	1,079.13	497,776
550,000	199.72	193,817	544.00	376,915	1,187.04	547,549

8.75% 8.75%

DEBT REDUCTION TABLE

TO REDUCE A 30 YEAR LOAN TO:

LOAN AMOUNT	25 YEARS		20 YEARS		15 YEARS	
	PRE-PAY	SAVE	PRE-PAY	SAVE	PRE-PAY	SAVE
50	0.02	16	0.05	30	0.10	43
100	0.04	38	0.10	69	0.21	99
200	0.07	69	0.19	135	0.42	198
300	0.10	99	0.29	204	0.63	297
400	0.14	143	0.39	282	0.85	409
500	0.18	181	0.48	347	1.06	508
600	0.21	212	0.58	417	1.27	607
700	0.25	256	0.68	495	1.49	720
800	0.28	286	0.77	560	1.70	818
900	0.31	316	0.87	629	1.91	917
1,000	0.36	368	0.97	709	2.13	1,030
2,000	0.71	728	1.94	1,416	4.25	2,058
3,000	1.06	1,089	2.91	2,125	6.38	3,088
4,000	1.42	1,463	3.88	2,843	8.51	4,130
5,000	1.77	1,824	4.85	3,551	10.64	5,160
6,000	2.12	2,184	5.82	4,259	12.76	6,188
7,000	2.49	2,565	6.79	4,977	14.90	7,232
8,000	2.84	2,926	7.76	5,685	17.02	8,260
9,000	3.19	3,287	8.73	6,393	19.15	9,290
10,000	3.54	3,648	9.70	7,103	21.27	10,319
15,000	5.32	5,485	14.55	10,663	31.91	15,490
20,000	7.08	7,301	19.40	14,214	42.54	20,648
25,000	8.86	9,139	24.25	17,775	53.19	25,822
30,000	10.63	10,962	29.10	21,326	63.82	30,981
35,000	12.41	12,800	33.95	24,886	74.46	36,153
45,000	15.95	16,454	43.65	31,998	95.74	46,485
55,000	19.49	20,107	53.36	39,114	117.01	56,815
65,000	23.04	23,768	63.06	46,225	138.29	67,147
75,000	26.58	27,422	72.76	53,337	159.56	77,477
85,000	30.13	31,084	82.46	60,449	180.84	87,810
100,000	35.44	36,561	97.01	71,113	212.74	103,299
120,000	42.53	43,876	116.41	85,336	255.29	123,961
140,000	49.62	51,191	135.81	99,559	297.84	144,623
160,000	56.70	58,498	155.21	113,783	340.39	165,286
180,000	63.79	65,812	174.61	128,006	382.94	185,948
200,000	70.88	73,128	194.02	142,234	425.49	206,611
225,000	79.75	82,279	218.27	160,018	478.68	232,445
250,000	88.60	91,411	242.52	177,793	531.87	258,268
275,000	97.47	100,564	266.78	195,581	585.06	284,102
300,000	106.33	109,702	291.03	213,356	638.24	309,923
350,000	124.05	127,986	339.53	248,915	744.62	361,580
400,000	141.77	146,269	388.04	284,478	850.99	413,235
450,000	159.49	164,552	436.54	320,036	957.36	464,890
500,000	177.21	182,836	485.05	355,599	1,063.74	516,547
550,000	194.93	201,119	533.55	391,159	1,170.11	568,202

9.00% 9.00%

DEBT REDUCTION TABLE

TO REDUCE A 30 YEAR LOAN TO:

LOAN AMOUNT	25 YEARS		20 YEARS		15 YEARS	
	PRE-PAY	SAVE	PRE-PAY	SAVE	PRE-PAY	SAVE
50	0.01	9	0.04	27	0.10	44
100	0.03	31	0.09	67	0.21	101
200	0.07	76	0.19	147	0.42	214
300	0.10	107	0.28	212	0.63	314
400	0.14	152	0.38	294	0.84	427
500	0.17	182	0.47	359	1.05	527
600	0.21	227	0.57	439	1.26	640
700	0.24	259	0.66	506	1.46	739
800	0.28	305	0.76	587	1.68	854
900	0.31	335	0.85	653	1.88	952
1,000	0.35	380	0.95	733	2.10	1,067
2,000	0.69	751	1.90	1,465	4.19	2,131
3,000	1.04	1,138	2.86	2,214	6.29	3,211
4,000	1.38	1,511	3.80	2,942	8.39	4,279
5,000	1.72	1,883	4.75	3,675	10.48	5,343
6,000	2.08	2,278	5.71	4,423	12.58	6,423
7,000	2.42	2,649	6.66	5,155	14.67	7,487
8,000	2.77	3,036	7.61	5,899	16.78	8,569
9,000	3.11	3,408	8.56	6,632	18.87	9,634
10,000	3.45	3,780	9.51	7,365	20.96	10,699
15,000	5.18	5,677	14.26	11,051	31.44	16,055
20,000	6.91	7,574	19.02	14,740	41.93	21,412
25,000	8.64	9,470	23.78	18,429	52.41	26,768
30,000	10.37	11,368	28.53	22,116	62.89	32,124
35,000	12.10	13,265	33.29	25,805	73.38	37,482
45,000	15.55	17,043	42.79	33,165	94.33	48,178
55,000	19.01	20,838	52.30	40,541	115.30	58,892
65,000	22.47	24,633	61.82	47,921	136.27	69,606
75,000	25.93	28,427	71.33	55,296	157.23	80,318
85,000	29.39	32,221	80.84	62,670	178.20	91,031
100,000	34.57	37,898	95.10	73,721	209.64	107,086
120,000	41.49	45,485	114.13	88,475	251.57	128,511
140,000	48.40	53,059	133.14	103,211	293.50	149,924
160,000	55.32	60,647	152.17	117,965	335.43	171,348
180,000	62.23	68,221	171.18	132,702	377.35	192,760
200,000	69.15	75,809	190.21	147,456	419.29	214,187
225,000	77.79	85,280	213.98	165,882	471.69	240,953
250,000	86.44	94,765	237.76	184,322	524.11	267,736
275,000	95.07	104,227	261.53	202,747	576.52	294,503
300,000	103.72	113,714	285.31	221,188	628.93	321,286
350,000	121.01	132,669	332.87	258,057	733.76	374,837
400,000	138.29	151,611	380.41	294,908	838.57	428,371
450,000	155.58	170,566	427.96	331,773	943.39	481,920
500,000	172.87	189,522	475.51	368,639	1,048.22	535,472
550,000	190.15	208,470	523.07	405,509	1,153.04	589,021

9.25% 9.25%

DEBT REDUCTION TABLE

TO REDUCE A 30 YEAR LOAN TO:

LOAN AMOUNT	25 YEARS		20 YEARS		15 YEARS	
	PRE-PAY	SAVE	PRE-PAY	SAVE	PRE-PAY	SAVE
50	0.01	10	0.04	28	0.10	45
100	0.03	32	0.09	68	0.20	100
200	0.07	77	0.19	149	0.41	215
300	0.10	115	0.28	227	0.62	330
400	0.13	146	0.37	294	0.82	430
500	0.17	193	0.46	372	1.03	546
600	0.20	231	0.56	454	1.24	661
700	0.24	278	0.66	537	1.45	776
800	0.27	308	0.74	599	1.65	875
900	0.30	346	0.84	681	1.86	991
1,000	0.34	393	0.93	759	2.07	1,106
2,000	0.67	777	1.86	1,518	4.13	2,209
3,000	1.01	1,169	2.79	2,277	6.19	3,312
4,000	1.35	1,569	3.73	3,052	8.26	4,432
5,000	1.68	1,953	4.66	3,811	10.32	5,536
6,000	2.02	2,346	5.59	4,570	12.39	6,641
7,000	2.36	2,746	6.53	5,345	14.46	7,761
8,000	2.70	3,139	7.45	6,100	16.52	8,865
9,000	3.03	3,523	8.38	6,859	18.58	9,968
10,000	3.37	3,923	9.32	7,633	20.65	11,087
15,000	5.05	5,875	13.98	11,444	30.97	16,623
20,000	6.74	7,846	18.64	15,267	41.30	22,175
25,000	8.43	9,814	23.30	19,089	51.63	27,726
30,000	10.11	11,768	27.96	22,900	61.95	33,262
35,000	11.80	13,737	32.62	26,721	72.28	38,813
45,000	15.17	17,660	41.94	34,355	92.93	49,900
55,000	18.54	21,582	51.25	41,983	113.58	60,987
65,000	21.91	25,512	60.58	49,633	134.24	72,090
75,000	25.28	29,434	69.90	57,265	154.89	83,177
85,000	28.65	33,358	79.21	64,894	175.54	94,265
100,000	33.71	39,249	93.19	76,350	206.52	110,904
120,000	40.44	47,085	111.83	91,616	247.82	133,078
140,000	47.19	54,946	130.47	106,893	289.12	155,265
160,000	53.93	62,792	149.10	122,155	330.42	177,440
180,000	60.67	70,644	167.75	137,438	371.73	199,630
200,000	67.41	78,488	186.38	152,698	413.03	221,804
225,000	75.84	88,310	209.69	171,803	464.67	249,546
250,000	84.27	98,124	232.98	190,887	516.30	277,271
275,000	92.70	107,938	256.28	209,975	567.92	304,995
300,000	101.12	117,743	279.58	229,063	619.55	332,720
350,000	117.97	137,364	326.17	267,236	722.81	388,172
400,000	134.82	156,984	372.76	305,409	826.06	443,621
450,000	151.68	176,619	419.37	343,601	929.33	499,088
500,000	168.53	196,239	465.96	381,773	1,032.59	554,540
550,000	185.39	215,868	512.55	419,946	1,135.84	609,989

DEBT REDUCTION TABLE

TO REDUCE A 30 YEAR LOAN TO:

LOAN AMOUNT	25 YEARS		20 YEARS		15 YEARS	
	PRE-PAY	SAVE	PRE-PAY	SAVE	PRE-PAY	SAVE
50	0.01	10	0.04	28	0.10	46
100	0.03	33	0.09	69	0.20	102
200	0.06	70	0.18	147	0.40	217
300	0.10	118	0.27	227	0.61	334
400	0.13	157	0.36	306	0.81	449
500	0.16	195	0.46	390	1.02	566
600	0.20	243	0.55	470	1.22	682
700	0.23	281	0.64	549	1.42	797
800	0.26	320	0.73	628	1.63	914
900	0.30	368	0.82	708	1.83	1,030
1,000	0.33	406	0.92	791	2.04	1,146
2,000	0.66	813	1.83	1,579	4.07	2,292
3,000	0.99	1,219	2.74	2,365	6.10	3,436
4,000	1.31	1,617	3.65	3,153	8.13	4,581
5,000	1.64	2,022	4.56	3,938	10.17	5,726
6,000	1.97	2,429	5.47	4,726	12.20	6,872
7,000	2.30	2,842	6.39	5,529	14.24	8,033
8,000	2.63	3,248	7.31	6,321	16.27	9,177
9,000	2.96	3,655	8.22	7,109	18.31	10,324
10,000	3.28	4,052	9.13	7,895	20.34	11,469
15,000	4.93	6,091	13.69	11,846	30.51	17,210
20,000	6.56	8,106	18.25	15,787	40.67	22,936
25,000	8.21	10,144	22.82	19,742	50.84	28,677
30,000	9.85	12,174	27.38	23,693	61.01	34,418
35,000	11.50	14,213	31.95	27,648	71.18	40,160
45,000	14.78	18,266	41.07	35,539	91.52	51,629
55,000	18.07	22,336	50.21	43,452	111.86	63,113
65,000	21.35	26,388	59.33	51,342	132.19	74,579
75,000	24.63	30,441	68.45	59,233	152.52	86,045
85,000	27.92	34,510	77.59	67,144	172.87	97,531
100,000	32.84	40,591	91.28	78,990	203.37	114,738
120,000	39.41	48,714	109.53	94,789	244.04	137,689
140,000	45.98	56,836	127.79	110,591	284.72	160,641
160,000	52.55	64,956	146.04	126,388	325.39	183,590
180,000	59.12	73,079	164.30	142,191	366.07	206,542
200,000	65.69	81,200	182.56	157,993	406.74	229,491
225,000	73.89	91,334	205.37	177,729	457.58	258,167
250,000	82.11	101,496	228.19	197,483	508.43	286,862
275,000	90.32	111,648	251.02	217,241	559.27	315,553
300,000	98.52	121,784	273.83	236,979	610.11	344,230
350,000	114.95	142,096	319.47	276,486	711.80	401,615
400,000	131.37	162,392	365.11	315,981	813.48	458,983
450,000	147.79	182,689	410.75	355,477	915.17	516,354
500,000	164.21	202,983	456.38	394,967	1,016.85	573,722
550,000	180.64	223,297	502.03	434,480	1,118.54	631,107

9.75% 9.75%

DEBT REDUCTION TABLE

TO REDUCE A 30 YEAR LOAN TO:

LOAN AMOUNT	25 YEARS		20 YEARS		15 YEARS	
	PRE-PAY	SAVE	PRE-PAY	SAVE	PRE-PAY	SAVE
50	0.02	24	0.05	43	0.10	59
100	0.04	49	0.09	81	0.20	117
200	0.07	88	0.18	162	0.40	235
300	0.10	128	0.27	243	0.60	352
400	0.13	167	0.36	324	0.80	469
500	0.16	206	0.45	404	1.00	586
600	0.19	246	0.54	486	1.20	704
700	0.22	285	0.62	561	1.40	821
800	0.25	324	0.71	642	1.60	938
900	0.29	373	0.80	723	1.80	1,055
1,000	0.32	413	0.89	804	2.00	1,173
2,000	0.64	834	1.79	1,625	4.00	2,360
3,000	0.96	1,253	2.68	2,441	6.01	3,550
4,000	1.28	1,676	3.58	3,264	8.01	4,739
5,000	1.60	2,097	4.47	4,081	10.01	5,927
6,000	1.92	2,517	5.37	4,902	12.02	7,117
7,000	2.23	2,921	6.25	5,701	14.01	8,287
8,000	2.56	3,351	7.15	6,523	16.01	9,475
9,000	2.88	3,773	8.04	7,340	18.02	10,666
10,000	3.20	4,193	8.94	8,161	20.02	11,854
15,000	4.80	6,290	13.40	12,237	30.03	17,781
20,000	6.39	8,377	17.87	16,317	40.04	23,708
25,000	8.00	10,492	22.34	20,411	50.06	29,652
30,000	9.60	12,588	26.81	24,491	60.06	35,576
35,000	11.19	14,675	31.28	28,572	70.07	41,503
45,000	14.40	18,886	40.22	36,746	90.10	53,375
55,000	17.59	23,070	49.15	44,903	110.11	65,227
65,000	20.78	27,254	58.08	53,059	130.13	77,080
75,000	23.99	31,466	67.02	61,233	150.16	88,953
85,000	27.18	35,649	75.95	69,388	170.17	100,803
100,000	31.98	41,946	89.36	81,643	200.21	118,602
120,000	38.38	50,342	107.24	97,978	240.25	142,325
140,000	44.78	58,736	125.11	114,308	280.29	166,048
160,000	51.17	67,122	142.98	130,639	320.34	189,774
180,000	57.57	75,517	160.86	146,974	360.38	213,496
200,000	63.97	83,912	178.73	163,304	400.42	237,220
225,000	71.96	94,393	201.07	183,715	450.47	266,869
250,000	79.96	104,886	223.41	204,126	500.52	296,520
275,000	87.95	115,367	245.75	224,536	550.57	326,170
300,000	95.95	125,859	268.09	244,948	600.62	355,820
350,000	111.94	146,832	312.76	285,764	700.72	415,119
400,000	127.93	167,814	357.45	326,603	800.84	474,439
450,000	143.92	188,787	402.13	367,425	900.94	533,739
500,000	159.91	209,760	446.81	408,246	1,001.04	593,039
550,000	175.91	230,751	491.50	449,085	1,101.15	652,356

10.00% 10.00%

DEBT REDUCTION TABLE

TO REDUCE A 30 YEAR LOAN TO:

LOAN AMOUNT	25 YEARS		20 YEARS		15 YEARS	
	PRE-PAY	SAVE	PRE-PAY	SAVE	PRE-PAY	SAVE
50	0.02	25	0.05	44	0.10	60
100	0.03	40	0.09	82	0.20	119
200	0.06	81	0.18	165	0.39	236
300	0.09	120	0.26	242	0.59	355
400	0.12	161	0.35	325	0.78	473
500	0.16	220	0.44	420	0.99	610
600	0.19	260	0.53	502	1.18	727
700	0.22	298	0.61	579	1.38	845
800	0.24	329	0.70	662	1.57	963
900	0.28	388	0.79	758	1.78	1,101
1,000	0.31	428	0.88	840	1.97	1,218
2,000	0.62	856	1.75	1,675	3.94	2,436
3,000	0.94	1,305	2.63	2,530	5.91	3,671
4,000	1.24	1,720	3.50	3,363	7.88	4,887
5,000	1.56	2,168	4.38	4,218	9.86	6,125
6,000	1.87	2,596	5.25	5,053	11.82	7,340
7,000	2.17	3,014	6.12	5,888	13.79	8,558
8,000	2.49	3,461	7.00	6,742	15.76	9,792
9,000	2.80	3,890	7.87	7,578	17.73	11,011
10,000	3.12	4,337	8.75	8,431	19.71	12,247
15,000	4.67	6,494	13.12	12,644	29.56	18,368
20,000	6.23	8,662	17.49	16,856	39.41	24,490
25,000	7.78	10,821	21.86	21,070	49.26	30,613
30,000	9.34	12,988	26.23	25,282	59.11	36,735
35,000	10.89	15,147	30.60	29,496	68.96	42,858
45,000	14.01	19,491	39.35	37,939	88.67	55,120
55,000	17.12	23,818	48.10	46,370	108.37	67,364
65,000	20.23	28,144	56.84	54,796	128.07	79,609
75,000	23.35	32,488	65.59	63,239	147.78	91,871
85,000	26.46	36,815	74.33	71,666	167.48	104,116
100,000	31.13	43,309	87.45	84,308	197.03	122,481
120,000	37.36	51,980	104.94	101,179	236.44	146,989
140,000	43.58	60,631	122.43	118,035	275.84	171,477
160,000	49.81	69,303	139.92	134,905	315.25	195,985
180,000	56.04	77,974	157.41	151,775	354.66	220,491
200,000	62.26	86,627	174.90	168,631	394.07	244,983
225,000	70.04	97,456	196.76	189,715	443.33	275,613
250,000	77.83	108,295	218.63	210,802	492.59	306,241
275,000	85.60	119,106	240.48	231,867	541.84	336,853
300,000	93.39	129,945	262.35	252,954	591.10	367,482
350,000	108.95	151,594	306.07	295,106	689.61	428,722
400,000	124.52	173,262	349.80	337,277	788.14	489,982
450,000	140.08	194,911	393.52	379,428	886.65	551,222
500,000	155.65	216,581	437.25	421,600	985.17	612,482
550,000	171.21	238,229	480.97	463,751	1,083.68	673,721

10.25% 10.25%

DEBT REDUCTION TABLE

TO REDUCE A 30 YEAR LOAN TO:

LOAN AMOUNT	25 YEARS		20 YEARS		15 YEARS	
	PRE-PAY	SAVE	PRE-PAY	SAVE	PRE-PAY	SAVE
50	0.02	26	0.05	45	0.10	61
100	0.03	41	0.09	84	0.19	119
200	0.06	82	0.17	162	0.38	238
300	0.09	131	0.26	260	0.58	375
400	0.12	172	0.34	338	0.77	494
500	0.15	214	0.42	417	0.96	613
600	0.18	264	0.51	515	1.16	752
700	0.21	305	0.60	599	1.35	871
800	0.25	364	0.69	697	1.55	1,008
900	0.27	394	0.77	775	1.74	1,127
1,000	0.30	435	0.85	854	1.93	1,246
2,000	0.60	880	1.71	1,728	3.87	2,512
3,000	0.91	1,336	2.56	2,596	5.81	3,779
4,000	1.21	1,780	3.42	3,470	7.75	5,044
5,000	1.51	2,225	4.28	4,344	9.69	6,311
6,000	1.82	2,681	5.13	5,214	11.63	7,578
7,000	2.12	3,126	5.99	6,088	13.57	8,844
8,000	2.43	3,581	6.85	6,960	15.51	10,109
9,000	2.73	4,025	7.70	7,829	17.45	11,375
10,000	3.02	4,450	8.55	8,683	19.38	12,622
15,000	4.54	6,696	12.83	13,043	29.08	18,953
20,000	6.05	8,920	17.10	17,382	38.77	25,264
25,000	7.57	11,166	21.39	21,746	48.46	31,593
30,000	9.08	13,390	25.66	26,085	58.15	37,904
35,000	10.60	15,636	29.94	30,444	67.85	44,234
45,000	13.63	20,106	38.49	39,142	87.23	56,874
55,000	16.66	24,577	47.05	47,846	106.62	69,516
65,000	19.68	29,035	55.60	56,543	126.00	82,155
75,000	22.71	33,506	64.16	65,248	145.39	94,798
85,000	25.74	37,976	72.71	73,946	164.77	107,437
100,000	30.28	44,671	85.54	86,988	193.85	126,390
120,000	36.33	53,601	102.65	104,390	232.62	151,672
140,000	42.39	62,541	119.76	121,791	271.39	176,953
160,000	48.45	71,482	136.86	139,188	310.16	202,235
180,000	54.50	80,412	153.97	156,590	348.93	227,516
200,000	60.56	89,352	171.08	173,991	387.70	252,798
225,000	68.14	100,537	192.47	195,752	436.16	284,408
250,000	75.70	111,692	213.85	217,492	484.62	316,000
275,000	83.28	122,878	235.24	239,254	533.09	347,613
300,000	90.84	134,032	256.63	260,999	581.55	379,206
350,000	105.99	156,383	299.40	304,500	678.47	442,407
400,000	121.13	178,723	342.17	348,002	775.40	505,613
450,000	136.27	201,065	384.94	391,504	872.32	568,816
500,000	151.41	223,403	427.71	435,004	969.25	632,020
550,000	166.55	245,745	470.48	478,507	1,066.18	695,226

10.50% 10.50%

DEBT REDUCTION TABLE

TO REDUCE A 30 YEAR LOAN TO:

LOAN AMOUNT	25 YEARS		20 YEARS		15 YEARS	
	PRE-PAY	SAVE	PRE-PAY	SAVE	PRE-PAY	SAVE
50	0.02	26	0.04	41	0.10	62
100	0.03	42	0.08	80	0.19	121
200	0.06	93	0.17	180	0.39	262
300	0.09	135	0.25	260	0.57	380
400	0.12	185	0.34	360	0.77	521
500	0.15	227	0.42	440	0.95	639
600	0.18	279	0.51	541	1.15	781
700	0.20	309	0.58	614	1.33	898
800	0.24	372	0.67	716	1.53	1,041
900	0.26	401	0.75	794	1.71	1,158
1,000	0.30	464	0.84	895	1.91	1,299
2,000	0.59	917	1.67	1,784	3.81	2,596
3,000	0.88	1,370	2.51	2,679	5.72	3,895
4,000	1.18	1,845	3.35	3,590	7.63	5,214
5,000	1.47	2,296	4.18	4,478	9.53	6,509
6,000	1.77	2,762	5.02	5,374	11.44	7,810
7,000	2.06	3,215	5.85	6,264	13.34	9,107
8,000	2.36	3,688	6.70	7,179	15.26	10,426
9,000	2.65	4,142	7.53	8,069	17.16	11,725
10,000	2.94	4,595	8.36	8,958	19.06	13,020
15,000	4.41	6,892	12.54	13,436	28.59	19,531
20,000	5.89	9,210	16.73	17,937	38.13	26,063
25,000	7.36	11,506	20.91	22,416	47.66	32,573
30,000	8.83	13,805	25.09	26,895	57.19	39,084
35,000	10.31	16,123	29.28	31,395	66.73	45,615
45,000	13.25	20,717	37.64	40,352	85.79	58,634
55,000	16.19	25,321	46.00	49,325	104.86	71,677
65,000	19.13	29,915	54.36	58,282	123.92	84,696
75,000	22.08	34,531	62.73	67,262	142.99	97,739
85,000	25.03	39,148	71.10	76,242	162.06	110,781
100,000	29.45	46,059	83.64	89,693	190.66	130,332
120,000	35.33	55,259	100.37	107,631	228.79	156,396
140,000	41.22	64,468	117.10	125,567	266.92	182,458
160,000	47.11	73,677	133.82	143,497	305.05	208,519
180,000	52.99	82,876	150.55	161,434	343.18	234,582
200,000	58.89	92,108	167.28	179,387	381.32	260,666
225,000	66.24	103,605	188.19	201,804	428.98	293,240
250,000	73.61	115,132	209.10	224,234	476.65	325,833
275,000	80.96	126,627	230.01	246,650	524.31	358,405
300,000	88.33	138,155	250.92	269,080	571.98	390,999
350,000	103.05	161,181	292.74	313,928	667.31	456,166
400,000	117.77	184,204	334.56	358,774	762.64	521,333
450,000	132.49	207,227	376.38	403,620	857.97	586,498
500,000	147.21	230,252	418.20	448,467	953.30	651,665
550,000	161.93	253,277	460.02	493,314	1,048.63	716,832

10.75% 10.75%

DEBT REDUCTION TABLE

TO REDUCE A 30 YEAR LOAN TO:

LOAN AMOUNT	25 YEARS		20 YEARS		15 YEARS	
	PRE-PAY	SAVE	PRE-PAY	SAVE	PRE-PAY	SAVE
50	0.02	27	0.04	41	0.10	63
100	0.03	43	0.08	82	0.19	123
200	0.06	95	0.17	183	0.38	264
300	0.08	126	0.24	259	0.56	384
400	0.11	177	0.33	361	0.75	524
500	0.15	243	0.41	458	0.94	667
600	0.17	273	0.49	539	1.12	787
700	0.20	327	0.57	637	1.31	929
800	0.23	378	0.66	739	1.50	1,070
900	0.25	409	0.73	814	1.68	1,190
1,000	0.29	473	0.82	917	1.87	1,331
2,000	0.58	957	1.64	1,850	3.75	2,684
3,000	0.86	1,418	2.45	2,761	5.62	4,016
4,000	1.15	1,904	3.27	3,695	7.50	5,371
5,000	1.43	2,364	4.09	4,611	9.37	6,701
6,000	1.72	2,849	4.91	5,545	11.25	8,055
7,000	2.00	3,310	5.72	6,456	13.12	9,387
8,000	2.29	3,795	6.54	7,390	15.00	10,741
9,000	2.57	4,254	7.36	8,305	16.87	12,070
10,000	2.86	4,739	8.18	9,239	18.75	13,425
15,000	4.29	7,103	12.26	13,845	28.12	20,127
20,000	5.72	9,478	16.35	18,474	37.49	26,849
25,000	7.15	11,843	20.43	23,080	46.86	33,550
30,000	8.58	14,217	24.52	27,707	56.24	40,273
35,000	10.02	16,604	28.62	32,341	65.62	46,997
45,000	12.88	21,344	36.79	41,576	84.36	60,421
55,000	15.74	26,082	44.96	50,809	103.11	73,845
65,000	18.60	30,823	53.13	60,044	121.85	87,269
75,000	21.45	35,549	61.31	69,283	140.60	100,693
85,000	24.32	40,311	69.49	78,540	159.35	114,139
100,000	28.61	47,414	81.74	92,379	187.46	134,264
120,000	34.34	56,916	98.10	110,876	224.96	161,135
140,000	40.05	66,382	114.45	129,350	262.45	187,983
160,000	45.77	75,860	130.79	147,817	299.94	214,830
180,000	51.50	85,361	147.15	166,314	337.44	241,702
200,000	57.22	94,839	163.49	184,781	374.93	268,549
225,000	64.37	106,694	183.93	207,884	421.80	302,123
250,000	71.53	118,558	204.37	230,985	468.66	335,691
275,000	78.68	130,412	224.80	254,081	515.53	369,263
300,000	85.83	142,266	245.24	277,184	562.40	402,836
350,000	100.14	165,983	286.12	323,387	656.13	469,977
400,000	114.45	189,703	326.99	369,586	749.87	537,123
450,000	128.75	213,408	367.87	415,789	843.60	604,264
500,000	143.06	237,127	408.74	461,987	937.33	671,405
550,000	157.36	260,836	449.61	508,186	1,031.07	738,551

11.00% 11.00%

DEBT REDUCTION TABLE

TO REDUCE A 30 YEAR LOAN TO:

LOAN AMOUNT	25 YEARS		20 YEARS		15 YEARS	
	PRE-PAY	SAVE	PRE-PAY	SAVE	PRE-PAY	SAVE
50	0.02	28	0.04	42	0.09	62
100	0.03	44	0.08	83	0.18	123
200	0.06	97	0.16	181	0.37	266
300	0.09	152	0.24	280	0.55	408
400	0.12	206	0.32	380	0.74	552
500	0.14	236	0.40	461	0.92	673
600	0.17	290	0.48	561	1.10	815
700	0.20	343	0.56	659	1.29	959
800	0.23	399	0.64	759	1.48	1,105
900	0.25	428	0.71	834	1.65	1,222
1,000	0.28	483	0.80	940	1.84	1,367
2,000	0.56	978	1.60	1,899	3.69	2,760
3,000	0.84	1,472	2.40	2,856	5.53	4,148
4,000	1.11	1,943	3.19	3,790	7.37	5,515
5,000	1.39	2,437	3.99	4,748	9.21	6,904
6,000	1.67	2,930	4.80	5,710	11.06	8,294
7,000	1.94	3,401	5.59	6,644	12.90	9,662
8,000	2.22	3,894	6.39	7,601	14.74	11,049
9,000	2.51	4,403	7.19	8,560	16.59	12,442
10,000	2.78	4,873	7.98	9,493	18.42	13,806
15,000	4.17	7,321	11.98	14,264	27.64	20,734
20,000	5.56	9,757	15.97	19,011	36.85	27,637
25,000	6.94	12,180	19.96	23,757	46.06	34,540
30,000	8.34	14,640	23.96	28,528	55.28	41,467
35,000	9.72	17,064	27.95	33,274	64.49	48,370
45,000	12.51	21,962	35.94	42,792	82.92	62,202
55,000	15.29	26,847	43.93	52,310	101.35	76,033
65,000	18.06	31,706	51.91	61,803	119.77	89,838
75,000	20.84	36,590	59.90	71,321	138.20	103,669
85,000	23.62	41,474	67.89	80,838	156.63	117,500
100,000	27.79	48,796	79.86	95,097	184.27	138,235
120,000	33.35	58,564	95.84	114,131	221.13	165,895
140,000	38.90	68,307	111.81	133,141	257.98	193,531
160,000	44.47	78,088	127.79	152,176	294.84	221,192
180,000	50.02	87,834	143.75	171,181	331.69	248,830
200,000	55.58	97,602	159.73	190,217	368.55	276,492
225,000	62.53	109,807	179.70	213,998	414.62	311,056
250,000	69.48	122,013	199.67	237,780	460.69	345,621
275,000	76.43	134,217	219.63	261,556	506.76	380,186
300,000	83.36	146,385	239.59	285,313	552.82	414,725
350,000	97.26	170,794	279.52	332,870	644.95	483,852
400,000	111.16	195,206	319.46	380,434	737.09	552,982
450,000	125.05	219,602	359.39	427,991	829.23	622,111
500,000	138.95	244,011	399.33	475,554	921.37	691,239
550,000	152.85	268,421	439.26	523,111	1,013.51	760,368

11.25% **11.25%**

DEBT REDUCTION TABLE

TO REDUCE A 30 YEAR LOAN TO:

LOAN AMOUNT	25 YEARS		20 YEARS		15 YEARS	
	PRE-PAY	SAVE	PRE-PAY	SAVE	PRE-PAY	SAVE
50	0.01	17	0.04	43	0.09	63
100	0.02	33	0.07	79	0.18	125
200	0.05	87	0.15	178	0.36	268
300	0.08	142	0.23	279	0.54	412
400	0.11	197	0.31	380	0.72	556
500	0.14	254	0.39	483	0.91	705
600	0.00	296	0.00	584	0.00	849
700	0.19	351	0.55	684	1.27	993
800	0.21	382	0.62	762	1.44	1,113
900	0.24	437	0.70	863	1.63	1,261
1,000	0.27	493	0.78	964	1.81	1,405
2,000	0.54	999	1.56	1,948	3.62	2,834
3,000	0.81	1,505	2.34	2,932	5.44	4,265
4,000	1.07	1,983	3.12	3,895	7.24	5,666
5,000	1.35	2,502	3.90	4,879	9.05	7,094
6,000	1.62	3,006	4.68	5,861	10.87	8,525
7,000	1.89	3,512	5.46	6,845	12.68	9,953
8,000	2.15	3,991	6.24	7,808	14.48	11,354
9,000	2.43	4,512	7.02	8,793	16.30	12,787
10,000	2.70	5,017	7.80	9,776	18.11	14,215
15,000	4.05	7,530	11.70	14,673	27.17	21,334
20,000	5.39	10,020	15.60	19,553	36.21	28,427
25,000	6.74	12,534	19.50	24,451	45.27	35,548
30,000	8.10	15,062	23.40	29,349	54.33	42,668
35,000	9.44	17,549	27.29	34,219	63.38	49,761
45,000	12.14	22,579	35.10	44,022	81.49	64,000
55,000	14.84	27,595	42.90	53,797	99.59	78,211
65,000	17.54	32,624	50.70	63,593	117.71	92,452
75,000	20.23	37,626	58.50	73,369	135.81	106,664
85,000	22.93	42,642	66.29	83,138	153.92	120,878
100,000	26.97	50,162	77.99	97,814	181.08	142,212
120,000	32.37	60,205	93.59	117,384	217.30	170,664
140,000	37.77	70,251	109.19	136,956	253.52	199,117
160,000	43.17	80,296	124.79	156,528	289.74	227,569
180,000	48.56	90,316	140.39	176,081	325.95	255,996
200,000	53.95	100,347	155.99	195,651	362.16	284,445
225,000	60.70	112,906	175.49	220,121	407.44	320,018
250,000	67.44	125,440	194.99	244,571	452.71	355,566
275,000	74.19	137,999	214.49	269,040	497.98	391,135
300,000	80.93	150,533	233.98	293,484	543.25	426,683
350,000	94.42	175,627	272.98	342,404	633.79	497,801
400,000	107.91	200,720	311.98	391,323	724.33	568,917
450,000	121.40	225,813	350.98	440,243	814.88	640,037
500,000	134.89	250,906	389.98	489,162	905.42	711,155
550,000	148.38	276,000	428.97	538,076	995.96	782,273

11.50% 11.50%

DEBT REDUCTION TABLE

TO REDUCE A 30 YEAR LOAN TO:

LOAN AMOUNT	25 YEARS		20 YEARS		15 YEARS	
	PRE-PAY	SAVE	PRE-PAY	SAVE	PRE-PAY	SAVE
50	0.01	17	0.04	44	0.09	64
100	0.02	34	0.07	80	0.17	124
200	0.05	89	0.15	182	0.35	269
300	0.07	131	0.22	278	0.53	416
400	0.10	189	0.30	382	0.71	564
500	0.13	245	0.38	485	0.89	711
600	0.15	289	0.45	582	1.06	856
700	0.18	346	0.53	685	1.24	1,002
800	0.21	404	0.61	790	1.42	1,151
900	0.23	446	0.68	886	1.60	1,298
1,000	0.26	503	0.76	990	1.78	1,445
2,000	0.52	1,020	1.52	2,001	3.56	2,915
3,000	0.79	1,551	2.29	3,018	5.34	4,384
4,000	1.04	2,041	3.04	4,002	7.11	5,827
5,000	1.31	2,572	3.81	5,019	8.89	7,297
6,000	1.57	3,089	4.57	6,030	10.68	8,769
7,000	1.83	3,593	5.33	7,020	12.45	10,212
8,000	2.09	4,112	6.09	8,031	14.23	11,682
9,000	2.36	4,641	6.85	9,040	16.01	13,150
10,000	2.62	5,157	7.62	10,057	17.79	14,620
15,000	3.93	7,731	11.42	15,072	26.68	21,919
20,000	5.24	10,318	15.23	20,111	35.58	29,242
25,000	6.54	12,875	19.03	25,122	44.47	36,538
30,000	7.86	15,475	22.84	30,162	53.37	43,863
35,000	9.16	18,034	26.65	35,181	62.26	51,160
45,000	11.78	23,192	34.26	45,234	80.05	65,782
55,000	14.39	28,337	41.87	55,285	97.84	80,402
65,000	17.02	33,521	49.49	65,364	115.64	95,050
75,000	19.64	38,680	57.11	75,422	133.43	109,671
85,000	22.25	43,826	64.72	85,475	151.22	124,293
100,000	26.17	51,543	76.13	100,539	177.89	146,208
120,000	31.42	61,886	91.37	120,676	213.48	175,476
140,000	36.65	72,191	106.60	140,788	249.06	204,720
160,000	41.89	82,506	121.82	160,890	284.64	233,960
180,000	47.12	92,809	137.05	181,001	320.22	263,203
200,000	52.35	103,111	152.27	201,104	355.79	292,442
225,000	58.90	116,015	171.31	226,254	400.27	329,008
250,000	65.45	128,918	190.35	251,405	444.75	365,575
275,000	71.98	141,778	209.38	276,526	489.22	402,113
300,000	78.53	154,680	228.41	301,669	533.69	438,676
350,000	91.62	180,459	266.48	351,943	622.64	511,782
400,000	104.71	206,251	304.55	402,237	711.59	584,911
450,000	117.80	232,028	342.62	452,509	800.54	658,016
500,000	130.89	257,821	380.69	502,802	889.49	731,146
550,000	143.97	283,585	418.76	553,075	978.44	804,251

11.75% 11.75%

DEBT REDUCTION TABLE

TO REDUCE A 30 YEAR LOAN TO:

LOAN AMOUNT	25 YEARS		20 YEARS		15 YEARS	
	PRE-PAY	SAVE	PRE-PAY	SAVE	PRE-PAY	SAVE
50	0.01	17	0.04	45	0.09	65
100	0.03	59	0.08	107	0.18	151
200	0.05	103	0.15	205	0.35	298
300	0.08	162	0.23	312	0.53	448
400	0.10	206	0.30	410	0.70	595
500	0.13	266	0.37	509	0.88	746
600	0.15	308	0.45	614	1.05	892
700	0.18	369	0.52	714	1.22	1,040
800	0.20	412	0.59	814	1.40	1,191
900	0.23	471	0.67	919	1.57	1,338
1,000	0.25	516	0.74	1,018	1.75	1,488
2,000	0.51	1,060	1.49	2,065	3.50	3,001
3,000	0.76	1,577	2.23	3,083	5.24	4,488
4,000	1.02	2,120	2.97	4,123	6.99	6,002
5,000	1.26	2,620	3.71	5,140	8.73	7,485
6,000	1.52	3,163	4.46	6,187	10.48	8,999
7,000	1.78	3,709	5.20	7,227	12.23	10,514
8,000	2.03	4,224	5.94	8,245	13.98	12,001
9,000	2.29	4,768	6.69	9,293	15.73	13,516
10,000	2.53	5,270	7.43	10,311	17.47	15,001
15,000	3.80	7,916	11.14	15,472	26.20	22,511
20,000	5.07	10,567	14.86	20,642	34.94	30,026
25,000	6.34	13,215	18.57	25,804	43.68	37,541
30,000	7.61	15,864	22.29	30,974	52.41	45,053
35,000	8.88	18,513	26.00	36,136	61.15	52,567
45,000	11.42	23,811	33.43	46,469	78.62	67,593
55,000	13.96	29,108	40.86	56,799	96.10	82,622
65,000	16.50	34,408	48.29	67,134	113.57	97,650
75,000	19.04	39,705	55.73	77,472	131.04	112,675
85,000	21.58	45,003	63.16	87,804	148.52	127,705
100,000	25.39	52,950	74.30	103,300	174.73	150,246
120,000	30.46	63,515	89.15	123,933	209.66	180,268
140,000	35.54	74,113	104.01	144,599	244.61	210,325
160,000	40.62	84,707	118.88	165,268	279.56	240,379
180,000	45.70	95,305	133.74	185,935	314.50	270,433
200,000	50.78	105,900	148.60	206,598	349.45	300,488
225,000	57.12	119,115	167.17	232,402	393.12	338,026
250,000	63.47	132,361	185.74	258,230	436.80	375,594
275,000	69.82	145,605	204.32	284,064	480.49	413,164
300,000	76.17	158,850	222.90	309,897	524.17	450,731
350,000	88.86	185,311	260.04	361,529	611.52	525,836
400,000	101.56	211,801	297.19	413,190	698.89	600,975
450,000	114.25	238,260	334.34	464,828	786.25	676,082
500,000	126.95	264,750	371.49	516,488	873.61	751,216
550,000	139.64	291,210	408.63	568,120	960.97	826,325

12.00% 12.00%

DEBT REDUCTION TABLE

TO REDUCE A 30 YEAR LOAN TO:

LOAN AMOUNT	25 YEARS		20 YEARS		15 YEARS	
	PRE-PAY	SAVE	PRE-PAY	SAVE	PRE-PAY	SAVE
50	0.01	18	0.04	45	0.09	66
100	0.03	61	0.08	109	0.18	154
200	0.05	106	0.15	210	0.35	304
300	0.07	151	0.22	311	0.52	453
400	0.10	212	0.29	412	0.69	603
500	0.12	258	0.36	513	0.86	754
600	0.14	302	0.43	613	1.03	903
700	0.17	362	0.50	714	1.20	1,053
800	0.20	438	0.58	847	1.38	1,234
900	0.22	482	0.65	947	1.55	1,383
1,000	0.25	544	0.73	1,055	1.72	1,533
2,000	0.49	1,072	1.45	2,103	3.43	3,064
3,000	0.74	1,630	2.18	3,182	5.15	4,625
4,000	0.98	2,157	2.90	4,228	6.86	6,154
5,000	1.23	2,701	3.62	5,277	8.57	7,685
6,000	1.48	3,259	4.35	6,355	10.30	9,249
7,000	1.72	3,789	5.07	7,405	12.01	10,781
8,000	1.97	4,347	5.80	8,481	13.73	12,340
9,000	2.22	4,889	6.52	9,528	15.44	13,869
10,000	2.46	5,417	7.24	10,577	17.15	15,399
15,000	3.69	8,135	10.87	15,886	25.73	23,117
20,000	4.92	10,851	14.49	21,186	34.31	30,832
25,000	6.15	13,569	18.12	26,496	42.89	38,550
30,000	7.38	16,285	21.74	31,796	51.47	46,265
35,000	8.61	19,002	25.37	37,105	60.04	53,978
45,000	11.08	24,450	32.61	47,704	77.20	69,409
55,000	13.54	29,883	39.86	58,313	94.36	84,840
65,000	16.00	35,318	47.11	68,923	111.51	100,270
75,000	18.46	40,752	54.36	79,533	128.67	115,703
85,000	20.92	46,169	61.60	90,109	145.82	131,103
100,000	24.61	54,321	72.47	106,021	171.55	154,249
120,000	29.53	65,185	86.97	127,238	205.87	185,111
140,000	34.46	76,070	101.47	148,456	240.18	215,973
160,000	39.37	86,904	115.95	169,634	274.48	246,802
180,000	44.30	97,787	130.45	190,852	308.80	277,665
200,000	49.22	108,654	144.95	212,070	343.11	308,527
225,000	55.38	122,255	163.07	238,591	386.00	347,105
250,000	61.53	135,822	181.18	265,077	428.89	385,652
275,000	67.68	149,404	199.30	291,594	471.78	424,228
300,000	73.84	163,005	217.42	318,114	514.67	462,806
350,000	86.14	190,157	253.66	371,128	600.44	539,929
400,000	98.44	217,308	289.89	424,134	686.22	617,054
450,000	110.75	244,491	326.13	477,170	772.00	694,207
500,000	123.06	271,659	362.37	530,184	857.78	771,332
550,000	135.37	298,843	398.61	583,223	943.56	848,487

DEBT REDUCTION TABLE

TO REDUCE A 30 YEAR LOAN TO:

LOAN AMOUNT	25 YEARS		20 YEARS		15 YEARS	
	PRE-PAY	SAVE	PRE-PAY	SAVE	PRE-PAY	SAVE
50	0.01	18	0.03	39	0.08	64
100	0.03	63	0.07	104	0.17	154
200	0.05	109	0.14	207	0.34	306
300	0.07	155	0.21	310	0.50	456
400	0.09	201	0.28	412	0.67	607
500	0.12	278	0.36	547	0.85	792
600	0.15	340	0.43	650	1.01	941
700	0.17	387	0.49	746	1.18	1,094
800	0.19	434	0.56	849	1.35	1,247
900	0.21	479	0.63	951	1.51	1,396
1,000	0.24	558	0.71	1,088	1.69	1,582
2,000	0.48	1,116	1.42	2,176	3.37	3,161
3,000	0.72	1,674	2.12	3,256	5.05	4,740
4,000	0.95	2,215	2.83	4,344	6.74	6,321
5,000	1.19	2,773	3.53	5,424	8.42	7,899
6,000	1.43	3,331	4.24	6,511	10.10	9,478
7,000	1.67	3,890	4.94	7,593	11.79	11,062
8,000	1.90	4,430	5.65	8,678	13.47	12,638
9,000	2.14	4,988	6.36	9,767	15.15	14,218
10,000	2.39	5,581	7.07	10,881	16.84	15,830
15,000	3.58	8,353	10.60	16,304	25.26	23,730
20,000	4.77	11,143	14.14	21,761	33.68	31,660
25,000	5.96	13,917	17.67	27,184	42.10	39,559
30,000	7.16	16,723	21.20	32,633	50.52	47,489
35,000	8.35	19,498	24.73	38,058	58.94	55,391
45,000	10.73	25,059	31.80	48,936	75.78	71,218
55,000	13.11	30,624	38.87	59,817	92.62	87,049
65,000	15.50	36,204	45.93	70,688	109.46	102,877
75,000	17.88	41,768	53.00	81,570	126.30	118,709
85,000	20.27	47,349	60.06	92,443	143.14	134,539
100,000	23.85	55,718	70.67	108,778	168.40	158,297
120,000	28.62	66,862	84.80	130,533	202.08	189,958
140,000	33.39	78,005	98.94	152,292	235.76	221,616
160,000	38.16	89,149	113.07	174,045	269.44	253,276
180,000	42.92	100,276	127.20	195,798	303.12	284,936
200,000	47.69	111,420	141.33	217,552	336.80	316,596
225,000	53.66	125,370	159.01	244,769	378.91	356,188
250,000	59.61	139,269	176.67	271,945	421.00	395,743
275,000	65.58	153,221	194.34	299,155	463.11	435,337
300,000	71.55	167,170	212.01	326,363	505.21	474,925
350,000	83.47	195,021	247.34	380,749	589.41	554,074
400,000	95.39	222,872	282.67	435,136	673.61	633,224
450,000	107.31	250,723	318.01	489,529	757.81	712,371
500,000	119.23	278,575	353.34	543,916	842.01	791,522
550,000	131.16	306,441	388.67	598,301	926.21	870,669

12.50% 12.50%

DEBT REDUCTION TABLE

TO REDUCE A 30 YEAR LOAN TO:

LOAN AMOUNT	25 YEARS		20 YEARS		15 YEARS	
	PRE-PAY	SAVE	PRE-PAY	SAVE	PRE-PAY	SAVE
50	0.01	19	0.03	40	0.08	65
100	0.03	64	0.07	106	0.17	156
200	0.05	111	0.14	211	0.33	308
300	0.07	159	0.20	309	0.49	461
400	0.10	240	0.28	448	0.67	650
500	0.12	286	0.35	552	0.83	802
600	0.14	335	0.41	651	0.99	955
700	0.16	382	0.48	755	1.15	1,106
800	0.19	463	0.55	886	1.33	1,296
900	0.21	509	0.62	991	1.49	1,447
1,000	0.23	556	0.69	1,096	1.65	1,599
2,000	0.46	1,129	1.38	2,219	3.31	3,232
3,000	0.70	1,721	2.07	3,342	4.96	4,863
4,000	0.92	2,261	2.75	4,432	6.61	6,465
5,000	1.15	2,834	3.44	5,554	8.26	8,094
6,000	1.39	3,424	4.13	6,676	9.92	9,727
7,000	1.62	4,002	4.82	7,802	11.57	11,361
8,000	1.84	4,538	5.51	8,897	13.22	12,959
9,000	2.08	5,130	6.20	10,021	14.87	14,590
10,000	2.31	5,704	6.89	11,145	16.53	16,225
15,000	3.47	8,574	10.34	16,734	24.79	24,350
20,000	4.62	11,407	13.77	22,280	33.05	32,444
25,000	5.77	14,260	17.22	27,869	41.32	40,573
30,000	6.93	17,129	20.67	33,459	49.58	48,700
35,000	8.08	19,963	24.10	39,006	57.84	56,794
45,000	10.39	25,685	31.00	50,183	74.37	73,048
55,000	12.70	31,389	37.88	61,320	90.89	89,270
65,000	15.02	37,129	44.78	72,500	107.42	105,525
75,000	17.32	42,815	51.66	83,634	123.95	121,748
85,000	19.64	48,553	58.55	94,805	140.48	138,004
100,000	23.10	57,107	68.89	111,538	165.27	162,353
120,000	27.72	68,534	82.66	133,845	198.32	194,829
140,000	32.33	79,924	96.43	156,126	231.37	227,274
160,000	36.95	91,348	110.21	178,439	264.42	259,748
180,000	41.57	102,775	123.99	200,755	297.47	292,225
200,000	46.19	114,201	137.77	223,070	330.53	324,704
225,000	51.97	128,496	154.99	250,966	371.85	365,310
250,000	57.74	142,755	172.21	278,835	413.16	405,880
275,000	63.52	157,048	189.43	306,729	454.48	446,483
300,000	69.29	171,309	206.65	334,600	495.79	487,053
350,000	80.83	199,844	241.09	390,364	578.42	568,228
400,000	92.38	228,400	275.53	446,131	661.05	649,404
450,000	103.94	256,991	309.98	501,932	743.69	730,615
500,000	115.49	285,542	344.42	557,695	826.33	811,791
550,000	127.03	314,082	378.86	613,463	908.96	892,968

DEBT REDUCTION TABLE

TO REDUCE A 30 YEAR LOAN TO:

LOAN AMOUNT	25 YEARS		20 YEARS		15 YEARS	
	PRE-PAY	SAVE	PRE-PAY	SAVE	PRE-PAY	SAVE
50	0.01	19	0.03	41	0.08	66
100	0.02	49	0.07	108	0.16	156
200	0.04	96	0.13	206	0.32	310
300	0.06	146	0.20	315	0.48	465
400	0.09	229	0.27	450	0.65	656
500	0.11	278	0.33	549	0.81	810
600	0.13	324	0.40	655	0.97	964
700	0.16	410	0.47	790	1.14	1,156
800	0.18	457	0.54	898	1.30	1,310
900	0.20	507	0.60	997	1.45	1,462
1,000	0.23	592	0.67	1,133	1.62	1,653
2,000	0.45	1,162	1.34	2,265	3.24	3,305
3,000	0.67	1,735	2.01	3,399	4.86	4,959
4,000	0.90	2,346	2.69	4,571	6.49	6,651
5,000	1.12	2,920	3.36	5,704	8.11	8,305
6,000	1.34	3,491	4.02	6,828	9.73	9,958
7,000	1.57	4,101	4.70	7,997	11.35	11,644
8,000	1.79	4,673	5.37	9,131	12.97	13,297
9,000	2.01	5,244	6.04	10,262	14.59	14,949
10,000	2.24	5,856	6.72	11,434	16.22	16,641
15,000	3.35	8,755	10.07	17,120	24.32	24,942
20,000	4.48	11,711	13.43	22,859	32.43	33,279
25,000	5.59	14,612	16.78	28,555	40.53	41,580
30,000	6.71	17,548	20.14	34,286	48.65	49,920
35,000	7.82	20,447	23.49	39,980	56.75	58,221
45,000	10.06	26,304	30.20	51,406	72.96	74,859
55,000	12.29	32,141	36.91	62,832	89.18	91,500
65,000	14.53	37,999	43.62	74,261	105.39	108,141
75,000	16.77	43,871	50.34	85,722	121.61	124,814
85,000	19.01	49,727	57.05	97,148	137.83	141,456
100,000	22.36	58,483	67.12	114,277	162.14	166,395
120,000	26.83	70,174	80.54	137,127	194.57	199,673
140,000	31.30	81,870	93.96	159,982	227.00	232,955
160,000	35.78	93,600	107.39	182,871	259.43	266,268
180,000	40.25	105,294	120.82	205,733	291.86	299,550
200,000	44.72	116,985	134.24	228,582	324.29	332,827
225,000	50.31	131,615	151.02	257,166	364.83	374,444
250,000	55.90	146,225	167.79	285,711	405.36	416,023
275,000	61.49	160,855	184.58	314,303	445.90	457,641
300,000	67.08	175,487	201.36	342,889	486.44	499,260
350,000	78.26	204,726	234.92	400,025	567.50	582,451
400,000	89.43	233,950	268.47	457,155	648.57	665,649
450,000	100.62	263,230	302.04	514,331	729.65	748,884
500,000	111.80	292,470	335.59	571,461	810.72	832,081
550,000	122.97	321,695	369.15	628,600	891.79	915,280

13.00% **13.00%**

DEBT REDUCTION TABLE

TO REDUCE A 30 YEAR LOAN TO:

LOAN AMOUNT	25 YEARS		20 YEARS		15 YEARS	
	PRE-PAY	SAVE	PRE-PAY	SAVE	PRE-PAY	SAVE
50	0.01	19	0.03	41	0.08	67
100	0.02	50	0.07	110	0.16	158
200	0.04	100	0.13	212	0.32	316
300	0.07	187	0.20	350	0.48	508
400	0.09	236	0.26	451	0.64	665
500	0.10	268	0.32	553	0.79	820
600	0.13	354	0.39	692	0.96	1,016
700	0.15	402	0.46	800	1.11	1,167
800	0.18	492	0.53	941	1.28	1,365
900	0.20	541	0.59	1,042	1.43	1,519
1,000	0.21	570	0.65	1,143	1.59	1,676
2,000	0.43	1,179	1.31	2,325	3.18	3,388
3,000	0.65	1,790	1.96	3,499	4.77	5,100
4,000	0.87	2,399	2.62	4,679	6.36	6,810
5,000	1.09	3,010	3.27	5,853	7.96	8,527
6,000	1.30	3,580	3.92	6,996	9.54	10,199
7,000	1.51	4,170	4.58	8,179	11.13	11,912
8,000	1.73	4,782	5.23	9,353	12.72	13,624
9,000	1.95	5,388	5.89	10,533	14.32	15,337
10,000	2.17	6,000	6.54	11,707	15.91	17,050
15,000	3.25	8,991	9.81	17,561	23.86	25,575
20,000	4.33	11,982	13.08	23,415	31.81	34,099
25,000	5.41	14,971	16.35	29,268	39.77	42,624
30,000	6.50	17,982	19.62	35,122	47.72	51,148
35,000	7.58	20,972	22.89	40,974	55.67	59,671
45,000	9.74	26,954	29.42	52,674	71.57	76,720
55,000	11.90	32,935	35.96	64,382	87.48	93,770
65,000	14.07	38,936	42.50	76,089	103.38	110,818
75,000	16.23	44,917	49.04	87,796	119.29	127,867
85,000	18.40	50,917	55.57	99,494	135.19	144,915
100,000	21.64	59,890	65.38	117,057	159.05	170,491
120,000	25.97	71,871	78.46	140,472	190.86	204,588
140,000	30.29	83,831	91.53	163,875	222.66	238,681
160,000	34.62	95,813	104.61	187,289	254.47	272,778
180,000	38.95	107,795	117.68	210,695	286.28	306,876
200,000	43.28	119,776	130.76	234,110	318.09	340,973
225,000	48.68	134,730	147.10	263,371	357.85	383,597
250,000	54.09	149,704	163.44	292,632	397.61	426,219
275,000	59.50	164,675	179.79	321,900	437.37	468,841
300,000	64.91	179,649	196.13	351,160	477.13	511,462
350,000	75.73	209,592	228.82	409,686	556.65	596,703
400,000	86.55	239,534	261.51	468,214	636.17	681,946
450,000	97.36	269,459	294.20	526,741	715.69	767,188
500,000	108.18	299,401	326.88	585,258	795.22	852,434
550,000	119.00	329,348	359.57	643,788	874.74	937,678

DEBT REDUCTION TABLE

TO REDUCE A 30 YEAR LOAN TO:

LOAN AMOUNT	25 YEARS		20 YEARS		15 YEARS	
	PRE-PAY	SAVE	PRE-PAY	SAVE	PRE-PAY	SAVE
50	0.01	20	0.03	42	0.08	68
100	0.02	51	0.06	103	0.16	161
200	0.04	103	0.12	208	0.31	319
300	0.07	193	0.19	350	0.47	514
400	0.08	224	0.25	453	0.62	671
500	0.11	314	0.32	596	0.78	868
600	0.13	366	0.38	700	0.94	1,029
700	0.14	396	0.44	803	1.09	1,186
800	0.17	487	0.51	946	1.25	1,383
900	0.19	538	0.57	1,050	1.40	1,540
1,000	0.21	610	0.64	1,194	1.56	1,737
2,000	0.42	1,220	1.27	2,379	3.12	3,475
3,000	0.63	1,829	1.91	3,573	4.68	5,212
4,000	0.83	2,418	2.54	4,758	6.23	6,946
5,000	1.05	3,069	3.19	5,994	7.80	8,725
6,000	1.26	3,678	3.82	7,178	9.36	10,462
7,000	1.46	4,266	4.46	8,372	10.92	12,199
8,000	1.67	4,873	5.09	9,555	12.47	13,930
9,000	1.89	5,527	5.73	10,784	14.04	15,712
10,000	2.10	6,134	6.37	11,975	15.60	17,446
15,000	3.14	9,185	9.55	17,962	23.40	26,173
20,000	4.19	12,253	12.73	23,946	31.19	34,893
25,000	5.23	15,298	15.91	29,926	38.99	43,615
30,000	6.28	18,368	19.09	35,912	46.79	52,341
35,000	7.32	21,413	22.28	41,903	54.58	61,058
45,000	9.42	27,573	28.65	53,915	70.19	78,550
55,000	11.51	33,688	35.01	65,882	85.78	95,994
65,000	13.60	39,804	41.37	77,850	101.37	113,438
75,000	15.69	45,921	47.74	89,827	116.97	130,887
85,000	17.79	52,075	54.11	101,833	132.57	148,370
100,000	20.93	61,258	63.66	119,795	155.96	174,538
120,000	25.12	73,533	76.39	143,772	187.16	209,473
140,000	29.30	85,766	89.12	167,718	218.35	244,367
160,000	33.49	98,036	101.85	191,693	249.54	279,295
180,000	37.67	110,269	114.58	215,639	280.73	314,188
200,000	41.86	122,542	127.32	239,624	311.93	349,121
225,000	47.08	137,822	143.22	269,544	350.91	392,735
250,000	52.32	153,164	159.14	299,515	389.91	436,392
275,000	57.55	168,484	175.06	329,485	428.90	480,046
300,000	62.78	183,784	190.97	359,413	467.88	523,659
350,000	73.25	214,445	222.80	419,343	545.87	610,970
400,000	83.71	245,065	254.63	479,240	623.85	698,240
450,000	94.17	275,686	286.45	539,131	701.83	785,511
500,000	104.64	306,348	318.29	599,071	779.82	872,822
550,000	115.10	336,968	350.11	658,959	857.80	960,092

DEBT REDUCTION TABLE

TO REDUCE A 30 YEAR LOAN TO:

LOAN AMOUNT	25 YEARS		20 YEARS		15 YEARS	
	PRE-PAY	SAVE	PRE-PAY	SAVE	PRE-PAY	SAVE
50	0.01	20	0.03	43	0.07	66
100	0.02	53	0.06	106	0.15	160
200	0.04	106	0.12	213	0.30	321
300	0.06	178	0.19	358	0.46	521
400	0.08	230	0.24	455	0.61	681
500	0.10	304	0.31	603	0.77	884
600	0.12	356	0.37	708	0.91	1,039
700	0.14	430	0.44	857	1.07	1,242
800	0.16	482	0.49	952	1.22	1,401
900	0.19	578	0.56	1,100	1.38	1,604
1,000	0.20	609	0.62	1,207	1.53	1,763
2,000	0.41	1,261	1.24	2,446	3.06	3,567
3,000	0.60	1,845	1.86	3,650	4.58	5,323
4,000	0.81	2,499	2.48	4,892	6.12	7,133
5,000	1.01	3,108	3.09	6,088	7.64	8,892
6,000	1.21	3,738	3.72	7,338	9.17	10,696
7,000	1.42	4,390	4.34	8,578	10.71	12,503
8,000	1.62	5,000	4.95	9,775	12.23	14,263
9,000	1.82	5,631	5.58	11,026	13.76	16,066
10,000	2.02	6,236	6.19	12,219	15.29	17,827
15,000	3.03	9,370	9.29	18,355	22.93	26,763
20,000	4.04	12,498	12.39	24,485	30.58	35,698
25,000	5.06	15,654	15.49	30,622	38.22	44,634
30,000	6.07	18,782	18.59	36,752	45.87	53,568
35,000	7.08	21,910	21.69	42,884	53.52	62,504
45,000	9.11	28,197	27.88	55,142	68.81	80,376
55,000	11.13	34,459	34.08	67,409	84.10	98,247
65,000	13.15	40,717	40.28	79,672	99.39	116,114
75,000	15.18	47,000	46.48	91,938	114.68	133,984
85,000	17.19	53,216	52.66	104,150	129.97	151,814
100,000	20.23	62,629	61.96	122,547	152.90	178,615
120,000	24.28	75,174	74.35	147,069	183.49	214,359
140,000	28.33	87,719	86.75	171,602	214.07	250,100
160,000	32.38	100,262	99.14	196,122	244.65	285,838
180,000	36.42	112,763	111.53	220,612	275.23	321,540
200,000	40.46	125,283	123.92	245,131	305.81	357,277
225,000	45.53	140,980	139.42	275,795	344.04	401,953
250,000	50.58	156,611	154.90	306,406	382.26	446,586
275,000	55.64	172,286	170.40	337,070	420.49	491,261
300,000	60.70	187,962	185.89	367,727	458.72	535,940
350,000	70.81	219,264	216.87	428,998	535.17	625,246
400,000	80.93	250,615	247.85	490,310	611.63	714,601
450,000	91.05	281,942	278.83	551,585	688.08	803,910
500,000	101.16	313,246	309.81	612,857	764.53	893,217
550,000	111.28	344,594	340.80	674,176	840.99	982,569

13.75% 13.75%

DEBT REDUCTION TABLE

TO REDUCE A 30 YEAR LOAN TO:

LOAN AMOUNT	25 YEARS		20 YEARS		15 YEARS	
	PRE-PAY	SAVE	PRE-PAY	SAVE	PRE-PAY	SAVE
50	0.01	20	0.03	43	0.07	66
100	0.02	54	0.06	109	0.15	164
200	0.03	88	0.12	218	0.29	324
300	0.06	184	0.18	358	0.45	529
400	0.07	216	0.24	466	0.59	687
500	0.10	315	0.30	608	0.75	895
600	0.11	346	0.36	716	0.89	1,053
700	0.14	446	0.42	860	1.05	1,262
800	0.15	475	0.48	967	1.19	1,418
900	0.18	574	0.54	1,109	1.35	1,627
1,000	0.19	605	0.60	1,218	1.49	1,786
2,000	0.39	1,258	1.20	2,471	2.99	3,618
3,000	0.58	1,891	1.81	3,737	4.49	5,451
4,000	0.78	2,545	2.41	4,992	5.99	7,285
5,000	0.98	3,195	3.02	6,255	7.49	9,116
6,000	1.17	3,826	3.62	7,510	8.99	10,949
7,000	1.37	4,479	4.22	8,764	10.49	12,781
8,000	1.57	5,133	4.83	10,030	11.99	14,615
9,000	1.75	5,717	5.42	11,237	13.48	16,400
10,000	1.95	6,371	6.03	12,503	14.98	18,234
15,000	2.93	9,593	9.05	18,797	22.48	27,398
20,000	3.91	12,787	12.06	25,043	29.97	36,514
25,000	4.89	16,010	15.08	31,336	37.47	45,679
30,000	5.86	19,182	18.09	37,580	44.96	54,793
35,000	6.85	22,426	21.11	43,875	52.46	63,958
45,000	8.79	28,774	27.13	56,367	67.44	82,191
55,000	10.75	35,191	33.16	68,906	82.43	100,472
65,000	12.71	41,610	39.19	81,447	97.42	118,754
75,000	14.66	48,004	45.22	93,985	112.41	137,033
85,000	16.62	54,424	51.25	106,528	127.39	155,312
100,000	19.55	64,014	60.29	125,312	149.87	182,708
120,000	23.46	76,826	72.35	150,390	179.85	219,269
140,000	27.38	89,663	84.41	175,472	209.83	255,832
160,000	31.28	102,427	96.46	200,501	239.79	292,340
180,000	35.19	115,241	108.52	225,582	269.77	328,902
200,000	39.11	128,077	120.59	250,673	299.75	365,465
225,000	43.99	144,062	135.66	281,997	337.22	411,142
250,000	48.88	160,071	150.73	313,322	374.68	456,815
275,000	53.78	176,128	165.81	344,696	412.16	502,541
300,000	58.66	192,116	180.88	376,022	449.63	548,220
350,000	68.44	224,134	211.02	438,673	524.56	639,573
400,000	78.21	256,130	241.17	501,334	599.49	730,924
450,000	87.99	288,172	271.32	564,033	674.44	822,328
500,000	97.76	320,170	301.46	626,685	749.37	913,681
550,000	107.55	352,237	331.61	689,385	824.31	1,005,083

DEBT REDUCTION TABLE

TO REDUCE A 30 YEAR LOAN TO:

LOAN AMOUNT	25 YEARS		20 YEARS		15 YEARS	
	PRE-PAY	SAVE	PRE-PAY	SAVE	PRE-PAY	SAVE
50	0.01	21	0.03	44	0.07	67
100	0.02	57	0.06	113	0.15	168
200	0.04	136	0.12	258	0.30	375
300	0.06	191	0.18	369	0.44	537
400	0.08	271	0.24	516	0.59	746
500	0.09	302	0.29	615	0.73	907
600	0.12	406	0.36	774	0.89	1,121
700	0.13	438	0.41	873	1.03	1,282
800	0.16	540	0.47	1,020	1.18	1,491
900	0.17	572	0.53	1,130	1.32	1,652
1,000	0.19	652	0.59	1,278	1.47	1,862
2,000	0.38	1,304	1.18	2,557	2.94	3,724
3,000	0.57	1,958	1.76	3,827	4.41	5,588
4,000	0.76	2,616	2.35	5,109	5.87	7,449
5,000	0.94	3,241	2.93	6,376	7.34	9,309
6,000	1.13	3,896	3.52	7,656	8.81	11,172
7,000	1.32	4,551	4.10	8,926	10.28	13,037
8,000	1.52	5,255	4.70	10,257	11.75	14,947
9,000	1.70	5,883	5.28	11,525	13.22	16,809
10,000	1.89	6,539	5.87	12,806	14.69	18,673
15,000	2.83	9,779	8.79	19,170	22.03	27,982
20,000	3.78	13,076	11.73	25,600	29.37	37,340
25,000	4.73	16,369	14.67	32,027	36.72	46,701
30,000	5.66	19,586	17.59	38,392	44.06	56,011
35,000	6.61	22,884	20.53	44,821	51.40	65,369
45,000	8.50	29,420	26.39	57,615	66.09	84,041
55,000	10.39	35,984	32.26	70,461	80.78	102,760
65,000	12.28	42,521	38.12	83,255	95.47	121,432
75,000	14.17	49,060	43.99	96,061	110.15	140,101
85,000	16.05	55,573	49.85	108,855	124.84	158,773
100,000	18.89	65,406	58.65	128,078	146.87	186,803
120,000	22.67	78,509	70.38	153,718	176.24	224,191
140,000	26.44	91,558	82.10	179,305	205.61	261,529
160,000	30.22	104,660	93.84	204,955	234.99	298,920
180,000	34.00	117,762	105.57	230,594	264.37	336,311
200,000	37.78	130,835	117.30	256,192	293.74	373,649
225,000	42.50	147,181	131.96	288,209	330.45	420,347
250,000	47.23	163,580	146.63	320,279	367.18	467,102
275,000	51.95	179,923	161.29	352,294	403.89	513,798
300,000	56.67	196,269	175.95	384,310	440.61	560,499
350,000	66.11	228,961	205.27	448,345	514.04	653,900
400,000	75.56	261,701	234.60	512,427	587.48	747,348
450,000	85.00	294,391	263.92	576,459	660.91	840,746
500,000	94.45	327,129	293.25	640,541	734.35	934,194
550,000	103.89	359,823	322.57	704,577	807.78	1,027,595

DEBT REDUCTION TABLE

TO REDUCE A 30 YEAR LOAN TO:

LOAN AMOUNT	25 YEARS		20 YEARS		15 YEARS	
	PRE-PAY	SAVE	PRE-PAY	SAVE	PRE-PAY	SAVE
50	0.01	21	0.03	45	0.07	68
100	0.02	58	0.06	115	0.14	167
200	0.04	141	0.12	265	0.29	380
300	0.05	173	0.17	368	0.43	544
400	0.08	281	0.23	521	0.58	760
500	0.09	314	0.28	622	0.72	924
600	0.11	398	0.35	786	0.87	1,140
700	0.13	452	0.40	886	1.01	1,302
800	0.15	538	0.46	1,042	1.15	1,516
900	0.16	569	0.51	1,141	1.29	1,679
1,000	0.18	654	0.57	1,295	1.44	1,895
2,000	0.36	1,307	1.14	2,592	2.88	3,790
3,000	0.54	1,961	1.71	3,887	4.31	5,681
4,000	0.73	2,668	2.28	5,224	5.76	7,628
5,000	0.91	3,317	2.85	6,515	7.19	9,515
6,000	1.09	3,971	3.42	7,811	8.63	11,410
7,000	1.28	4,679	4.00	9,161	10.08	13,359
8,000	1.46	5,330	4.56	10,444	11.51	15,248
9,000	1.64	5,986	5.13	11,742	12.95	17,146
10,000	1.83	6,693	5.71	13,090	14.39	19,088
15,000	2.73	9,985	8.55	19,595	21.58	28,605
20,000	3.65	13,358	11.41	26,168	28.78	38,177
25,000	4.56	16,678	14.25	32,676	35.97	47,694
30,000	5.47	20,026	17.11	39,246	43.17	57,265
35,000	6.38	23,344	19.96	45,763	50.36	66,781
45,000	8.21	30,068	25.67	58,899	64.76	85,926
55,000	10.04	36,762	31.37	71,977	79.14	105,010
65,000	11.86	43,427	37.07	85,055	93.53	124,097
75,000	13.68	50,091	42.77	98,132	107.92	143,184
85,000	15.50	56,760	48.48	111,222	122.31	162,274
100,000	18.24	66,801	57.03	130,860	143.89	190,928
120,000	21.89	80,160	68.44	157,029	172.67	229,104
140,000	25.53	93,493	79.84	183,184	201.45	267,279
160,000	29.19	106,906	91.26	209,408	230.23	305,507
180,000	32.83	120,239	102.66	235,563	259.01	343,682
200,000	36.48	133,599	114.06	261,721	287.78	381,855
225,000	41.04	150,306	128.32	294,448	323.76	429,602
250,000	45.60	167,015	142.58	327,179	359.73	477,347
275,000	50.17	183,747	156.84	359,907	395.71	525,094
300,000	54.72	200,400	171.09	392,582	431.67	572,784
350,000	63.84	233,814	199.61	458,038	503.62	668,273
400,000	72.97	267,251	228.13	523,494	575.57	763,762
450,000	82.08	300,611	256.64	588,898	647.51	859,200
500,000	91.20	334,027	285.16	654,355	719.46	954,690
550,000	100.33	367,467	313.68	719,813	791.41	1,050,182

DEBT REDUCTION TABLE

TO REDUCE A 30 YEAR LOAN TO:

LOAN AMOUNT	25 YEARS		20 YEARS		15 YEARS	
	PRE-PAY	SAVE	PRE-PAY	SAVE	PRE-PAY	SAVE
50	0.01	21	0.02	35	0.07	69
100	0.02	61	0.05	108	0.14	171
200	0.04	147	0.11	263	0.29	390
300	0.05	179	0.16	366	0.42	552
400	0.07	266	0.22	525	0.57	773
500	0.09	326	0.27	629	0.70	938
600	0.11	413	0.33	787	0.85	1,159
700	0.12	444	0.38	890	0.98	1,320
800	0.14	534	0.44	1,049	1.13	1,543
900	0.15	566	0.49	1,153	1.26	1,706
1,000	0.18	680	0.55	1,312	1.41	1,928
2,000	0.35	1,330	1.10	2,622	2.82	3,854
3,000	0.53	2,039	1.66	3,989	4.23	5,834
4,000	0.70	2,689	2.21	5,297	5.64	7,758
5,000	0.88	3,405	2.77	6,672	7.05	9,745
6,000	1.05	4,053	3.32	7,981	8.46	11,669
7,000	1.24	4,791	3.88	9,350	9.87	13,651
8,000	1.41	5,442	4.43	10,660	11.28	15,577
9,000	1.58	6,094	4.98	11,970	12.68	17,499
10,000	1.76	6,803	5.54	13,338	14.10	19,483
15,000	2.64	10,203	8.31	20,006	21.14	29,219
20,000	3.52	13,610	11.08	26,680	28.19	38,966
25,000	4.41	17,064	13.86	33,402	35.24	48,756
30,000	5.28	20,442	16.63	40,074	42.29	58,501
35,000	6.16	23,844	19.40	46,744	49.33	68,239
45,000	7.92	30,646	24.94	60,082	63.42	87,717
55,000	9.68	37,480	30.49	73,478	77.52	107,254
65,000	11.44	44,283	36.03	86,818	91.61	126,733
75,000	13.21	51,147	41.58	100,214	105.71	146,271
85,000	14.96	57,923	47.12	113,553	119.80	165,750
100,000	17.61	68,188	55.44	133,621	140.95	195,032
120,000	21.13	81,824	66.53	160,356	169.14	234,048
140,000	24.65	95,463	77.62	187,092	197.33	273,064
160,000	28.18	109,127	88.71	213,826	225.52	312,080
180,000	31.69	122,708	99.79	240,503	253.70	351,039
200,000	35.21	136,347	110.88	267,239	281.89	390,057
225,000	39.61	153,387	124.74	300,644	317.12	438,811
250,000	44.02	170,486	138.61	334,108	352.37	487,629
275,000	48.42	187,524	152.47	367,511	387.60	536,380
300,000	52.82	204,563	166.33	400,916	422.84	585,139
350,000	61.63	238,670	194.05	467,726	493.31	682,654
400,000	70.43	272,752	221.77	534,537	563.78	780,167
450,000	79.23	306,830	249.48	601,335	634.25	877,679
500,000	88.04	340,968	277.21	668,202	704.73	975,250
550,000	96.84	375,047	304.93	735,011	775.20	1,072,762

DEBT REDUCTION TABLE

TO REDUCE A 30 YEAR LOAN TO:

LOAN AMOUNT	25 YEARS		20 YEARS		15 YEARS	
	PRE-PAY	SAVE	PRE-PAY	SAVE	PRE-PAY	SAVE
50	0.01	22	0.02	36	0.07	70
100	0.02	63	0.05	111	0.14	175
200	0.04	153	0.11	272	0.28	396
300	0.05	187	0.16	378	0.41	561
400	0.07	277	0.22	541	0.56	789
500	0.08	309	0.27	646	0.69	953
600	0.10	400	0.33	810	0.83	1,177
700	0.12	461	0.37	904	0.96	1,343
800	0.14	555	0.43	1,071	1.11	1,574
900	0.15	585	0.48	1,174	1.24	1,737
1,000	0.17	679	0.54	1,341	1.38	1,963
2,000	0.34	1,390	1.08	2,727	2.77	3,983
3,000	0.51	2,067	1.62	4,066	4.14	5,940
4,000	0.68	2,782	2.16	5,458	5.53	7,967
5,000	0.85	3,460	2.69	6,784	6.90	9,923
6,000	1.02	4,172	3.24	8,187	8.29	11,946
7,000	1.19	4,849	3.77	9,512	9.66	13,901
8,000	1.36	5,562	4.31	10,902	11.05	15,926
9,000	1.53	6,242	4.85	12,244	12.42	17,884
10,000	1.70	6,954	5.39	13,633	13.81	19,908
15,000	2.54	10,384	8.08	20,416	20.70	29,824
20,000	3.40	13,906	10.78	27,263	27.61	39,808
25,000	4.25	17,397	13.47	34,096	34.51	49,785
30,000	5.09	20,829	16.16	40,882	41.41	59,708
35,000	5.95	24,347	18.86	47,726	48.31	69,685
45,000	7.64	31,272	24.24	61,346	62.11	89,586
55,000	9.34	38,224	29.63	74,977	75.91	109,488
65,000	11.05	45,241	35.03	88,671	89.72	129,453
75,000	12.74	52,164	40.41	102,290	103.52	149,353
85,000	14.44	59,116	45.80	115,921	117.32	169,253
100,000	16.99	69,562	53.88	136,386	138.03	199,138
120,000	20.38	83,439	64.65	163,636	165.63	238,940
140,000	23.79	97,401	75.43	190,946	193.24	278,801
160,000	27.18	111,279	86.20	218,198	220.84	318,605
180,000	30.58	125,216	96.98	245,509	248.45	358,468
200,000	33.97	139,091	107.76	272,769	276.05	398,268
225,000	38.22	156,489	121.22	306,855	310.56	448,055
250,000	42.48	173,947	134.70	341,012	345.07	497,897
275,000	46.72	191,319	148.17	375,111	379.58	547,685
300,000	50.97	208,714	161.64	409,205	414.09	597,468
350,000	59.46	243,480	188.58	477,399	483.10	697,035
400,000	67.95	278,248	215.52	545,592	552.11	796,602
450,000	76.45	313,042	242.45	613,773	621.12	896,168
500,000	84.95	347,870	269.40	682,026	690.14	995,796
550,000	93.44	382,633	296.34	750,217	759.16	1,095,365

7.00% 7.00%

DEBT REDUCTION TABLE

TO REDUCE A 15 YEAR LOAN TO:

LOAN AMOUNT	12.5 YEARS		10 YEARS		7.5 YEARS	
	PRE-PAY	SAVE	PRE-PAY	SAVE	PRE-PAY	SAVE
50	0.06	6	0.14	12	0.27	17
100	0.11	12	0.27	23	0.54	33
200	0.21	23	0.53	45	1.07	66
300	0.31	34	0.79	67	1.60	99
400	0.41	45	1.05	89	2.13	131
500	0.52	57	1.31	112	2.66	164
600	0.62	68	1.57	134	3.19	197
700	0.72	80	1.83	156	3.72	230
800	0.82	91	2.09	178	4.26	263
900	0.93	103	2.36	202	4.80	297
1,000	1.04	115	2.63	225	5.33	330
2,000	2.07	230	5.25	449	10.65	659
3,000	3.10	344	7.87	673	15.98	989
4,000	4.13	458	10.49	898	21.30	1,318
5,000	5.16	572	13.11	1,122	26.62	1,647
6,000	6.20	688	15.74	1,348	31.96	1,978
7,000	7.24	803	18.36	1,572	37.28	2,308
8,000	8.27	917	20.98	1,796	42.60	2,637
9,000	9.30	1,032	23.60	2,021	47.93	2,967
10,000	10.33	1,146	26.22	2,245	53.25	3,296
15,000	15.50	1,720	39.34	3,369	79.88	4,945
20,000	20.67	2,293	52.45	4,491	106.50	6,593
25,000	25.83	2,866	65.57	5,615	133.13	8,242
30,000	31.00	3,440	78.68	6,738	159.76	9,890
35,000	36.17	4,013	91.79	7,861	186.39	11,539
45,000	46.50	5,159	118.01	10,106	239.63	14,835
55,000	56.83	6,306	144.24	12,352	292.89	18,132
65,000	67.17	7,453	170.47	14,598	346.14	21,429
75,000	77.49	8,598	196.69	16,843	399.38	24,725
85,000	87.83	9,745	222.92	19,090	452.64	28,022
100,000	103.33	11,465	262.26	22,459	532.52	32,968
120,000	124.00	13,758	314.71	26,950	639.02	39,561
140,000	144.67	16,052	367.16	31,442	745.53	46,155
160,000	165.33	18,344	419.61	35,934	852.03	52,748
180,000	185.99	20,637	472.06	40,425	958.53	59,341
200,000	206.66	22,930	524.51	44,917	1,065.04	65,936
225,000	232.49	25,796	590.08	50,532	1,198.16	74,177
250,000	258.32	28,662	655.64	56,146	1,331.29	82,419
275,000	284.16	31,530	721.21	61,762	1,464.43	90,662
300,000	309.99	34,396	786.77	67,376	1,597.55	98,903
350,000	361.66	40,129	917.90	78,606	1,863.82	115,388
400,000	413.32	45,861	1,049.02	89,835	2,130.07	131,871
450,000	464.99	51,594	1,180.16	101,065	2,396.33	148,355
500,000	516.65	57,326	1,311.28	112,294	2,662.59	164,839
550,000	568.32	63,059	1,442.41	123,524	2,928.85	181,323

7.25% 7.25%

DEBT REDUCTION TABLE

TO REDUCE A 15 YEAR LOAN TO:

LOAN AMOUNT	12.5 YEARS		10 YEARS		7.5 YEARS	
	PRE-PAY	SAVE	PRE-PAY	SAVE	PRE-PAY	SAVE
50	0.05	6	0.13	11	0.27	17
100	0.10	11	0.26	23	0.53	34
200	0.21	24	0.52	46	1.06	68
300	0.31	36	0.79	71	1.60	103
400	0.41	47	1.04	93	2.12	137
500	0.51	59	1.31	117	2.65	171
600	0.62	72	1.57	141	3.19	206
700	0.71	82	1.82	163	3.71	239
800	0.82	95	2.09	187	4.24	274
900	0.93	108	2.35	211	4.78	309
1,000	1.03	120	2.62	235	5.31	344
2,000	2.06	240	5.23	469	10.62	687
3,000	3.08	359	7.84	703	15.93	1,031
4,000	4.11	478	10.45	937	21.23	1,375
5,000	5.14	598	13.06	1,171	26.54	1,718
6,000	6.16	717	15.67	1,405	31.85	2,062
7,000	7.19	837	18.28	1,640	37.15	2,405
8,000	8.23	958	20.90	1,875	42.47	2,750
9,000	9.25	1,077	23.51	2,109	47.78	3,094
10,000	10.28	1,197	26.12	2,343	53.09	3,438
15,000	15.42	1,795	39.18	3,515	79.63	5,157
20,000	20.55	2,393	52.23	4,686	106.17	6,875
25,000	25.70	2,992	65.29	5,858	132.71	8,595
30,000	30.84	3,591	78.35	7,030	159.26	10,314
35,000	35.97	4,188	91.40	8,201	185.79	12,033
45,000	46.26	5,386	117.52	10,545	238.88	15,472
55,000	56.53	6,583	143.63	12,888	291.96	18,909
65,000	66.80	7,778	169.74	15,231	345.05	22,347
75,000	77.09	8,977	195.86	17,575	398.14	25,786
85,000	87.36	10,173	221.97	19,918	451.22	29,224
100,000	102.78	11,968	261.15	23,434	530.84	34,381
120,000	123.34	14,362	313.38	28,121	637.02	41,258
140,000	143.90	16,756	365.61	32,808	743.19	48,134
160,000	164.45	19,149	417.83	37,493	849.35	55,009
180,000	185.01	21,544	470.06	42,181	955.52	61,886
200,000	205.56	23,937	522.30	46,868	1,061.69	68,763
225,000	231.26	26,929	587.58	52,726	1,194.40	77,357
250,000	256.96	29,922	652.87	58,585	1,327.12	85,954
275,000	282.65	32,913	718.15	64,443	1,459.82	94,548
300,000	308.35	35,906	783.45	70,303	1,592.54	103,145
350,000	359.73	41,889	914.01	82,018	1,857.96	120,334
400,000	411.12	47,873	1,044.59	93,735	2,123.38	137,525
450,000	462.52	53,859	1,175.16	105,452	2,388.80	154,716
500,000	513.91	59,843	1,305.74	117,170	2,654.23	171,907
550,000	565.30	65,827	1,436.31	128,887	2,919.65	189,098

DEBT REDUCTION TABLE

TO REDUCE A 15 YEAR LOAN TO:

LOAN AMOUNT	12.5 YEARS		10 YEARS		7.5 YEARS	
	PRE-PAY	SAVE	PRE-PAY	SAVE	PRE-PAY	SAVE
50	0.05	6	0.13	12	0.26	17
100	0.10	12	0.26	24	0.53	36
200	0.20	24	0.52	48	1.06	71
300	0.30	36	0.78	72	1.58	106
400	0.41	50	1.04	98	2.12	143
500	0.51	62	1.30	122	2.65	179
600	0.61	74	1.56	146	3.17	214
700	0.72	88	1.82	171	3.71	251
800	0.82	100	2.08	195	4.23	286
900	0.92	112	2.34	219	4.76	321
1,000	1.02	124	2.60	243	5.29	357
2,000	2.04	249	5.20	488	10.58	715
3,000	3.06	373	7.80	732	15.87	1,073
4,000	4.08	498	10.40	976	21.16	1,431
5,000	5.11	623	13.00	1,220	26.45	1,789
6,000	6.13	748	15.60	1,464	31.74	2,147
7,000	7.15	873	18.20	1,708	37.03	2,505
8,000	8.17	997	20.80	1,953	42.33	2,864
9,000	9.20	1,123	23.40	2,197	47.62	3,222
10,000	10.22	1,247	26.00	2,441	52.91	3,580
15,000	15.33	1,871	39.00	3,662	79.37	5,371
20,000	20.44	2,495	52.00	4,883	105.82	7,161
25,000	25.55	3,119	65.00	6,104	132.28	8,952
30,000	30.66	3,743	78.00	7,325	158.74	10,743
35,000	35.78	4,367	91.00	8,546	185.19	12,533
45,000	46.00	5,615	117.00	10,988	238.11	16,114
55,000	56.22	6,863	143.00	13,431	291.02	19,695
65,000	66.44	8,110	169.01	15,874	343.93	23,277
75,000	76.67	9,359	195.01	18,315	396.85	26,858
85,000	86.88	10,605	221.00	20,756	449.75	30,438
100,000	102.21	12,477	260.00	24,419	529.12	35,809
120,000	122.66	14,973	312.01	29,304	634.95	42,972
140,000	143.11	17,469	364.01	34,188	740.77	50,134
160,000	163.55	19,965	416.01	39,072	846.60	57,296
180,000	183.99	22,460	468.01	43,956	952.42	64,458
200,000	204.43	24,955	520.01	48,840	1,058.24	71,620
225,000	229.99	28,075	585.01	54,945	1,190.53	80,573
250,000	255.54	31,193	650.01	61,049	1,322.80	89,524
275,000	281.10	34,314	715.01	67,154	1,455.08	98,477
300,000	306.65	37,433	780.02	73,260	1,587.37	107,430
350,000	357.76	43,672	910.02	85,470	1,851.92	125,335
400,000	408.87	49,911	1,040.03	97,681	2,116.49	143,241
450,000	459.98	56,150	1,170.02	109,890	2,381.05	161,146
500,000	511.08	62,388	1,300.02	122,099	2,645.60	179,050
550,000	562.20	68,628	1,430.03	134,310	2,910.17	196,956

DEBT REDUCTION TABLE

TO REDUCE A 15 YEAR LOAN TO:

LOAN AMOUNT	12.5 YEARS		10 YEARS		7.5 YEARS	
	PRE-PAY	SAVE	PRE-PAY	SAVE	PRE-PAY	SAVE
50	0.05	6	0.13	12	0.26	17
100	0.10	12	0.26	25	0.52	36
200	0.20	25	0.52	50	1.05	74
300	0.30	38	0.78	76	1.58	111
400	0.41	52	1.04	101	2.11	148
500	0.51	65	1.30	127	2.64	186
600	0.61	78	1.56	153	3.17	223
700	0.72	92	1.82	178	3.70	261
800	0.81	103	2.07	202	4.21	296
900	0.91	116	2.33	228	4.74	334
1,000	1.01	129	2.59	254	5.27	371
2,000	2.03	259	5.18	508	10.55	745
3,000	3.05	390	7.77	763	15.82	1,118
4,000	4.06	519	10.35	1,016	21.09	1,489
5,000	5.08	649	12.94	1,270	26.37	1,862
6,000	6.10	779	15.53	1,525	31.64	2,235
7,000	7.12	910	18.12	1,779	36.92	2,608
8,000	8.13	1,039	20.70	2,032	42.18	2,979
9,000	9.15	1,169	23.29	2,287	47.46	3,352
10,000	10.17	1,300	25.89	2,542	52.74	3,725
15,000	15.24	1,948	38.82	3,811	79.10	5,587
20,000	20.33	2,598	51.77	5,083	105.47	7,450
25,000	25.41	3,248	64.71	6,354	131.84	9,313
30,000	30.49	3,897	77.65	7,625	158.20	11,175
35,000	35.57	4,547	90.59	8,896	184.57	13,039
45,000	45.74	5,847	116.47	11,437	237.30	16,764
55,000	55.90	7,145	142.35	13,978	290.04	20,489
65,000	66.07	8,446	168.24	16,521	342.78	24,215
75,000	76.23	9,744	194.12	19,062	395.51	27,940
85,000	86.39	11,043	220.01	21,604	448.24	31,665
100,000	101.64	12,992	258.83	25,416	527.35	37,253
120,000	121.96	15,590	310.59	30,499	632.81	44,703
140,000	142.29	18,189	362.36	35,583	738.28	52,155
160,000	162.62	20,788	414.13	40,666	843.75	59,605
180,000	182.95	23,387	465.90	45,750	949.22	67,056
200,000	203.27	25,984	517.66	50,833	1,054.69	74,506
225,000	228.68	29,232	582.36	57,187	1,186.52	83,819
250,000	254.10	32,482	647.08	63,542	1,318.37	93,134
275,000	279.51	35,730	711.79	69,897	1,450.20	102,448
300,000	304.92	38,978	776.49	76,250	1,582.04	111,761
350,000	355.73	45,474	905.91	88,959	1,845.71	130,388
400,000	406.55	51,970	1,035.32	101,667	2,109.38	149,014
450,000	457.37	58,466	1,164.73	114,375	2,373.05	167,641
500,000	508.19	64,963	1,294.16	127,085	2,636.73	186,269
550,000	559.01	71,459	1,423.57	139,793	2,900.40	204,895

8.00% **8.00%**

DEBT REDUCTION TABLE

TO REDUCE A 15 YEAR LOAN TO:

LOAN AMOUNT	12.5 YEARS		10 YEARS		7.5 YEARS	
	PRE-PAY	SAVE	PRE-PAY	SAVE	PRE-PAY	SAVE
50	0.05	7	0.13	13	0.27	19
100	0.10	13	0.26	26	0.53	38
200	0.20	26	0.51	51	1.05	76
300	0.31	41	0.77	79	1.58	116
400	0.40	53	1.03	105	2.10	154
500	0.51	68	1.29	132	2.63	193
600	0.61	81	1.54	158	3.15	231
700	0.71	95	1.81	185	3.68	271
800	0.81	108	2.06	211	4.20	309
900	0.91	121	2.31	236	4.73	347
1,000	1.01	135	2.58	264	5.26	387
2,000	2.02	270	5.15	528	10.51	773
3,000	3.04	406	7.73	793	15.77	1,162
4,000	4.04	540	10.31	1,057	21.02	1,548
5,000	5.05	675	12.88	1,320	26.27	1,934
6,000	6.07	812	15.46	1,586	31.54	2,323
7,000	7.07	945	18.03	1,849	36.79	2,710
8,000	8.08	1,080	20.61	2,113	42.04	3,096
9,000	9.10	1,217	23.19	2,378	47.30	3,484
10,000	10.10	1,351	25.76	2,642	52.55	3,870
15,000	15.16	2,027	38.65	3,964	78.83	5,807
20,000	20.20	2,701	51.52	5,284	105.10	7,741
25,000	25.26	3,378	64.40	6,605	131.38	9,677
30,000	30.31	4,053	77.29	7,927	157.66	11,613
35,000	35.37	4,730	90.17	9,248	183.93	13,549
45,000	45.47	6,081	115.93	11,890	236.48	17,420
55,000	55.58	7,433	141.70	14,534	289.04	21,292
65,000	65.68	8,783	167.45	17,175	341.59	25,162
75,000	75.79	10,135	193.22	19,818	394.14	29,034
85,000	85.89	11,486	218.98	22,460	446.69	32,904
100,000	101.04	13,512	257.62	26,423	525.52	38,711
120,000	121.25	16,215	309.15	31,708	630.62	46,453
140,000	141.46	18,918	360.67	36,993	735.72	54,196
160,000	161.67	21,620	412.20	42,278	840.83	61,938
180,000	181.88	24,323	463.72	47,563	945.93	69,681
200,000	202.09	27,026	515.25	52,848	1,051.04	77,423
225,000	227.35	30,404	579.66	59,455	1,182.42	87,102
250,000	252.60	33,781	644.05	66,059	1,313.79	96,779
275,000	277.87	37,161	708.46	72,666	1,445.17	106,457
300,000	303.13	40,539	772.87	79,272	1,576.56	116,136
350,000	353.65	47,295	901.68	92,484	1,839.31	135,491
400,000	404.18	54,053	1,030.50	105,697	2,102.08	154,848
450,000	454.69	60,808	1,159.31	118,909	2,364.83	174,203
500,000	505.21	67,564	1,288.11	132,120	2,627.59	193,559
550,000	555.74	74,322	1,416.93	145,333	2,890.35	212,916

DEBT REDUCTION TABLE

TO REDUCE A 15 YEAR LOAN TO:

LOAN AMOUNT	12.5 YEARS		10 YEARS		7.5 YEARS	
	PRE-PAY	SAVE	PRE-PAY	SAVE	PRE-PAY	SAVE
50	0.05	7	0.13	13	0.26	19
100	0.10	13	0.25	26	0.52	39
200	0.20	27	0.51	54	1.04	79
300	0.30	41	0.76	81	1.57	119
400	0.40	55	1.02	108	2.09	159
500	0.50	69	1.28	136	2.61	199
600	0.60	83	1.53	163	3.14	240
700	0.70	97	1.79	191	3.66	280
800	0.80	111	2.05	218	4.19	320
900	0.90	125	2.30	246	4.71	360
1,000	1.00	139	2.56	273	5.23	400
2,000	2.01	281	5.13	548	10.47	803
3,000	3.01	421	7.69	823	15.71	1,205
4,000	4.02	562	10.26	1,098	20.95	1,607
5,000	5.02	702	12.82	1,372	26.18	2,009
6,000	6.03	843	15.39	1,647	31.42	2,411
7,000	7.04	984	17.95	1,921	36.66	2,813
8,000	8.03	1,122	20.51	2,194	41.89	3,213
9,000	9.04	1,263	23.07	2,469	47.13	3,616
10,000	10.04	1,403	25.64	2,744	52.36	4,017
15,000	15.06	2,105	38.45	4,115	78.54	6,026
20,000	20.09	2,808	51.28	5,488	104.73	8,037
25,000	25.11	3,510	64.10	6,860	130.91	10,045
30,000	30.13	4,211	76.91	8,231	157.09	12,054
35,000	35.16	4,914	89.74	9,605	183.28	14,065
45,000	45.19	6,317	115.37	12,348	235.64	18,082
55,000	55.24	7,721	141.01	15,093	288.01	22,102
65,000	65.28	9,125	166.65	17,836	340.36	26,119
75,000	75.33	10,530	192.29	20,581	392.73	30,138
85,000	85.37	11,933	217.93	23,326	445.10	34,157
100,000	100.43	14,038	256.38	27,441	523.64	40,183
120,000	120.52	16,847	307.67	32,931	628.37	48,222
140,000	140.61	19,655	358.94	38,419	733.10	56,258
160,000	160.69	22,462	410.22	43,907	837.83	64,295
180,000	180.78	25,270	461.49	49,395	942.55	72,332
200,000	200.86	28,077	512.77	54,883	1,047.28	80,369
225,000	225.98	31,588	576.87	61,744	1,178.20	90,416
250,000	251.08	35,097	640.96	68,604	1,309.10	100,461
275,000	276.19	38,607	705.06	75,465	1,440.02	110,508
300,000	301.30	42,117	769.15	82,325	1,570.92	120,553
350,000	351.52	49,136	897.35	96,046	1,832.74	140,646
400,000	401.73	56,155	1,025.54	109,767	2,094.56	160,738
450,000	451.95	63,175	1,153.73	123,488	2,356.39	180,831
500,000	502.17	70,195	1,281.93	137,210	2,618.21	200,923
550,000	552.38	77,214	1,410.12	150,931	2,880.03	221,016

8.50% 8.50%

DEBT REDUCTION TABLE

TO REDUCE A 15 YEAR LOAN TO:

LOAN AMOUNT	12.5 YEARS		10 YEARS		7.5 YEARS	
	PRE-PAY	SAVE	PRE-PAY	SAVE	PRE-PAY	SAVE
50	0.06	7	0.12	13	0.26	20
100	0.10	14	0.25	28	0.52	41
200	0.20	29	0.51	57	1.05	83
300	0.30	43	0.76	84	1.56	124
400	0.40	58	1.02	114	2.09	167
500	0.50	72	1.27	141	2.61	207
600	0.60	87	1.53	171	3.13	250
700	0.70	102	1.78	198	3.65	291
800	0.80	117	2.04	227	4.18	333
900	0.90	131	2.29	255	4.69	374
1,000	1.00	146	2.55	284	5.22	416
2,000	2.00	291	5.10	569	10.43	833
3,000	2.99	436	7.65	853	15.65	1,249
4,000	4.00	584	10.21	1,139	20.87	1,667
5,000	4.99	728	12.76	1,423	26.09	2,083
6,000	5.99	874	15.31	1,708	31.30	2,499
7,000	6.98	1,018	17.85	1,991	36.52	2,916
8,000	7.99	1,166	20.41	2,278	41.74	3,334
9,000	8.98	1,311	22.96	2,562	46.96	3,750
10,000	9.98	1,456	25.51	2,846	52.17	4,166
15,000	14.97	2,185	38.26	4,269	78.25	6,249
20,000	19.97	2,915	51.03	5,694	104.35	8,334
25,000	24.95	3,642	63.78	7,117	130.43	10,417
30,000	29.94	4,370	76.53	8,540	156.51	12,500
35,000	34.94	5,100	89.29	9,965	182.60	14,585
45,000	44.91	6,556	114.80	12,811	234.77	18,751
55,000	54.90	8,014	140.32	15,659	286.95	22,919
65,000	64.87	9,469	165.82	18,504	339.11	27,085
75,000	74.86	10,928	191.34	21,352	391.29	31,253
85,000	84.84	12,385	216.85	24,200	443.46	35,421
100,000	99.82	14,572	255.12	28,470	521.72	41,672
120,000	119.78	17,485	306.14	34,164	626.06	50,006
140,000	139.74	20,399	357.16	39,858	730.40	58,340
160,000	159.70	23,313	408.19	45,552	834.74	66,674
180,000	179.66	26,227	459.21	51,245	939.09	75,008
200,000	199.63	29,142	510.24	56,941	1,043.44	83,344
225,000	224.57	32,783	574.01	64,057	1,173.86	93,761
250,000	249.53	36,427	637.80	71,176	1,304.30	104,180
275,000	274.48	40,069	701.57	78,292	1,434.72	114,597
300,000	299.44	43,712	765.36	85,411	1,565.15	125,016
350,000	349.34	50,997	892.91	99,646	1,826.01	145,852
400,000	399.25	58,283	1,020.47	113,881	2,086.87	166,688
450,000	449.15	65,568	1,148.03	128,116	2,347.73	187,524
500,000	499.06	72,854	1,275.59	142,352	2,608.59	208,360
550,000	548.96	80,138	1,403.15	156,587	2,869.44	229,196

8.75% 8.75%

DEBT REDUCTION TABLE

TO REDUCE A 15 YEAR LOAN TO:

LOAN AMOUNT	12.5 YEARS		10 YEARS		7.5 YEARS	
	PRE-PAY	SAVE	PRE-PAY	SAVE	PRE-PAY	SAVE
50	0.05	8	0.13	15	0.26	22
100	0.10	15	0.26	30	0.52	43
200	0.20	31	0.51	59	1.04	86
300	0.30	46	0.76	88	1.56	129
400	0.40	61	1.02	118	2.08	172
500	0.50	76	1.27	147	2.60	216
600	0.60	91	1.52	177	3.12	259
700	0.70	106	1.78	206	3.64	302
800	0.79	120	2.03	236	4.16	345
900	0.89	135	2.28	265	4.68	388
1,000	0.99	151	2.54	295	5.20	431
2,000	1.99	303	5.08	590	10.40	864
3,000	2.97	452	7.61	884	15.59	1,294
4,000	3.97	605	10.16	1,181	20.79	1,727
5,000	4.96	755	12.69	1,474	25.98	2,157
6,000	5.95	906	15.23	1,770	31.19	2,590
7,000	6.94	1,057	17.76	2,064	36.38	3,021
8,000	7.93	1,208	20.31	2,361	41.58	3,453
9,000	8.92	1,358	22.84	2,654	46.77	3,884
10,000	9.92	1,511	25.38	2,950	51.97	4,316
15,000	14.88	2,266	38.08	4,426	77.96	6,476
20,000	19.84	3,022	50.77	5,902	103.95	8,635
25,000	24.79	3,776	63.45	7,376	129.93	10,792
30,000	29.75	4,532	76.15	8,852	155.92	12,951
35,000	34.71	5,287	88.84	10,328	181.91	15,110
45,000	44.63	6,798	114.22	13,278	233.88	19,427
55,000	54.55	8,310	139.60	16,230	285.86	23,745
65,000	64.46	9,819	164.98	19,179	337.83	28,061
75,000	74.38	11,330	190.37	22,132	389.81	32,380
85,000	84.29	12,840	215.74	25,081	441.78	36,696
100,000	99.18	15,108	253.82	29,509	519.75	43,174
120,000	119.01	18,129	304.59	35,411	623.70	51,808
140,000	138.85	21,151	355.35	41,312	727.64	60,443
160,000	158.68	24,172	406.11	47,214	831.59	69,077
180,000	178.52	27,194	456.88	53,116	935.54	77,712
200,000	198.35	30,215	507.64	59,017	1,039.49	86,347
225,000	223.15	33,993	571.10	66,395	1,169.43	97,140
250,000	247.93	37,767	634.54	73,770	1,299.35	107,932
275,000	272.73	41,545	698.00	81,148	1,429.29	118,726
300,000	297.52	45,322	761.46	88,526	1,559.23	129,520
350,000	347.10	52,874	888.36	103,279	1,819.10	151,106
400,000	396.69	60,429	1,015.28	118,034	2,078.97	172,693
450,000	446.29	67,984	1,142.19	132,789	2,338.85	194,281
500,000	495.87	75,537	1,269.09	147,542	2,598.71	215,866
550,000	545.46	83,091	1,396.01	162,298	2,858.59	237,454

9.00% 9.00%

DEBT REDUCTION TABLE

TO REDUCE A 15 YEAR LOAN TO:

LOAN AMOUNT	12.5 YEARS		10 YEARS		7.5 YEARS	
	PRE-PAY	SAVE	PRE-PAY	SAVE	PRE-PAY	SAVE
50	0.05	8	0.13	15	0.26	22
100	0.10	15	0.25	30	0.52	44
200	0.20	32	0.51	61	1.04	89
300	0.29	46	0.76	91	1.55	133
400	0.40	63	1.01	122	2.07	178
500	0.49	77	1.26	152	2.58	222
600	0.59	93	1.52	183	3.11	268
700	0.69	110	1.77	214	3.63	313
800	0.79	125	2.02	244	4.14	357
900	0.89	141	2.28	275	4.66	402
1,000	0.98	155	2.52	304	5.17	446
2,000	1.97	313	5.05	611	10.35	893
3,000	2.96	470	7.58	917	15.53	1,340
4,000	3.94	625	10.10	1,221	20.70	1,786
5,000	4.92	781	12.62	1,527	25.88	2,233
6,000	5.91	938	15.15	1,833	31.06	2,680
7,000	6.90	1,096	17.68	2,139	36.24	3,128
8,000	7.88	1,251	20.20	2,444	41.41	3,574
9,000	8.87	1,408	22.72	2,749	46.59	4,021
10,000	9.85	1,564	25.25	3,055	51.77	4,468
15,000	14.78	2,348	37.88	4,584	77.66	6,703
20,000	19.70	3,129	50.50	6,111	103.54	8,937
25,000	24.63	3,912	63.12	7,639	129.43	11,172
30,000	29.56	4,695	75.75	9,167	155.32	13,407
35,000	34.48	5,476	88.37	10,694	181.20	15,640
45,000	44.34	7,043	113.63	13,751	232.98	20,110
55,000	54.19	8,607	138.87	16,806	284.75	24,579
65,000	64.04	10,172	164.12	19,862	336.52	29,047
75,000	73.90	11,738	189.37	22,918	388.30	33,517
85,000	83.75	13,303	214.62	25,973	440.07	37,985
100,000	98.52	15,649	252.49	30,557	517.72	44,688
120,000	118.23	18,780	302.99	36,668	621.27	53,627
140,000	137.93	21,909	353.49	42,779	724.81	62,564
160,000	157.64	25,039	403.99	48,891	828.36	71,502
180,000	177.35	28,170	454.49	55,003	931.91	80,440
200,000	197.04	31,298	504.98	61,113	1,035.44	89,377
225,000	221.68	35,212	568.11	68,754	1,164.88	100,550
250,000	246.31	39,124	631.23	76,392	1,294.31	111,722
275,000	270.94	43,036	694.35	84,031	1,423.74	122,894
300,000	295.57	46,949	757.48	91,672	1,553.17	134,067
350,000	344.83	54,773	883.72	106,949	1,812.03	156,410
400,000	394.09	62,598	1,009.97	122,228	2,070.89	178,755
450,000	443.36	70,424	1,136.21	137,507	2,329.76	201,100
500,000	492.61	78,247	1,262.45	152,784	2,588.61	223,444
550,000	541.88	86,073	1,388.70	168,063	2,847.48	245,789

9.25% 9.25%

DEBT REDUCTION TABLE

TO REDUCE A 15 YEAR LOAN TO:

LOAN AMOUNT	12.5 YEARS		10 YEARS		7.5 YEARS	
	PRE-PAY	SAVE	PRE-PAY	SAVE	PRE-PAY	SAVE
50	0.05	8	0.13	15	0.26	22
100	0.10	16	0.26	32	0.52	46
200	0.20	33	0.51	64	1.03	92
300	0.30	49	0.76	95	1.55	138
400	0.39	64	1.01	126	2.06	184
500	0.49	81	1.26	158	2.58	230
600	0.59	97	1.51	189	3.09	276
700	0.68	112	1.76	221	3.61	323
800	0.78	129	2.01	252	4.12	369
900	0.88	145	2.26	283	4.64	415
1,000	0.98	162	2.51	315	5.15	461
2,000	1.96	324	5.02	631	10.31	923
3,000	2.94	486	7.53	948	15.47	1,386
4,000	3.92	648	10.05	1,265	20.63	1,848
5,000	4.90	811	12.56	1,581	25.79	2,311
6,000	5.87	971	15.06	1,895	30.94	2,772
7,000	6.85	1,133	17.58	2,212	36.09	3,234
8,000	7.83	1,296	20.09	2,529	41.25	3,697
9,000	8.81	1,458	22.60	2,845	46.41	4,159
10,000	9.79	1,620	25.12	3,162	51.57	4,622
15,000	14.68	2,430	37.67	4,742	77.35	6,932
20,000	19.58	3,240	50.23	6,323	103.13	9,243
25,000	24.47	4,050	62.79	7,904	128.92	11,555
30,000	29.36	4,859	75.34	9,484	154.70	13,865
35,000	34.25	5,668	87.90	11,065	180.48	16,176
45,000	44.04	7,289	113.01	14,226	232.05	20,798
55,000	53.82	8,908	138.12	17,388	283.61	25,419
65,000	63.61	10,528	163.24	20,550	335.18	30,041
75,000	73.39	12,146	188.35	23,710	386.74	34,663
85,000	83.18	13,767	213.46	26,872	438.31	39,284
100,000	97.86	16,196	251.13	31,614	515.65	46,217
120,000	117.43	19,435	301.36	37,937	618.78	55,460
140,000	137.01	22,677	351.59	44,262	721.92	64,706
160,000	156.58	25,915	401.82	50,585	825.05	73,949
180,000	176.15	29,154	452.04	56,907	928.18	83,192
200,000	195.72	32,393	502.27	63,230	1,031.31	92,435
225,000	220.18	36,442	565.05	71,133	1,160.22	103,990
250,000	244.64	40,490	627.83	79,037	1,289.14	115,544
275,000	269.12	44,542	690.62	86,942	1,418.06	127,100
300,000	293.58	48,590	753.41	94,846	1,546.97	138,654
350,000	342.51	56,689	878.97	110,653	1,804.79	161,763
400,000	391.44	64,788	1,004.54	126,461	2,062.63	184,873
450,000	440.37	72,886	1,130.11	142,269	2,320.45	207,981
500,000	489.29	80,983	1,255.67	158,075	2,578.28	231,090
550,000	538.23	89,083	1,381.24	173,884	2,836.11	254,200

9.50% 9.50%

DEBT REDUCTION TABLE

TO REDUCE A 15 YEAR LOAN TO:

LOAN AMOUNT	12.5 YEARS		10 YEARS		7.5 YEARS	
	PRE-PAY	SAVE	PRE-PAY	SAVE	PRE-PAY	SAVE
50	0.05	8	0.12	15	0.25	22
100	0.10	17	0.25	32	0.51	47
200	0.20	34	0.50	65	1.03	95
300	0.29	49	0.75	97	1.54	142
400	0.39	67	1.00	130	2.06	191
500	0.48	82	1.24	161	2.56	237
600	0.58	100	1.50	196	3.08	286
700	0.68	117	1.75	229	3.60	335
800	0.78	134	2.00	261	4.11	381
900	0.88	151	2.25	294	4.62	429
1,000	0.97	167	2.49	325	5.13	476
2,000	1.94	334	4.99	653	10.27	954
3,000	2.92	503	7.49	980	15.41	1,432
4,000	3.89	670	9.99	1,307	20.55	1,911
5,000	4.86	837	12.48	1,633	25.67	2,386
6,000	5.83	1,004	14.98	1,960	30.81	2,864
7,000	6.80	1,172	17.48	2,287	35.95	3,343
8,000	7.78	1,341	19.98	2,614	41.09	3,821
9,000	8.74	1,506	22.47	2,940	46.21	4,296
10,000	9.72	1,675	24.97	3,267	51.35	4,775
15,000	14.58	2,512	37.46	4,901	77.03	7,163
20,000	19.44	3,350	49.95	6,536	102.71	9,551
25,000	24.30	4,188	62.44	8,171	128.39	11,940
30,000	29.16	5,025	74.93	9,805	154.07	14,328
35,000	34.02	5,863	87.42	11,440	179.74	16,716
45,000	43.73	7,536	112.38	14,706	231.09	21,491
55,000	53.45	9,211	137.36	17,975	282.45	26,268
65,000	63.17	10,887	162.34	21,244	333.80	31,044
75,000	72.89	12,562	187.32	24,513	385.16	35,821
85,000	82.60	14,235	212.28	27,779	436.51	40,595
100,000	97.18	16,748	249.75	32,682	513.54	47,760
120,000	116.62	20,099	299.71	39,221	616.26	57,314
140,000	136.06	23,449	349.65	45,756	718.96	66,865
160,000	155.50	26,800	399.61	52,294	821.67	76,418
180,000	174.93	30,148	449.55	58,829	924.38	85,969
200,000	194.37	33,499	499.51	65,367	1,027.09	95,523
225,000	218.66	37,686	561.94	73,537	1,155.47	107,462
250,000	242.95	41,871	624.37	81,707	1,283.86	119,402
275,000	267.26	46,061	686.82	89,879	1,412.25	131,343
300,000	291.55	50,247	749.25	98,049	1,540.63	143,283
350,000	340.14	58,622	874.13	114,391	1,797.40	167,164
400,000	388.74	66,998	999.01	130,734	2,054.18	191,045
450,000	437.32	75,370	1,123.88	147,074	2,310.94	214,924
500,000	485.91	83,745	1,248.75	163,416	2,567.72	238,805
550,000	534.51	92,121	1,373.63	179,758	2,824.49	262,686

9.75% 9.75%

DEBT REDUCTION TABLE

TO REDUCE A 15 YEAR LOAN TO:

LOAN AMOUNT	12.5 YEARS		10 YEARS		7.5 YEARS	
	PRE-PAY	SAVE	PRE-PAY	SAVE	PRE-PAY	SAVE
50	0.05	9	0.13	17	0.26	25
100	0.10	18	0.25	34	0.52	50
200	0.20	35	0.50	68	1.03	99
300	0.29	52	0.75	101	1.54	148
400	0.39	70	1.00	135	2.05	197
500	0.48	86	1.24	168	2.56	246
600	0.58	104	1.49	202	3.07	295
700	0.68	121	1.74	236	3.58	345
800	0.77	138	1.99	270	4.09	394
900	0.87	155	2.23	302	4.60	443
1,000	0.96	172	2.48	336	5.11	492
2,000	1.93	346	4.97	675	10.23	986
3,000	2.89	518	7.45	1,011	15.34	1,478
4,000	3.86	692	9.93	1,349	20.46	1,972
5,000	4.83	866	12.42	1,688	25.57	2,466
6,000	5.79	1,038	14.90	2,025	30.68	2,950
7,000	6.76	1,212	17.38	2,362	35.80	3,452
8,000	7.72	1,385	19.87	2,701	40.92	3,946
9,000	8.68	1,556	22.35	3,037	46.02	4,437
10,000	9.65	1,730	24.84	3,376	51.14	4,931
15,000	14.47	2,595	37.25	5,063	76.71	7,397
20,000	19.30	3,461	49.67	6,751	102.28	9,862
25,000	24.12	4,325	62.08	8,438	127.84	12,327
30,000	28.95	5,192	74.51	10,129	153.42	14,795
35,000	33.78	6,058	86.92	11,816	178.99	17,261
45,000	43.42	40,807	111.75	15,191	230.12	22,192
55,000	53.08	9,520	136.59	18,569	281.27	27,125
65,000	62.72	11,249	161.42	21,944	332.40	32,056
75,000	72.37	12,979	186.25	25,319	383.54	36,987
85,000	82.02	14,711	211.09	28,697	434.68	41,920
100,000	96.49	17,305	248.34	33,760	511.39	49,317
120,000	115.79	20,767	298.01	40,512	613.67	59,181
140,000	135.10	24,230	347.68	47,265	715.95	69,045
160,000	154.39	27,689	397.34	54,016	818.22	78,907
180,000	173.69	31,151	447.01	60,769	920.50	88,771
200,000	192.99	34,613	496.68	67,521	1,022.78	98,635
225,000	217.11	38,939	558.77	75,962	1,150.62	110,964
250,000	241.24	43,267	620.85	84,402	1,278.47	123,294
275,000	265.36	47,593	682.94	92,843	1,406.32	135,624
300,000	289.49	51,921	745.02	101,283	1,534.17	147,953
350,000	337.74	60,574	869.19	118,163	1,789.86	172,612
400,000	385.98	69,226	993.35	135,042	2,045.55	197,269
450,000	434.22	77,878	1,117.53	151,923	2,301.24	221,928
500,000	482.47	86,532	1,241.70	168,804	2,556.94	246,588
550,000	530.72	95,186	1,365.87	185,685	2,812.63	271,247

10.00% 10.00%

DEBT REDUCTION TABLE

TO REDUCE A 15 YEAR LOAN TO:

LOAN AMOUNT	12.5 YEARS		10 YEARS		7.5 YEARS	
	PRE-PAY	SAVE	PRE-PAY	SAVE	PRE-PAY	SAVE
50	0.05	9	0.13	18	0.26	25
100	0.10	18	0.25	34	0.51	50
200	0.20	37	0.50	70	1.02	102
300	0.29	53	0.74	104	1.53	152
400	0.39	72	0.99	139	2.04	204
500	0.48	89	1.23	173	2.54	253
600	0.58	108	1.48	209	3.06	305
700	0.67	124	1.73	243	3.56	355
800	0.77	143	1.98	279	4.08	407
900	0.86	160	2.22	312	4.58	456
1,000	0.96	179	2.47	348	5.09	508
2,000	1.91	356	4.94	696	10.18	1,016
3,000	2.88	537	7.41	1,046	15.28	1,527
4,000	3.83	714	9.88	1,393	20.37	2,035
5,000	4.78	891	12.34	1,740	25.45	2,542
6,000	5.75	1,072	14.82	2,091	30.55	3,053
7,000	6.70	1,249	17.28	2,438	35.64	3,561
8,000	7.67	1,430	19.76	2,788	40.74	4,071
9,000	8.62	1,608	22.22	3,135	45.83	4,579
10,000	9.57	1,785	24.69	3,483	50.91	5,087
15,000	14.36	2,678	37.03	5,225	76.37	7,631
20,000	19.15	3,572	49.38	6,968	101.83	10,175
25,000	23.94	4,465	61.72	8,710	127.29	12,720
30,000	28.73	5,359	74.07	10,453	152.75	15,265
35,000	33.52	6,252	86.41	12,195	178.21	17,809
45,000	43.10	8,039	111.10	15,680	229.13	22,898
55,000	52.68	9,826	135.79	19,165	280.05	27,987
65,000	62.26	11,613	160.48	22,650	330.97	33,076
75,000	71.84	13,400	185.18	26,136	381.89	38,165
85,000	81.42	15,187	209.87	29,620	432.81	43,253
100,000	95.79	17,868	246.90	34,847	509.19	50,887
120,000	114.95	21,442	296.28	41,817	611.03	61,065
140,000	134.11	25,016	345.67	48,787	712.86	71,242
160,000	153.27	28,590	395.05	55,757	814.70	81,420
180,000	172.43	32,164	444.43	62,727	916.54	91,598
200,000	191.58	35,736	493.80	69,694	1,018.37	101,773
225,000	215.53	40,203	555.53	78,407	1,145.67	114,495
250,000	239.48	44,671	617.25	87,119	1,272.97	127,218
275,000	263.43	49,138	678.98	95,831	1,400.26	139,940
300,000	287.38	53,606	740.71	104,544	1,527.56	152,662
350,000	335.28	62,541	864.16	121,968	1,782.16	178,106
400,000	383.17	71,474	987.60	139,390	2,036.75	203,549
450,000	431.07	80,409	1,111.06	156,815	2,291.34	228,993
500,000	478.97	89,344	1,234.51	174,239	2,545.94	254,437
550,000	526.87	98,279	1,357.97	191,664	2,800.53	279,881

10.25% 10.25%

DEBT REDUCTION TABLE

TO REDUCE A 15 YEAR LOAN TO:

LOAN AMOUNT	12.5 YEARS		10 YEARS		7.5 YEARS	
	PRE-PAY	SAVE	PRE-PAY	SAVE	PRE-PAY	SAVE
50	0.05	9	0.12	17	0.25	25
100	0.10	19	0.25	36	0.51	53
200	0.20	38	0.50	73	1.02	105
300	0.29	56	0.74	108	1.53	158
400	0.39	75	0.99	144	2.03	210
500	0.48	93	1.23	180	2.54	263
600	0.58	112	1.48	216	3.05	315
700	0.67	130	1.72	252	3.55	367
800	0.77	149	1.97	288	4.06	420
900	0.86	167	2.21	324	4.57	472
1,000	0.96	185	2.46	360	5.07	525
2,000	1.91	370	4.91	719	10.14	1,049
3,000	2.86	554	7.37	1,079	15.21	1,574
4,000	3.81	738	9.82	1,438	20.28	2,099
5,000	4.76	922	12.27	1,796	25.35	2,623
6,000	5.71	1,107	14.73	2,157	30.42	3,148
7,000	6.66	1,291	17.18	2,515	35.49	3,672
8,000	7.61	1,475	19.64	2,875	40.56	4,197
9,000	8.56	1,659	22.09	3,234	45.63	4,722
10,000	9.51	1,843	24.54	3,593	50.69	5,246
15,000	14.26	2,764	36.81	5,390	76.04	7,869
20,000	19.01	3,685	49.08	7,187	101.38	10,492
25,000	23.77	4,609	61.36	8,986	126.74	13,117
30,000	28.53	5,531	73.63	10,782	152.08	15,740
35,000	33.28	6,452	85.90	12,579	177.43	18,363
45,000	42.79	8,296	110.45	16,175	228.13	23,612
55,000	52.29	10,138	134.99	19,768	278.82	28,858
65,000	61.81	11,984	159.54	23,364	329.52	34,106
75,000	71.31	13,826	184.08	26,957	380.21	39,352
85,000	80.82	15,670	208.63	30,553	430.91	44,600
100,000	95.08	18,435	245.44	35,943	506.94	52,469
120,000	114.10	22,123	294.52	43,131	608.33	62,963
140,000	133.11	25,809	343.61	50,320	709.72	73,457
160,000	152.13	29,496	392.70	57,509	811.11	83,951
180,000	171.15	33,184	441.79	64,698	912.50	94,445
200,000	190.16	36,870	490.88	71,887	1,013.89	104,939
225,000	213.94	41,482	552.24	80,875	1,140.63	118,059
250,000	237.71	46,090	613.60	89,861	1,267.36	131,176
275,000	261.48	50,699	674.96	98,846	1,394.10	144,293
300,000	285.25	55,307	736.32	107,832	1,520.83	157,410
350,000	332.79	64,526	859.04	125,805	1,774.31	183,647
400,000	380.33	73,743	981.76	143,777	2,027.78	209,881
450,000	427.88	82,963	1,104.48	161,750	2,281.26	236,118
500,000	475.42	92,180	1,227.20	179,721	2,534.72	262,351
550,000	522.95	101,396	1,349.91	197,692	2,788.19	288,586

10.50% 10.50%

DEBT REDUCTION TABLE

TO REDUCE A 15 YEAR LOAN TO:

LOAN AMOUNT	12.5 YEARS		10 YEARS		7.5 YEARS	
	PRE-PAY	SAVE	PRE-PAY	SAVE	PRE-PAY	SAVE
50	0.04	8	0.12	17	0.25	26
100	0.09	18	0.24	36	0.51	53
200	0.18	36	0.48	72	1.01	106
300	0.28	56	0.73	110	1.52	162
400	0.37	74	0.97	146	2.02	214
500	0.47	94	1.22	185	2.53	270
600	0.56	112	1.46	221	3.03	323
700	0.66	133	1.71	259	3.54	378
800	0.75	151	1.95	295	4.04	431
900	0.85	171	2.20	334	4.55	487
1,000	0.94	189	2.44	369	5.05	539
2,000	1.89	380	4.88	741	10.10	1,081
3,000	2.83	569	7.32	1,110	15.14	1,620
4,000	3.78	761	9.76	1,481	20.19	2,162
5,000	4.72	951	12.20	1,853	25.24	2,704
6,000	5.66	1,139	14.64	2,222	30.28	3,243
7,000	6.61	1,331	17.08	2,594	35.33	3,784
8,000	7.55	1,520	19.51	2,962	40.37	4,324
9,000	8.49	1,710	21.96	3,334	45.42	4,865
10,000	9.44	1,901	24.40	3,705	50.47	5,407
15,000	14.16	2,852	36.60	5,558	75.70	8,110
20,000	18.88	3,803	48.79	7,410	100.94	10,814
25,000	23.59	4,752	60.99	9,263	126.17	13,517
30,000	28.31	5,703	73.19	11,115	151.40	16,220
35,000	33.03	6,653	85.39	12,968	176.64	18,923
45,000	42.47	8,555	109.78	16,672	227.10	24,330
55,000	51.90	10,455	134.18	20,378	277.57	29,737
65,000	61.34	12,356	158.57	24,082	328.03	35,143
75,000	70.77	14,256	182.97	27,788	378.50	40,550
85,000	80.21	16,157	207.36	31,492	428.97	45,957
100,000	94.36	19,008	243.95	37,050	504.66	54,066
120,000	113.24	22,810	292.74	44,459	605.60	64,880
140,000	132.11	26,612	341.53	51,869	706.53	75,693
160,000	150.98	30,413	390.32	59,279	807.46	86,506
180,000	169.85	34,214	439.11	66,689	908.39	97,319
200,000	188.72	38,015	487.90	74,099	1,009.32	108,132
225,000	212.31	42,767	548.89	83,362	1,135.49	121,649
250,000	235.90	47,519	609.88	92,624	1,261.65	135,165
275,000	259.49	52,271	670.87	101,887	1,387.82	148,682
300,000	283.08	57,023	731.85	111,149	1,513.98	162,198
350,000	330.26	66,527	853.83	129,674	1,766.31	189,232
400,000	377.44	76,031	975.80	148,198	2,018.64	216,265
450,000	424.62	85,534	1,097.78	166,723	2,270.97	243,298
500,000	471.80	95,038	1,219.75	185,248	2,523.30	270,331
550,000	518.98	104,542	1,341.73	203,773	2,775.63	297,364

10.75% 10.75%

DEBT REDUCTION TABLE

TO REDUCE A 15 YEAR LOAN TO:

LOAN AMOUNT	12.5 YEARS		10 YEARS		7.5 YEARS	
	PRE-PAY	SAVE	PRE-PAY	SAVE	PRE-PAY	SAVE
50	0.04	8	0.12	17	0.25	26
100	0.09	18	0.24	36	0.50	54
200	0.18	37	0.48	74	1.00	109
300	0.28	58	0.73	113	1.50	165
400	0.37	77	0.97	152	2.01	222
500	0.47	98	1.21	190	2.51	277
600	0.56	117	1.45	229	3.01	333
700	0.66	137	1.70	267	3.52	389
800	0.75	157	1.94	305	4.02	445
900	0.85	177	2.18	344	4.52	501
1,000	0.94	197	2.42	382	5.03	557
2,000	1.88	393	4.85	763	10.05	1,113
3,000	2.81	587	7.27	1,145	15.07	1,670
4,000	3.75	784	9.70	1,526	20.10	2,227
5,000	4.68	979	12.12	1,908	25.12	2,783
6,000	5.62	1,175	14.55	2,290	30.14	3,340
7,000	6.56	1,371	16.97	2,671	35.16	3,896
8,000	7.49	1,566	19.40	3,053	40.19	4,453
9,000	8.43	1,763	21.82	3,434	45.21	5,010
10,000	9.36	1,958	24.24	3,815	50.23	5,566
15,000	14.04	2,936	36.37	5,723	75.35	8,349
20,000	18.73	3,917	48.49	7,633	100.47	11,135
25,000	23.41	4,896	60.61	9,541	125.59	13,918
30,000	28.09	5,875	72.73	11,448	150.70	16,701
35,000	32.77	6,854	84.85	13,356	175.81	19,484
45,000	42.13	8,812	109.10	17,174	226.05	25,053
55,000	51.49	10,770	133.34	20,989	276.28	30,619
65,000	60.86	12,730	157.59	24,806	326.52	36,188
75,000	70.22	14,687	181.83	28,622	376.75	41,754
85,000	79.58	16,646	206.07	32,439	426.99	47,323
100,000	93.63	19,585	242.44	38,164	502.34	55,675
120,000	112.36	23,502	290.93	45,797	602.81	66,810
140,000	131.08	27,418	339.41	53,430	703.27	77,945
160,000	149.81	31,335	387.90	61,062	803.74	89,079
180,000	168.53	35,251	436.39	68,695	904.21	100,215
200,000	187.26	39,169	484.88	76,328	1,004.67	111,349
225,000	210.66	44,063	545.49	85,869	1,130.25	125,267
250,000	234.07	48,961	606.10	95,411	1,255.85	139,188
275,000	257.48	53,857	666.71	104,951	1,381.43	153,106
300,000	280.88	58,752	727.32	114,492	1,507.01	167,024
350,000	327.70	68,545	848.54	133,575	1,758.18	194,862
400,000	374.51	78,336	969.76	152,655	2,009.34	222,698
450,000	421.33	88,130	1,090.97	171,739	2,260.51	250,537
500,000	468.14	97,922	1,212.19	190,822	2,511.69	278,376
550,000	514.95	107,713	1,333.41	209,902	2,762.85	306,212

11.00% 11.00%

DEBT REDUCTION TABLE

TO REDUCE A 15 YEAR LOAN TO:

LOAN AMOUNT	12.5 YEARS		10 YEARS		7.5 YEARS	
	PRE-PAY	SAVE	PRE-PAY	SAVE	PRE-PAY	SAVE
50	0.05	10	0.12	19	0.25	28
100	0.09	19	0.24	39	0.50	56
200	0.18	39	0.48	77	1.00	113
300	0.28	61	0.73	119	1.50	172
400	0.37	80	0.97	157	2.00	229
500	0.46	99	1.20	195	2.50	285
600	0.56	122	1.45	236	3.00	344
700	0.65	141	1.69	275	3.50	400
800	0.74	160	1.93	313	4.00	457
900	0.84	182	2.17	354	4.50	516
1,000	0.93	202	2.41	392	5.00	572
2,000	1.85	401	4.82	784	10.00	1,144
3,000	2.79	605	7.23	1,178	15.00	1,718
4,000	3.71	805	9.64	1,571	20.00	2,291
5,000	4.65	1,009	12.05	1,965	25.00	2,865
6,000	5.57	1,209	14.46	2,357	30.00	3,437
7,000	6.50	1,410	16.86	2,748	34.99	4,009
8,000	7.43	1,613	19.28	3,143	40.00	4,583
9,000	8.36	1,815	21.68	3,535	45.00	5,156
10,000	9.29	2,017	24.10	3,930	50.00	5,730
15,000	13.94	3,026	36.14	5,893	75.00	8,594
20,000	18.58	4,033	48.19	7,858	100.00	11,459
25,000	23.23	5,043	60.23	9,822	125.00	14,324
30,000	27.87	6,050	72.28	11,787	150.00	17,189
35,000	32.51	7,058	84.32	13,751	174.99	20,053
45,000	41.80	9,074	108.41	17,679	224.99	25,783
55,000	51.09	11,091	132.50	21,608	274.99	31,513
65,000	60.38	13,108	156.59	25,537	324.98	37,242
75,000	69.67	15,125	180.68	29,465	374.98	42,972
85,000	78.95	17,140	204.77	33,394	424.98	48,701
100,000	92.89	20,166	240.91	39,287	499.97	57,295
120,000	111.46	24,198	289.09	47,145	599.97	68,755
140,000	130.04	28,231	337.27	55,002	699.96	80,214
160,000	148.62	32,264	385.45	62,860	799.96	91,673
180,000	167.19	36,296	433.63	70,717	899.95	103,132
200,000	185.77	40,330	481.81	78,574	999.94	114,591
225,000	208.99	45,371	542.03	88,395	1,124.94	128,915
250,000	232.21	50,412	602.26	98,218	1,249.93	143,239
275,000	255.43	55,453	662.48	108,039	1,374.92	157,563
300,000	278.65	60,494	722.71	117,861	1,499.91	171,886
350,000	325.10	70,579	843.17	137,507	1,749.91	200,537
400,000	371.54	80,661	963.62	157,150	1,999.89	229,185
450,000	417.98	90,743	1,084.07	176,793	2,249.88	257,832
500,000	464.42	100,825	1,204.52	196,436	2,499.86	286,480
550,000	510.86	110,907	1,324.97	216,080	2,749.84	315,128

11.25% 11.25%

DEBT REDUCTION TABLE

TO REDUCE A 15 YEAR LOAN TO:

LOAN AMOUNT	12.5 YEARS		10 YEARS		7.5 YEARS	
	PRE-PAY	SAVE	PRE-PAY	SAVE	PRE-PAY	SAVE
50	0.05	11	0.12	20	0.25	29
100	0.09	19	0.24	39	0.49	57
200	0.18	40	0.48	80	0.99	116
300	0.28	63	0.72	121	1.49	176
400	0.37	83	0.96	162	1.99	235
500	0.46	103	1.19	200	2.48	292
600	0.55	123	1.44	242	2.98	352
700	0.65	146	1.68	283	3.48	412
800	0.74	167	1.92	324	3.98	471
900	0.83	186	2.15	362	4.47	528
1,000	0.92	206	2.39	403	4.97	587
2,000	1.84	414	4.79	808	9.95	1,178
3,000	2.76	621	7.18	1,211	14.92	1,765
4,000	3.68	829	9.57	1,615	19.90	2,356
5,000	4.61	1,038	11.97	2,021	24.88	2,946
6,000	5.52	1,243	14.36	2,423	29.85	3,533
7,000	6.45	1,452	16.75	2,828	34.83	4,124
8,000	7.37	1,660	19.15	3,233	39.81	4,714
9,000	8.29	1,866	21.54	3,636	44.78	5,301
10,000	9.21	2,074	23.93	4,040	49.76	5,892
15,000	13.82	3,112	35.90	6,061	74.63	8,837
20,000	18.43	4,151	47.87	8,084	99.52	11,786
25,000	23.03	5,187	59.84	10,104	124.39	14,731
30,000	27.64	6,225	71.80	12,124	149.27	17,677
35,000	32.24	7,261	83.77	14,145	174.14	20,623
45,000	41.46	9,337	107.71	18,188	223.91	26,517
55,000	50.68	11,414	131.64	22,231	273.67	32,412
65,000	59.88	13,486	155.57	26,271	323.42	38,303
75,000	69.10	15,563	179.51	30,314	373.18	44,197
85,000	78.31	17,637	203.44	34,355	422.93	50,088
100,000	92.13	20,750	239.34	40,418	497.57	58,929
120,000	110.56	24,900	287.21	48,502	597.08	70,714
140,000	128.98	29,049	335.08	56,585	696.59	82,500
160,000	147.41	33,200	382.95	64,669	796.11	94,286
180,000	165.83	37,349	430.82	72,753	895.62	106,071
200,000	184.27	41,502	478.69	80,839	995.14	117,860
225,000	207.30	46,689	538.53	90,943	1,119.53	132,591
250,000	230.33	51,875	598.36	101,046	1,243.92	147,322
275,000	253.37	57,065	658.20	111,153	1,368.32	162,057
300,000	276.39	62,250	718.03	121,256	1,492.71	176,788
350,000	322.46	72,626	837.71	141,467	1,741.49	206,253
400,000	368.53	83,002	957.38	161,677	1,990.28	235,719
450,000	414.59	93,376	1,077.05	181,885	2,239.06	265,182
500,000	460.66	103,752	1,196.72	202,095	2,487.84	294,647
550,000	506.73	114,128	1,316.40	222,306	2,736.63	324,113

11.50% 11.50%

DEBT REDUCTION TABLE

TO REDUCE A 15 YEAR LOAN TO:

LOAN AMOUNT	12.5 YEARS		10 YEARS		7.5 YEARS	
	PRE-PAY	SAVE	PRE-PAY	SAVE	PRE-PAY	SAVE
50	0.04	9	0.12	20	0.25	29
100	0.09	21	0.24	42	0.50	60
200	0.18	42	0.48	83	0.99	120
300	0.27	63	0.71	123	1.48	180
400	0.36	84	0.95	165	1.98	241
500	0.45	105	1.18	205	2.47	300
600	0.55	128	1.43	250	2.97	363
700	0.64	149	1.67	291	3.47	424
800	0.73	170	1.90	331	3.96	483
900	0.82	191	2.14	373	4.45	543
1,000	0.91	212	2.37	413	4.95	604
2,000	1.83	427	4.75	829	9.90	1,210
3,000	2.74	639	7.13	1,246	14.85	1,816
4,000	3.66	854	9.51	1,662	19.81	2,422
5,000	4.57	1,067	11.89	2,078	24.76	3,029
6,000	5.48	1,279	14.26	2,492	29.70	3,632
7,000	6.39	1,492	16.64	2,908	34.66	4,239
8,000	7.31	1,707	19.02	3,324	39.61	4,845
9,000	8.23	1,921	21.40	3,740	44.56	5,451
10,000	9.14	2,135	23.78	4,156	49.52	6,058
15,000	13.71	3,202	35.67	6,234	74.27	9,086
20,000	18.28	4,269	47.56	8,312	99.03	12,115
25,000	22.84	5,334	59.44	10,389	123.78	15,143
30,000	27.41	6,402	71.33	12,468	148.54	18,172
35,000	31.98	7,469	83.22	14,545	173.30	21,201
45,000	41.12	9,603	106.99	18,701	222.81	27,258
55,000	50.25	11,736	130.77	22,857	272.32	33,315
65,000	59.39	13,871	154.55	27,013	321.83	39,372
75,000	68.52	16,003	178.32	31,168	371.34	45,429
85,000	77.66	18,137	202.10	35,324	420.86	51,487
100,000	91.37	21,340	237.77	41,560	495.13	60,575
120,000	109.65	25,609	285.32	49,871	594.16	72,690
140,000	127.92	29,876	332.87	58,183	693.18	84,805
160,000	146.19	34,144	380.42	66,494	792.20	96,919
180,000	164.46	38,410	427.97	74,805	891.23	109,034
200,000	182.74	42,680	475.53	83,119	990.26	121,151
225,000	205.58	48,015	534.97	93,509	1,114.04	136,294
250,000	228.42	53,349	594.41	103,898	1,237.82	151,437
275,000	251.26	58,684	653.85	114,287	1,361.60	166,581
300,000	274.11	64,021	713.30	124,679	1,485.39	181,727
350,000	319.79	74,690	832.18	145,458	1,732.95	212,013
400,000	365.48	85,361	951.06	166,239	1,980.52	242,302
450,000	411.16	96,030	1,069.94	187,017	2,228.08	272,589
500,000	456.85	106,701	1,188.83	207,799	2,475.65	302,878
550,000	502.53	117,370	1,307.70	228,577	2,723.21	333,164

11.75% DEBT REDUCTION TABLE 11.75%

TO REDUCE A 15 YEAR LOAN TO:

LOAN AMOUNT	12.5 YEARS		10 YEARS		7.5 YEARS	
	PRE-PAY	SAVE	PRE-PAY	SAVE	PRE-PAY	SAVE
50	0.04	9	0.12	20	0.24	29
100	0.09	21	0.24	42	0.49	61
200	0.18	43	0.48	86	0.99	124
300	0.27	64	0.71	127	1.48	185
400	0.36	87	0.95	171	1.97	248
500	0.45	108	1.18	211	2.46	309
600	0.54	130	1.42	255	2.96	372
700	0.64	155	1.66	300	3.45	435
800	0.72	174	1.89	340	3.94	496
900	0.82	198	2.13	384	4.44	560
1,000	0.90	217	2.36	425	4.92	620
2,000	1.81	437	4.72	852	9.85	1,243
3,000	2.72	658	7.08	1,280	14.78	1,866
4,000	3.62	876	9.45	1,708	19.71	2,488
5,000	4.53	1,096	11.81	2,135	24.63	3,110
6,000	5.44	1,316	14.17	2,563	29.56	3,733
7,000	6.35	1,537	16.54	2,990	34.49	4,356
8,000	7.24	1,752	18.89	3,415	39.41	4,976
9,000	8.15	1,972	21.25	3,842	44.34	5,599
10,000	9.06	2,193	23.61	4,269	49.26	6,222
15,000	13.59	3,290	35.43	6,407	73.90	9,335
20,000	18.12	4,387	47.23	8,541	98.53	12,446
25,000	22.65	5,483	59.04	10,676	123.16	15,556
30,000	27.18	6,580	70.85	12,813	147.80	18,670
35,000	31.71	7,676	82.66	14,947	172.43	21,781
45,000	40.77	9,870	106.28	19,219	221.70	28,005
55,000	49.83	12,063	129.89	23,488	270.96	34,226
65,000	58.89	14,257	153.51	27,760	320.22	40,450
75,000	67.95	16,450	177.13	32,032	369.49	46,675
85,000	77.01	18,643	200.74	36,300	418.75	52,896
100,000	90.60	21,933	236.16	42,706	492.65	62,231
120,000	108.72	26,321	283.40	51,250	591.18	74,679
140,000	126.84	30,707	330.63	59,791	689.71	87,125
160,000	144.95	35,092	377.86	68,331	788.24	99,570
180,000	163.08	39,481	425.10	76,875	886.77	112,019
200,000	181.20	43,868	472.32	85,415	985.30	124,465
225,000	203.85	49,352	531.37	96,093	1,108.47	140,024
250,000	226.50	54,836	590.41	106,771	1,231.63	155,583
275,000	249.14	60,317	649.45	117,446	1,354.79	171,139
300,000	271.80	65,802	708.49	128,124	1,477.95	186,698
350,000	317.10	76,770	826.58	149,480	1,724.28	217,816
400,000	362.40	87,737	944.65	170,832	1,970.60	248,931
450,000	407.69	98,701	1,062.73	192,185	2,216.93	280,047
500,000	453.00	109,671	1,180.82	213,541	2,463.26	311,165
550,000	498.29	120,636	1,298.90	234,894	2,709.58	342,281

12.00% 12.00%

DEBT REDUCTION TABLE

TO REDUCE A 15 YEAR LOAN TO:

LOAN AMOUNT	12.5 YEARS		10 YEARS		7.5 YEARS	
	PRE-PAY	SAVE	PRE-PAY	SAVE	PRE-PAY	SAVE
50	0.04	9	0.11	19	0.24	29
100	0.08	19	0.23	42	0.49	61
200	0.17	42	0.46	85	0.98	125
300	0.26	65	0.70	129	1.47	189
400	0.35	87	0.93	173	1.96	253
500	0.44	110	1.17	217	2.45	317
600	0.53	133	1.40	261	2.94	381
700	0.62	155	1.64	305	3.43	445
800	0.71	177	1.87	348	3.92	509
900	0.80	200	2.11	393	4.41	573
1,000	0.89	223	2.34	436	4.90	637
2,000	1.79	449	4.69	876	9.80	1,276
3,000	2.69	674	7.04	1,315	14.70	1,916
4,000	3.59	900	9.38	1,754	19.61	2,556
5,000	4.49	1,126	11.73	2,193	24.51	3,195
6,000	5.38	1,349	14.07	2,629	29.40	3,831
7,000	6.28	1,575	16.41	3,068	34.31	4,471
8,000	7.18	1,801	18.76	3,507	39.21	5,110
9,000	8.08	2,027	21.11	3,947	44.11	5,750
10,000	8.98	2,252	23.46	4,386	49.02	6,390
15,000	13.47	3,379	35.18	6,578	73.52	9,584
20,000	17.96	4,505	46.91	8,772	98.03	12,779
25,000	22.45	5,631	58.63	10,964	122.53	15,973
30,000	26.94	6,757	70.36	13,157	147.04	19,168
35,000	31.44	7,887	82.09	15,353	171.55	22,366
45,000	40.42	10,139	105.54	19,738	220.56	28,755
55,000	49.40	12,392	129.00	24,125	269.57	35,144
65,000	58.39	14,647	152.46	28,513	318.59	41,537
75,000	67.37	16,900	175.91	32,898	367.60	47,926
85,000	76.34	19,150	199.36	37,284	416.62	54,315
100,000	89.82	22,532	234.54	43,865	490.14	63,902
120,000	107.78	27,037	281.45	52,637	588.16	76,681
140,000	125.75	31,545	328.36	61,410	686.19	89,462
160,000	143.72	36,053	375.27	70,184	784.22	102,244
180,000	161.67	40,556	422.17	78,955	882.25	115,023
200,000	179.64	45,064	469.08	87,729	980.28	127,805
225,000	202.10	50,698	527.72	98,696	1,102.81	143,781
250,000	224.54	56,327	586.35	109,661	1,225.34	159,754
275,000	247.00	61,962	644.99	120,628	1,347.88	175,731
300,000	269.46	67,596	703.62	131,594	1,470.41	191,707
350,000	314.37	78,862	820.90	153,528	1,715.49	223,659
400,000	359.28	90,128	938.16	175,458	1,960.55	255,609
450,000	404.19	101,394	1,055.44	197,393	2,205.62	287,561
500,000	449.09	112,658	1,172.70	219,323	2,450.69	319,511
550,000	494.01	123,926	1,289.98	241,257	2,695.76	351,463

DEBT REDUCTION TABLE

TO REDUCE A 15 YEAR LOAN TO:

LOAN AMOUNT	12.5 YEARS		10 YEARS		7.5 YEARS	
	PRE-PAY	SAVE	PRE-PAY	SAVE	PRE-PAY	SAVE
50	0.05	12	0.12	23	0.25	33
100	0.09	23	0.23	44	0.49	65
200	0.18	46	0.46	88	0.97	129
300	0.27	70	0.70	135	1.47	197
400	0.36	93	0.93	179	1.95	261
500	0.44	113	1.16	222	2.43	325
600	0.54	140	1.40	270	2.93	393
700	0.62	161	1.63	314	3.41	457
800	0.71	183	1.86	358	3.90	522
900	0.80	208	2.10	405	4.39	590
1,000	0.89	231	2.33	449	4.87	654
2,000	1.78	462	4.66	900	9.75	1,311
3,000	2.67	694	6.99	1,351	14.63	1,967
4,000	3.56	924	9.31	1,799	19.50	2,621
5,000	4.45	1,156	11.64	2,250	24.38	3,278
6,000	5.34	1,387	13.98	2,702	29.26	3,935
7,000	6.23	1,618	16.30	3,150	34.13	4,588
8,000	7.12	1,849	18.63	3,601	39.01	5,245
9,000	8.01	2,081	20.96	4,052	43.89	5,902
10,000	8.91	2,315	23.29	4,503	48.76	6,558
15,000	13.35	3,469	34.93	6,752	73.14	9,836
20,000	17.81	4,628	46.58	9,006	97.52	13,117
25,000	22.26	5,783	58.22	11,256	121.90	16,395
30,000	26.71	6,940	69.87	13,509	146.28	19,675
35,000	31.16	8,096	81.51	15,759	170.66	22,953
45,000	40.06	10,409	104.80	20,262	219.42	29,511
55,000	48.97	12,723	128.09	24,765	268.17	36,069
65,000	57.87	15,036	151.38	29,267	316.93	42,627
75,000	66.77	17,349	174.67	33,771	365.69	49,186
85,000	75.68	19,664	197.96	38,273	414.45	55,744
100,000	89.04	23,136	232.90	45,030	487.59	65,583
120,000	106.84	27,761	279.48	54,036	585.11	78,700
140,000	124.65	32,388	326.06	63,042	682.63	91,817
160,000	142.45	37,014	372.64	72,047	780.15	104,934
180,000	160.26	41,641	419.22	81,053	877.67	118,051
200,000	178.07	46,269	465.80	90,059	975.18	131,167
225,000	200.32	52,050	524.02	101,315	1,097.08	147,561
250,000	222.58	57,835	582.25	112,574	1,218.98	163,959
275,000	244.84	63,618	640.47	123,830	1,340.87	180,353
300,000	267.10	69,402	698.70	135,089	1,462.77	196,750
350,000	311.61	80,968	815.15	157,604	1,706.57	229,542
400,000	356.13	92,536	931.60	180,118	1,950.36	262,333
450,000	400.64	104,102	1,048.05	202,634	2,194.16	295,126
500,000	445.16	115,670	1,164.50	225,148	2,437.95	327,917
550,000	489.68	127,237	1,280.95	247,663	2,681.74	360,708

DEBT REDUCTION TABLE

TO REDUCE A 15 YEAR LOAN TO:

LOAN AMOUNT	12.5 YEARS		10 YEARS		7.5 YEARS	
	PRE-PAY	SAVE	PRE-PAY	SAVE	PRE-PAY	SAVE
50	0.05	13	0.12	23	0.24	32
100	0.09	23	0.23	45	0.48	65
200	0.18	47	0.46	91	0.97	133
300	0.27	72	0.70	139	1.46	201
400	0.35	94	0.92	182	1.94	267
500	0.44	117	1.15	228	2.42	334
600	0.53	142	1.39	277	2.91	402
700	0.62	166	1.62	323	3.40	471
800	0.70	188	1.85	368	3.88	535
900	0.79	212	2.08	414	4.36	603
1,000	0.88	236	2.31	461	4.85	671
2,000	1.76	472	4.62	921	9.70	1,343
3,000	2.65	713	6.94	1,386	14.55	2,017
4,000	3.53	949	9.25	1,846	19.40	2,688
5,000	4.41	1,186	11.56	2,309	24.25	3,363
6,000	5.29	1,423	13.87	2,770	29.10	4,034
7,000	6.18	1,662	16.19	3,234	33.95	4,708
8,000	7.06	1,898	18.50	3,695	38.80	5,380
9,000	7.94	2,136	20.81	4,158	43.65	6,054
10,000	8.82	2,372	23.12	4,618	48.50	6,725
15,000	13.24	3,562	34.69	6,930	72.75	10,091
20,000	17.65	4,748	46.25	9,239	97.00	13,453
25,000	22.05	5,932	57.81	11,549	121.25	16,816
30,000	26.47	7,121	69.37	13,860	145.50	20,182
35,000	30.88	8,308	80.93	16,169	169.75	23,545
45,000	39.71	10,683	104.06	20,790	218.25	30,273
55,000	48.53	13,056	127.18	25,410	266.76	37,001
65,000	57.36	15,432	150.31	30,032	315.26	43,730
75,000	66.17	17,802	173.43	34,650	363.75	50,454
85,000	75.00	20,178	196.55	39,270	412.26	57,183
100,000	88.23	23,738	231.24	46,201	485.01	67,274
120,000	105.89	28,488	277.49	55,443	582.01	80,730
140,000	123.53	33,234	323.73	64,681	679.01	94,184
160,000	141.18	37,984	369.98	73,923	776.01	107,640
180,000	158.83	42,733	416.24	83,166	873.02	121,097
200,000	176.47	47,478	462.48	92,404	970.02	134,551
225,000	198.53	53,413	520.29	103,955	1,091.27	151,370
250,000	220.59	59,349	578.10	115,505	1,212.52	168,189
275,000	242.65	65,284	635.91	127,056	1,333.77	185,008
300,000	264.71	71,219	693.72	138,607	1,455.03	201,828
350,000	308.83	83,089	809.34	161,708	1,697.53	235,466
400,000	352.95	94,960	924.96	184,810	1,940.04	269,105
450,000	397.07	106,830	1,040.58	207,911	2,182.54	302,742
500,000	441.18	118,698	1,156.19	231,010	2,425.04	336,378
550,000	485.30	130,568	1,271.81	254,111	2,667.54	370,016

12.75% 12.75%

DEBT REDUCTION TABLE

TO REDUCE A 15 YEAR LOAN TO:

LOAN AMOUNT	12.5 YEARS		10 YEARS		7.5 YEARS	
	PRE-PAY	SAVE	PRE-PAY	SAVE	PRE-PAY	SAVE
50	0.04	11	0.11	22	0.24	33
100	0.09	25	0.23	47	0.49	69
200	0.18	50	0.46	94	0.97	138
300	0.26	72	0.69	141	1.45	206
400	0.35	97	0.92	189	1.93	275
500	0.44	122	1.15	236	2.41	343
600	0.52	144	1.38	283	2.89	412
700	0.61	169	1.60	329	3.37	480
800	0.70	194	1.83	376	3.85	549
900	0.79	220	2.07	427	4.35	621
1,000	0.88	244	2.30	474	4.83	690
2,000	1.75	487	4.59	947	9.65	1,379
3,000	2.62	729	6.89	1,421	14.47	2,060
4,000	3.50	974	9.18	1,894	19.29	2,757
5,000	4.37	1,216	11.47	2,366	24.12	3,446
6,000	5.24	1,458	13.77	2,840	28.94	4,136
7,000	6.12	1,704	16.07	3,316	33.77	4,828
8,000	7.00	1,948	18.37	3,791	38.59	5,517
9,000	7.87	2,191	20.66	4,263	43.42	6,207
10,000	8.74	2,433	22.95	4,736	48.24	6,896
15,000	13.12	3,653	34.43	7,106	72.36	10,346
20,000	17.49	4,870	45.91	9,476	96.48	13,795
25,000	21.86	6,088	57.39	11,845	120.60	17,245
30,000	26.23	7,304	68.86	14,212	144.71	20,691
35,000	30.60	8,521	80.34	16,582	168.84	24,141
45,000	39.35	10,958	103.30	21,321	217.08	31,040
55,000	48.08	13,389	126.25	26,057	265.31	37,936
65,000	56.83	15,826	149.21	30,797	313.56	44,835
75,000	65.58	18,263	172.17	35,537	361.80	51,735
85,000	74.32	20,696	195.12	40,273	410.03	58,630
100,000	87.44	24,350	229.56	47,382	482.40	68,979
120,000	104.92	29,218	275.47	56,858	578.87	82,774
140,000	122.41	34,089	321.38	66,333	675.35	96,569
160,000	139.90	38,961	367.30	75,813	771.84	110,368
180,000	157.38	43,829	413.21	85,288	868.31	124,163
200,000	174.87	48,699	459.12	94,764	964.79	137,958
225,000	196.73	54,786	516.51	106,609	1,085.39	155,203
250,000	218.59	60,874	573.90	118,455	1,205.98	172,447
275,000	240.44	66,959	631.29	130,301	1,326.58	189,692
300,000	262.30	73,047	688.68	142,146	1,447.18	206,936
350,000	306.03	85,226	803.47	165,841	1,688.39	241,430
400,000	349.74	97,399	918.25	189,532	1,929.58	275,919
450,000	393.46	109,574	1,033.03	213,223	2,170.78	310,408
500,000	437.18	121,749	1,147.81	236,914	2,411.97	344,898
550,000	480.89	133,923	1,262.58	260,604	2,653.17	379,387

13.00% 13.00%

DEBT REDUCTION TABLE

TO REDUCE A 15 YEAR LOAN TO:

LOAN AMOUNT	12.5 YEARS		10 YEARS		7.5 YEARS	
	PRE-PAY	SAVE	PRE-PAY	SAVE	PRE-PAY	SAVE
50	0.04	11	0.11	22	0.24	33
100	0.09	25	0.23	48	0.48	69
200	0.17	48	0.45	94	0.95	138
300	0.26	74	0.68	144	1.44	211
400	0.34	97	0.91	192	1.91	280
500	0.43	124	1.14	242	2.40	352
600	0.52	148	1.36	288	2.87	421
700	0.61	175	1.60	340	3.36	494
800	0.69	197	1.82	386	3.83	562
900	0.78	224	2.05	436	4.32	636
1,000	0.86	247	2.28	484	4.79	704
2,000	1.73	498	4.56	971	9.59	1,412
3,000	2.60	749	6.84	1,457	14.39	2,120
4,000	3.47	1,000	9.12	1,943	19.19	2,828
5,000	4.33	1,247	11.39	2,426	23.98	3,532
6,000	5.20	1,497	13.67	2,913	28.78	4,240
7,000	6.07	1,748	15.95	3,399	33.58	4,948
8,000	6.93	1,997	18.23	3,886	38.38	5,655
9,000	7.79	2,244	20.50	4,368	43.17	6,360
10,000	8.66	2,495	22.79	4,856	47.97	7,068
15,000	13.00	3,746	34.18	7,285	71.96	10,603
20,000	17.33	4,993	45.58	9,714	95.95	14,138
25,000	21.65	6,238	56.96	12,140	119.93	17,670
30,000	25.99	7,488	68.36	14,569	143.92	21,206
35,000	30.32	8,737	79.75	16,998	167.91	24,741
45,000	38.99	11,235	102.54	21,857	215.89	31,812
55,000	47.64	13,728	125.32	26,711	263.86	38,880
65,000	56.31	16,227	148.11	31,570	311.84	45,951
75,000	64.97	18,721	170.90	36,426	359.81	53,018
85,000	73.63	21,217	193.69	41,285	407.79	60,089
100,000	86.62	24,961	227.86	48,568	479.75	70,692
120,000	103.95	29,954	273.43	58,282	575.69	84,830
140,000	121.28	34,949	319.02	68,000	671.65	98,972
160,000	138.60	39,941	364.59	77,713	767.60	113,110
180,000	155.93	44,934	410.16	87,427	863.55	127,249
200,000	173.25	49,925	455.73	97,140	959.50	141,387
225,000	194.91	56,167	512.70	109,283	1,079.43	159,061
250,000	216.57	62,408	569.66	121,425	1,199.37	176,734
275,000	238.22	68,648	626.63	133,569	1,319.31	194,409
300,000	259.88	74,890	683.60	145,712	1,439.25	212,083
350,000	303.19	87,371	797.53	169,997	1,679.12	247,430
400,000	346.51	99,854	911.46	194,283	1,919.00	282,778
450,000	389.82	112,335	1,025.40	218,569	2,158.87	318,125
500,000	433.13	124,815	1,139.32	242,851	2,398.74	353,469
550,000	476.44	137,296	1,253.26	267,137	2,638.61	388,816

DEBT REDUCTION TABLE

TO REDUCE A 15 YEAR LOAN TO:

LOAN AMOUNT	12.5 YEARS		10 YEARS		7.5 YEARS	
	PRE-PAY	SAVE	PRE-PAY	SAVE	PRE-PAY	SAVE
50	0.04	11	0.11	22	0.23	33
100	0.08	23	0.22	47	0.47	69
200	0.17	50	0.45	98	0.95	142
300	0.26	77	0.68	148	1.43	216
400	0.35	103	0.91	199	1.91	289
500	0.43	128	1.13	248	2.39	362
600	0.51	151	1.35	296	2.86	432
700	0.60	178	1.58	346	3.34	504
800	0.69	205	1.81	396	3.82	577
900	0.77	229	2.04	447	4.29	650
1,000	0.86	256	2.26	497	4.77	723
2,000	1.72	511	4.52	993	9.54	1,447
3,000	2.57	765	6.78	1,490	14.31	2,170
4,000	3.44	1,025	9.05	1,991	19.09	2,897
5,000	4.29	1,278	11.31	2,488	23.86	3,621
6,000	5.15	1,534	13.57	2,984	28.62	4,343
7,000	6.00	1,788	15.83	3,481	33.39	5,066
8,000	6.87	2,047	18.10	3,982	38.17	5,794
9,000	7.72	2,301	20.36	4,479	42.94	6,517
10,000	8.58	2,557	22.61	4,974	47.71	7,240
15,000	12.87	3,835	33.92	7,462	71.56	10,860
20,000	17.16	5,115	45.23	9,952	95.42	14,483
25,000	21.45	6,393	56.54	12,440	119.27	18,103
30,000	25.74	7,672	67.84	14,927	143.12	21,723
35,000	30.04	8,954	79.16	17,418	166.98	25,346
45,000	38.61	11,509	101.77	22,393	214.68	32,586
55,000	47.20	14,069	124.38	27,369	262.39	39,829
65,000	55.78	16,628	147.00	32,347	310.10	47,073
75,000	64.36	19,184	169.61	37,322	357.80	54,312
85,000	72.94	21,743	192.23	42,300	405.51	61,556
100,000	85.81	25,580	226.15	49,765	477.07	72,419
120,000	102.97	30,695	271.38	59,717	572.49	86,902
140,000	120.13	35,810	316.61	69,669	667.90	101,385
160,000	137.30	40,929	361.85	79,626	763.32	115,871
180,000	154.46	46,044	407.08	89,578	858.73	130,354
200,000	171.62	51,159	452.30	99,529	954.14	144,837
225,000	193.08	57,557	508.85	111,973	1,073.41	162,943
250,000	214.52	63,948	565.38	124,412	1,192.68	181,047
275,000	235.98	70,345	621.92	136,855	1,311.95	199,153
300,000	257.44	76,743	678.46	149,298	1,431.22	217,260
350,000	300.34	89,531	791.54	174,181	1,669.75	253,469
400,000	343.25	102,322	904.61	199,062	1,908.29	289,678
450,000	386.15	115,111	1,017.69	223,945	2,146.82	325,887
500,000	429.05	127,900	1,130.76	248,827	2,385.36	362,097
550,000	471.96	140,690	1,243.84	273,709	2,623.89	398,305

DEBT REDUCTION TABLE

TO REDUCE A 15 YEAR LOAN TO:

LOAN AMOUNT	12.5 YEARS		10 YEARS		7.5 YEARS	
	PRE-PAY	SAVE	PRE-PAY	SAVE	PRE-PAY	SAVE
50	0.05	15	0.12	26	0.24	37
100	0.09	27	0.23	51	0.48	74
200	0.17	52	0.45	101	0.95	147
300	0.25	77	0.67	151	1.42	221
400	0.34	103	0.90	202	1.90	294
500	0.42	128	1.12	252	2.37	368
600	0.51	157	1.35	306	2.85	445
700	0.60	184	1.57	356	3.32	518
800	0.68	209	1.80	408	3.80	593
900	0.76	234	2.02	457	4.27	666
1,000	0.85	261	2.24	507	4.74	739
2,000	1.70	523	4.49	1,019	9.49	1,482
3,000	2.55	786	6.74	1,530	14.24	2,225
4,000	3.40	1,047	8.97	2,036	18.97	2,963
5,000	4.25	1,309	11.22	2,547	23.72	3,706
6,000	5.10	1,572	13.47	3,058	28.47	4,450
7,000	5.95	1,833	15.71	3,566	33.20	5,188
8,000	6.80	2,096	17.95	4,076	37.95	5,931
9,000	7.65	2,358	20.20	4,587	42.70	6,674
10,000	8.50	2,619	22.44	5,094	47.43	7,412
15,000	12.75	3,930	33.67	7,645	71.16	11,123
20,000	17.00	5,240	44.88	10,191	94.87	14,829
25,000	21.25	6,551	56.11	12,742	118.60	18,539
30,000	25.50	7,860	67.33	15,290	142.31	22,245
35,000	29.74	9,168	78.55	17,837	166.02	25,951
45,000	38.24	11,788	100.99	22,934	213.46	33,368
55,000	46.74	14,409	123.43	28,031	260.90	40,784
65,000	55.25	17,032	145.88	33,129	308.34	48,201
75,000	63.75	19,652	168.32	38,226	355.78	55,617
85,000	72.24	22,269	190.76	43,320	403.21	63,029
100,000	84.99	26,201	224.43	50,968	474.37	74,156
120,000	101.99	31,441	269.31	61,160	569.24	88,985
140,000	118.99	36,682	314.20	71,355	664.11	103,817
160,000	135.99	41,923	359.08	81,549	758.99	118,650
180,000	152.98	47,160	403.96	91,740	853.86	133,478
200,000	169.98	52,401	448.85	101,936	948.73	148,310
225,000	191.23	58,952	504.96	114,678	1,067.32	166,849
250,000	212.48	65,503	561.06	127,420	1,185.92	185,389
275,000	233.72	72,051	617.17	140,162	1,304.51	203,927
300,000	254.97	78,602	673.27	152,903	1,423.10	222,466
350,000	297.47	91,704	785.49	178,388	1,660.28	259,543
400,000	339.96	104,803	897.70	203,872	1,897.46	296,621
450,000	382.45	117,903	1,009.91	229,355	2,134.64	333,699
500,000	424.95	131,004	1,122.12	254,839	2,371.83	370,776
550,000	467.44	144,103	1,234.33	280,323	2,609.01	407,854

13.75% 13.75%

DEBT REDUCTION TABLE

TO REDUCE A 15 YEAR LOAN TO:

LOAN AMOUNT	12.5 YEARS		10 YEARS		7.5 YEARS	
	PRE-PAY	SAVE	PRE-PAY	SAVE	PRE-PAY	SAVE
50	0.04	13	0.11	25	0.24	37
100	0.08	25	0.22	51	0.47	74
200	0.17	54	0.45	105	0.95	152
300	0.25	79	0.67	155	1.41	225
400	0.34	108	0.90	210	1.89	304
500	0.42	133	1.11	259	2.36	378
600	0.51	163	1.34	314	2.83	456
700	0.59	187	1.56	364	3.30	530
800	0.68	216	1.79	419	3.78	608
900	0.76	241	2.00	468	4.24	681
1,000	0.85	270	2.23	522	4.72	759
2,000	1.69	538	4.46	1,044	9.44	1,518
3,000	2.53	806	6.69	1,567	14.15	2,277
4,000	3.37	1,074	8.91	2,088	18.87	3,036
5,000	4.21	1,342	11.14	2,610	23.59	3,796
6,000	5.05	1,609	13.37	3,132	28.30	4,554
7,000	5.90	1,880	15.59	3,653	33.02	5,313
8,000	6.74	2,147	17.82	4,175	37.73	6,072
9,000	7.58	2,415	20.05	4,697	42.45	6,831
10,000	8.42	2,683	22.27	5,218	47.17	7,590
15,000	12.63	4,025	33.41	7,827	70.75	11,385
20,000	16.84	5,367	44.54	10,436	94.33	15,180
25,000	21.04	6,706	55.67	13,044	117.91	18,975
30,000	25.25	8,047	66.81	15,653	141.49	22,769
35,000	29.46	9,389	77.94	18,261	165.07	26,564
45,000	37.87	12,070	100.21	23,479	212.23	34,154
55,000	46.29	14,753	122.47	28,695	259.39	41,743
65,000	54.70	17,433	144.74	33,912	306.56	49,333
75,000	63.12	20,117	167.01	39,130	353.72	56,923
85,000	71.54	22,801	189.28	44,350	400.89	64,517
100,000	84.17	26,827	222.68	52,177	471.63	75,901
120,000	101.00	32,190	267.22	62,612	565.96	91,081
140,000	117.83	37,554	311.75	73,046	660.28	106,260
160,000	134.67	42,922	356.29	83,484	754.61	121,443
180,000	151.50	48,286	400.83	93,919	848.94	136,623
200,000	168.33	53,650	445.36	104,353	943.26	151,802
225,000	189.36	60,353	501.03	117,397	1,061.16	170,776
250,000	210.41	67,063	556.71	130,444	1,179.08	189,755
275,000	231.45	73,768	612.37	143,486	1,296.98	208,729
300,000	252.49	80,474	668.04	156,530	1,414.89	227,704
350,000	294.57	93,887	779.38	182,620	1,650.71	265,656
400,000	336.66	107,302	890.73	208,711	1,886.53	303,609
450,000	378.73	120,711	1,002.06	234,797	2,122.33	341,557
500,000	420.82	134,125	1,113.41	260,887	2,358.15	379,509
550,000	462.90	147,538	1,224.75	286,977	2,593.97	417,462

14.00% 14.00%

DEBT REDUCTION TABLE

TO REDUCE A 15 YEAR LOAN TO:

LOAN AMOUNT	12.5 YEARS		10 YEARS		7.5 YEARS	
	PRE-PAY	SAVE	PRE-PAY	SAVE	PRE-PAY	SAVE
50	0.04	13	0.11	26	0.24	38
100	0.08	25	0.22	51	0.47	75
200	0.17	55	0.44	105	0.94	153
300	0.25	81	0.66	158	1.41	231
400	0.34	111	0.89	213	1.88	310
500	0.42	138	1.11	267	2.35	388
600	0.50	163	1.32	317	2.81	462
700	0.58	190	1.54	371	3.28	541
800	0.67	220	1.77	426	3.75	619
900	0.75	246	1.99	480	4.22	698
1,000	0.84	276	2.21	534	4.69	776
2,000	1.67	549	4.42	1,067	9.38	1,551
3,000	2.50	822	6.62	1,598	14.06	2,327
4,000	3.34	1,100	8.84	2,136	18.76	3,107
5,000	4.17	1,373	11.05	2,669	23.45	3,882
6,000	5.00	1,646	13.25	3,202	28.13	4,658
7,000	5.83	1,919	15.46	3,735	32.82	5,433
8,000	6.67	2,197	17.68	4,272	37.51	6,212
9,000	7.50	2,470	19.88	4,804	42.20	6,989
10,000	8.33	2,744	22.09	5,338	46.89	7,764
15,000	12.50	4,116	33.13	8,005	70.33	11,645
20,000	16.67	5,491	44.19	10,679	93.78	15,532
25,000	20.83	6,862	55.23	13,347	117.22	19,413
30,000	25.00	8,235	66.27	16,015	140.66	23,295
35,000	29.17	9,609	77.33	18,689	164.11	27,181
45,000	37.50	12,353	99.41	24,025	210.99	34,944
55,000	45.84	15,101	121.51	29,367	257.88	42,712
65,000	54.16	17,841	143.60	34,704	304.76	50,475
75,000	62.50	20,589	165.69	40,044	351.65	58,243
85,000	70.83	23,332	187.78	45,381	398.53	66,006
100,000	83.33	27,450	220.92	53,391	468.86	77,655
120,000	100.00	32,944	265.11	64,073	562.65	93,191
140,000	116.67	38,435	309.30	74,752	656.42	108,722
160,000	133.33	43,923	353.48	85,430	750.19	124,253
180,000	150.00	49,414	397.66	96,107	843.96	139,783
200,000	166.66	54,903	441.84	106,784	937.73	155,314
225,000	187.50	61,769	497.08	120,136	1,054.96	174,732
250,000	208.33	68,630	552.31	133,483	1,172.17	194,144
275,000	229.17	75,496	607.54	146,833	1,289.39	213,561
300,000	249.99	82,355	662.77	160,180	1,406.60	232,974
350,000	291.66	96,082	773.23	186,876	1,641.04	271,803
400,000	333.33	109,810	883.69	213,574	1,875.47	310,633
450,000	374.99	123,535	994.15	240,270	2,109.91	349,463
500,000	416.66	137,263	1,104.62	266,969	2,344.34	388,293
550,000	458.33	150,990	1,215.08	293,666	2,578.77	427,122

14.25% 14.25%

DEBT REDUCTION TABLE

TO REDUCE A 15 YEAR LOAN TO:

LOAN AMOUNT	12.5 YEARS		10 YEARS		7.5 YEARS	
	PRE-PAY	SAVE	PRE-PAY	SAVE	PRE-PAY	SAVE
50	0.04	13	0.11	26	0.23	37
100	0.09	30	0.22	54	0.47	79
200	0.17	57	0.44	108	0.93	158
300	0.25	84	0.66	163	1.40	237
400	0.33	111	0.88	217	1.86	315
500	0.41	139	1.09	271	2.33	395
600	0.49	166	1.31	324	2.79	473
700	0.57	193	1.53	379	3.26	552
800	0.66	225	1.76	438	3.73	635
900	0.74	252	1.97	490	4.20	714
1,000	0.83	281	2.19	545	4.66	793
2,000	1.65	560	4.38	1,089	9.32	1,585
3,000	2.48	844	6.58	1,639	13.98	2,382
4,000	3.30	1,122	8.76	2,182	18.64	3,175
5,000	4.13	1,405	10.96	2,731	23.31	3,971
6,000	4.95	1,684	13.15	3,275	27.96	4,763
7,000	5.77	1,963	15.34	3,820	32.62	5,556
8,000	6.60	2,246	17.53	4,368	37.29	6,353
9,000	7.42	2,525	19.72	4,912	41.94	7,145
10,000	8.25	2,808	21.92	5,462	46.61	7,942
15,000	12.38	4,213	32.87	8,191	69.91	11,912
20,000	16.50	5,616	43.83	10,922	93.22	15,884
25,000	20.62	7,019	54.79	13,653	116.52	19,855
30,000	24.75	8,424	65.74	16,382	139.82	23,825
35,000	28.87	9,827	76.70	19,113	163.13	27,797
45,000	37.12	12,635	98.61	24,573	209.73	35,737
55,000	45.38	15,448	120.54	30,040	256.35	43,684
65,000	53.62	18,253	142.45	35,500	302.95	51,625
75,000	61.87	21,061	164.36	40,960	349.56	59,567
85,000	70.12	23,869	186.28	46,422	396.16	67,508
100,000	82.50	28,084	219.16	54,618	466.08	79,425
120,000	98.99	33,698	262.98	65,538	559.29	95,308
140,000	115.49	39,314	306.81	76,460	652.51	111,192
160,000	131.99	44,932	350.64	87,385	745.73	127,079
180,000	148.49	50,548	394.47	98,308	838.94	142,963
200,000	164.99	56,166	438.31	109,234	932.16	158,850
225,000	185.61	63,185	493.09	122,885	1,048.67	178,704
250,000	206.24	70,208	547.88	136,541	1,165.20	198,563
275,000	226.86	77,227	602.67	150,194	1,281.71	218,417
300,000	247.49	84,250	657.46	163,850	1,398.24	238,275
350,000	288.74	98,293	767.03	191,158	1,631.28	277,988
400,000	329.98	112,332	876.61	218,467	1,864.32	317,701
450,000	371.23	126,374	986.18	245,774	2,097.35	357,413
500,000	412.48	140,417	1,095.76	273,083	2,330.39	397,125
550,000	453.73	154,458	1,205.34	300,392	2,563.43	436,838

14.50% **14.50%**

DEBT REDUCTION TABLE

TO REDUCE A 15 YEAR LOAN TO:

LOAN AMOUNT	12.5 YEARS		10 YEARS		7.5 YEARS	
	PRE-PAY	SAVE	PRE-PAY	SAVE	PRE-PAY	SAVE
50	0.04	13	0.11	26	0.23	38
100	0.08	27	0.22	55	0.46	79
200	0.16	55	0.43	108	0.92	158
300	0.25	86	0.65	166	1.39	242
400	0.32	112	0.87	221	1.85	322
500	0.41	144	1.09	279	2.32	405
600	0.49	171	1.30	332	2.78	485
700	0.58	203	1.53	392	3.25	569
800	0.65	228	1.74	445	3.71	647
900	0.74	260	1.96	503	4.17	731
1,000	0.82	288	2.17	557	4.63	810
2,000	1.63	572	4.34	1,113	9.26	1,620
3,000	2.45	861	6.52	1,674	13.90	2,434
4,000	3.26	1,145	8.69	2,230	18.53	3,244
5,000	4.08	1,434	10.87	2,791	23.16	4,058
6,000	4.89	1,719	13.04	3,347	27.79	4,868
7,000	5.72	2,010	15.22	3,908	32.43	5,682
8,000	6.53	2,295	17.38	4,463	37.06	6,492
9,000	7.35	2,584	19.56	5,024	41.69	7,306
10,000	8.16	2,869	21.73	5,581	46.32	8,116
15,000	12.25	4,307	32.61	8,376	69.49	12,179
20,000	16.33	5,741	43.47	11,166	92.65	16,236
25,000	20.41	7,177	54.34	13,960	115.82	20,299
30,000	24.49	8,611	65.21	16,751	138.97	24,356
35,000	28.58	10,050	76.08	19,545	162.14	28,419
45,000	36.74	12,921	97.82	25,130	208.47	36,539
55,000	44.91	15,793	119.55	30,713	254.79	44,658
65,000	53.08	18,667	141.29	36,299	301.12	52,779
75,000	61.24	21,537	163.03	41,884	347.45	60,899
85,000	69.41	24,410	184.76	47,468	393.77	69,019
100,000	81.65	28,714	217.36	55,842	463.26	81,198
120,000	97.98	34,457	260.84	67,012	555.91	97,438
140,000	114.31	40,200	304.31	78,181	648.56	113,678
160,000	130.64	45,944	347.78	89,350	741.22	129,919
180,000	146.97	51,687	391.26	100,520	833.87	146,159
200,000	163.31	57,433	434.73	111,689	926.52	162,399
225,000	183.72	64,611	489.08	125,653	1,042.34	182,702
250,000	204.13	71,789	543.41	139,611	1,158.15	203,000
275,000	224.55	78,971	597.76	153,576	1,273.97	223,303
300,000	244.96	86,149	652.10	167,536	1,389.79	243,602
350,000	285.79	100,508	760.78	195,458	1,621.42	284,202
400,000	326.62	114,867	869.47	223,382	1,853.05	324,803
450,000	367.44	129,224	978.15	251,305	2,084.68	365,404
500,000	408.27	143,583	1,086.83	279,227	2,316.31	406,005
550,000	449.10	157,942	1,195.52	307,152	2,547.94	446,605

14.75% 14.75%

DEBT REDUCTION TABLE

TO REDUCE A 15 YEAR LOAN TO:

LOAN AMOUNT	12.5 YEARS		10 YEARS		7.5 YEARS	
	PRE-PAY	SAVE	PRE-PAY	SAVE	PRE-PAY	SAVE
50	0.04	13	0.10	25	0.23	38
100	0.08	28	0.21	54	0.46	80
200	0.16	57	0.43	112	0.92	164
300	0.24	87	0.65	171	1.38	248
400	0.32	114	0.86	224	1.84	328
500	0.40	144	1.08	284	2.30	412
600	0.48	174	1.29	340	2.76	496
700	0.57	206	1.51	399	3.23	580
800	0.64	231	1.72	453	3.68	660
900	0.72	261	1.94	511	4.14	744
1,000	0.81	293	2.16	570	4.60	828
2,000	1.61	583	4.31	1,138	9.20	1,655
3,000	2.42	878	6.47	1,711	13.81	2,487
4,000	3.23	1,172	8.62	2,279	18.41	3,315
5,000	4.04	1,467	10.78	2,853	23.02	4,147
6,000	4.84	1,757	12.93	3,421	27.62	4,975
7,000	5.66	2,055	15.09	3,994	32.23	5,807
8,000	6.46	2,345	17.24	4,562	36.83	6,635
9,000	7.27	2,640	19.40	5,136	41.44	7,467
10,000	8.08	2,933	21.55	5,704	46.04	8,295
15,000	12.12	4,402	32.34	8,562	69.06	12,446
20,000	16.16	5,868	43.11	11,413	92.08	16,593
25,000	20.20	7,337	53.89	14,269	115.11	20,746
30,000	24.24	8,803	64.67	17,122	138.12	24,892
35,000	28.28	10,272	75.45	19,978	161.15	29,044
45,000	36.37	13,210	97.01	25,687	207.19	37,343
55,000	44.45	16,145	118.57	31,395	253.23	45,642
65,000	52.53	19,080	140.12	37,102	299.28	53,941
75,000	60.61	22,016	161.68	42,811	345.32	62,240
85,000	68.69	24,951	183.24	48,520	391.36	70,539
100,000	80.81	29,352	215.57	57,080	460.42	82,985
120,000	96.97	35,223	258.68	68,496	552.51	99,583
140,000	113.13	41,093	301.80	79,913	644.59	116,180
160,000	129.30	46,966	344.91	91,329	736.68	132,778
180,000	145.46	52,837	388.03	102,747	828.76	149,376
200,000	161.62	58,707	431.14	114,163	920.85	165,974
225,000	181.82	66,044	485.03	128,431	1,035.95	186,719
250,000	202.03	73,386	538.93	142,705	1,151.06	207,468
275,000	222.23	80,723	592.82	156,974	1,266.16	228,213
300,000	242.43	88,059	646.71	171,242	1,381.26	248,958
350,000	282.83	102,735	754.49	199,783	1,611.48	290,453
400,000	323.24	117,414	862.28	228,325	1,841.69	331,947
450,000	363.65	132,093	970.07	256,868	2,071.90	373,441
500,000	404.05	146,769	1,077.86	285,410	2,302.12	414,936
550,000	444.45	161,442	1,185.63	313,946	2,532.32	456,426

10.00% 10.00%

MONTHLY LOAN PAYMENT TABLE

DOLLARS REQUIRED TO AMORTIZE LOAN

LOAN AMOUNT	TERM OF LOAN IN YEARS					
	1	3	5	15	20	30
50	4.40	1.62	1.07	0.54	0.49	0.44
100	8.80	3.23	2.13	1.08	0.97	0.88
200	17.59	6.46	4.25	2.15	1.94	1.76
300	26.38	9.69	6.38	3.23	2.90	2.64
400	35.17	12.91	8.50	4.30	3.87	3.52
500	43.96	16.14	10.63	5.38	4.83	4.39
600	52.75	19.37	12.75	6.45	5.80	5.27
700	61.55	22.59	14.88	7.53	6.76	6.15
800	70.34	25.82	17.00	8.60	7.73	7.03
900	79.13	29.05	19.13	9.68	8.69	7.90
1,000	87.92	32.27	21.25	10.75	9.66	8.78
2,000	175.84	64.54	42.50	21.50	19.31	17.56
3,000	263.75	96.81	63.75	32.24	28.96	26.33
4,000	351.67	129.07	84.99	42.99	38.61	35.11
5,000	439.58	161.34	106.24	53.74	48.26	43.88
6,000	527.50	193.61	127.49	64.48	57.91	52.66
7,000	615.42	225.88	148.73	75.23	67.56	61.44
8,000	703.33	258.14	169.98	85.97	77.21	70.21
9,000	791.25	290.41	191.23	96.72	86.86	78.99
10,000	879.16	322.68	212.48	107.47	96.51	87.76
15,000	1,318.74	484.01	318.71	161.20	144.76	131.64
20,000	1,758.32	645.35	424.95	214.93	193.01	175.52
25,000	2,197.90	806.68	531.18	268.66	241.26	219.40
30,000	2,637.48	968.02	637.42	322.39	289.51	263.28
35,000	3,077.06	1,129.36	743.65	376.12	337.76	307.16
45,000	3,956.22	1,452.03	956.12	483.58	434.26	394.91
55,000	4,835.38	1,774.70	1,168.59	591.04	530.77	482.67
65,000	5,714.54	2,097.37	1,381.06	698.50	627.27	570.43
75,000	6,593.70	2,420.04	1,593.53	805.96	723.77	658.18
85,000	7,472.86	2,742.72	1,806.00	913.42	820.27	745.94
100,000	8,791.59	3,226.72	2,124.71	1,074.61	965.03	877.58
120,000	10,549.91	3,872.07	2,549.65	1,289.53	1,158.03	1,053.09
140,000	12,308.23	4,517.41	2,974.59	1,504.45	1,351.04	1,228.61
160,000	14,066.55	5,162.75	3,399.53	1,719.37	1,544.04	1,404.12
180,000	15,824.86	5,808.10	3,824.47	1,934.29	1,737.04	1,579.63
200,000	17,583.18	6,453.44	4,249.41	2,149.22	1,930.05	1,755.15
225,000	19,781.08	7,260.12	4,780.59	2,417.87	2,171.30	1,974.54
250,000	21,978.98	8,066.80	5,311.77	2,686.52	2,412.56	2,193.93
275,000	24,176.87	8,873.48	5,842.94	2,955.17	2,653.81	2,413.33
300,000	26,374.77	9,680.16	6,374.12	3,223.82	2,895.07	2,632.72
350,000	30,770.57	11,293.52	7,436.47	3,761.12	3,377.58	3,071.51
400,000	35,166.36	12,906.88	8,498.82	4,298.43	3,860.09	3,510.29
450,000	39,562.15	14,520.24	9,561.18	4,835.73	4,342.60	3,949.08
500,000	43,957.95	16,133.60	10,623.53	5,373.03	4,825.11	4,387.86
550,000	48,353.74	17,746.96	11,685.88	5,910.33	5,307.62	4,826.65

MONTHLY LOAN PAYMENT TABLES

INSTRUCTIONS

The monthly mortgage payments you'll find listed in this section are based on *self-amortizing* loans (those which are completely paid off by the end of their terms). Here's how to proceed:

- Let's say you are thinking about borrowing $75,000 at 10.00% for a term of 30 years.
- Turn to the table that has 10.00% at both the upper left and upper right hand corners. (Reproduced on the preceding page.)
- Look down the left hand (*Loan Amount*) column until you see $75,000.
- Read across to the right until you are under the 30 year (*Term of Loan*) column.
- You'll find $658.18, which is the monthly payment required to pay off a $75,000, 10.00% loan, written for a 30 year term.

FOR LOAN AMOUNTS NOT LISTED:

Let's say you're thinking of borrowing $73,450, at 10.00% for 30 years. Assuming the correct interest rate and term, any combination which adds up to the number you are seeking will get you within pennies of the correct number. So, using the same table, find the values for $65,000, $8,000, $400, and $50; then add them together. Here's what you would find:

	Loan Amount	Monthly Payment
	$65,000	$570.43
	8,000	70.21
	400	3.52
	50	0.44
Total :	$73,450	$644.60

There are two other solutions that will work for virtually any loan: 1) use the Mortage Factor Tables (the last set of tables in PART THREE); or 2) use the *Banker's Secret Software.*

7.00% 7.00%

MONTHLY LOAN PAYMENT TABLE

DOLLARS REQUIRED TO AMORTIZE LOAN

LOAN AMOUNT	TERM OF LOAN IN YEARS					
	1	3	5	15	20	30
50	4.33	1.55	1.00	0.45	0.39	0.34
100	8.66	3.09	1.99	0.90	0.78	0.67
200	17.31	6.18	3.97	1.80	1.56	1.34
300	25.96	9.27	5.95	2.70	2.33	2.00
400	34.62	12.36	7.93	3.60	3.11	2.67
500	43.27	15.44	9.91	4.50	3.88	3.33
600	51.92	18.53	11.89	5.40	4.66	4.00
700	60.57	21.62	13.87	6.30	5.43	4.66
800	69.23	24.71	15.85	7.20	6.21	5.33
900	77.88	27.79	17.83	8.09	6.98	5.99
1,000	86.53	30.88	19.81	8.99	7.76	6.66
2,000	173.06	61.76	39.61	17.98	15.51	13.31
3,000	259.59	92.64	59.41	26.97	23.26	19.96
4,000	346.11	123.51	79.21	35.96	31.02	26.62
5,000	432.64	154.39	99.01	44.95	38.77	33.27
6,000	519.17	185.27	118.81	53.93	46.52	39.92
7,000	605.69	216.14	138.61	62.92	54.28	46.58
8,000	692.22	247.02	158.41	71.91	62.03	53.23
9,000	778.75	277.90	178.22	80.90	69.78	59.88
10,000	865.27	308.78	198.02	89.89	77.53	66.54
15,000	1,297.91	463.16	297.02	134.83	116.30	99.80
20,000	1,730.54	617.55	396.03	179.77	155.06	133.07
25,000	2,163.17	771.93	495.03	224.71	193.83	166.33
30,000	2,595.81	926.32	594.04	269.65	232.59	199.60
35,000	3,028.44	1,080.70	693.05	314.59	271.36	232.86
45,000	3,893.71	1,389.47	891.06	404.48	348.89	299.39
55,000	4,758.98	1,698.25	1,089.07	494.36	426.42	365.92
65,000	5,624.24	2,007.02	1,287.08	584.24	503.95	432.45
75,000	6,489.51	2,315.79	1,485.09	674.13	581.48	498.98
85,000	7,354.78	2,624.56	1,683.11	764.01	659.01	565.51
100,000	8,652.68	3,087.71	1,980.12	898.83	775.30	665.31
120,000	10,383.21	3,705.26	2,376.15	1,078.60	930.36	798.37
140,000	12,113.75	4,322.80	2,772.17	1,258.36	1,085.42	931.43
160,000	13,844.28	4,940.34	3,168.20	1,438.13	1,240.48	1,064.49
180,000	15,574.82	5,557.88	3,564.22	1,617.90	1,395.54	1,197.55
200,000	17,305.35	6,175.42	3,960.24	1,797.66	1,550.60	1,330.61
225,000	19,468.52	6,947.35	4,455.27	2,022.37	1,744.43	1,496.94
250,000	21,631.69	7,719.28	4,950.30	2,247.08	1,938.25	1,663.26
275,000	23,794.86	8,491.21	5,445.33	2,471.78	2,132.08	1,829.59
300,000	25,958.03	9,263.13	5,940.36	2,696.49	2,325.90	1,995.91
350,000	30,284.37	10,806.99	6,930.42	3,145.90	2,713.55	2,328.56
400,000	34,610.70	12,350.84	7,920.48	3,595.32	3,101.20	2,661.21
450,000	38,937.04	13,894.70	8,910.54	4,044.73	3,488.85	2,993.87
500,000	43,263.38	15,438.55	9,900.60	4,494.15	3,876.50	3,326.52
550,000	47,589.72	16,982.41	10,890.66	4,943.56	4,264.15	3,659.17

7.25% 7.25%

MONTHLY LOAN PAYMENT TABLE

DOLLARS REQUIRED TO AMORTIZE LOAN

LOAN AMOUNT	TERM OF LOAN IN YEARS					
	1	3	5	15	20	30
50	4.34	1.55	1.00	0.46	0.40	0.35
100	8.67	3.10	2.00	0.92	0.80	0.69
200	17.33	6.20	3.99	1.83	1.59	1.37
300	26.00	9.30	5.98	2.74	2.38	2.05
400	34.66	12.40	7.97	3.66	3.17	2.73
500	43.33	15.50	9.96	4.57	3.96	3.42
600	51.99	18.60	11.96	5.48	4.75	4.10
700	60.65	21.70	13.95	6.40	5.54	4.78
800	69.32	24.80	15.94	7.31	6.33	5.46
900	77.98	27.90	17.93	8.22	7.12	6.14
1,000	86.65	31.00	19.92	9.13	7.91	6.83
2,000	173.29	61.99	39.84	18.26	15.81	13.65
3,000	259.93	92.98	59.76	27.39	23.72	20.47
4,000	346.57	123.97	79.68	36.52	31.62	27.29
5,000	433.22	154.96	99.60	45.65	39.52	34.11
6,000	519.86	185.95	119.52	54.78	47.43	40.94
7,000	606.50	216.95	139.44	63.91	55.33	47.76
8,000	693.14	247.94	159.36	73.03	63.24	54.58
9,000	779.78	278.93	179.28	82.16	71.14	61.40
10,000	866.43	309.92	199.20	91.29	79.04	68.22
15,000	1,299.64	464.88	298.80	136.93	118.56	102.33
20,000	1,732.85	619.84	398.39	182.58	158.08	136.44
25,000	2,166.06	774.79	497.99	228.22	197.60	170.55
30,000	2,599.27	929.75	597.59	273.86	237.12	204.66
35,000	3,032.48	1,084.71	697.18	319.51	276.64	238.77
45,000	3,898.90	1,394.62	896.38	410.79	355.67	306.98
55,000	4,765.32	1,704.54	1,095.57	502.08	434.71	375.20
65,000	5,631.74	2,014.45	1,294.76	593.37	513.75	443.42
75,000	6,498.16	2,324.37	1,493.96	684.65	592.79	511.64
85,000	7,364.58	2,634.28	1,693.15	775.94	671.82	579.85
100,000	8,664.21	3,099.16	1,991.94	912.87	790.38	682.18
120,000	10,397.05	3,718.99	2,390.33	1,095.44	948.46	818.62
140,000	12,129.89	4,338.82	2,788.72	1,278.01	1,106.53	955.05
160,000	13,862.73	4,958.65	3,187.10	1,460.59	1,264.61	1,091.49
180,000	15,595.57	5,578.48	3,585.49	1,643.16	1,422.68	1,227.92
200,000	17,328.41	6,198.31	3,983.88	1,825.73	1,580.76	1,364.36
225,000	19,494.46	6,973.10	4,481.86	2,053.95	1,778.35	1,534.90
250,000	21,660.51	7,747.89	4,979.85	2,282.16	1,975.94	1,705.45
275,000	23,826.57	8,522.68	5,477.83	2,510.38	2,173.54	1,875.99
300,000	25,992.62	9,297.46	5,975.81	2,738.59	2,371.13	2,046.53
350,000	30,324.72	10,847.04	6,971.78	3,195.03	2,766.32	2,387.62
400,000	34,656.82	12,396.62	7,967.75	3,651.46	3,161.51	2,728.71
450,000	38,988.92	13,946.19	8,963.72	4,107.89	3,556.70	3,069.80
500,000	43,321.02	15,495.77	9,959.69	4,564.32	3,951.88	3,410.89
550,000	47,653.13	17,045.35	10,955.65	5,020.75	4,347.07	3,751.97

7.50% 7.50%

MONTHLY LOAN PAYMENT TABLE

DOLLARS REQUIRED TO AMORTIZE LOAN

LOAN AMOUNT	TERM OF LOAN IN YEARS					
	1	3	5	15	20	30
50	4.34	1.56	1.01	0.47	0.41	0.35
100	8.68	3.12	2.01	0.93	0.81	0.70
200	17.36	6.23	4.01	1.86	1.62	1.40
300	26.03	9.34	6.02	2.79	2.42	2.10
400	34.71	12.45	8.02	3.71	3.23	2.80
500	43.38	15.56	10.02	4.64	4.03	3.50
600	52.06	18.67	12.03	5.57	4.84	4.20
700	60.74	21.78	14.03	6.49	5.64	4.90
800	69.41	24.89	16.04	7.42	6.45	5.60
900	78.09	28.00	18.04	8.35	7.26	6.30
1,000	86.76	31.11	20.04	9.28	8.06	7.00
2,000	173.52	62.22	40.08	18.55	16.12	13.99
3,000	260.28	93.32	60.12	27.82	24.17	20.98
4,000	347.03	124.43	80.16	37.09	32.23	27.97
5,000	433.79	155.54	100.19	46.36	40.28	34.97
6,000	520.55	186.64	120.23	55.63	48.34	41.96
7,000	607.31	217.75	140.27	64.90	56.40	48.95
8,000	694.06	248.85	160.31	74.17	64.45	55.94
9,000	780.82	279.96	180.35	83.44	72.51	62.93
10,000	867.58	311.07	200.38	92.71	80.56	69.93
15,000	1,301.37	466.60	300.57	139.06	120.84	104.89
20,000	1,735.15	622.13	400.76	185.41	161.12	139.85
25,000	2,168.94	777.66	500.95	231.76	201.40	174.81
30,000	2,602.73	933.19	601.14	278.11	241.68	209.77
35,000	3,036.51	1,088.72	701.33	324.46	281.96	244.73
45,000	3,904.09	1,399.78	901.71	417.16	362.52	314.65
55,000	4,771.66	1,710.85	1,102.09	509.86	443.08	384.57
65,000	5,639.24	2,021.91	1,302.47	602.56	523.64	454.49
75,000	6,506.81	2,332.97	1,502.85	695.26	604.20	524.42
85,000	7,374.39	2,644.03	1,703.23	787.97	684.76	594.34
100,000	8,675.75	3,110.63	2,003.80	927.02	805.60	699.22
120,000	10,410.90	3,732.75	2,404.56	1,112.42	966.72	839.06
140,000	12,146.04	4,354.88	2,805.32	1,297.82	1,127.84	978.91
160,000	13,881.19	4,977.00	3,206.08	1,483.22	1,288.95	1,118.75
180,000	15,616.34	5,599.12	3,606.84	1,668.63	1,450.07	1,258.59
200,000	17,351.49	6,221.25	4,007.59	1,854.03	1,611.19	1,398.43
225,000	19,520.42	6,998.90	4,508.54	2,085.78	1,812.59	1,573.24
250,000	21,689.36	7,776.56	5,009.49	2,317.54	2,013.99	1,748.04
275,000	23,858.29	8,554.21	5,510.44	2,549.29	2,215.39	1,922.84
300,000	26,027.23	9,331.87	6,011.39	2,781.04	2,416.78	2,097.65
350,000	30,365.10	10,887.18	7,013.29	3,244.55	2,819.58	2,447.26
400,000	34,702.97	12,442.49	8,015.18	3,708.05	3,222.38	2,796.86
450,000	39,040.84	13,997.80	9,017.08	4,171.56	3,625.17	3,146.47
500,000	43,378.71	15,553.11	10,018.98	4,635.07	4,027.97	3,496.08
550,000	47,716.58	17,108.42	11,020.88	5,098.57	4,430.77	3,845.68

7.75% 7.75%

MONTHLY LOAN PAYMENT TABLE

DOLLARS REQUIRED TO AMORTIZE LOAN

LOAN AMOUNT	TERM OF LOAN IN YEARS					
	1	3	5	15	20	30
50	4.35	1.57	1.01	0.48	0.42	0.36
100	8.69	3.13	2.02	0.95	0.83	0.72
200	17.38	6.25	4.04	1.89	1.65	1.44
300	26.07	9.37	6.05	2.83	2.47	2.15
400	34.75	12.49	8.07	3.77	3.29	2.87
500	43.44	15.62	10.08	4.71	4.11	3.59
600	52.13	18.74	12.10	5.65	4.93	4.30
700	60.82	21.86	14.11	6.59	5.75	5.02
800	69.50	24.98	16.13	7.54	6.57	5.74
900	78.19	28.10	18.15	8.48	7.39	6.45
1,000	86.88	31.23	20.16	9.42	8.21	7.17
2,000	173.75	62.45	40.32	18.83	16.42	14.33
3,000	260.62	93.67	60.48	28.24	24.63	21.50
4,000	347.50	124.89	80.63	37.66	32.84	28.66
5,000	434.37	156.11	100.79	47.07	41.05	35.83
6,000	521.24	187.33	120.95	56.48	49.26	42.99
7,000	608.12	218.55	141.10	65.89	57.47	50.15
8,000	694.99	249.77	161.26	75.31	65.68	57.32
9,000	781.86	281.00	181.42	84.72	73.89	64.48
10,000	868.73	312.22	201.57	94.13	82.10	71.65
15,000	1,303.10	468.32	302.36	141.20	123.15	107.47
20,000	1,737.46	624.43	403.14	188.26	164.19	143.29
25,000	2,171.83	780.53	503.93	235.32	205.24	179.11
30,000	2,606.19	936.64	604.71	282.39	246.29	214.93
35,000	3,040.56	1,092.75	705.50	329.45	287.34	250.75
45,000	3,909.28	1,404.96	907.07	423.58	369.43	322.39
55,000	4,778.01	1,717.17	1,108.64	517.71	451.53	394.03
65,000	5,646.74	2,029.38	1,310.21	611.83	533.62	465.67
75,000	6,515.47	2,341.59	1,511.78	705.96	615.72	537.31
85,000	7,384.20	2,653.80	1,713.35	800.09	697.81	608.96
100,000	8,687.29	3,122.12	2,015.70	941.28	820.95	716.42
120,000	10,424.75	3,746.54	2,418.84	1,129.54	985.14	859.70
140,000	12,162.21	4,370.97	2,821.98	1,317.79	1,149.33	1,002.98
160,000	13,899.67	4,995.39	3,225.12	1,506.05	1,313.52	1,146.26
180,000	15,637.12	5,619.81	3,628.26	1,694.30	1,477.71	1,289.55
200,000	17,374.58	6,244.24	4,031.40	1,882.56	1,641.90	1,432.83
225,000	19,546.40	7,024.77	4,535.32	2,117.88	1,847.14	1,611.93
250,000	21,718.23	7,805.30	5,039.24	2,353.19	2,052.38	1,791.04
275,000	23,890.05	8,585.83	5,543.17	2,588.51	2,257.61	1,970.14
300,000	26,061.87	9,366.35	6,047.09	2,823.83	2,462.85	2,149.24
350,000	30,405.51	10,927.41	7,054.94	3,294.47	2,873.32	2,507.45
400,000	34,749.16	12,488.47	8,062.79	3,765.11	3,283.80	2,865.65
450,000	39,092.80	14,049.53	9,070.64	4,235.75	3,694.27	3,223.86
500,000	43,436.45	15,610.59	10,078.48	4,706.38	4,104.75	3,582.07
550,000	47,780.09	17,171.65	11,086.33	5,177.02	4,515.22	3,940.27

8.00% 8.00%

MONTHLY LOAN PAYMENT TABLE

DOLLARS REQUIRED TO AMORTIZE LOAN

LOAN AMOUNT	TERM OF LOAN IN YEARS					
	1	3	5	15	20	30
50	4.35	1.57	1.02	0.48	0.42	0.37
100	8.70	3.14	2.03	0.96	0.84	0.74
200	17.40	6.27	4.06	1.92	1.68	1.47
300	26.10	9.41	6.09	2.87	2.51	2.21
400	34.80	12.54	8.12	3.83	3.35	2.94
500	43.50	15.67	10.14	4.78	4.19	3.67
600	52.20	18.81	12.17	5.74	5.02	4.41
700	60.90	21.94	14.20	6.69	5.86	5.14
800	69.60	25.07	16.23	7.65	6.70	5.88
900	78.29	28.21	18.25	8.61	7.53	6.61
1,000	86.99	31.34	20.28	9.56	8.37	7.34
2,000	173.98	62.68	40.56	19.12	16.73	14.68
3,000	260.97	94.01	60.83	28.67	25.10	22.02
4,000	347.96	125.35	81.11	38.23	33.46	29.36
5,000	434.95	156.69	101.39	47.79	41.83	36.69
6,000	521.94	188.02	121.66	57.34	50.19	44.03
7,000	608.92	219.36	141.94	66.90	58.56	51.37
8,000	695.91	250.70	162.22	76.46	66.92	58.71
9,000	782.90	282.03	182.49	86.01	75.28	66.04
10,000	869.89	313.37	202.77	95.57	83.65	73.38
15,000	1,304.83	470.05	304.15	143.35	125.47	110.07
20,000	1,739.77	626.73	405.53	191.14	167.29	146.76
25,000	2,174.72	783.41	506.91	238.92	209.12	183.45
30,000	2,609.66	940.10	608.30	286.70	250.94	220.13
35,000	3,044.60	1,096.78	709.68	334.48	292.76	256.82
45,000	3,914.48	1,410.14	912.44	430.05	376.40	330.20
55,000	4,784.37	1,723.51	1,115.21	525.61	460.05	403.58
65,000	5,654.25	2,036.87	1,317.97	621.18	543.69	476.95
75,000	6,524.14	2,350.23	1,520.73	716.74	627.34	550.33
85,000	7,394.02	2,663.60	1,723.50	812.31	710.98	623.70
100,000	8,698.85	3,133.64	2,027.64	955.66	836.45	733.77
120,000	10,438.62	3,760.37	2,433.17	1,146.79	1,003.73	880.52
140,000	12,178.39	4,387.10	2,838.70	1,337.92	1,171.02	1,027.28
160,000	13,918.15	5,013.82	3,244.23	1,529.05	1,338.31	1,174.03
180,000	15,657.92	5,640.55	3,649.76	1,720.18	1,505.60	1,320.78
200,000	17,397.69	6,267.28	4,055.28	1,911.31	1,672.89	1,467.53
225,000	19,572.40	7,050.69	4,562.19	2,150.22	1,882.00	1,650.98
250,000	21,747.11	7,834.10	5,069.10	2,389.14	2,091.11	1,834.42
275,000	23,921.82	8,617.51	5,576.01	2,628.05	2,300.22	2,017.86
300,000	26,096.53	9,400.91	6,082.92	2,866.96	2,509.33	2,201.30
350,000	30,445.96	10,967.73	7,096.74	3,344.79	2,927.55	2,568.18
400,000	34,795.38	12,534.55	8,110.56	3,822.61	3,345.77	2,935.06
450,000	39,144.80	14,101.37	9,124.38	4,300.44	3,763.99	3,301.95
500,000	43,494.22	15,668.19	10,138.20	4,778.27	4,182.21	3,668.83
550,000	47,843.64	17,235.01	11,152.02	5,256.09	4,600.43	4,035.71

8.25% 8.25%

MONTHLY LOAN PAYMENT TABLE

DOLLARS REQUIRED TO AMORTIZE LOAN

LOAN AMOUNT	TERM OF LOAN IN YEARS					
	1	3	5	15	20	30
50	4.36	1.58	1.02	0.49	0.43	0.38
100	8.72	3.15	2.04	0.98	0.86	0.76
200	17.43	6.30	4.08	1.95	1.71	1.51
300	26.14	9.44	6.12	2.92	2.56	2.26
400	34.85	12.59	8.16	3.89	3.41	3.01
500	43.56	15.73	10.20	4.86	4.27	3.76
600	52.27	18.88	12.24	5.83	5.12	4.51
700	60.98	22.02	14.28	6.80	5.97	5.26
800	69.69	25.17	16.32	7.77	6.82	6.02
900	78.40	28.31	18.36	8.74	7.67	6.77
1,000	87.11	31.46	20.40	9.71	8.53	7.52
2,000	174.21	62.91	40.80	19.41	17.05	15.03
3,000	261.32	94.36	61.19	29.11	25.57	22.54
4,000	348.42	125.81	81.59	38.81	34.09	30.06
5,000	435.53	157.26	101.99	48.51	42.61	37.57
6,000	522.63	188.72	122.38	58.21	51.13	45.08
7,000	609.73	220.17	142.78	67.91	59.65	52.59
8,000	696.84	251.62	163.18	77.62	68.17	60.11
9,000	783.94	283.07	183.57	87.32	76.69	67.62
10,000	871.05	314.52	203.97	97.02	85.21	75.13
15,000	1,306.57	471.78	305.95	145.53	127.81	112.69
20,000	1,742.09	629.04	407.93	194.03	170.42	150.26
25,000	2,177.61	786.30	509.91	242.54	213.02	187.82
30,000	2,613.13	943.56	611.89	291.05	255.62	225.38
35,000	3,048.65	1,100.82	713.87	339.55	298.23	262.95
45,000	3,919.69	1,415.34	917.84	436.57	383.43	338.07
55,000	4,790.73	1,729.86	1,121.80	533.58	468.64	413.20
65,000	5,661.77	2,044.37	1,325.76	630.60	553.85	488.33
75,000	6,532.81	2,358.89	1,529.72	727.61	639.05	563.45
85,000	7,403.85	2,673.41	1,733.69	824.62	724.26	638.58
100,000	8,710.41	3,145.19	2,039.63	970.15	852.07	751.27
120,000	10,452.49	3,774.22	2,447.56	1,164.17	1,022.48	901.52
140,000	12,194.57	4,403.26	2,855.48	1,358.20	1,192.90	1,051.78
160,000	13,936.66	5,032.30	3,263.41	1,552.23	1,363.31	1,202.03
180,000	15,678.74	5,661.33	3,671.33	1,746.26	1,533.72	1,352.28
200,000	17,420.82	6,290.37	4,079.26	1,940.29	1,704.14	1,502.54
225,000	19,598.42	7,076.67	4,589.16	2,182.82	1,917.15	1,690.35
250,000	21,776.02	7,862.96	5,099.07	2,425.36	2,130.17	1,878.17
275,000	23,953.62	8,649.26	5,608.97	2,667.89	2,343.19	2,065.99
300,000	26,131.22	9,435.55	6,118.88	2,910.43	2,556.20	2,253.80
350,000	30,486.43	11,008.14	7,138.69	3,395.50	2,982.23	2,629.44
400,000	34,841.63	12,580.73	8,158.51	3,880.57	3,408.27	3,005.07
450,000	39,196.83	14,153.33	9,178.32	4,365.64	3,834.30	3,380.70
500,000	43,552.04	15,725.92	10,198.13	4,850.71	4,260.33	3,756.34
550,000	47,907.24	17,298.51	11,217.94	5,335.78	4,686.37	4,131.97

8.50% 8.50%

MONTHLY LOAN PAYMENT TABLE

DOLLARS REQUIRED TO AMORTIZE LOAN

LOAN AMOUNT	TERM OF LOAN IN YEARS					
	1	3	5	15	20	30
50	4.37	1.58	1.03	0.50	0.44	0.39
100	8.73	3.16	2.06	0.99	0.87	0.77
200	17.45	6.32	4.11	1.97	1.74	1.54
300	26.17	9.48	6.16	2.96	2.61	2.31
400	34.89	12.63	8.21	3.94	3.48	3.08
500	43.61	15.79	10.26	4.93	4.34	3.85
600	52.34	18.95	12.31	5.91	5.21	4.62
700	61.06	22.10	14.37	6.90	6.08	5.39
800	69.78	25.26	16.42	7.88	6.95	6.16
900	78.50	28.42	18.47	8.87	7.82	6.93
1,000	87.22	31.57	20.52	9.85	8.68	7.69
2,000	174.44	63.14	41.04	19.70	17.36	15.38
3,000	261.66	94.71	61.55	29.55	26.04	23.07
4,000	348.88	126.28	82.07	39.39	34.72	30.76
5,000	436.10	157.84	102.59	49.24	43.40	38.45
6,000	523.32	189.41	123.10	59.09	52.07	46.14
7,000	610.54	220.98	143.62	68.94	60.75	53.83
8,000	697.76	252.55	164.14	78.78	69.43	61.52
9,000	784.98	284.11	184.65	88.63	78.11	69.21
10,000	872.20	315.68	205.17	98.48	86.79	76.90
15,000	1,308.30	473.52	307.75	147.72	130.18	115.34
20,000	1,744.40	631.36	410.34	196.95	173.57	153.79
25,000	2,180.50	789.19	512.92	246.19	216.96	192.23
30,000	2,616.60	947.03	615.50	295.43	260.35	230.68
35,000	3,052.70	1,104.87	718.08	344.66	303.74	269.12
45,000	3,924.90	1,420.54	923.25	443.14	390.53	346.02
55,000	4,797.09	1,736.22	1,128.41	541.61	477.31	422.91
65,000	5,669.29	2,051.89	1,333.58	640.09	564.09	499.80
75,000	6,541.49	2,367.57	1,538.74	738.56	650.87	576.69
85,000	7,413.69	2,683.25	1,743.91	837.03	737.65	653.58
100,000	8,721.98	3,156.76	2,051.66	984.74	867.83	768.92
120,000	10,466.38	3,788.11	2,461.99	1,181.69	1,041.39	922.70
140,000	12,210.77	4,419.46	2,872.32	1,378.64	1,214.96	1,076.48
160,000	13,955.17	5,050.81	3,282.65	1,575.59	1,388.52	1,230.27
180,000	15,699.57	5,682.16	3,692.98	1,772.54	1,562.09	1,384.05
200,000	17,443.96	6,313.51	4,103.31	1,969.48	1,735.65	1,537.83
225,000	19,624.46	7,102.70	4,616.22	2,215.67	1,952.61	1,730.06
250,000	21,804.95	7,891.89	5,129.14	2,461.85	2,169.56	1,922.29
275,000	23,985.45	8,681.08	5,642.05	2,708.04	2,386.52	2,114.52
300,000	26,165.94	9,470.27	6,154.96	2,954.22	2,603.47	2,306.75
350,000	30,526.93	11,048.64	7,180.79	3,446.59	3,037.39	2,691.20
400,000	34,887.92	12,627.02	8,206.62	3,938.96	3,471.30	3,075.66
450,000	39,248.91	14,205.40	9,232.44	4,431.33	3,905.21	3,460.12
500,000	43,609.90	15,783.77	10,258.27	4,923.70	4,339.12	3,844.57
550,000	47,970.89	17,362.15	11,284.10	5,416.07	4,773.03	4,229.03

8.75% 8.75%

MONTHLY LOAN PAYMENT TABLE

DOLLARS REQUIRED TO AMORTIZE LOAN

LOAN AMOUNT	TERM OF LOAN IN YEARS					
	1	3	5	15	20	30
50	4.37	1.59	1.04	0.50	0.45	0.40
100	8.74	3.17	2.07	1.00	0.89	0.79
200	17.47	6.34	4.13	2.00	1.77	1.58
300	26.21	9.51	6.20	3.00	2.66	2.37
400	34.94	12.68	8.26	4.00	3.54	3.15
500	43.67	15.85	10.32	5.00	4.42	3.94
600	52.41	19.02	12.39	6.00	5.31	4.73
700	61.14	22.18	14.45	7.00	6.19	5.51
800	69.87	25.35	16.51	8.00	7.07	6.30
900	78.61	28.52	18.58	9.00	7.96	7.09
1,000	87.34	31.69	20.64	10.00	8.84	7.87
2,000	174.68	63.37	41.28	19.99	17.68	15.74
3,000	262.01	95.06	61.92	29.99	26.52	23.61
4,000	349.35	126.74	82.55	39.98	35.35	31.47
5,000	436.68	158.42	103.19	49.98	44.19	39.34
6,000	524.02	190.11	123.83	59.97	53.03	47.21
7,000	611.35	221.79	144.47	69.97	61.86	55.07
8,000	698.69	253.47	165.10	79.96	70.70	62.94
9,000	786.03	285.16	185.74	89.96	79.54	70.81
10,000	873.36	316.84	206.38	99.95	88.38	78.68
15,000	1,310.04	475.26	309.56	149.92	132.56	118.01
20,000	1,746.72	633.68	412.75	199.89	176.75	157.35
25,000	2,183.39	792.09	515.94	249.87	220.93	196.68
30,000	2,620.07	950.51	619.12	299.84	265.12	236.02
35,000	3,056.75	1,108.93	722.31	349.81	309.30	275.35
45,000	3,930.11	1,425.76	928.68	449.76	397.67	354.02
55,000	4,803.46	1,742.60	1,135.05	549.70	486.05	432.69
65,000	5,676.82	2,059.43	1,341.43	649.65	574.42	511.36
75,000	6,550.17	2,376.27	1,547.80	749.59	662.79	590.03
85,000	7,423.53	2,693.10	1,754.17	849.54	751.16	668.70
100,000	8,733.56	3,168.36	2,063.73	999.45	883.72	786.71
120,000	10,480.28	3,802.03	2,476.47	1,199.34	1,060.46	944.05
140,000	12,226.99	4,435.70	2,889.22	1,399.23	1,237.20	1,101.39
160,000	13,973.70	5,069.37	3,301.96	1,599.12	1,413.94	1,258.73
180,000	15,720.41	5,703.04	3,714.71	1,799.01	1,590.68	1,416.07
200,000	17,467.12	6,336.71	4,127.45	1,998.90	1,767.43	1,573.41
225,000	19,650.51	7,128.79	4,643.38	2,248.76	1,988.35	1,770.08
250,000	21,833.90	7,920.88	5,159.31	2,498.63	2,209.28	1,966.76
275,000	24,017.29	8,712.97	5,675.24	2,748.49	2,430.21	2,163.43
300,000	26,200.68	9,505.06	6,191.17	2,998.35	2,651.14	2,360.11
350,000	30,567.46	11,089.23	7,223.04	3,498.08	3,092.99	2,753.46
400,000	34,934.24	12,673.41	8,254.90	3,997.80	3,534.85	3,146.81
450,000	39,301.02	14,257.58	9,286.76	4,497.52	3,976.70	3,540.16
500,000	43,667.80	15,841.76	10,318.62	4,997.25	4,418.56	3,933.51
550,000	48,034.58	17,425.93	11,350.48	5,496.97	4,860.41	4,326.86

9.00% 9.00%

MONTHLY LOAN PAYMENT TABLE

DOLLARS REQUIRED TO AMORTIZE LOAN

LOAN AMOUNT	TERM OF LOAN IN YEARS					
	1	3	5	15	20	30
50	4.38	1.59	1.04	0.51	0.45	0.41
100	8.75	3.18	2.08	1.02	0.90	0.81
200	17.50	6.36	4.16	2.03	1.80	1.61
300	26.24	9.54	6.23	3.05	2.70	2.42
400	34.99	12.72	8.31	4.06	3.60	3.22
500	43.73	15.90	10.38	5.08	4.50	4.03
600	52.48	19.08	12.46	6.09	5.40	4.83
700	61.22	22.26	14.54	7.10	6.30	5.64
800	69.97	25.44	16.61	8.12	7.20	6.44
900	78.71	28.62	18.69	9.13	8.10	7.25
1,000	87.46	31.80	20.76	10.15	9.00	8.05
2,000	174.91	63.60	41.52	20.29	18.00	16.10
3,000	262.36	95.40	62.28	30.43	27.00	24.14
4,000	349.81	127.20	83.04	40.58	35.99	32.19
5,000	437.26	159.00	103.80	50.72	44.99	40.24
6,000	524.71	190.80	124.56	60.86	53.99	48.28
7,000	612.17	222.60	145.31	71.00	62.99	56.33
8,000	699.62	254.40	166.07	81.15	71.98	64.37
9,000	787.07	286.20	186.83	91.29	80.98	72.42
10,000	874.52	318.00	207.59	101.43	89.98	80.47
15,000	1,311.78	477.00	311.38	152.14	134.96	120.70
20,000	1,749.03	636.00	415.17	202.86	179.95	160.93
25,000	2,186.29	795.00	518.96	253.57	224.94	201.16
30,000	2,623.55	954.00	622.76	304.28	269.92	241.39
35,000	3,060.81	1,113.00	726.55	355.00	314.91	281.62
45,000	3,935.32	1,430.99	934.13	456.42	404.88	362.09
55,000	4,809.84	1,748.99	1,141.71	557.85	494.85	442.55
65,000	5,684.35	2,066.99	1,349.30	659.28	584.83	523.01
75,000	6,558.87	2,384.98	1,556.88	760.70	674.80	603.47
85,000	7,433.38	2,702.98	1,764.47	862.13	764.77	683.93
100,000	8,745.15	3,179.98	2,075.84	1,014.27	899.73	804.63
120,000	10,494.18	3,815.97	2,491.01	1,217.12	1,079.68	965.55
140,000	12,243.21	4,451.97	2,906.17	1,419.98	1,259.62	1,126.48
160,000	13,992.24	5,087.96	3,321.34	1,622.83	1,439.57	1,287.40
180,000	15,741.27	5,723.96	3,736.51	1,825.68	1,619.51	1,448.33
200,000	17,490.30	6,359.95	4,151.68	2,028.54	1,799.46	1,609.25
225,000	19,676.59	7,154.94	4,670.63	2,282.10	2,024.39	1,810.41
250,000	21,862.87	7,949.94	5,189.59	2,535.67	2,249.32	2,011.56
275,000	24,049.16	8,744.93	5,708.55	2,789.24	2,474.25	2,212.72
300,000	26,235.45	9,539.92	6,227.51	3,042.80	2,699.18	2,413.87
350,000	30,608.02	11,129.91	7,265.43	3,549.94	3,149.05	2,816.18
400,000	34,980.60	12,719.90	8,303.35	4,057.07	3,598.91	3,218.50
450,000	39,353.17	14,309.88	9,341.26	4,564.20	4,048.77	3,620.81
500,000	43,725.74	15,899.87	10,379.18	5,071.34	4,498.63	4,023.12
550,000	48,098.32	17,489.86	11,417.10	5,578.47	4,948.50	4,425.43

9.25% 9.25%

MONTHLY LOAN PAYMENT TABLE

DOLLARS REQUIRED TO AMORTIZE LOAN

LOAN AMOUNT	TERM OF LOAN IN YEARS					
	1	3	5	15	20	30
50	4.38	1.60	1.05	0.52	0.46	0.42
100	8.76	3.20	2.09	1.03	0.92	0.83
200	17.52	6.39	4.18	2.06	1.84	1.65
300	26.28	9.58	6.27	3.09	2.75	2.47
400	35.03	12.77	8.36	4.12	3.67	3.30
500	43.79	15.96	10.44	5.15	4.58	4.12
600	52.55	19.15	12.53	6.18	5.50	4.94
700	61.30	22.35	14.62	7.21	6.42	5.76
800	70.06	25.54	16.71	8.24	7.33	6.59
900	78.82	28.73	18.80	9.27	8.25	7.41
1,000	87.57	31.92	20.88	10.30	9.16	8.23
2,000	175.14	63.84	41.76	20.59	18.32	16.46
3,000	262.71	95.75	62.64	30.88	27.48	24.69
4,000	350.27	127.67	83.52	41.17	36.64	32.91
5,000	437.84	159.59	104.40	51.46	45.80	41.14
6,000	525.41	191.50	125.28	61.76	54.96	49.37
7,000	612.98	223.42	146.16	72.05	64.12	57.59
8,000	700.54	255.33	167.04	82.34	73.27	65.82
9,000	788.11	287.25	187.92	92.63	82.43	74.05
10,000	875.68	319.17	208.80	102.92	91.59	82.27
15,000	1,313.52	478.75	313.20	154.38	137.39	123.41
20,000	1,751.35	638.33	417.60	205.84	183.18	164.54
25,000	2,189.19	797.91	522.00	257.30	228.97	205.67
30,000	2,627.03	957.49	626.40	308.76	274.77	246.81
35,000	3,064.87	1,117.07	730.80	360.22	320.56	287.94
45,000	3,940.54	1,436.23	939.60	463.14	412.15	370.21
55,000	4,816.21	1,755.40	1,148.40	566.06	503.73	452.48
65,000	5,691.89	2,074.56	1,357.20	668.98	595.32	534.74
75,000	6,567.56	2,393.72	1,566.00	771.90	686.91	617.01
85,000	7,443.24	2,712.88	1,774.80	874.82	778.49	699.28
100,000	8,756.75	3,191.63	2,087.99	1,029.20	915.87	822.68
120,000	10,508.10	3,829.95	2,505.59	1,235.04	1,099.05	987.22
140,000	12,259.45	4,468.27	2,923.19	1,440.87	1,282.22	1,151.75
160,000	14,010.80	5,106.60	3,340.79	1,646.71	1,465.39	1,316.29
180,000	15,762.15	5,744.92	3,758.39	1,852.55	1,648.57	1,480.82
200,000	17,513.50	6,383.25	4,175.98	2,058.39	1,831.74	1,645.36
225,000	19,702.68	7,181.15	4,697.98	2,315.69	2,060.71	1,851.02
250,000	21,891.87	7,979.06	5,219.98	2,572.99	2,289.67	2,056.69
275,000	24,081.05	8,776.96	5,741.98	2,830.28	2,518.64	2,262.36
300,000	26,270.24	9,574.87	6,263.97	3,087.58	2,747.61	2,468.03
350,000	30,648.61	11,170.68	7,307.97	3,602.18	3,205.54	2,879.37
400,000	35,026.99	12,766.49	8,351.96	4,116.77	3,663.47	3,290.71
450,000	39,405.36	14,362.30	9,395.96	4,631.37	4,121.41	3,702.04
500,000	43,783.73	15,958.11	10,439.95	5,145.97	4,579.34	4,113.38
550,000	48,162.10	17,553.92	11,483.95	5,660.56	5,037.27	4,524.72

9.50% 9.50%

MONTHLY LOAN PAYMENT TABLE

DOLLARS REQUIRED TO AMORTIZE LOAN

LOAN AMOUNT	TERM OF LOAN IN YEARS					
	1	3	5	15	20	30
50	4.39	1.61	1.06	0.53	0.47	0.43
100	8.77	3.21	2.11	1.05	0.94	0.85
200	17.54	6.41	4.21	2.09	1.87	1.69
300	26.31	9.61	6.31	3.14	2.80	2.53
400	35.08	12.82	8.41	4.18	3.73	3.37
500	43.85	16.02	10.51	5.23	4.67	4.21
600	52.62	19.22	12.61	6.27	5.60	5.05
700	61.38	22.43	14.71	7.31	6.53	5.89
800	70.15	25.63	16.81	8.36	7.46	6.73
900	78.92	28.83	18.91	9.40	8.39	7.57
1,000	87.69	32.04	21.01	10.45	9.33	8.41
2,000	175.37	64.07	42.01	20.89	18.65	16.82
3,000	263.06	96.10	63.01	31.33	27.97	25.23
4,000	350.74	128.14	84.01	41.77	37.29	33.64
5,000	438.42	160.17	105.01	52.22	46.61	42.05
6,000	526.11	192.20	126.02	62.66	55.93	50.46
7,000	613.79	224.24	147.02	73.10	65.25	58.86
8,000	701.47	256.27	168.02	83.54	74.58	67.27
9,000	789.16	288.30	189.02	93.99	83.90	75.68
10,000	876.84	320.33	210.02	104.43	93.22	84.09
15,000	1,315.26	480.50	315.03	156.64	139.82	126.13
20,000	1,753.68	640.66	420.04	208.85	186.43	168.18
25,000	2,192.09	800.83	525.05	261.06	233.04	210.22
30,000	2,630.51	960.99	630.06	313.27	279.64	252.26
35,000	3,068.93	1,121.16	735.07	365.48	326.25	294.30
45,000	3,945.76	1,441.49	945.09	469.91	419.46	378.39
55,000	4,822.60	1,761.82	1,155.11	574.33	512.68	462.47
65,000	5,699.43	2,082.15	1,365.13	678.75	605.89	546.56
75,000	6,576.27	2,402.48	1,575.14	783.17	699.10	630.65
85,000	7,453.10	2,722.81	1,785.16	887.60	792.32	714.73
100,000	8,768.36	3,203.30	2,100.19	1,044.23	932.14	840.86
120,000	10,522.03	3,843.96	2,520.23	1,253.07	1,118.56	1,009.03
140,000	12,275.70	4,484.62	2,940.27	1,461.92	1,304.99	1,177.20
160,000	14,029.37	5,125.28	3,360.30	1,670.76	1,491.41	1,345.37
180,000	15,783.04	5,765.94	3,780.34	1,879.61	1,677.84	1,513.54
200,000	17,536.71	6,406.59	4,200.38	2,088.45	1,864.27	1,681.71
225,000	19,728.80	7,207.42	4,725.42	2,349.51	2,097.30	1,891.93
250,000	21,920.88	8,008.24	5,250.47	2,610.57	2,330.33	2,102.14
275,000	24,112.97	8,809.07	5,775.52	2,871.62	2,563.37	2,312.35
300,000	26,305.06	9,609.89	6,300.56	3,132.68	2,796.40	2,522.57
350,000	30,689.23	11,211.54	7,350.66	3,654.79	3,262.46	2,942.99
400,000	35,073.41	12,813.18	8,400.75	4,176.90	3,728.53	3,363.42
450,000	39,457.59	14,414.83	9,450.84	4,699.02	4,194.60	3,783.85
500,000	43,841.76	16,016.48	10,500.94	5,221.13	4,660.66	4,204.28
550,000	48,225.94	17,618.13	11,551.03	5,743.24	5,126.73	4,624.70

9.75% 9.75%

MONTHLY LOAN PAYMENT TABLE

DOLLARS REQUIRED TO AMORTIZE LOAN

LOAN AMOUNT	TERM OF LOAN IN YEARS					
	1	3	5	15	20	30
50	4.39	1.61	1.06	0.53	0.48	0.43
100	8.78	3.22	2.12	1.06	0.95	0.86
200	17.56	6.43	4.23	2.12	1.90	1.72
300	26.34	9.65	6.34	3.18	2.85	2.58
400	35.12	12.86	8.45	4.24	3.80	3.44
500	43.90	16.08	10.57	5.30	4.75	4.30
600	52.68	19.29	12.68	6.36	5.70	5.16
700	61.46	22.51	14.79	7.42	6.64	6.02
800	70.24	25.72	16.90	8.48	7.59	6.88
900	79.02	28.94	19.02	9.54	8.54	7.74
1,000	87.80	32.15	21.13	10.60	9.49	8.60
2,000	175.60	64.30	42.25	21.19	18.98	17.19
3,000	263.40	96.45	63.38	31.79	28.46	25.78
4,000	351.20	128.60	84.50	42.38	37.95	34.37
5,000	439.00	160.75	105.63	52.97	47.43	42.96
6,000	526.80	192.90	126.75	63.57	56.92	51.55
7,000	614.60	225.05	147.87	74.16	66.40	60.15
8,000	702.40	257.20	169.00	84.75	75.89	68.74
9,000	790.20	289.35	190.12	95.35	85.37	77.33
10,000	878.00	321.50	211.25	105.94	94.86	85.92
15,000	1,317.00	482.25	316.87	158.91	142.28	128.88
20,000	1,756.00	643.00	422.49	211.88	189.71	171.84
25,000	2,195.00	803.75	528.11	264.85	237.13	214.79
30,000	2,633.99	964.50	633.73	317.81	284.56	257.75
35,000	3,072.99	1,125.25	739.35	370.78	331.99	300.71
45,000	3,950.99	1,446.75	950.60	476.72	426.84	386.62
55,000	4,828.99	1,768.25	1,161.84	582.65	521.69	472.54
65,000	5,706.98	2,089.75	1,373.08	688.59	616.54	558.46
75,000	6,584.98	2,411.25	1,584.32	794.53	711.39	644.37
85,000	7,462.98	2,732.75	1,795.57	900.46	806.24	730.29
100,000	8,779.97	3,215.00	2,112.43	1,059.37	948.52	859.16
120,000	10,535.96	3,858.00	2,534.91	1,271.24	1,138.23	1,030.99
140,000	12,291.96	4,501.00	2,957.40	1,483.11	1,327.93	1,202.82
160,000	14,047.95	5,144.00	3,379.88	1,694.99	1,517.63	1,374.65
180,000	15,803.94	5,786.99	3,802.37	1,906.86	1,707.34	1,546.48
200,000	17,559.94	6,429.99	4,224.85	2,118.73	1,897.04	1,718.31
225,000	19,754.93	7,233.74	4,752.96	2,383.57	2,134.17	1,933.10
250,000	21,949.92	8,037.49	5,281.07	2,648.41	2,371.30	2,147.89
275,000	24,144.91	8,841.24	5,809.17	2,913.25	2,608.43	2,362.68
300,000	26,339.90	9,644.99	6,337.28	3,178.09	2,845.56	2,577.47
350,000	30,729.88	11,252.48	7,393.49	3,707.77	3,319.81	3,007.05
400,000	35,119.87	12,859.98	8,449.70	4,237.46	3,794.07	3,436.62
450,000	39,509.85	14,467.48	9,505.91	4,767.14	4,268.33	3,866.20
500,000	43,899.83	16,074.98	10,562.13	5,296.82	4,742.59	4,295.78
550,000	48,289.82	17,682.47	11,618.34	5,826.50	5,216.85	4,725.35

10.00% 10.00%

MONTHLY LOAN PAYMENT TABLE

DOLLARS REQUIRED TO AMORTIZE LOAN

LOAN AMOUNT	TERM OF LOAN IN YEARS					
	1	3	5	15	20	30
50	4.40	1.62	1.07	0.54	0.49	0.44
100	8.80	3.23	2.13	1.08	0.97	0.88
200	17.59	6.46	4.25	2.15	1.94	1.76
300	26.38	9.69	6.38	3.23	2.90	2.64
400	35.17	12.91	8.50	4.30	3.87	3.52
500	43.96	16.14	10.63	5.38	4.83	4.39
600	52.75	19.37	12.75	6.45	5.80	5.27
700	61.55	22.59	14.88	7.53	6.76	6.15
800	70.34	25.82	17.00	8.60	7.73	7.03
900	79.13	29.05	19.13	9.68	8.69	7.90
1,000	87.92	32.27	21.25	10.75	9.66	8.78
2,000	175.84	64.54	42.50	21.50	19.31	17.56
3,000	263.75	96.81	63.75	32.24	28.96	26.33
4,000	351.67	129.07	84.99	42.99	38.61	35.11
5,000	439.58	161.34	106.24	53.74	48.26	43.88
6,000	527.50	193.61	127.49	64.48	57.91	52.66
7,000	615.42	225.88	148.73	75.23	67.56	61.44
8,000	703.33	258.14	169.98	85.97	77.21	70.21
9,000	791.25	290.41	191.23	96.72	86.86	78.99
10,000	879.16	322.68	212.48	107.47	96.51	87.76
15,000	1,318.74	484.01	318.71	161.20	144.76	131.64
20,000	1,758.32	645.35	424.95	214.93	193.01	175.52
25,000	2,197.90	806.68	531.18	268.66	241.26	219.40
30,000	2,637.48	968.02	637.42	322.39	289.51	263.28
35,000	3,077.06	1,129.36	743.65	376.12	337.76	307.16
45,000	3,956.22	1,452.03	956.12	483.58	434.26	394.91
55,000	4,835.38	1,774.70	1,168.59	591.04	530.77	482.67
65,000	5,714.54	2,097.37	1,381.06	698.50	627.27	570.43
75,000	6,593.70	2,420.04	1,593.53	805.96	723.77	658.18
85,000	7,472.86	2,742.72	1,806.00	913.42	820.27	745.94
100,000	8,791.59	3,226.72	2,124.71	1,074.61	965.03	877.58
120,000	10,549.91	3,872.07	2,549.65	1,289.53	1,158.03	1,053.09
140,000	12,308.23	4,517.41	2,974.59	1,504.45	1,351.04	1,228.61
160,000	14,066.55	5,162.75	3,399.53	1,719.37	1,544.04	1,404.12
180,000	15,824.86	5,808.10	3,824.47	1,934.29	1,737.04	1,579.63
200,000	17,583.18	6,453.44	4,249.41	2,149.22	1,930.05	1,755.15
225,000	19,781.08	7,260.12	4,780.59	2,417.87	2,171.30	1,974.54
250,000	21,978.98	8,066.80	5,311.77	2,686.52	2,412.56	2,193.93
275,000	24,176.87	8,873.48	5,842.94	2,955.17	2,653.81	2,413.33
300,000	26,374.77	9,680.16	6,374.12	3,223.82	2,895.07	2,632.72
350,000	30,770.57	11,293.52	7,436.47	3,761.12	3,377.58	3,071.51
400,000	35,166.36	12,906.88	8,498.82	4,298.43	3,860.09	3,510.29
450,000	39,562.15	14,520.24	9,561.18	4,835.73	4,342.60	3,949.08
500,000	43,957.95	16,133.60	10,623.53	5,373.03	4,825.11	4,387.86
550,000	48,353.74	17,746.96	11,685.88	5,910.33	5,307.62	4,826.65

10.25% 10.25%

MONTHLY LOAN PAYMENT TABLE

DOLLARS REQUIRED TO AMORTIZE LOAN

LOAN AMOUNT	TERM OF LOAN IN YEARS					
	1	3	5	15	20	30
50	4.41	1.62	1.07	0.55	0.50	0.45
100	8.81	3.24	2.14	1.09	0.99	0.90
200	17.61	6.48	4.28	2.18	1.97	1.80
300	26.41	9.72	6.42	3.27	2.95	2.69
400	35.22	12.96	8.55	4.36	3.93	3.59
500	44.02	16.20	10.69	5.45	4.91	4.49
600	52.82	19.44	12.83	6.54	5.89	5.38
700	61.63	22.67	14.96	7.63	6.88	6.28
800	70.43	25.91	17.10	8.72	7.86	7.17
900	79.23	29.15	19.24	9.81	8.84	8.07
1,000	88.04	32.39	21.38	10.90	9.82	8.97
2,000	176.07	64.77	42.75	21.80	19.64	17.93
3,000	264.10	97.16	64.12	32.70	29.45	26.89
4,000	352.13	129.54	85.49	43.60	39.27	35.85
5,000	440.17	161.93	106.86	54.50	49.09	44.81
6,000	528.20	194.31	128.23	65.40	58.90	53.77
7,000	616.23	226.70	149.60	76.30	68.72	62.73
8,000	704.26	259.08	170.97	87.20	78.54	71.69
9,000	792.29	291.47	192.34	98.10	88.35	80.65
10,000	880.33	323.85	213.71	109.00	98.17	89.62
15,000	1,320.49	485.78	320.56	163.50	147.25	134.42
20,000	1,760.65	647.70	427.41	218.00	196.33	179.23
25,000	2,200.81	809.62	534.26	272.49	245.42	224.03
30,000	2,640.97	971.55	641.11	326.99	294.50	268.84
35,000	3,081.13	1,133.47	747.96	381.49	343.58	313.64
45,000	3,961.45	1,457.32	961.67	490.48	441.74	403.25
55,000	4,841.78	1,781.16	1,175.37	599.48	539.91	492.86
65,000	5,722.10	2,105.01	1,389.07	708.47	638.07	582.47
75,000	6,602.42	2,428.86	1,602.77	817.47	736.24	672.08
85,000	7,482.74	2,752.70	1,816.48	926.46	834.40	761.69
100,000	8,803.23	3,238.47	2,137.03	1,089.96	981.65	896.11
120,000	10,563.87	3,886.17	2,564.44	1,307.95	1,177.98	1,075.33
140,000	12,324.51	4,533.86	2,991.84	1,525.94	1,374.31	1,254.55
160,000	14,085.16	5,181.56	3,419.25	1,743.93	1,570.63	1,433.77
180,000	15,845.80	5,829.25	3,846.65	1,961.92	1,766.96	1,612.99
200,000	17,606.45	6,476.94	4,274.06	2,179.91	1,963.29	1,792.21
225,000	19,807.25	7,286.56	4,808.31	2,452.39	2,208.70	2,016.23
250,000	22,008.06	8,096.18	5,342.57	2,724.88	2,454.11	2,240.26
275,000	24,208.86	8,905.79	5,876.83	2,997.37	2,699.52	2,464.28
300,000	26,409.67	9,715.41	6,411.08	3,269.86	2,944.94	2,688.31
350,000	30,811.28	11,334.65	7,479.60	3,814.83	3,435.76	3,136.36
400,000	35,212.89	12,953.88	8,548.11	4,359.81	3,926.58	3,584.41
450,000	39,614.50	14,573.11	9,616.62	4,904.78	4,417.40	4,032.46
500,000	44,016.11	16,192.35	10,685.14	5,449.76	4,908.22	4,480.51
550,000	48,417.72	17,811.58	11,753.65	5,994.74	5,399.04	4,928.56

10.50% 10.50%

MONTHLY LOAN PAYMENT TABLE

DOLLARS REQUIRED TO AMORTIZE LOAN

LOAN AMOUNT	TERM OF LOAN IN YEARS 1	3	5	15	20	30
50	4.41	1.63	1.08	0.56	0.50	0.46
100	8.82	3.26	2.15	1.11	1.00	0.92
200	17.63	6.51	4.30	2.22	2.00	1.83
300	26.45	9.76	6.45	3.32	3.00	2.75
400	35.26	13.01	8.60	4.43	4.00	3.66
500	44.08	16.26	10.75	5.53	5.00	4.58
600	52.89	19.51	12.90	6.64	6.00	5.49
700	61.71	22.76	15.05	7.74	6.99	6.41
800	70.52	26.01	17.20	8.85	7.99	7.32
900	79.34	29.26	19.35	9.95	8.99	8.24
1,000	88.15	32.51	21.50	11.06	9.99	9.15
2,000	176.30	65.01	42.99	22.11	19.97	18.30
3,000	264.45	97.51	64.49	33.17	29.96	27.45
4,000	352.60	130.01	85.98	44.22	39.94	36.59
5,000	440.75	162.52	107.47	55.27	49.92	45.74
6,000	528.90	195.02	128.97	66.33	59.91	54.89
7,000	617.05	227.52	150.46	77.38	69.89	64.04
8,000	705.19	260.02	171.96	88.44	79.88	73.18
9,000	793.34	292.53	193.45	99.49	89.86	82.33
10,000	881.49	325.03	214.94	110.54	99.84	91.48
15,000	1,322.23	487.54	322.41	165.81	149.76	137.22
20,000	1,762.98	650.05	429.88	221.08	199.68	182.95
25,000	2,203.72	812.57	537.35	276.35	249.60	228.69
30,000	2,644.46	975.08	644.82	331.62	299.52	274.43
35,000	3,085.21	1,137.59	752.29	386.89	349.44	320.16
45,000	3,966.69	1,462.61	967.23	497.43	449.28	411.64
55,000	4,848.18	1,787.64	1,182.17	607.97	549.11	503.11
65,000	5,729.66	2,112.66	1,397.11	718.51	648.95	594.59
75,000	6,611.15	2,437.69	1,612.05	829.05	748.79	686.06
85,000	7,492.64	2,762.71	1,826.99	939.59	848.63	777.53
100,000	8,814.87	3,250.25	2,149.40	1,105.40	998.38	914.74
120,000	10,577.84	3,900.30	2,579.27	1,326.48	1,198.06	1,097.69
140,000	12,340.81	4,550.35	3,009.15	1,547.56	1,397.74	1,280.64
160,000	14,103.78	5,200.40	3,439.03	1,768.64	1,597.41	1,463.59
180,000	15,866.75	5,850.44	3,868.91	1,989.72	1,797.09	1,646.54
200,000	17,629.73	6,500.49	4,298.79	2,210.80	1,996.76	1,829.48
225,000	19,833.44	7,313.05	4,836.13	2,487.15	2,246.36	2,058.17
250,000	22,037.16	8,125.62	5,373.48	2,763.50	2,495.95	2,286.85
275,000	24,240.87	8,938.18	5,910.83	3,039.85	2,745.55	2,515.54
300,000	26,444.59	9,750.74	6,448.18	3,316.20	2,995.14	2,744.22
350,000	30,852.02	11,375.86	7,522.87	3,868.90	3,494.33	3,201.59
400,000	35,259.45	13,000.98	8,597.57	4,421.60	3,993.52	3,658.96
450,000	39,666.88	14,626.10	9,672.26	4,974.30	4,492.71	4,116.33
500,000	44,074.31	16,251.23	10,746.96	5,527.00	4,991.90	4,573.70
550,000	48,481.74	17,876.35	11,821.65	6,079.70	5,491.09	5,031.07

10.75% 10.75%

MONTHLY LOAN PAYMENT TABLE

DOLLARS REQUIRED TO AMORTIZE LOAN

LOAN AMOUNT	TERM OF LOAN IN YEARS					
	1	3	5	15	20	30
50	4.42	1.64	1.09	0.57	0.51	0.47
100	8.83	3.27	2.17	1.13	1.02	0.94
200	17.66	6.53	4.33	2.25	2.04	1.87
300	26.48	9.79	6.49	3.37	3.05	2.81
400	35.31	13.05	8.65	4.49	4.07	3.74
500	44.14	16.32	10.81	5.61	5.08	4.67
600	52.96	19.58	12.98	6.73	6.10	5.61
700	61.79	22.84	15.14	7.85	7.11	6.54
800	70.62	26.10	17.30	8.97	8.13	7.47
900	79.44	29.36	19.46	10.09	9.14	8.41
1,000	88.27	32.63	21.62	11.21	10.16	9.34
2,000	176.54	65.25	43.24	22.42	20.31	18.67
3,000	264.80	97.87	64.86	33.63	30.46	28.01
4,000	353.07	130.49	86.48	44.84	40.61	37.34
5,000	441.33	163.11	108.09	56.05	50.77	46.68
6,000	529.60	195.73	129.71	67.26	60.92	56.01
7,000	617.86	228.35	151.33	78.47	71.07	65.35
8,000	706.13	260.97	172.95	89.68	81.22	74.68
9,000	794.39	293.59	194.57	100.89	91.38	84.02
10,000	882.66	326.21	216.18	112.10	101.53	93.35
15,000	1,323.98	489.31	324.27	168.15	152.29	140.03
20,000	1,765.31	652.41	432.36	224.19	203.05	186.70
25,000	2,206.63	815.52	540.45	280.24	253.81	233.38
30,000	2,647.96	978.62	648.54	336.29	304.57	280.05
35,000	3,089.28	1,141.72	756.63	392.34	355.34	326.72
45,000	3,971.93	1,467.93	972.81	504.43	456.86	420.07
55,000	4,854.58	1,794.13	1,188.99	616.53	558.38	513.42
65,000	5,737.24	2,120.33	1,405.17	728.62	659.90	606.77
75,000	6,619.89	2,446.54	1,621.35	840.72	761.43	700.12
85,000	7,502.54	2,772.74	1,837.53	952.81	862.95	793.46
100,000	8,826.51	3,262.05	2,161.80	1,120.95	1,015.23	933.49
120,000	10,591.82	3,914.46	2,594.16	1,345.14	1,218.28	1,120.18
140,000	12,357.12	4,566.87	3,026.52	1,569.33	1,421.33	1,306.88
160,000	14,122.42	5,219.28	3,458.88	1,793.52	1,624.37	1,493.58
180,000	15,887.72	5,871.69	3,891.24	2,017.71	1,827.42	1,680.27
200,000	17,653.02	6,524.10	4,323.60	2,241.90	2,030.46	1,866.97
225,000	19,859.65	7,339.61	4,864.04	2,522.14	2,284.27	2,100.34
250,000	22,066.28	8,155.12	5,404.49	2,802.37	2,538.08	2,333.71
275,000	24,272.90	8,970.63	5,944.94	3,082.61	2,791.88	2,567.08
300,000	26,479.53	9,786.14	6,485.39	3,362.85	3,045.69	2,800.45
350,000	30,892.79	11,417.16	7,566.29	3,923.32	3,553.31	3,267.19
400,000	35,306.04	13,048.19	8,647.19	4,483.80	4,060.92	3,733.93
450,000	39,719.29	14,679.21	9,728.08	5,044.27	4,568.54	4,200.67
500,000	44,132.55	16,310.23	10,808.98	5,604.74	5,076.15	4,667.41
550,000	48,545.80	17,941.25	11,889.88	6,165.22	5,583.76	5,134.15

11.00% 11.00%

MONTHLY LOAN PAYMENT TABLE

DOLLARS REQUIRED TO AMORTIZE LOAN

LOAN AMOUNT	TERM OF LOAN IN YEARS					
	1	3	5	15	20	30
50	4.42	1.64	1.09	0.57	0.52	0.48
100	8.84	3.28	2.18	1.14	1.04	0.96
200	17.68	6.55	4.35	2.28	2.07	1.91
300	26.52	9.83	6.53	3.41	3.10	2.86
400	35.36	13.10	8.70	4.55	4.13	3.81
500	44.20	16.37	10.88	5.69	5.17	4.77
600	53.03	19.65	13.05	6.82	6.20	5.72
700	61.87	22.92	15.22	7.96	7.23	6.67
800	70.71	26.20	17.40	9.10	8.26	7.62
900	79.55	29.47	19.57	10.23	9.29	8.58
1,000	88.39	32.74	21.75	11.37	10.33	9.53
2,000	176.77	65.48	43.49	22.74	20.65	19.05
3,000	265.15	98.22	65.23	34.10	30.97	28.57
4,000	353.53	130.96	86.97	45.47	41.29	38.10
5,000	441.91	163.70	108.72	56.83	51.61	47.62
6,000	530.29	196.44	130.46	68.20	61.94	57.14
7,000	618.68	229.18	152.20	79.57	72.26	66.67
8,000	707.06	261.91	173.94	90.93	82.58	76.19
9,000	795.44	294.65	195.69	102.30	92.90	85.71
10,000	883.82	327.39	217.43	113.66	103.22	95.24
15,000	1,325.73	491.09	326.14	170.49	154.83	142.85
20,000	1,767.64	654.78	434.85	227.32	206.44	190.47
25,000	2,209.55	818.47	543.57	284.15	258.05	238.09
30,000	2,651.45	982.17	652.28	340.98	309.66	285.70
35,000	3,093.36	1,145.86	760.99	397.81	361.27	333.32
45,000	3,977.18	1,473.25	978.41	511.47	464.49	428.55
55,000	4,861.00	1,800.63	1,195.84	625.13	567.71	523.78
65,000	5,744.81	2,128.02	1,413.26	738.79	670.93	619.02
75,000	6,628.63	2,455.41	1,630.69	852.45	774.15	714.25
85,000	7,512.45	2,782.80	1,848.11	966.11	877.37	809.48
100,000	8,838.17	3,273.88	2,174.25	1,136.60	1,032.19	952.33
120,000	10,605.80	3,928.65	2,609.10	1,363.92	1,238.63	1,142.79
140,000	12,373.44	4,583.43	3,043.94	1,591.24	1,445.07	1,333.26
160,000	14,141.07	5,238.20	3,478.79	1,818.56	1,651.51	1,523.72
180,000	15,908.70	5,892.97	3,913.64	2,045.88	1,857.94	1,714.19
200,000	17,676.34	6,547.75	4,348.49	2,273.20	2,064.38	1,904.65
225,000	19,885.88	7,366.22	4,892.05	2,557.35	2,322.43	2,142.73
250,000	22,095.42	8,184.68	5,435.61	2,841.50	2,580.48	2,380.81
275,000	24,304.96	9,003.15	5,979.17	3,125.65	2,838.52	2,618.89
300,000	26,514.50	9,821.62	6,522.73	3,409.80	3,096.57	2,856.98
350,000	30,933.59	11,458.56	7,609.85	3,978.09	3,612.66	3,333.14
400,000	35,352.67	13,095.49	8,696.97	4,546.39	4,128.76	3,809.30
450,000	39,771.75	14,732.43	9,784.10	5,114.69	4,644.85	4,285.46
500,000	44,190.83	16,369.36	10,871.22	5,682.99	5,160.95	4,761.62
550,000	48,609.92	18,006.30	11,958.34	6,251.29	5,677.04	5,237.78

11.25% 11.25%

MONTHLY LOAN PAYMENT TABLE

DOLLARS REQUIRED TO AMORTIZE LOAN

LOAN AMOUNT	TERM OF LOAN IN YEARS					
	1	3	5	15	20	30
50	4.43	1.65	1.10	0.58	0.53	0.49
100	8.85	3.29	2.19	1.16	1.05	0.98
200	17.70	6.58	4.38	2.31	2.10	1.95
300	26.55	9.86	6.57	3.46	3.15	2.92
400	35.40	13.15	8.75	4.61	4.20	3.89
500	44.25	16.43	10.94	5.77	5.25	4.86
600	53.10	19.72	13.13	6.92	6.30	5.83
700	61.95	23.01	15.31	8.07	7.35	6.80
800	70.80	26.29	17.50	9.22	8.40	7.78
900	79.65	29.58	19.69	10.38	9.45	8.75
1,000	88.50	32.86	21.87	11.53	10.50	9.72
2,000	177.00	65.72	43.74	23.05	20.99	19.43
3,000	265.50	98.58	65.61	34.58	31.48	29.14
4,000	354.00	131.43	87.47	46.10	41.98	38.86
5,000	442.50	164.29	109.34	57.62	52.47	48.57
6,000	530.99	197.15	131.21	69.15	62.96	58.28
7,000	619.49	230.01	153.08	80.67	73.45	67.99
8,000	707.99	262.86	174.94	92.19	83.95	77.71
9,000	796.49	295.72	196.81	103.72	94.44	87.42
10,000	884.99	328.58	218.68	115.24	104.93	97.13
15,000	1,327.48	492.86	328.01	172.86	157.39	145.69
20,000	1,769.97	657.15	437.35	230.47	209.86	194.26
25,000	2,212.46	821.44	546.69	288.09	262.32	242.82
30,000	2,654.95	985.72	656.02	345.71	314.78	291.38
35,000	3,097.45	1,150.01	765.36	403.33	367.24	339.95
45,000	3,982.43	1,478.58	984.03	518.56	472.17	437.07
55,000	4,867.41	1,807.15	1,202.71	633.79	577.10	534.20
65,000	5,752.40	2,135.73	1,421.38	749.03	682.02	631.32
75,000	6,637.38	2,464.30	1,640.05	864.26	786.95	728.45
85,000	7,522.36	2,792.87	1,858.73	979.50	891.87	825.58
100,000	8,849.84	3,285.73	2,186.74	1,152.35	1,049.26	971.27
120,000	10,619.80	3,942.87	2,624.08	1,382.82	1,259.11	1,165.52
140,000	12,389.77	4,600.02	3,061.43	1,613.29	1,468.96	1,359.77
160,000	14,159.74	5,257.16	3,498.77	1,843.76	1,678.81	1,554.02
180,000	15,929.70	5,914.31	3,936.12	2,074.23	1,888.67	1,748.28
200,000	17,699.67	6,571.45	4,373.47	2,304.69	2,098.52	1,942.53
225,000	19,912.13	7,392.88	4,920.15	2,592.78	2,360.83	2,185.34
250,000	22,124.58	8,214.31	5,466.83	2,880.87	2,623.15	2,428.16
275,000	24,337.04	9,035.74	6,013.51	3,168.95	2,885.46	2,670.97
300,000	26,549.50	9,857.18	6,560.20	3,457.04	3,147.77	2,913.79
350,000	30,974.41	11,500.04	7,653.56	4,033.21	3,672.40	3,399.42
400,000	35,399.33	13,142.90	8,746.93	4,609.38	4,197.03	3,885.05
450,000	39,824.25	14,785.76	9,840.29	5,185.56	4,721.66	4,370.68
500,000	44,249.16	16,428.62	10,933.66	5,761.73	5,246.29	4,856.31
550,000	48,674.08	18,071.48	12,027.02	6,337.90	5,770.91	5,341.94

11.50% 11.50%

MONTHLY LOAN PAYMENT TABLE

DOLLARS REQUIRED TO AMORTIZE LOAN

LOAN AMOUNT	TERM OF LOAN IN YEARS					
	1	3	5	15	20	30
50	4.44	1.65	1.10	0.59	0.54	0.50
100	8.87	3.30	2.20	1.17	1.07	1.00
200	17.73	6.60	4.40	2.34	2.14	1.99
300	26.59	9.90	6.60	3.51	3.20	2.98
400	35.45	13.20	8.80	4.68	4.27	3.97
500	44.31	16.49	11.00	5.85	5.34	4.96
600	53.17	19.79	13.20	7.01	6.40	5.95
700	62.04	23.09	15.40	8.18	7.47	6.94
800	70.90	26.39	17.60	9.35	8.54	7.93
900	79.76	29.68	19.80	10.52	9.60	8.92
1,000	88.62	32.98	22.00	11.69	10.67	9.91
2,000	177.24	65.96	43.99	23.37	21.33	19.81
3,000	265.85	98.93	65.98	35.05	32.00	29.71
4,000	354.47	131.91	87.98	46.73	42.66	39.62
5,000	443.08	164.89	109.97	58.41	53.33	49.52
6,000	531.70	197.86	131.96	70.10	63.99	59.42
7,000	620.31	230.84	153.95	81.78	74.66	69.33
8,000	708.93	263.81	175.95	93.46	85.32	79.23
9,000	797.54	296.79	197.94	105.14	95.98	89.13
10,000	886.16	329.77	219.93	116.82	106.65	99.03
15,000	1,329.23	494.65	329.89	175.23	159.97	148.55
20,000	1,772.31	659.53	439.86	233.64	213.29	198.06
25,000	2,215.38	824.41	549.82	292.05	266.61	247.58
30,000	2,658.46	989.29	659.78	350.46	319.93	297.09
35,000	3,101.53	1,154.17	769.75	408.87	373.26	346.61
45,000	3,987.68	1,483.93	989.67	525.69	479.90	445.64
55,000	4,873.83	1,813.69	1,209.60	642.51	586.54	544.67
65,000	5,759.98	2,143.45	1,429.52	759.33	693.18	643.69
75,000	6,646.13	2,473.21	1,649.45	876.15	799.83	742.72
85,000	7,532.28	2,802.97	1,869.38	992.97	906.47	841.75
100,000	8,861.51	3,297.61	2,199.27	1,168.19	1,066.43	990.30
120,000	10,633.81	3,957.13	2,639.12	1,401.83	1,279.72	1,188.35
140,000	12,406.11	4,616.65	3,078.97	1,635.47	1,493.01	1,386.41
160,000	14,178.41	5,276.17	3,518.82	1,869.11	1,706.29	1,584.47
180,000	15,950.71	5,935.69	3,958.67	2,102.75	1,919.58	1,782.53
200,000	17,723.02	6,595.21	4,398.53	2,336.38	2,132.86	1,980.59
225,000	19,938.39	7,419.61	4,948.34	2,628.43	2,399.47	2,228.16
250,000	22,153.77	8,244.01	5,498.16	2,920.48	2,666.08	2,475.73
275,000	24,369.14	9,068.41	6,047.97	3,212.53	2,932.69	2,723.31
300,000	26,584.52	9,892.81	6,597.79	3,504.57	3,199.29	2,970.88
350,000	31,015.27	11,541.61	7,697.42	4,088.67	3,732.51	3,466.03
400,000	35,446.03	13,190.41	8,797.05	4,672.76	4,265.72	3,961.17
450,000	39,876.78	14,839.21	9,896.68	5,256.86	4,798.94	4,456.32
500,000	44,307.53	16,488.01	10,996.31	5,840.95	5,332.15	4,951.46
550,000	48,738.28	18,136.81	12,095.94	6,425.05	5,865.37	5,446.61

11.75% 11.75%

MONTHLY LOAN PAYMENT TABLE

DOLLARS REQUIRED TO AMORTIZE LOAN

LOAN AMOUNT	TERM OF LOAN IN YEARS					
	1	3	5	15	20	30
50	4.44	1.66	1.11	0.60	0.55	0.51
100	8.88	3.31	2.22	1.19	1.09	1.01
200	17.75	6.62	4.43	2.37	2.17	2.02
300	26.62	9.93	6.64	3.56	3.26	3.03
400	35.50	13.24	8.85	4.74	4.34	4.04
500	44.37	16.55	11.06	5.93	5.42	5.05
600	53.24	19.86	13.28	7.11	6.51	6.06
700	62.12	23.17	15.49	8.29	7.59	7.07
800	70.99	26.48	17.70	9.48	8.67	8.08
900	79.86	29.79	19.91	10.66	9.76	9.09
1,000	88.74	33.10	22.12	11.85	10.84	10.10
2,000	177.47	66.20	44.24	23.69	21.68	20.19
3,000	266.20	99.29	66.36	35.53	32.52	30.29
4,000	354.93	132.39	88.48	47.37	43.35	40.38
5,000	443.66	165.48	110.60	59.21	54.19	50.48
6,000	532.40	198.58	132.71	71.05	65.03	60.57
7,000	621.13	231.67	154.83	82.89	75.86	70.66
8,000	709.86	264.77	176.95	94.74	86.70	80.76
9,000	798.59	297.86	199.07	106.58	97.54	90.85
10,000	887.32	330.96	221.19	118.42	108.38	100.95
15,000	1,330.98	496.43	331.78	177.62	162.56	151.42
20,000	1,774.64	661.91	442.37	236.83	216.75	201.89
25,000	2,218.30	827.38	552.96	296.04	270.93	252.36
30,000	2,661.96	992.86	663.55	355.24	325.12	302.83
35,000	3,105.62	1,158.33	774.15	414.45	379.30	353.30
45,000	3,992.94	1,489.28	995.33	532.86	487.67	454.24
55,000	4,880.26	1,820.23	1,216.51	651.28	596.04	555.18
65,000	5,767.58	2,151.18	1,437.70	769.69	704.41	656.12
75,000	6,654.90	2,482.13	1,658.88	888.10	812.79	757.06
85,000	7,542.21	2,813.08	1,880.06	1,006.52	921.16	858.00
100,000	8,873.19	3,309.51	2,211.84	1,184.14	1,083.71	1,009.41
120,000	10,647.83	3,971.41	2,654.20	1,420.96	1,300.45	1,211.30
140,000	12,422.47	4,633.31	3,096.57	1,657.79	1,517.19	1,413.18
160,000	14,197.11	5,295.21	3,538.94	1,894.62	1,733.94	1,615.06
180,000	15,971.74	5,957.11	3,981.30	2,131.44	1,950.68	1,816.94
200,000	17,746.38	6,619.01	4,423.67	2,368.27	2,167.42	2,018.82
225,000	19,964.68	7,446.39	4,976.63	2,664.30	2,438.35	2,271.18
250,000	22,182.97	8,273.76	5,529.59	2,960.33	2,709.27	2,523.53
275,000	24,401.27	9,101.14	6,082.54	3,256.37	2,980.20	2,775.88
300,000	26,619.57	9,928.51	6,635.50	3,552.40	3,251.13	3,028.23
350,000	31,056.16	11,583.27	7,741.42	4,144.46	3,792.98	3,532.94
400,000	35,492.76	13,238.02	8,847.33	4,736.53	4,334.83	4,037.64
450,000	39,929.35	14,892.77	9,953.25	5,328.60	4,876.69	4,542.35
500,000	44,365.94	16,547.52	11,059.17	5,920.66	5,418.54	5,047.05
550,000	48,802.54	18,202.27	12,165.08	6,512.73	5,960.39	5,551.76

12.00% 12.00%

MONTHLY LOAN PAYMENT TABLE

DOLLARS REQUIRED TO AMORTIZE LOAN

LOAN AMOUNT	TERM OF LOAN IN YEARS					
	1	3	5	15	20	30
50	4.45	1.67	1.12	0.61	0.56	0.52
100	8.89	3.33	2.23	1.21	1.11	1.03
200	17.77	6.65	4.45	2.41	2.21	2.06
300	26.66	9.97	6.68	3.61	3.31	3.09
400	35.54	13.29	8.90	4.81	4.41	4.12
500	44.43	16.61	11.13	6.01	5.51	5.15
600	53.31	19.93	13.35	7.21	6.61	6.18
700	62.20	23.26	15.58	8.41	7.71	7.21
800	71.08	26.58	17.80	9.61	8.81	8.23
900	79.97	29.90	20.03	10.81	9.91	9.26
1,000	88.85	33.22	22.25	12.01	11.02	10.29
2,000	177.70	66.43	44.49	24.01	22.03	20.58
3,000	266.55	99.65	66.74	36.01	33.04	30.86
4,000	355.40	132.86	88.98	48.01	44.05	41.15
5,000	444.25	166.08	111.23	60.01	55.06	51.44
6,000	533.10	199.29	133.47	72.02	66.07	61.72
7,000	621.95	232.51	155.72	84.02	77.08	72.01
8,000	710.80	265.72	177.96	96.02	88.09	82.29
9,000	799.64	298.93	200.21	108.02	99.10	92.58
10,000	888.49	332.15	222.45	120.02	110.11	102.87
15,000	1,332.74	498.22	333.67	180.03	165.17	154.30
20,000	1,776.98	664.29	444.89	240.04	220.22	205.73
25,000	2,221.22	830.36	556.12	300.05	275.28	257.16
30,000	2,665.47	996.43	667.34	360.06	330.33	308.59
35,000	3,109.71	1,162.51	778.56	420.06	385.39	360.02
45,000	3,998.20	1,494.65	1,001.01	540.08	495.49	462.88
55,000	4,886.69	1,826.79	1,223.45	660.10	605.60	565.74
65,000	5,775.18	2,158.94	1,445.89	780.11	715.71	668.60
75,000	6,663.66	2,491.08	1,668.34	900.13	825.82	771.46
85,000	7,552.15	2,823.22	1,890.78	1,020.15	935.93	874.33
100,000	8,884.88	3,321.44	2,224.45	1,200.17	1,101.09	1,028.62
120,000	10,661.86	3,985.72	2,669.34	1,440.21	1,321.31	1,234.34
140,000	12,438.84	4,650.01	3,114.23	1,680.24	1,541.53	1,440.06
160,000	14,215.81	5,314.29	3,559.12	1,920.27	1,761.74	1,645.79
180,000	15,992.79	5,978.58	4,004.01	2,160.31	1,981.96	1,851.51
200,000	17,769.76	6,642.87	4,448.89	2,400.34	2,202.18	2,057.23
225,000	19,990.98	7,473.22	5,005.01	2,700.38	2,477.45	2,314.38
250,000	22,212.20	8,303.58	5,561.12	3,000.43	2,752.72	2,571.54
275,000	24,433.42	9,133.94	6,117.23	3,300.47	3,027.99	2,828.69
300,000	26,654.64	9,964.30	6,673.34	3,600.51	3,303.26	3,085.84
350,000	31,097.08	11,625.01	7,785.56	4,200.59	3,853.81	3,600.15
400,000	35,539.52	13,285.73	8,897.78	4,800.68	4,404.35	4,114.46
450,000	39,981.96	14,946.44	10,010.01	5,400.76	4,954.89	4,628.76
500,000	44,424.40	16,607.16	11,122.23	6,000.85	5,505.44	5,143.07
550,000	48,866.84	18,267.88	12,234.45	6,600.93	6,055.98	5,657.37

12.25% 12.25%

MONTHLY LOAN PAYMENT TABLE

DOLLARS REQUIRED TO AMORTIZE LOAN

LOAN AMOUNT	TERM OF LOAN IN YEARS					
	1	3	5	15	20	30
50	4.45	1.67	1.12	0.61	0.56	0.53
100	8.90	3.34	2.24	1.22	1.12	1.05
200	17.80	6.67	4.48	2.44	2.24	2.10
300	26.69	10.01	6.72	3.65	3.36	3.15
400	35.59	13.34	8.95	4.87	4.48	4.20
500	44.49	16.67	11.19	6.09	5.60	5.24
600	53.38	20.01	13.43	7.30	6.72	6.29
700	62.28	23.34	15.66	8.52	7.83	7.34
800	71.18	26.67	17.90	9.74	8.95	8.39
900	80.07	30.01	20.14	10.95	10.07	9.44
1,000	88.97	33.34	22.38	12.17	11.19	10.48
2,000	177.94	66.67	44.75	24.33	22.38	20.96
3,000	266.90	100.01	67.12	36.49	33.56	31.44
4,000	355.87	133.34	89.49	48.66	44.75	41.92
5,000	444.83	166.67	111.86	60.82	55.93	52.40
6,000	533.80	200.01	134.23	72.98	67.12	62.88
7,000	622.77	233.34	156.60	85.15	78.30	73.36
8,000	711.73	266.68	178.97	97.31	89.49	83.84
9,000	800.70	300.01	201.34	109.47	100.68	94.32
10,000	889.66	333.34	223.71	121.63	111.86	104.79
15,000	1,334.49	500.01	335.57	182.45	167.79	157.19
20,000	1,779.32	666.68	447.42	243.26	223.72	209.58
25,000	2,224.15	833.35	559.28	304.08	279.65	261.98
30,000	2,668.98	1,000.02	671.13	364.89	335.57	314.37
35,000	3,113.81	1,166.69	782.99	425.71	391.50	366.77
45,000	4,003.47	1,500.03	1,006.70	547.34	503.36	471.56
55,000	4,893.12	1,833.37	1,230.41	668.97	615.22	576.35
65,000	5,782.78	2,166.70	1,454.12	790.60	727.07	681.14
75,000	6,672.44	2,500.04	1,677.83	912.23	838.93	785.93
85,000	7,562.10	2,833.38	1,901.54	1,033.86	950.78	890.72
100,000	8,896.58	3,333.39	2,237.10	1,216.30	1,118.57	1,047.90
120,000	10,675.90	4,000.07	2,684.52	1,459.56	1,342.28	1,257.48
140,000	12,455.21	4,666.74	3,131.94	1,702.82	1,566.00	1,467.06
160,000	14,234.53	5,333.42	3,579.36	1,946.08	1,789.71	1,676.64
180,000	16,013.85	6,000.10	4,026.78	2,189.34	2,013.42	1,886.22
200,000	17,793.16	6,666.77	4,474.20	2,432.60	2,237.13	2,095.80
225,000	20,017.31	7,500.12	5,033.48	2,736.68	2,516.78	2,357.77
250,000	22,241.45	8,333.47	5,592.75	3,040.75	2,796.42	2,619.75
275,000	24,465.60	9,166.81	6,152.03	3,344.83	3,076.06	2,881.72
300,000	26,689.74	10,000.16	6,711.30	3,648.90	3,355.70	3,143.69
350,000	31,138.03	11,666.85	7,829.85	4,257.05	3,914.98	3,667.64
400,000	35,586.32	13,333.54	8,948.40	4,865.20	4,474.26	4,191.59
450,000	40,034.61	15,000.23	10,066.95	5,473.35	5,033.55	4,715.54
500,000	44,482.90	16,666.93	11,185.50	6,081.50	5,592.83	5,239.49
550,000	48,931.19	18,333.62	12,304.05	6,689.65	6,152.11	5,763.44

12.50% 12.50%

MONTHLY LOAN PAYMENT TABLE

DOLLARS REQUIRED TO AMORTIZE LOAN

LOAN AMOUNT	TERM OF LOAN IN YEARS					
	1	3	5	15	20	30
50	4.46	1.68	1.13	0.62	0.57	0.54
100	8.91	3.35	2.25	1.24	1.14	1.07
200	17.82	6.70	4.50	2.47	2.28	2.14
300	26.73	10.04	6.75	3.70	3.41	3.21
400	35.64	13.39	9.00	4.94	4.55	4.27
500	44.55	16.73	11.25	6.17	5.69	5.34
600	53.45	20.08	13.50	7.40	6.82	6.41
700	62.36	23.42	15.75	8.63	7.96	7.48
800	71.27	26.77	18.00	9.87	9.09	8.54
900	80.18	30.11	20.25	11.10	10.23	9.61
1,000	89.09	33.46	22.50	12.33	11.37	10.68
2,000	178.17	66.91	45.00	24.66	22.73	21.35
3,000	267.25	100.37	67.50	36.98	34.09	32.02
4,000	356.34	133.82	90.00	49.31	45.45	42.70
5,000	445.42	167.27	112.49	61.63	56.81	53.37
6,000	534.50	200.73	134.99	73.96	68.17	64.04
7,000	623.59	234.18	157.49	86.28	79.53	74.71
8,000	712.67	267.63	179.99	98.61	90.90	85.39
9,000	801.75	301.09	202.49	110.93	102.26	96.06
10,000	890.83	334.54	224.98	123.26	113.62	106.73
15,000	1,336.25	501.81	337.47	184.88	170.43	160.09
20,000	1,781.66	669.08	449.96	246.51	227.23	213.46
25,000	2,227.08	836.35	562.45	308.14	284.04	266.82
30,000	2,672.49	1,003.61	674.94	369.76	340.85	320.18
35,000	3,117.91	1,170.88	787.43	431.39	397.65	373.55
45,000	4,008.73	1,505.42	1,012.41	554.64	511.27	480.27
55,000	4,899.56	1,839.95	1,237.39	677.89	624.88	587.00
65,000	5,790.39	2,174.49	1,462.37	801.14	738.50	693.72
75,000	6,681.22	2,509.03	1,687.35	924.40	852.11	800.45
85,000	7,572.05	2,843.56	1,912.33	1,047.65	965.72	907.17
100,000	8,908.29	3,345.37	2,249.80	1,232.53	1,136.15	1,067.26
120,000	10,689.95	4,014.44	2,699.76	1,479.03	1,363.37	1,280.71
140,000	12,471.61	4,683.51	3,149.72	1,725.54	1,590.60	1,494.17
160,000	14,253.26	5,352.59	3,599.68	1,972.04	1,817.83	1,707.62
180,000	16,034.92	6,021.66	4,049.63	2,218.54	2,045.06	1,921.07
200,000	17,816.58	6,690.73	4,499.59	2,465.05	2,272.29	2,134.52
225,000	20,043.65	7,527.07	5,062.04	2,773.18	2,556.32	2,401.33
250,000	22,270.72	8,363.41	5,624.49	3,081.31	2,840.36	2,668.15
275,000	24,497.79	9,199.75	6,186.94	3,389.44	3,124.39	2,934.96
300,000	26,724.86	10,036.09	6,749.39	3,697.57	3,408.43	3,201.78
350,000	31,179.01	11,708.77	7,874.28	4,313.83	3,976.50	3,735.41
400,000	35,633.15	13,381.46	8,999.18	4,930.09	4,544.57	4,269.04
450,000	40,087.29	15,054.14	10,124.08	5,546.35	5,112.64	4,802.66
500,000	44,541.44	16,726.82	11,248.97	6,162.62	5,680.71	5,336.29
550,000	48,995.58	18,399.50	12,373.87	6,778.88	6,248.78	5,869.92

12.75% 12.75%

MONTHLY LOAN PAYMENT TABLE

DOLLARS REQUIRED TO AMORTIZE LOAN

LOAN AMOUNT	TERM OF LOAN IN YEARS					
	1	3	5	15	20	30
50	4.47	1.68	1.14	0.63	0.58	0.55
100	8.93	3.36	2.27	1.25	1.16	1.09
200	17.85	6.72	4.53	2.50	2.31	2.18
300	26.77	10.08	6.79	3.75	3.47	3.27
400	35.69	13.43	9.06	5.00	4.62	4.35
500	44.61	16.79	11.32	6.25	5.77	5.44
600	53.53	20.15	13.58	7.50	6.93	6.53
700	62.45	23.51	15.84	8.75	8.08	7.61
800	71.37	26.86	18.11	10.00	9.24	8.70
900	80.29	30.22	20.37	11.24	10.39	9.79
1,000	89.21	33.58	22.63	12.49	11.54	10.87
2,000	178.41	67.15	45.26	24.98	23.08	21.74
3,000	267.61	100.73	67.88	37.47	34.62	32.61
4,000	356.81	134.30	90.51	49.96	46.16	43.47
5,000	446.01	167.87	113.13	62.45	57.70	54.34
6,000	535.21	201.45	135.76	74.94	69.23	65.21
7,000	624.41	235.02	158.38	87.42	80.77	76.07
8,000	713.61	268.59	181.01	99.91	92.31	86.94
9,000	802.81	302.17	203.63	112.40	103.85	97.81
10,000	892.01	335.74	226.26	124.89	115.39	108.67
15,000	1,338.01	503.61	339.38	187.33	173.08	163.01
20,000	1,784.01	671.48	452.51	249.77	230.77	217.34
25,000	2,230.01	839.35	565.64	312.21	288.46	271.68
30,000	2,676.01	1,007.21	678.76	374.66	346.15	326.01
35,000	3,122.01	1,175.08	791.89	437.10	403.84	380.35
45,000	4,014.01	1,510.82	1,018.14	561.98	519.22	489.02
55,000	4,906.01	1,846.56	1,244.40	686.87	634.60	597.69
65,000	5,798.01	2,182.29	1,470.65	811.75	749.98	706.36
75,000	6,690.01	2,518.03	1,696.90	936.63	865.36	815.02
85,000	7,582.01	2,853.77	1,923.16	1,061.52	980.74	923.69
100,000	8,920.01	3,357.37	2,262.54	1,248.84	1,153.82	1,086.70
120,000	10,704.01	4,028.84	2,715.04	1,498.61	1,384.58	1,304.04
140,000	12,488.01	4,700.32	3,167.55	1,748.38	1,615.34	1,521.38
160,000	14,272.01	5,371.79	3,620.05	1,998.14	1,846.10	1,738.71
180,000	16,056.01	6,043.26	4,072.56	2,247.91	2,076.87	1,956.05
200,000	17,840.01	6,714.74	4,525.07	2,497.68	2,307.63	2,173.39
225,000	20,070.01	7,554.08	5,090.70	2,809.89	2,596.08	2,445.06
250,000	22,300.01	8,393.42	5,656.33	3,122.10	2,884.53	2,716.74
275,000	24,530.01	9,232.76	6,221.96	3,434.31	3,172.99	2,988.41
300,000	26,760.01	10,072.10	6,787.60	3,746.52	3,461.44	3,260.08
350,000	31,220.01	11,750.79	7,918.86	4,370.93	4,038.35	3,803.43
400,000	35,680.02	13,429.47	9,050.13	4,995.35	4,615.25	4,346.78
450,000	40,140.02	15,108.15	10,181.39	5,619.77	5,192.16	4,890.12
500,000	44,600.02	16,786.84	11,312.66	6,244.19	5,769.06	5,433.47
550,000	49,060.02	18,465.52	12,443.92	6,868.61	6,345.97	5,976.82

13.00% 13.00%

MONTHLY LOAN PAYMENT TABLE

DOLLARS REQUIRED TO AMORTIZE LOAN

LOAN AMOUNT	TERM OF LOAN IN YEARS					
	1	3	5	15	20	30
50	4.47	1.69	1.14	0.64	0.59	0.56
100	8.94	3.37	2.28	1.27	1.18	1.11
200	17.87	6.74	4.56	2.54	2.35	2.22
300	26.80	10.11	6.83	3.80	3.52	3.32
400	35.73	13.48	9.11	5.07	4.69	4.43
500	44.66	16.85	11.38	6.33	5.86	5.54
600	53.60	20.22	13.66	7.60	7.03	6.64
700	62.53	23.59	15.93	8.86	8.21	7.75
800	71.46	26.96	18.21	10.13	9.38	8.85
900	80.39	30.33	20.48	11.39	10.55	9.96
1,000	89.32	33.70	22.76	12.66	11.72	11.07
2,000	178.64	67.39	45.51	25.31	23.44	22.13
3,000	267.96	101.09	68.26	37.96	35.15	33.19
4,000	357.27	134.78	91.02	50.61	46.87	44.25
5,000	446.59	168.47	113.77	63.27	58.58	55.31
6,000	535.91	202.17	136.52	75.92	70.30	66.38
7,000	625.23	235.86	159.28	88.57	82.02	77.44
8,000	714.54	269.56	182.03	101.22	93.73	88.50
9,000	803.86	303.25	204.78	113.88	105.45	99.56
10,000	893.18	336.94	227.54	126.53	117.16	110.62
15,000	1,339.76	505.41	341.30	189.79	175.74	165.93
20,000	1,786.35	673.88	455.07	253.05	234.32	221.24
25,000	2,232.94	842.35	568.83	316.32	292.90	276.55
30,000	2,679.52	1,010.82	682.60	379.58	351.48	331.86
35,000	3,126.11	1,179.29	796.36	442.84	410.06	387.17
45,000	4,019.28	1,516.23	1,023.89	569.36	527.21	497.79
55,000	4,912.46	1,853.17	1,251.42	695.89	644.37	608.41
65,000	5,805.63	2,190.11	1,478.95	822.41	761.53	719.03
75,000	6,698.80	2,527.05	1,706.49	948.94	878.69	829.65
85,000	7,591.97	2,863.99	1,934.02	1,075.46	995.84	940.27
100,000	8,931.73	3,369.40	2,275.31	1,265.25	1,171.58	1,106.20
120,000	10,718.08	4,043.28	2,730.37	1,518.30	1,405.90	1,327.44
140,000	12,504.42	4,717.16	3,185.44	1,771.34	1,640.21	1,548.68
160,000	14,290.77	5,391.04	3,640.50	2,024.39	1,874.53	1,769.92
180,000	16,077.11	6,064.92	4,095.56	2,277.44	2,108.84	1,991.16
200,000	17,863.46	6,738.80	4,550.62	2,530.49	2,343.16	2,212.40
225,000	20,096.39	7,581.14	5,119.45	2,846.80	2,636.05	2,488.95
250,000	22,329.32	8,423.49	5,688.27	3,163.11	2,928.94	2,765.50
275,000	24,562.26	9,265.84	6,257.10	3,479.42	3,221.84	3,042.05
300,000	26,795.19	10,108.19	6,825.93	3,795.73	3,514.73	3,318.60
350,000	31,261.05	11,792.89	7,963.58	4,428.35	4,100.52	3,871.70
400,000	35,726.92	13,477.59	9,101.23	5,060.97	4,686.31	4,424.80
450,000	40,192.78	15,162.28	10,238.89	5,693.59	5,272.10	4,977.90
500,000	44,658.64	16,846.98	11,376.54	6,326.22	5,857.88	5,531.00
550,000	49,124.51	18,531.68	12,514.20	6,958.84	6,443.67	6,084.10

13.25% 13.25%

MONTHLY LOAN PAYMENT TABLE

DOLLARS REQUIRED TO AMORTIZE LOAN

LOAN AMOUNT	TERM OF LOAN IN YEARS					
	1	3	5	15	20	30
50	4.48	1.70	1.15	0.65	0.60	0.57
100	8.95	3.39	2.29	1.29	1.19	1.13
200	17.89	6.77	4.58	2.57	2.38	2.26
300	26.84	10.15	6.87	3.85	3.57	3.38
400	35.78	13.53	9.16	5.13	4.76	4.51
500	44.72	16.91	11.45	6.41	5.95	5.63
600	53.67	20.29	13.73	7.70	7.14	6.76
700	62.61	23.68	16.02	8.98	8.33	7.89
800	71.55	27.06	18.31	10.26	9.52	9.01
900	80.50	30.44	20.60	11.54	10.71	10.14
1,000	89.44	33.82	22.89	12.82	11.90	11.26
2,000	178.87	67.63	45.77	25.64	23.79	22.52
3,000	268.31	101.45	68.65	38.46	35.69	33.78
4,000	357.74	135.26	91.53	51.27	47.58	45.04
5,000	447.18	169.08	114.41	64.09	59.40	56.29
6,000	536.61	202.89	137.29	76.91	71.37	67.55
7,000	626.05	236.71	160.17	89.73	83.27	78.81
8,000	715.48	270.52	183.06	102.54	95.16	90.07
9,000	804.92	304.34	205.94	115.36	107.05	101.32
10,000	894.35	338.15	228.02	128.18	118.95	112.58
15,000	1,341.52	507.22	343.22	192.27	178.42	168.87
20,000	1,788.70	676.29	457.63	256.35	237.89	225.16
25,000	2,235.87	845.37	572.04	320.44	297.36	281.45
30,000	2,683.04	1,014.44	686.44	384.53	356.83	337.74
35,000	3,130.22	1,183.51	800.85	448.61	416.31	394.03
45,000	4,024.56	1,521.66	1,029.66	576.79	535.25	506.60
55,000	4,918.91	1,859.80	1,258.47	704.96	654.19	619.18
65,000	5,813.25	2,197.95	1,487.29	833.13	773.13	731.76
75,000	6,707.60	2,536.09	1,716.10	961.31	892.08	844.34
85,000	7,601.95	2,874.24	1,944.91	1,089.48	1,011.02	956.91
100,000	8,943.47	3,381.45	2,288.13	1,281.74	1,189.44	1,125.78
120,000	10,732.16	4,057.74	2,745.76	1,538.09	1,427.32	1,350.93
140,000	12,520.85	4,734.03	3,203.38	1,794.44	1,665.21	1,576.09
160,000	14,309.54	5,410.32	3,661.01	2,050.78	1,903.09	1,801.24
180,000	16,098.23	6,086.61	4,118.63	2,307.13	2,140.98	2,026.40
200,000	17,886.93	6,762.90	4,576.26	2,563.48	2,378.87	2,251.55
225,000	20,122.79	7,608.27	5,148.29	2,883.91	2,676.22	2,533.00
250,000	22,358.66	8,453.63	5,720.32	3,204.35	2,973.58	2,814.44
275,000	24,594.52	9,298.99	6,292.35	3,524.78	3,270.94	3,095.88
300,000	26,830.39	10,144.35	6,864.38	3,845.21	3,568.30	3,377.33
350,000	31,302.12	11,835.08	8,008.44	4,486.08	4,163.01	3,940.21
400,000	35,773.85	13,525.80	9,152.51	5,126.95	4,757.73	4,503.10
450,000	40,245.58	15,216.53	10,296.57	5,767.82	5,352.44	5,065.99
500,000	44,717.31	16,907.25	11,440.63	6,408.69	5,947.16	5,628.87
550,000	49,189.04	18,597.98	12,584.70	7,049.56	6,541.87	6,191.76

13.50% 13.50%

MONTHLY LOAN PAYMENT TABLE

DOLLARS REQUIRED TO AMORTIZE LOAN

LOAN AMOUNT	TERM OF LOAN IN YEARS					
	1	3	5	15	20	30
50	4.48	1.70	1.16	0.65	0.61	0.58
100	8.96	3.40	2.31	1.30	1.21	1.15
200	17.92	6.79	4.61	2.60	2.42	2.30
300	26.87	10.19	6.91	3.90	3.63	3.44
400	35.83	13.58	9.21	5.20	4.83	4.59
500	44.78	16.97	11.51	6.50	6.04	5.73
600	53.74	20.37	13.81	7.79	7.25	6.88
700	62.69	23.76	16.11	9.09	8.46	8.02
800	71.65	27.15	18.41	10.39	9.66	9.17
900	80.60	30.55	20.71	11.69	10.87	10.31
1,000	89.56	33.94	23.01	12.99	12.08	11.46
2,000	179.11	67.88	46.02	25.97	24.15	22.91
3,000	268.66	101.81	69.03	38.95	36.23	34.37
4,000	358.21	135.75	92.04	51.94	48.30	45.82
5,000	447.77	169.68	115.05	64.92	60.37	57.28
6,000	537.32	203.62	138.06	77.90	72.45	68.73
7,000	626.87	237.55	161.07	90.89	84.52	80.18
8,000	716.42	271.49	184.08	103.87	96.59	91.64
9,000	805.97	305.42	207.09	116.85	108.67	103.09
10,000	895.53	339.36	230.10	129.84	120.74	114.55
15,000	1,343.29	509.03	345.15	194.75	181.11	171.82
20,000	1,791.05	678.71	460.20	259.67	241.48	229.09
25,000	2,238.81	848.39	575.25	324.58	301.85	286.36
30,000	2,686.57	1,018.06	690.30	389.50	362.22	343.63
35,000	3,134.33	1,187.74	805.35	454.42	422.59	400.90
45,000	4,029.85	1,527.09	1,035.45	584.25	543.32	515.44
55,000	4,925.37	1,866.45	1,265.55	714.08	664.06	629.98
65,000	5,820.89	2,205.80	1,495.64	843.91	784.80	744.52
75,000	6,716.41	2,545.15	1,725.74	973.74	905.54	859.06
85,000	7,611.93	2,884.50	1,955.84	1,103.58	1,026.27	973.61
100,000	8,955.21	3,393.53	2,300.99	1,298.32	1,207.38	1,145.42
120,000	10,746.25	4,072.24	2,761.19	1,557.99	1,448.85	1,374.50
140,000	12,537.29	4,750.95	3,221.38	1,817.65	1,690.33	1,603.58
160,000	14,328.33	5,429.65	3,681.58	2,077.31	1,931.80	1,832.66
180,000	16,119.37	6,108.36	4,141.78	2,336.98	2,173.28	2,061.75
200,000	17,910.41	6,787.06	4,601.97	2,596.64	2,414.75	2,290.83
225,000	20,149.21	7,635.44	5,177.22	2,921.22	2,716.60	2,577.18
250,000	22,388.01	8,483.83	5,752.47	3,245.80	3,018.44	2,863.54
275,000	24,626.81	9,332.21	6,327.71	3,570.38	3,320.29	3,149.89
300,000	26,865.61	10,180.59	6,902.96	3,894.96	3,622.13	3,436.24
350,000	31,343.21	11,877.36	8,053.45	4,544.12	4,225.82	4,008.95
400,000	35,820.82	13,574.12	9,203.94	5,193.28	4,829.50	4,581.65
450,000	40,298.42	15,270.88	10,354.44	5,842.44	5,433.19	5,154.36
500,000	44,776.02	16,967.65	11,504.93	6,491.60	6,036.88	5,727.07
550,000	49,253.62	18,664.41	12,655.42	7,140.76	6,640.57	6,299.77

MONTHLY LOAN PAYMENT TABLE

DOLLARS REQUIRED TO AMORTIZE LOAN

LOAN AMOUNT	TERM OF LOAN IN YEARS					
	1	3	5	15	20	30
50	4.49	1.71	1.16	0.66	0.62	0.59
100	8.97	3.41	2.32	1.32	1.23	1.17
200	17.94	6.82	4.63	2.63	2.46	2.34
300	26.91	10.22	6.95	3.95	3.68	3.50
400	35.87	13.63	9.26	5.26	4.91	4.67
500	44.84	17.03	11.57	6.58	6.13	5.83
600	53.81	20.44	13.89	7.89	7.36	7.00
700	62.77	23.84	16.20	9.21	8.58	8.16
800	71.74	27.25	18.52	10.52	9.81	9.33
900	80.71	30.66	20.83	11.84	11.03	10.49
1,000	89.67	34.06	23.14	13.15	12.26	11.66
2,000	179.34	68.12	46.28	26.30	24.51	23.31
3,000	269.01	102.17	69.42	39.45	36.77	34.96
4,000	358.68	136.23	92.56	52.60	49.02	46.61
5,000	448.35	170.29	115.70	65.75	61.28	58.26
6,000	538.02	204.34	138.84	78.90	73.53	69.91
7,000	627.69	238.40	161.98	92.05	85.78	81.56
8,000	717.36	272.46	185.12	105.20	98.04	93.21
9,000	807.03	306.51	208.25	118.35	110.29	104.87
10,000	896.70	340.57	231.39	131.50	122.55	116.52
15,000	1,345.05	510.85	347.09	197.25	183.82	174.77
20,000	1,793.40	681.13	462.78	263.00	245.09	233.03
25,000	2,241.74	851.41	578.48	328.75	306.36	291.28
30,000	2,690.09	1,021.69	694.17	394.50	367.63	349.54
35,000	3,138.44	1,191.98	809.86	460.25	428.90	407.79
45,000	4,035.13	1,532.54	1,041.25	591.75	551.44	524.31
55,000	4,931.83	1,873.10	1,272.64	723.25	673.98	640.82
65,000	5,828.52	2,213.67	1,504.03	854.75	796.52	757.33
75,000	6,725.22	2,554.23	1,735.42	986.25	919.06	873.84
85,000	7,621.92	2,894.79	1,966.81	1,117.74	1,041.60	990.35
100,000	8,966.96	3,405.64	2,313.89	1,314.99	1,225.41	1,165.12
120,000	10,760.35	4,086.76	2,776.67	1,577.99	1,470.49	1,398.14
140,000	12,553.74	4,767.89	3,239.44	1,840.99	1,715.57	1,631.16
160,000	14,347.13	5,449.02	3,702.22	2,103.98	1,960.65	1,864.19
180,000	16,140.52	6,130.14	4,165.00	2,366.98	2,205.73	2,097.21
200,000	17,933.91	6,811.27	4,627.77	2,629.98	2,450.82	2,330.23
225,000	20,175.65	7,662.68	5,206.25	2,958.73	2,757.17	2,621.51
250,000	22,417.39	8,514.09	5,784.72	3,287.47	3,063.52	2,912.79
275,000	24,659.13	9,365.50	6,363.19	3,616.22	3,369.87	3,204.06
300,000	26,900.86	10,216.90	6,941.66	3,944.97	3,676.22	3,495.34
350,000	31,384.34	11,919.72	8,098.60	4,602.46	4,288.92	4,077.90
400,000	35,867.82	13,622.54	9,255.54	5,259.95	4,901.63	4,660.46
450,000	40,351.29	15,325.35	10,412.49	5,917.45	5,514.33	5,243.01
500,000	44,834.77	17,028.17	11,569.43	6,574.94	6,127.03	5,825.57
550,000	49,318.25	18,730.99	12,726.37	7,232.43	6,739.73	6,408.12

14.00% 14.00%

MONTHLY LOAN PAYMENT TABLE

DOLLARS REQUIRED TO AMORTIZE LOAN

LOAN AMOUNT	TERM OF LOAN IN YEARS					
	1	3	5	15	20	30
50	4.49	1.71	1.17	0.67	0.63	0.60
100	8.98	3.42	2.33	1.34	1.25	1.19
200	17.96	6.84	4.66	2.67	2.49	2.37
300	26.94	10.26	6.99	4.00	3.74	3.56
400	35.92	13.68	9.31	5.33	4.98	4.74
500	44.90	17.09	11.64	6.66	6.22	5.93
600	53.88	20.51	13.97	8.00	7.47	7.11
700	62.86	23.93	16.29	9.33	8.71	8.30
800	71.83	27.35	18.62	10.66	9.95	9.48
900	80.81	30.76	20.95	11.99	11.20	10.67
1,000	89.79	34.18	23.27	13.32	12.44	11.85
2,000	179.58	68.36	46.54	26.64	24.88	23.70
3,000	269.37	102.54	69.81	39.96	37.31	35.55
4,000	359.15	136.72	93.08	53.27	49.75	47.40
5,000	448.94	170.89	116.35	66.59	62.18	59.25
6,000	538.73	205.07	139.61	79.91	74.62	71.10
7,000	628.51	239.25	162.88	93.23	87.05	82.95
8,000	718.30	273.43	186.15	106.54	99.49	94.79
9,000	808.09	307.60	209.42	119.86	111.92	106.64
10,000	897.88	341.78	232.69	133.18	124.36	118.49
15,000	1,346.81	512.67	349.03	199.77	186.53	177.74
20,000	1,795.75	683.56	465.37	266.35	248.71	236.98
25,000	2,244.68	854.45	581.71	332.94	310.89	296.22
30,000	2,693.62	1,025.33	698.05	399.53	373.06	355.47
35,000	3,142.55	1,196.22	814.39	466.11	435.24	414.71
45,000	4,040.43	1,538.00	1,047.08	599.29	559.59	533.20
55,000	4,938.30	1,879.77	1,279.76	732.46	683.94	651.68
65,000	5,836.17	2,221.55	1,512.44	865.64	808.29	770.17
75,000	6,734.04	2,563.33	1,745.12	998.81	932.65	888.66
85,000	7,631.91	2,905.10	1,977.81	1,131.99	1,057.00	1,007.15
100,000	8,978.72	3,417.77	2,326.83	1,331.75	1,243.53	1,184.88
120,000	10,774.46	4,101.32	2,792.20	1,598.09	1,492.23	1,421.85
140,000	12,570.20	4,784.87	3,257.56	1,864.44	1,740.93	1,658.83
160,000	14,365.94	5,468.43	3,722.93	2,130.79	1,989.64	1,895.80
180,000	16,161.69	6,151.98	4,188.29	2,397.14	2,238.34	2,132.77
200,000	17,957.43	6,835.53	4,653.66	2,663.49	2,487.05	2,369.75
225,000	20,202.11	7,689.97	5,235.36	2,996.42	2,797.93	2,665.97
250,000	22,446.78	8,544.41	5,817.07	3,329.36	3,108.81	2,962.18
275,000	24,691.46	9,398.85	6,398.77	3,662.29	3,419.69	3,258.40
300,000	26,936.14	10,253.29	6,980.48	3,995.23	3,730.57	3,554.62
350,000	31,425.50	11,962.18	8,143.89	4,661.10	4,352.33	4,147.06
400,000	35,914.85	13,671.06	9,307.31	5,326.97	4,974.09	4,739.49
450,000	40,404.21	15,379.94	10,470.72	5,992.84	5,595.85	5,331.93
500,000	44,893.56	17,088.82	11,634.13	6,658.71	6,217.61	5,924.36
550,000	49,382.92	18,797.70	12,797.54	7,324.58	6,839.37	6,516.80

MONTHLY LOAN PAYMENT TABLE

DOLLARS REQUIRED TO AMORTIZE LOAN

LOAN AMOUNT	TERM OF LOAN IN YEARS					
	1	3	5	15	20	30
50	4.50	1.72	1.17	0.68	0.64	0.61
100	9.00	3.43	2.34	1.35	1.27	1.21
200	17.99	6.86	4.68	2.70	2.53	2.41
300	26.98	10.29	7.02	4.05	3.79	3.62
400	35.97	13.72	9.36	5.40	5.05	4.82
500	44.96	17.15	11.70	6.75	6.31	6.03
600	53.95	20.58	14.04	8.10	7.58	7.23
700	62.94	24.01	16.38	9.45	8.84	8.44
800	71.93	27.44	18.72	10.79	10.10	9.64
900	80.92	30.87	21.06	12.14	11.36	10.85
1,000	89.91	34.30	23.40	13.49	12.62	12.05
2,000	179.81	68.60	46.80	26.98	25.24	24.10
3,000	269.72	102.90	70.20	40.46	37.86	36.15
4,000	359.62	137.20	93.60	53.95	50.47	48.19
5,000	449.53	171.50	117.00	67.43	63.09	60.24
6,000	539.43	205.80	140.39	80.92	75.71	72.29
7,000	629.34	240.10	163.79	94.41	88.33	84.33
8,000	719.24	274.40	187.19	107.89	100.94	96.38
9,000	809.15	308.70	210.59	121.38	113.56	108.43
10,000	899.05	343.00	233.99	134.86	126.18	120.47
15,000	1,348.58	514.49	350.98	202.29	189.26	180.71
20,000	1,798.10	685.99	467.97	269.72	252.35	240.94
25,000	2,247.62	857.48	584.96	337.15	315.43	301.18
30,000	2,697.15	1,028.98	701.95	404.58	378.52	361.41
35,000	3,146.67	1,200.48	818.94	472.01	441.61	421.65
45,000	4,045.72	1,543.47	1,052.92	606.87	567.78	542.11
55,000	4,944.77	1,886.46	1,286.90	741.72	693.95	662.58
65,000	5,843.82	2,229.45	1,520.88	876.58	820.12	783.05
75,000	6,742.86	2,572.44	1,754.86	1,011.44	946.29	903.52
85,000	7,641.91	2,915.44	1,988.84	1,146.30	1,072.47	1,023.99
100,000	8,990.48	3,429.92	2,339.81	1,348.58	1,261.72	1,204.69
120,000	10,788.58	4,115.91	2,807.77	1,618.30	1,514.07	1,445.63
140,000	12,586.68	4,801.89	3,275.73	1,888.02	1,766.41	1,686.57
160,000	14,384.77	5,487.87	3,743.70	2,157.73	2,018.76	1,927.50
180,000	16,182.87	6,173.86	4,211.66	2,427.45	2,271.10	2,168.44
200,000	17,980.96	6,859.84	4,679.62	2,697.16	2,523.44	2,409.38
225,000	20,228.58	7,717.32	5,264.57	3,034.31	2,838.87	2,710.55
250,000	22,476.20	8,574.80	5,849.52	3,371.45	3,154.30	3,011.72
275,000	24,723.82	9,432.28	6,434.47	3,708.60	3,469.73	3,312.89
300,000	26,971.44	10,289.76	7,019.42	4,045.74	3,785.16	3,614.07
350,000	31,466.68	12,004.72	8,189.33	4,720.03	4,416.02	4,216.41
400,000	35,961.92	13,719.68	9,359.23	5,394.32	5,046.88	4,818.75
450,000	40,457.16	15,434.64	10,529.13	6,068.61	5,677.74	5,421.10
500,000	44,952.40	17,149.59	11,699.04	6,742.90	6,308.60	6,023.44
550,000	49,447.64	18,864.55	12,868.94	7,417.19	6,939.46	6,625.78

14.50% 14.50%

MONTHLY LOAN PAYMENT TABLE

DOLLARS REQUIRED TO AMORTIZE LOAN

LOAN AMOUNT	TERM OF LOAN IN YEARS					
	1	3	5	15	20	30
50	4.51	1.73	1.18	0.69	0.64	0.62
100	9.01	3.45	2.36	1.37	1.28	1.23
200	18.01	6.89	4.71	2.74	2.56	2.45
300	27.01	10.33	7.06	4.10	3.84	3.68
400	36.01	13.77	9.42	5.47	5.12	4.90
500	45.02	17.22	11.77	6.83	6.40	6.13
600	54.02	20.66	14.12	8.20	7.68	7.35
700	63.02	24.10	16.47	9.56	8.96	8.58
800	72.02	27.54	18.83	10.93	10.24	9.80
900	81.03	30.98	21.18	12.29	11.52	11.03
1,000	90.03	34.43	23.53	13.66	12.80	12.25
2,000	180.05	68.85	47.06	27.32	25.60	24.50
3,000	270.07	103.27	70.59	40.97	38.40	36.74
4,000	360.10	137.69	94.12	54.63	51.20	48.99
5,000	450.12	172.11	117.65	68.28	64.00	61.23
6,000	540.14	206.53	141.17	81.94	76.80	73.48
7,000	630.16	240.95	164.70	95.59	89.60	85.72
8,000	720.19	275.37	188.23	109.25	102.40	97.97
9,000	810.21	309.79	211.76	122.90	115.20	110.22
10,000	900.23	344.21	235.29	136.56	128.00	122.46
15,000	1,350.34	516.32	352.93	204.83	192.00	183.69
20,000	1,800.46	688.42	470.57	273.11	256.00	244.92
25,000	2,250.57	860.53	588.21	341.38	320.00	306.14
30,000	2,700.68	1,032.63	705.85	409.66	384.00	367.37
35,000	3,150.79	1,204.74	823.49	477.93	448.00	428.60
45,000	4,051.02	1,548.95	1,058.78	614.48	576.00	551.06
55,000	4,951.25	1,893.16	1,294.06	751.03	704.00	673.51
65,000	5,851.47	2,237.37	1,529.34	887.58	832.00	795.97
75,000	6,751.70	2,581.58	1,764.63	1,024.13	960.00	918.42
85,000	7,651.92	2,925.79	1,999.91	1,160.68	1,088.00	1,040.88
100,000	9,002.26	3,442.10	2,352.83	1,365.51	1,280.00	1,224.56
120,000	10,802.71	4,130.52	2,823.40	1,638.61	1,536.00	1,469.47
140,000	12,603.16	4,818.94	3,293.96	1,911.71	1,792.00	1,714.38
160,000	14,403.61	5,507.36	3,764.53	2,184.81	2,048.00	1,959.29
180,000	16,204.06	6,195.78	4,235.10	2,457.91	2,304.00	2,204.21
200,000	18,004.51	6,884.20	4,705.66	2,731.01	2,560.00	2,449.12
225,000	20,255.08	7,744.72	5,293.87	3,072.38	2,880.00	2,755.26
250,000	22,505.64	8,605.25	5,882.08	3,413.76	3,200.00	3,061.39
275,000	24,756.21	9,465.77	6,470.28	3,755.13	3,520.00	3,367.53
300,000	27,006.77	10,326.30	7,058.49	4,096.51	3,840.00	3,673.67
350,000	31,507.90	12,047.35	8,234.90	4,779.26	4,480.00	4,285.95
400,000	36,009.02	13,768.40	9,411.32	5,462.01	5,120.00	4,898.23
450,000	40,510.15	15,489.44	10,587.73	6,144.76	5,759.99	5,510.51
500,000	45,011.28	17,210.49	11,764.15	6,827.51	6,399.99	6,122.78
550,000	49,512.41	18,931.54	12,940.56	7,510.26	7,039.99	6,735.06

14.75% 14.75%

MONTHLY LOAN PAYMENT TABLE

DOLLARS REQUIRED TO AMORTIZE LOAN

LOAN AMOUNT	TERM OF LOAN IN YEARS					
	1	3	5	15	20	30
50	4.51	1.73	1.19	0.70	0.65	0.63
100	9.02	3.46	2.37	1.39	1.30	1.25
200	18.03	6.91	4.74	2.77	2.60	2.49
300	27.05	10.37	7.10	4.15	3.90	3.74
400	36.06	13.82	9.47	5.54	5.20	4.98
500	45.08	17.28	11.83	6.92	6.50	6.23
600	54.09	20.73	14.20	8.30	7.80	7.47
700	63.10	24.19	16.57	9.68	9.09	8.72
800	72.12	27.64	18.93	11.07	10.39	9.96
900	81.13	31.09	21.30	12.45	11.69	11.21
1,000	90.15	34.55	23.66	13.83	12.99	12.45
2,000	180.29	69.09	47.32	27.66	25.97	24.89
3,000	270.43	103.63	70.98	41.48	38.96	37.34
4,000	360.57	138.18	94.64	55.31	51.94	49.78
5,000	450.71	172.72	118.30	69.13	64.92	62.23
6,000	540.85	207.26	141.96	82.96	77.91	74.67
7,000	630.99	241.81	165.62	96.78	90.89	87.12
8,000	721.13	276.35	189.28	110.61	103.87	99.56
9,000	811.27	310.89	212.94	124.43	116.86	112.01
10,000	901.41	345.44	236.59	138.26	129.84	124.45
15,000	1,352.11	518.16	354.89	207.38	194.76	186.68
20,000	1,802.81	690.87	473.18	276.51	259.68	248.90
25,000	2,253.51	863.58	591.48	345.63	324.59	311.12
30,000	2,704.22	1,036.30	709.77	414.76	389.51	373.35
35,000	3,154.92	1,209.01	828.07	483.88	454.43	435.57
45,000	4,056.32	1,554.44	1,064.66	622.13	584.26	560.02
55,000	4,957.73	1,899.87	1,301.24	760.38	714.10	684.47
65,000	5,859.13	2,245.30	1,537.83	898.63	843.94	808.91
75,000	6,760.53	2,590.73	1,774.42	1,036.88	973.77	933.36
85,000	7,661.94	2,936.16	2,011.01	1,175.13	1,103.61	1,057.81
100,000	9,014.04	3,454.31	2,365.90	1,382.51	1,298.36	1,244.48
120,000	10,816.85	4,145.17	2,839.07	1,659.01	1,558.03	1,493.38
140,000	12,619.66	4,836.03	3,312.25	1,935.51	1,817.70	1,742.27
160,000	14,422.47	5,526.89	3,785.43	2,212.01	2,077.37	1,991.17
180,000	16,225.27	6,217.75	4,258.61	2,488.51	2,337.04	2,240.06
200,000	18,028.08	6,908.61	4,731.79	2,765.01	2,596.72	2,488.96
225,000	20,281.59	7,772.19	5,323.26	3,110.64	2,921.30	2,800.08
250,000	22,535.10	8,635.76	5,914.73	3,456.26	3,245.89	3,111.19
275,000	24,788.61	9,499.34	6,506.20	3,801.89	3,570.48	3,422.31
300,000	27,042.12	10,362.91	7,097.68	4,147.52	3,895.07	3,733.43
350,000	31,549.14	12,090.06	8,280.62	4,838.77	4,544.25	4,355.67
400,000	36,056.16	13,817.22	9,463.57	5,530.02	5,193.43	4,977.91
450,000	40,563.18	15,544.37	10,646.51	6,221.27	5,842.60	5,600.15
500,000	45,070.20	17,271.52	11,829.46	6,912.52	6,491.78	6,222.38
550,000	49,577.22	18,998.67	13,012.40	7,603.78	7,140.96	6,844.62

BI-WEEKLY PAYMENT TABLE

TYPICAL 30 YEAR LOAN COMPARED TO A BI-WEEKLY

LOAN AMOUNT	MONTHLY PAYMENT	TOTAL INTEREST	BI-WKLY PAYMENT	TERM YR/WK	INTEREST SAVED	YR/WK SAVED
50	0.44	106.15	0.22	20/44	37.04	9/08
100	0.88	211.51	0.44	20/40	74.11	9/12
200	1.76	423.11	0.88	20/40	147.86	9/12
300	2.64	634.34	1.32	20/40	221.71	9/12
400	3.52	845.98	1.76	20/40	295.83	9/12
500	4.39	1,075.72	2.20	20/40	388.05	9/12
600	5.27	1,287.18	2.64	20/40	461.68	9/12
700	6.15	1,497.65	3.08	20/40	534.83	9/12
800	7.03	1,710.05	3.52	20/40	609.50	9/12
900	7.90	1,939.71	3.95	20/50	689.28	9/02
1,000	8.78	2,151.04	4.39	20/48	762.94	9/04
2,000	17.56	4,302.17	8.78	20/50	1,525.23	9/02
3,000	26.33	6,473.18	13.17	20/50	2,308.50	9/02
4,000	35.11	8,623.13	17.56	20/50	3,070.41	9/02
5,000	43.88	10,793.87	21.94	20/50	3,839.34	9/02
6,000	52.66	12,944.63	26.33	20/50	4,602.25	9/02
7,000	61.44	15,095.87	30.72	20/50	5,364.60	9/02
8,000	70.21	17,266.16	35.11	20/50	6,146.77	9/02
9,000	78.99	19,417.99	39.50	20/50	6,910.04	9/02
10,000	87.76	21,587.63	43.88	20/50	7,678.52	9/02
15,000	131.64	32,380.73	65.82	20/50	11,516.85	9/02
20,000	175.52	43,173.79	87.76	20/50	15,355.62	9/02
25,000	219.40	53,968.35	109.70	20/50	19,195.77	9/02
30,000	263.28	64,761.40	131.64	20/50	23,034.20	9/02
35,000	307.16	75,556.32	153.58	20/50	26,874.76	9/02
45,000	394.91	97,161.06	197.46	20/50	34,570.24	9/02
55,000	482.67	118,748.77	241.34	20/50	42,249.36	9/02
65,000	570.43	140,336.06	285.22	20/50	49,926.93	9/02
75,000	658.18	161,941.57	329.09	20/50	57,611.03	9/02
85,000	745.94	183,529.16	372.97	20/50	65,289.44	9/02
100,000	877.58	215,909.34	438.79	20/50	76,805.96	9/02
120,000	1,053.09	259,102.77	526.55	20/50	92,180.97	9/02
140,000	1,228.61	302,277.09	614.31	20/50	107,537.41	9/02
160,000	1,404.12	345,470.91	702.06	20/50	122,899.93	9/02
180,000	1,579.63	388,663.44	789.82	20/50	138,274.51	9/02
200,000	1,755.15	431,838.23	877.58	20/50	153,631.14	9/02
225,000	1,974.54	485,826.00	987.27	20/50	172,833.42	9/02
250,000	2,193.93	539,812.00	1,096.97	20/50	192,046.70	9/02
275,000	2,413.33	593,780.77	1,206.67	20/50	211,242.36	9/02
300,000	2,632.72	647,767.27	1,316.36	20/50	230,443.09	9/02
350,000	3,071.51	755,722.30	1,535.76	20/50	268,853.87	9/02
400,000	3,510.29	863,695.39	1,755.15	20/50	307,267.93	9/02
450,000	3,949.08	971,650.18	1,974.54	20/50	345,664.46	9/02
500,000	4,387.86	1,079,625.42	2,193.93	20/50	384,081.35	9/02
550,000	4,826.65	1,187,579.43	2,413.33	20/50	422,491.06	9/02

BI-WEEKLY PAYMENT TABLES

INSTRUCTIONS

While we've repeatedly cautioned you against "pseudo bi-weeklies," real bi-weekly loans are available and do work. These tables will let you see at a glance how much money a bi-weekly loan will save you compared to an equivalent monthly mortgage that is not pre-paid at all.

Here's how to proceed: Let's say you're shopping for a $75,000 loan and have your choice of borrowing $75,000 at 10% for a 30 year term, repayable monthly, or of borrowing that same amount at the same rate, repayable bi-weekly.

- Turn to the table that has 10.00% at both the upper left and the upper right hand corners. (Reproduced on the preceding page for your convenience.)
- Look down the left hand column (*Loan Amount*) until you see $75,000.
- Reading across towards the right, you'll come to the *Monthly Payment* and *Total Interest* columns.
- Here you'll find that a regular monthly payment of $658.18 would retire this loan in 30 years (all of these tables are designed for 30 year loans) at a total cost of $161,941.57 in interest charges.
- Continuing across to the right, you'll next come to the *Bi-Weekly Payment* column, followed by the *Term (Yr/Wk)*, *Interest Saved*, and *Yr/Wk Saved* columns.
- Under these columns, you'll find that a bi-weekly payment of $329.09 (half the monthly payment), would pay this loan off in 20 years/50 weeks -- saving you $57,611.03 in interest and 9 years/2 weeks -- compared to a monthly loan that is not pre-paid at all.

Remember that you can obtain virtually the equivalent of bi-weekly savings by pre-paying on your own. To determine what advance you should send in, divide your monthly payment by 12, and add that amount to each of your regularly scheduled monthly payments. In the above example, that would mean a *Regular* pre-payment of $54.85 ($658.18 ÷ 12), which would save $57,210.71 and 8 years/11 months. **As always, the more you pre-pay, the more you'll save.**

7.00% 7.00%

BI-WEEKLY PAYMENT TABLE

TYPICAL 30 YEAR LOAN COMPARED TO A BI-WEEKLY

LOAN AMOUNT	MONTHLY PAYMENT	TOTAL INTEREST	BI-WKLY PAYMENT	TERM YR/WK	INTEREST SAVED	YR/WK SAVED
50	0.34	64.15	0.17	22/22	15.09	7/30
100	0.67	135.66	0.34	22/26	37.00	7/26
200	1.34	271.35	0.67	23/16	65.64	6/36
300	2.00	415.32	1.00	23/32	102.01	6/20
400	2.67	550.55	1.34	23/16	139.28	6/36
500	3.33	694.42	1.67	23/26	175.59	6/26
600	4.00	830.05	2.00	23/32	203.72	6/20
700	4.66	974.15	2.33	23/36	240.28	6/16
800	5.33	1,109.74	2.67	23/28	277.78	6/24
900	5.99	1,253.57	3.00	23/32	314.01	6/20
1,000	6.66	1,388.90	3.33	23/34	341.80	6/18
2,000	13.31	2,786.95	6.66	23/34	692.67	6/18
3,000	19.96	4,184.42	9.98	23/38	1,033.41	6/14
4,000	26.62	5,573.59	13.31	23/36	1,375.56	6/16
5,000	33.27	6,970.97	16.64	23/36	1,726.47	6/16
6,000	39.92	8,369.02	19.96	23/38	2,067.38	6/14
7,000	46.58	9,758.16	23.29	23/38	2,409.46	6/14
8,000	53.23	11,155.63	26.62	23/36	2,759.50	6/16
9,000	59.88	12,553.63	29.94	23/38	3,100.50	6/14
10,000	66.54	13,942.56	33.27	23/38	3,442.53	6/14
15,000	99.80	20,922.13	49.90	23/38	5,167.25	6/14
20,000	133.07	27,893.87	66.54	23/38	6,894.56	6/14
25,000	166.33	34,873.31	83.17	23/38	8,618.59	6/14
30,000	199.60	41,845.14	99.80	23/38	10,335.67	6/14
35,000	232.86	48,824.63	116.43	23/38	12,060.56	6/14
45,000	299.39	62,775.57	149.70	23/38	15,511.20	6/14
55,000	365.92	76,726.65	182.96	23/38	18,952.84	6/14
65,000	432.45	90,678.26	216.23	23/38	22,404.82	6/14
75,000	498.98	104,628.89	249.49	23/38	25,845.52	6/14
85,000	565.51	118,580.49	282.76	23/38	29,297.29	6/14
100,000	665.31	139,502.20	332.66	23/38	34,464.71	6/14
120,000	798.37	167,404.66	399.19	23/38	41,357.32	6/14
140,000	931.43	195,306.89	465.72	23/38	48,250.53	6/14
160,000	1,064.49	223,208.98	532.25	23/38	55,142.82	6/14
180,000	1,197.55	251,111.15	598.78	23/38	62,035.09	6/14
200,000	1,330.61	279,013.30	665.31	23/38	68,928.48	6/14
225,000	1,496.94	313,886.95	748.47	23/38	77,537.04	6/14
250,000	1,663.26	348,769.07	831.63	23/38	86,155.31	6/14
275,000	1,829.59	383,642.09	914.80	23/38	94,773.64	6/14
300,000	1,995.91	418,524.05	997.96	23/38	103,391.47	6/14
350,000	2,328.56	488,279.73	1,164.28	23/38	120,618.76	6/14
400,000	2,661.21	558,035.91	1,330.61	23/38	137,855.53	6/14
450,000	2,993.87	627,782.70	1,496.94	23/38	155,083.80	6/14
500,000	3,326.52	697,538.22	1,663.26	23/38	172,310.54	6/14
550,000	3,659.17	767,293.35	1,829.59	23/38	189,546.34	6/14

7.25% 7.25%

BI-WEEKLY PAYMENT TABLE

TYPICAL 30 YEAR LOAN COMPARED TO A BI-WEEKLY

LOAN AMOUNT	MONTHLY PAYMENT	TOTAL INTEREST	BI-WKLY PAYMENT	TERM YR/WK	INTEREST SAVED	YR/WK SAVED
50	0.35	65.69	0.18	20/34	19.09	9/18
100	0.69	138.77	0.35	22/02	38.35	7/50
200	1.37	286.16	0.69	22/44	76.84	7/08
300	2.05	433.54	1.03	23/06	114.94	6/46
400	2.73	581.09	1.37	23/14	153.19	6/38
500	3.42	719.65	1.71	23/18	182.22	6/34
600	4.10	867.22	2.05	23/22	220.49	6/30
700	4.78	1,014.77	2.39	23/24	258.61	6/28
800	5.46	1,162.41	2.73	23/26	296.62	6/26
900	6.14	1,309.92	3.07	23/26	334.73	6/26
1,000	6.83	1,448.25	3.42	23/18	373.49	6/34
2,000	13.65	2,905.80	6.83	23/22	746.41	6/30
3,000	20.47	4,362.84	10.24	23/24	1,119.38	6/28
4,000	27.29	5,820.31	13.65	23/26	1,492.23	6/26
5,000	34.11	7,278.27	17.06	23/26	1,865.11	6/26
6,000	40.94	8,726.34	20.47	23/26	2,228.46	6/26
7,000	47.76	10,183.67	23.88	23/26	2,601.22	6/26
8,000	54.58	11,641.57	27.29	23/26	2,975.07	6/26
9,000	61.40	13,098.54	30.70	23/26	3,346.90	6/26
10,000	68.22	14,556.05	34.11	23/26	3,720.63	6/26
15,000	102.33	21,834.36	51.17	23/26	5,585.52	6/26
20,000	136.44	29,112.16	68.22	23/26	7,440.07	6/26
25,000	170.55	36,390.83	85.28	23/26	9,305.78	6/26
30,000	204.66	43,668.78	102.33	23/26	11,160.87	6/26
35,000	238.77	50,946.47	119.39	23/26	13,025.43	6/26
45,000	306.98	65,511.59	153.49	23/26	16,744.29	6/26
55,000	375.20	80,068.30	187.60	23/26	20,465.37	6/26
65,000	443.42	94,624.21	221.71	23/26	24,185.42	6/26
75,000	511.64	109,180.72	255.82	23/26	27,905.42	6/26
85,000	579.85	123,745.79	289.93	23/26	31,634.59	6/26
100,000	682.18	145,580.04	341.09	23/26	37,210.03	6/26
120,000	818.62	174,692.22	409.31	23/26	44,649.64	6/26
140,000	955.05	203,814.02	477.53	23/26	52,100.12	6/26
160,000	1,091.49	232,925.84	545.75	23/26	59,539.38	6/26
180,000	1,227.92	262,047.80	613.96	23/26	66,979.45	6/26
200,000	1,364.36	291,159.91	682.18	23/26	74,419.44	6/26
225,000	1,534.90	327,560.03	767.45	23/26	83,724.46	6/26
250,000	1,705.45	363,950.38	852.73	23/26	93,029.48	6/26
275,000	1,875.99	400,349.72	938.00	23/26	102,334.08	6/26
300,000	2,046.53	436,749.23	1,023.27	23/26	111,638.60	6/26
350,000	2,387.62	509,539.14	1,193.81	23/26	130,238.26	6/26
400,000	2,728.71	582,329.20	1,364.36	23/26	148,848.43	6/26
450,000	3,069.80	655,119.42	1,534.90	23/26	167,448.44	6/26
500,000	3,410.89	727,909.32	1,705.45	23/26	186,058.54	6/26
550,000	3,751.97	800,708.85	1,875.99	23/26	204,667.60	6/26

7.50% 7.50%

BI-WEEKLY PAYMENT TABLE

TYPICAL 30 YEAR LOAN COMPARED TO A BI-WEEKLY

LOAN AMOUNT	MONTHLY PAYMENT	TOTAL INTEREST	BI-WKLY PAYMENT	TERM YR/WK	INTEREST SAVED	YR/WK SAVED
50	0.35	75.78	0.18	21/30	24.85	8/22
100	0.70	151.02	0.35	23/14	39.57	6/38
200	1.40	302.11	0.70	23/12	79.58	6/40
300	2.10	453.18	1.05	23/12	119.49	6/40
400	2.80	603.78	1.40	23/12	158.89	6/40
500	3.50	754.92	1.75	23/12	198.84	6/40
600	4.20	905.91	2.10	23/12	238.66	6/40
700	4.90	1,056.83	2.45	23/12	278.16	6/40
800	5.60	1,207.38	2.80	23/12	317.83	6/40
900	6.30	1,358.89	3.15	23/12	357.96	6/40
1,000	7.00	1,509.89	3.50	23/12	397.86	6/40
2,000	13.99	3,028.33	7.00	23/12	804.05	6/40
3,000	20.98	4,548.31	10.49	23/16	1,201.45	6/36
4,000	27.97	6,067.33	13.99	23/14	1,608.29	6/38
5,000	34.97	7,576.67	17.49	23/14	2,005.45	6/38
6,000	41.96	9,095.81	20.98	23/16	2,402.41	6/36
7,000	48.95	10,615.14	24.48	23/14	2,809.83	6/38
8,000	55.94	12,134.72	27.97	23/16	3,206.56	6/36
9,000	62.93	13,654.14	31.47	23/16	3,614.17	6/36
10,000	69.93	15,163.23	34.97	23/14	4,010.83	6/38
15,000	104.89	22,749.79	52.45	23/16	6,016.06	6/36
20,000	139.85	30,336.50	69.93	23/16	8,021.21	6/36
25,000	174.81	37,923.13	87.41	23/16	10,027.24	6/36
30,000	209.77	45,509.84	104.89	23/16	12,032.66	6/36
35,000	244.73	53,095.98	122.37	23/16	14,037.04	6/36
45,000	314.65	68,269.49	157.33	23/16	18,047.93	6/36
55,000	384.57	83,442.49	192.29	23/16	22,058.62	6/36
65,000	454.49	98,615.61	227.25	23/16	26,069.24	6/36
75,000	524.42	113,779.03	262.21	23/16	30,070.04	6/36
85,000	594.34	128,952.40	297.17	23/16	34,080.95	6/36
100,000	699.22	151,712.05	349.61	23/16	40,096.52	6/36
120,000	839.06	182,058.02	419.53	23/16	48,117.37	6/36
140,000	978.91	212,394.88	489.46	23/16	56,139.40	6/36
160,000	1,118.75	242,741.13	559.38	23/16	64,160.66	6/36
180,000	1,258.59	273,086.82	629.30	23/16	72,181.33	6/36
200,000	1,398.43	303,433.66	699.22	23/16	80,203.15	6/36
225,000	1,573.24	341,356.58	786.62	23/16	90,219.59	6/36
250,000	1,748.04	379,289.78	874.02	23/16	100,246.63	6/36
275,000	1,922.84	417,222.30	961.42	23/16	110,272.35	6/36
300,000	2,097.65	455,145.46	1,048.83	23/16	120,299.43	6/36
350,000	2,447.26	531,001.07	1,223.63	23/16	140,342.19	6/36
400,000	2,796.86	606,866.84	1,398.43	23/16	160,395.50	6/36
450,000	3,146.47	682,722.44	1,573.24	23/16	180,448.60	6/36
500,000	3,496.08	758,578.74	1,748.04	23/16	200,491.79	6/36
550,000	3,845.68	834,444.32	1,922.84	23/16	220,544.76	6/36

7.75% 7.75%

BI-WEEKLY PAYMENT TABLE

TYPICAL 30 YEAR LOAN COMPARED TO A BI-WEEKLY

LOAN AMOUNT	MONTHLY PAYMENT	TOTAL INTEREST	BI-WKLY PAYMENT	TERM YR/WK	INTEREST SAVED	YR/WK SAVED
50	0.36	77.24	0.18	22/46	20.28	7/06
100	0.72	154.28	0.36	22/40	41.16	7/12
200	1.44	308.41	0.72	22/40	82.55	7/12
300	2.15	473.12	1.08	22/40	134.35	7/12
400	2.87	626.95	1.44	22/40	175.35	7/12
500	3.59	781.22	1.80	22/40	216.73	7/12
600	4.30	945.83	2.15	23/04	257.90	6/48
700	5.02	1,099.92	2.51	23/00	299.14	7/00
800	5.74	1,253.78	2.87	23/00	340.18	7/00
900	6.45	1,418.76	3.23	22/50	392.31	7/02
1,000	7.17	1,573.26	3.59	22/48	433.83	7/04
2,000	14.33	3,156.17	7.17	23/02	866.72	6/50
3,000	21.50	4,729.27	10.75	23/04	1,289.98	6/48
4,000	28.66	6,312.71	14.33	23/04	1,723.31	6/48
5,000	35.83	7,885.29	17.92	23/02	2,156.75	6/50
6,000	42.99	9,469.05	21.50	23/02	2,590.67	6/50
7,000	50.15	11,052.56	25.08	23/04	3,024.16	6/48
8,000	57.32	12,625.37	28.66	23/04	3,446.39	6/48
9,000	64.48	14,209.00	32.24	23/04	3,880.30	6/48
10,000	71.65	15,781.83	35.83	23/04	4,313.67	6/48
15,000	107.47	23,677.72	53.74	23/04	6,470.30	6/48
20,000	143.29	31,573.70	71.65	23/04	8,626.94	6/48
25,000	179.11	39,469.89	89.56	23/04	10,783.87	6/48
30,000	214.93	47,366.16	107.47	23/04	12,940.56	6/48
35,000	250.75	55,262.23	125.38	23/04	15,096.91	6/48
45,000	322.39	71,054.11	161.20	23/04	19,410.51	6/48
55,000	394.03	86,846.69	197.02	23/04	23,724.89	6/48
65,000	465.67	102,639.08	232.84	23/04	28,037.85	6/48
75,000	537.31	118,430.43	268.66	23/04	32,350.73	6/48
85,000	608.96	134,212.02	304.48	23/04	36,653.88	6/48
100,000	716.42	157,900.20	358.21	23/04	43,123.30	6/48
120,000	859.70	189,484.36	429.85	23/04	51,750.22	6/48
140,000	1,002.98	221,069.18	501.49	23/04	60,377.40	6/48
160,000	1,146.26	252,652.67	573.13	23/04	69,003.87	6/48
180,000	1,289.55	284,226.85	644.78	23/04	77,630.83	6/48
200,000	1,432.83	315,810.66	716.42	23/04	86,257.07	6/48
225,000	1,611.93	355,291.22	805.97	23/04	97,040.89	6/48
250,000	1,791.04	394,761.11	895.52	23/04	107,814.29	6/48
275,000	1,970.14	434,241.66	985.07	23/04	118,597.81	6/48
300,000	2,149.24	473,721.42	1,074.62	23/04	129,380.72	6/48
350,000	2,507.45	552,672.06	1,253.73	23/04	150,947.90	6/48
400,000	2,865.65	631,632.55	1,432.83	23/04	172,515.06	6/48
450,000	3,223.86	710,582.59	1,611.93	23/04	194,071.98	6/48
500,000	3,582.07	789,532.66	1,791.04	23/04	215,638.77	6/48
550,000	3,940.27	868,493.16	1,970.14	23/04	237,205.34	6/48

8.00% 8.00%

BI-WEEKLY PAYMENT TABLE

TYPICAL 30 YEAR LOAN COMPARED TO A BI-WEEKLY

LOAN AMOUNT	MONTHLY PAYMENT	TOTAL INTEREST	BI-WKLY PAYMENT	TERM YR/WK	INTEREST SAVED	YR/WK SAVED
50	0.37	78.81	0.19	20/40	26.22	9/12
100	0.74	157.59	0.37	22/18	42.87	7/34
200	1.47	325.46	0.74	22/16	96.35	7/36
300	2.21	483.15	1.11	22/16	139.49	7/36
400	2.94	651.02	1.47	22/40	182.18	7/12
500	3.67	819.58	1.84	22/34	236.29	7/18
600	4.41	976.51	2.21	22/32	278.77	7/20
700	5.14	1,145.01	2.57	22/42	322.12	7/10
800	5.88	1,302.13	2.94	22/40	364.44	7/12
900	6.61	1,470.48	3.31	22/36	418.34	7/16
1,000	7.34	1,639.13	3.67	22/44	461.75	7/08
2,000	14.68	3,277.76	7.34	22/44	923.09	7/08
3,000	22.02	4,916.77	11.01	22/44	1,384.95	7/08
4,000	29.36	6,555.34	14.68	22/44	1,846.51	7/08
5,000	36.69	8,205.80	18.35	22/44	2,319.03	7/08
6,000	44.03	9,844.84	22.02	22/44	2,781.11	7/08
7,000	51.37	11,483.68	25.69	22/44	3,242.55	7/08
8,000	58.71	13,122.39	29.36	22/44	3,704.06	7/08
9,000	66.04	14,773.12	33.02	22/44	4,167.07	7/08
10,000	73.38	16,411.69	36.69	22/44	4,627.57	7/08
15,000	110.07	24,617.40	55.04	22/44	6,947.15	7/08
20,000	146.76	32,822.46	73.38	22/44	9,254.93	7/08
25,000	183.45	41,028.33	91.73	22/44	11,574.58	7/08
30,000	220.13	49,246.03	110.07	22/44	13,894.90	7/08
35,000	256.82	57,452.01	128.41	22/44	16,203.52	7/08
45,000	330.20	73,864.09	165.10	22/44	20,831.44	7/08
55,000	403.58	90,274.86	201.79	22/44	25,458.92	7/08
65,000	476.95	106,697.65	238.48	22/44	30,098.05	7/08
75,000	550.33	123,109.44	275.17	22/44	34,725.77	7/08
85,000	623.70	139,531.77	311.85	22/44	39,353.81	7/08
100,000	733.77	164,149.32	366.89	22/44	46,300.86	7/08
120,000	880.52	196,983.99	440.26	22/44	55,557.23	7/08
140,000	1,027.28	229,806.91	513.64	22/44	64,813.06	7/08
160,000	1,174.03	262,641.08	587.02	22/44	74,079.31	7/08
180,000	1,320.78	295,475.33	660.39	22/44	83,335.01	7/08
200,000	1,467.53	328,309.52	733.77	22/44	92,601.94	7/08
225,000	1,650.98	369,338.11	825.49	22/44	104,165.79	7/08
250,000	1,834.42	410,377.95	917.21	22/44	115,740.74	7/08
275,000	2,017.86	451,418.50	1,008.93	22/44	127,315.71	7/08
300,000	2,201.30	492,458.53	1,100.65	22/44	138,891.53	7/08
350,000	2,568.18	574,538.97	1,284.09	22/44	162,042.22	7/08
400,000	2,935.06	656,619.15	1,467.53	22/44	185,192.96	7/08
450,000	3,301.95	738,687.92	1,650.98	22/44	208,342.93	7/08
500,000	3,668.83	820,768.80	1,834.42	22/44	231,493.85	7/08
550,000	4,035.71	902,848.64	2,017.86	22/44	254,644.47	7/08

8.25% 8.25%

BI-WEEKLY PAYMENT TABLE

TYPICAL 30 YEAR LOAN COMPARED TO A BI-WEEKLY

LOAN AMOUNT	MONTHLY PAYMENT	TOTAL INTEREST	BI-WKLY PAYMENT	TERM YR/WK	INTEREST SAVED	YR/WK SAVED
50	0.38	80.26	0.19	22/00	21.68	8/00
100	0.76	160.71	0.38	21/48	44.39	8/04
200	1.51	332.18	0.76	21/46	99.98	8/06
300	2.26	504.01	1.13	22/24	144.85	7/28
400	3.01	676.09	1.51	22/16	200.85	7/36
500	3.76	847.90	1.88	22/30	245.69	7/22
600	4.51	1,019.92	2.26	22/24	301.68	7/28
700	5.26	1,192.12	2.63	22/32	346.99	7/20
800	6.02	1,352.15	3.01	22/28	390.99	7/24
900	6.77	1,523.65	3.39	22/24	446.28	7/28
1,000	7.52	1,695.84	3.76	22/30	491.68	7/22
2,000	15.03	3,403.65	7.52	22/30	995.08	7/22
3,000	22.54	5,111.33	11.27	22/32	1,487.43	7/20
4,000	30.06	6,806.40	15.03	22/32	1,977.77	7/20
5,000	37.57	8,514.62	18.79	22/32	2,482.20	7/20
6,000	45.08	10,222.74	22.54	22/32	2,974.16	7/20
7,000	52.59	11,930.52	26.30	22/32	3,478.02	7/20
8,000	60.11	13,626.05	30.06	22/32	3,969.42	7/20
9,000	67.62	15,333.69	33.81	22/32	4,460.94	7/20
10,000	75.13	17,041.58	37.57	22/32	4,964.56	7/20
15,000	112.69	25,568.88	56.35	22/32	7,448.14	7/20
20,000	150.26	34,083.19	75.13	22/32	9,918.48	7/20
25,000	187.82	42,610.58	93.91	22/32	12,401.59	7/20
30,000	225.38	51,136.33	112.69	22/32	14,883.07	7/20
35,000	262.95	59,651.54	131.48	22/32	17,365.56	7/20
45,000	338.07	76,706.04	169.04	22/32	22,332.50	7/20
55,000	413.20	93,746.52	206.60	22/32	27,284.94	7/20
65,000	488.33	110,788.20	244.17	22/32	32,249.30	7/20
75,000	563.45	127,842.31	281.73	22/32	37,215.18	7/20
85,000	638.58	144,883.86	319.29	22/32	42,169.35	7/20
100,000	751.27	170,451.76	375.64	22/32	49,615.56	7/20
120,000	901.52	204,546.73	450.76	22/32	59,534.28	7/20
140,000	1,051.78	238,630.07	525.89	22/32	69,452.79	7/20
160,000	1,202.03	272,725.29	601.02	22/32	79,382.79	7/20
180,000	1,352.28	306,820.57	676.14	22/32	89,302.05	7/20
200,000	1,502.54	340,904.12	751.27	22/32	99,220.56	7/20
225,000	1,690.35	383,526.05	845.18	22/32	111,633.59	7/20
250,000	1,878.17	426,135.58	939.09	22/32	124,034.05	7/20
275,000	2,065.99	468,745.86	1,033.00	22/32	136,435.95	7/20
300,000	2,253.80	511,367.34	1,126.90	22/32	148,836.78	7/20
350,000	2,629.44	596,587.46	1,314.72	22/32	173,638.64	7/20
400,000	3,005.07	681,819.64	1,502.54	22/32	198,452.98	7/20
450,000	3,380.70	767,051.64	1,690.35	22/32	223,255.55	7/20
500,000	3,756.34	852,271.44	1,878.17	22/32	248,057.26	7/20
550,000	4,131.97	937,503.82	2,065.99	22/32	272,871.80	7/20

8.50% 8.50%

BI-WEEKLY PAYMENT TABLE

TYPICAL 30 YEAR LOAN COMPARED TO A BI-WEEKLY

LOAN AMOUNT	MONTHLY PAYMENT	TOTAL INTEREST	BI-WKLY PAYMENT	TERM YR/WK	INTEREST SAVED	YR/WK SAVED
50	0.39	81.84	0.20	20/02	27.70	9/50
100	0.77	175.68	0.39	21/26	57.97	8/26
200	1.54	350.62	0.77	22/16	104.40	7/36
300	2.31	526.35	1.16	22/02	162.58	7/50
400	3.08	701.67	1.54	22/16	209.19	7/36
500	3.85	877.07	1.93	22/08	267.12	7/44
600	4.62	1,052.42	2.31	22/16	313.75	7/36
700	5.39	1,228.26	2.70	22/10	372.11	7/42
800	6.16	1,403.55	3.08	22/16	418.86	7/36
900	6.93	1,578.58	3.47	22/10	476.55	7/42
1,000	7.69	1,766.67	3.85	22/16	535.41	7/36
2,000	15.38	3,534.09	7.69	22/20	1,060.86	7/32
3,000	23.07	5,300.61	11.54	22/18	1,595.92	7/34
4,000	30.76	7,067.78	15.38	22/20	2,119.92	7/32
5,000	38.45	8,834.41	19.23	22/20	2,655.78	7/32
6,000	46.14	10,601.82	23.07	22/20	3,180.65	7/32
7,000	53.83	12,368.70	26.92	22/20	3,716.30	7/32
8,000	61.52	14,135.46	30.76	22/20	4,239.99	7/32
9,000	69.21	15,902.27	34.61	22/20	4,776.13	7/32
10,000	76.90	17,669.97	38.45	22/20	5,301.21	7/32
15,000	115.34	26,517.55	57.67	22/20	7,958.59	7/32
20,000	153.79	35,352.21	76.90	22/20	10,614.66	7/32
25,000	192.23	44,200.07	96.12	22/20	13,271.87	7/32
30,000	230.68	53,035.02	115.34	22/20	15,916.79	7/32
35,000	269.12	61,883.02	134.56	22/20	18,574.90	7/32
45,000	346.02	79,552.57	173.01	22/20	23,875.40	7/32
55,000	422.91	97,235.00	211.46	22/20	29,188.86	7/32
65,000	499.80	114,917.62	249.90	22/20	34,491.24	7/32
75,000	576.69	132,600.64	288.35	22/20	39,805.23	7/32
85,000	653.58	150,283.36	326.79	22/20	45,107.35	7/32
100,000	768.92	176,800.06	384.46	22/20	53,065.34	7/32
120,000	922.70	212,165.86	461.35	22/20	63,681.08	7/32
140,000	1,076.48	247,531.28	538.24	22/20	74,297.68	7/32
160,000	1,230.27	282,883.52	615.14	22/20	84,911.67	7/32
180,000	1,384.05	318,248.40	692.03	22/20	95,527.73	7/32
200,000	1,537.83	353,613.70	768.92	22/20	106,143.79	7/32
225,000	1,730.06	397,813.28	865.03	22/20	119,403.56	7/32
250,000	1,922.29	442,013.87	961.15	22/20	132,676.16	7/32
275,000	2,114.52	486,214.99	1,057.26	22/20	145,938.00	7/32
300,000	2,306.75	530,413.91	1,153.38	22/20	159,209.37	7/32
350,000	2,691.20	618,827.20	1,345.60	22/20	185,742.94	7/32
400,000	3,075.66	707,227.58	1,537.83	22/20	212,275.95	7/32
450,000	3,460.12	795,627.43	1,730.06	22/20	238,808.74	7/32
500,000	3,844.57	884,040.95	1,922.29	22/20	265,354.47	7/32
550,000	4,229.03	972,441.10	2,114.52	22/20	291,887.11	7/32

8.75% 8.75%

BI-WEEKLY PAYMENT TABLE

TYPICAL 30 YEAR LOAN COMPARED TO A BI-WEEKLY

LOAN AMOUNT	MONTHLY PAYMENT	TOTAL INTEREST	BI-WKLY PAYMENT	TERM YR/WK	INTEREST SAVED	YR/WK SAVED
50	0.40	83.29	0.20	21/10	23.28	8/42
100	0.79	179.04	0.40	21/06	59.71	8/46
200	1.58	357.68	0.79	21/46	108.36	8/06
300	2.37	536.28	1.19	21/32	167.88	8/20
400	3.15	728.23	1.58	21/46	229.89	8/06
500	3.94	906.96	1.97	22/02	278.20	7/50
600	4.73	1,086.27	2.37	21/46	338.50	8/06
700	5.51	1,278.00	2.76	22/00	400.05	8/00
800	6.30	1,456.74	3.15	22/06	448.00	7/46
900	7.09	1,635.07	3.55	22/00	507.59	8/00
1,000	7.87	1,828.39	3.94	22/04	570.47	7/48
2,000	15.74	3,655.37	7.87	22/08	1,128.21	7/44
3,000	23.61	5,483.89	11.81	22/06	1,698.56	7/46
4,000	31.47	7,326.11	15.74	22/08	2,271.38	8/42
5,000	39.34	9,154.03	19.67	22/08	2,829.64	7/44
6,000	47.21	10,981.78	23.61	22/08	3,400.02	7/44
7,000	55.07	12,822.92	27.54	22/08	3,971.49	7/44
8,000	62.94	14,651.11	31.47	22/08	4,530.19	7/44
9,000	70.81	16,479.10	35.41	22/08	5,100.55	7/44
10,000	78.68	18,307.85	39.34	22/08	5,659.61	7/44
15,000	118.01	27,474.93	59.01	22/08	8,502.66	7/44
20,000	157.35	36,628.47	78.68	22/08	11,331.98	7/44
25,000	196.68	45,796.18	98.34	22/08	14,163.95	7/44
30,000	236.02	54,950.11	118.01	22/08	16,993.96	7/44
35,000	275.35	64,117.46	137.68	22/08	19,837.37	7/44
45,000	354.02	82,438.93	177.01	22/08	25,498.14	7/44
55,000	432.69	100,760.24	216.35	22/08	31,171.43	7/44
65,000	511.36	119,081.12	255.68	22/08	36,832.64	7/44
75,000	590.03	137,402.28	295.02	22/08	42,505.51	7/44
85,000	668.70	155,724.12	334.35	22/08	48,167.58	7/44
100,000	786.71	183,199.31	393.36	22/08	56,670.40	7/44
120,000	944.05	219,841.63	472.03	22/08	68,004.36	7/44
140,000	1,101.39	256,483.65	550.70	22/08	79,338.76	7/44
160,000	1,258.73	293,126.99	629.37	22/08	90,673.94	7/44
180,000	1,416.07	329,768.85	708.04	22/08	102,007.71	7/44
200,000	1,573.41	366,411.78	786.71	22/08	113,342.17	7/44
225,000	1,770.08	412,221.37	885.04	22/08	127,507.44	7/44
250,000	1,966.76	458,018.39	983.38	22/08	141,672.69	7/44
275,000	2,163.43	503,828.17	1,081.72	22/08	155,850.04	7/44
300,000	2,360.11	549,624.21	1,180.06	22/08	170,013.19	7/44
350,000	2,753.46	641,231.01	1,376.73	22/08	198,344.16	7/44
400,000	3,146.81	732,837.01	1,573.41	22/08	226,685.60	7/44
450,000	3,540.16	824,443.21	1,770.08	22/08	255,016.00	7/44
500,000	3,933.51	916,049.53	1,966.76	22/08	283,357.15	7/44
550,000	4,326.86	1,007,656.31	2,163.43	22/08	311,687.97	7/44

9.00% 9.00%

BI-WEEKLY PAYMENT TABLE

TYPICAL 30 YEAR LOAN COMPARED TO A BI-WEEKLY

LOAN AMOUNT	MONTHLY PAYMENT	TOTAL INTEREST	BI-WKLY PAYMENT	TERM YR/WK	INTEREST SAVED	YR/WK SAVED
50	0.41	84.87	0.21	19/20	29.14	10/32
100	0.81	182.52	0.41	20/38	61.89	9/14
200	1.61	378.44	0.81	21/26	126.35	8/26
300	2.42	560.09	1.21	21/40	176.10	8/12
400	3.22	756.57	1.61	17/34	240.62	12/18
500	4.03	937.87	2.02	21/34	301.65	8/18
600	4.83	1,134.10	2.42	21/40	365.89	8/12
700	5.64	1,316.61	2.82	21/44	416.65	8/08
800	6.44	1,513.21	3.22	21/48	480.82	8/04
900	7.25	1,694.93	3.63	21/40	542.93	8/12
1,000	8.05	1,891.33	4.03	21/42	607.06	8/10
2,000	16.10	3,781.45	8.05	21/46	1,201.52	8/06
3,000	24.14	5,687.91	12.07	21/48	1,811.17	8/04
4,000	32.19	7,579.44	16.10	21/46	2,418.63	8/06
5,000	40.24	9,470.36	20.12	21/48	3,012.97	8/04
6,000	48.28	11,376.31	24.14	21/48	3,622.85	8/04
7,000	56.33	13,266.87	28.17	21/48	4,229.19	8/04
8,000	64.37	15,172.93	32.19	21/48	4,839.15	8/04
9,000	72.42	17,064.10	36.21	21/48	5,434.41	8/04
10,000	80.47	18,955.16	40.24	21/48	6,040.85	8/04
15,000	120.70	28,440.47	60.35	21/48	9,057.43	8/04
20,000	160.93	37,924.72	80.47	21/48	12,084.42	8/04
25,000	201.16	47,409.41	100.58	21/48	15,100.93	8/04
30,000	241.39	56,894.84	120.70	21/48	18,128.37	8/04
35,000	281.62	66,379.31	140.81	21/48	21,144.38	8/04
45,000	362.09	85,333.85	181.05	21/48	27,184.36	8/04
55,000	442.55	104,304.19	221.28	21/48	33,228.84	8/04
65,000	523.01	123,274.48	261.51	21/48	39,272.79	8/04
75,000	603.47	142,244.19	301.74	21/48	45,316.72	8/04
85,000	683.93	161,213.19	341.97	21/48	51,359.89	8/04
100,000	804.63	189,653.61	402.32	21/48	60,416.55	8/04
120,000	965.55	227,592.22	482.78	21/48	72,503.14	8/04
140,000	1,126.48	265,517.70	563.24	21/48	84,576.33	8/04
160,000	1,287.40	303,456.50	643.70	21/48	96,663.11	8/04
180,000	1,448.33	341,381.91	724.17	21/48	108,748.28	8/04
200,000	1,609.25	379,321.00	804.63	21/48	120,835.16	8/04
225,000	1,810.41	426,731.09	905.21	21/48	135,936.13	8/04
250,000	2,011.56	474,155.20	1,005.78	21/48	151,038.39	8/04
275,000	2,212.72	521,564.10	1,106.36	21/48	166,138.84	8/04
300,000	2,413.87	568,989.51	1,206.94	21/48	181,254.45	8/04
350,000	2,816.18	663,823.08	1,408.09	21/48	211,457.90	8/04
400,000	3,218.50	758,642.37	1,609.25	21/48	241,658.93	8/04
450,000	3,620.81	853,476.29	1,810.41	21/48	271,874.42	8/04
500,000	4,023.12	948,310.14	2,011.56	21/48	302,078.06	8/04
550,000	4,425.43	1,043,144.43	2,212.72	21/48	332,293.58	8/04

9.25% 9.25%

BI-WEEKLY PAYMENT TABLE

TYPICAL 30 YEAR LOAN COMPARED TO A BI-WEEKLY

LOAN AMOUNT	MONTHLY PAYMENT	TOTAL INTEREST	BI-WKLY PAYMENT	TERM YR/WK	INTEREST SAVED	YR/WK SAVED
50	0.42	86.54	0.21	20/22	25.11	9/30
100	0.83	185.55	0.42	20/18	63.48	9/34
200	1.65	384.94	0.83	21/06	129.90	8/46
300	2.47	585.50	1.24	21/20	197.19	8/32
400	3.30	770.22	1.65	21/26	248.53	8/26
500	4.12	970.85	2.06	21/30	315.67	8/22
600	4.94	1,171.22	2.47	21/34	382.60	8/18
700	5.76	1,371.60	2.88	21/36	449.55	8/16
800	6.59	1,555.88	3.30	21/26	512.62	8/26
900	7.41	1,756.58	3.71	21/28	579.53	8/24
1,000	8.23	1,956.69	4.12	21/30	646.28	8/22
2,000	16.46	3,913.28	8.23	21/34	1,280.23	8/18
3,000	24.69	5,869.29	12.35	21/34	1,926.06	8/18
4,000	32.91	7,841.53	16.46	21/34	2,575.09	8/18
5,000	41.14	9,798.39	20.57	21/36	3,209.14	8/16
6,000	49.37	11,754.88	24.69	21/34	3,855.73	8/18
7,000	57.59	13,727.47	28.80	21/36	4,505.46	8/16
8,000	65.82	15,684.14	32.91	21/36	5,138.94	8/16
9,000	74.05	17,640.19	37.03	21/36	5,784.92	8/16
10,000	82.27	19,612.65	41.14	21/36	6,434.60	8/16
15,000	123.41	29,410.72	61.71	21/36	9,643.75	8/16
20,000	164.54	39,225.44	82.27	21/36	12,857.16	8/16
25,000	205.67	49,039.36	102.84	21/36	16,081.97	8/16
30,000	246.81	58,837.62	123.41	21/36	19,290.87	8/16
35,000	287.94	68,651.32	143.97	21/36	22,503.33	8/16
45,000	370.21	88,264.29	185.11	21/36	28,937.76	8/16
55,000	452.48	107,876.12	226.24	21/36	35,359.56	8/16
65,000	534.74	127,504.83	267.37	21/36	41,797.70	8/16
75,000	617.01	147,116.26	308.51	21/36	48,231.68	8/16
85,000	699.28	166,729.97	349.64	21/36	54,654.31	8/16
100,000	822.68	196,156.38	411.34	21/36	64,301.27	8/16
120,000	987.22	235,381.22	493.61	21/36	77,157.34	8/16
140,000	1,151.75	274,621.73	575.88	21/36	90,029.83	8/16
160,000	1,316.29	313,846.81	658.15	21/36	102,886.24	8/16
180,000	1,480.82	353,087.69	740.41	21/36	115,745.78	8/16
200,000	1,645.36	392,311.78	822.68	21/36	128,601.60	8/16
225,000	1,851.02	441,367.22	925.51	21/36	144,686.96	8/16
250,000	2,056.69	490,405.50	1,028.35	21/36	160,766.96	8/16
275,000	2,262.36	539,444.42	1,131.18	21/36	176,836.79	8/16
300,000	2,468.03	588,483.26	1,234.02	21/36	192,917.33	8/16
350,000	2,879.37	686,561.49	1,439.69	21/36	225,067.97	8/16
400,000	3,290.71	784,639.74	1,645.36	21/36	257,219.26	8/16
450,000	3,702.04	882,733.04	1,851.02	21/36	289,371.71	8/16
500,000	4,113.38	980,811.33	2,056.69	21/36	321,522.96	8/16
550,000	4,524.72	1,078,889.20	2,262.36	21/36	353,672.82	8/16

9.50% 9.50%

BI-WEEKLY PAYMENT TABLE

TYPICAL 30 YEAR LOAN COMPARED TO A BI-WEEKLY

LOAN AMOUNT	MONTHLY PAYMENT	TOTAL INTEREST	BI-WKLY PAYMENT	TERM YR/WK	INTEREST SAVED	YR/WK SAVED
50	0.43	88.08	0.22	18/40	30.88	11/12
100	0.85	189.13	0.43	20/00	65.79	10/00
200	1.69	392.08	0.85	20/38	134.17	9/14
300	2.53	596.04	1.27	21/00	203.58	9/00
400	3.37	800.00	1.69	21/06	272.67	8/46
500	4.21	1,004.25	2.11	21/10	342.03	8/42
600	5.05	1,208.58	2.53	21/14	411.82	8/38
700	5.89	1,412.45	2.95	21/16	480.61	8/36
800	6.73	1,616.21	3.37	21/16	549.47	8/36
900	7.57	1,820.89	3.79	21/24	619.23	8/28
1,000	8.41	2,024.41	4.21	21/20	687.74	8/32
2,000	16.82	4,049.90	8.41	21/24	1,364.08	8/28
3,000	25.23	6,073.83	12.62	21/24	2,051.60	8/28
4,000	33.64	8,098.88	16.82	21/24	2,727.78	8/28
5,000	42.05	10,122.21	21.03	21/22	3,414.41	8/30
6,000	50.46	12,147.93	25.23	21/24	4,091.07	8/28
7,000	58.86	14,188.98	29.43	21/24	4,783.30	8/28
8,000	67.27	16,213.27	33.64	21/24	5,471.06	8/28
9,000	75.68	18,238.36	37.84	21/24	6,146.98	8/28
10,000	84.09	20,262.96	42.05	21/24	6,834.86	8/28
15,000	126.13	30,402.39	63.07	21/24	10,254.30	8/28
20,000	168.18	40,526.98	84.09	21/24	13,658.24	8/28
25,000	210.22	50,666.36	105.11	21/24	17,077.37	8/28
30,000	252.26	60,805.81	126.13	21/24	20,496.44	8/28
35,000	294.30	70,945.76	147.15	21/24	23,915.78	8/28
45,000	378.39	91,208.88	189.20	21/24	30,751.40	8/28
55,000	462.47	111,489.55	231.24	21/24	37,591.66	8/28
65,000	546.56	131,752.09	273.28	21/24	44,413.36	8/28
75,000	630.65	152,015.43	315.33	21/24	51,248.19	8/28
85,000	714.73	172,295.40	357.37	21/24	58,088.07	8/28
100,000	840.86	202,697.08	420.43	21/24	68,328.85	8/28
120,000	1,009.03	243,241.23	504.52	21/24	82,004.40	8/28
140,000	1,177.20	283,784.04	588.60	21/24	95,665.77	8/28
160,000	1,345.37	324,326.24	672.69	21/24	109,339.36	8/28
180,000	1,513.54	364,869.81	756.77	21/24	123,001.36	8/28
200,000	1,681.71	405,411.98	840.86	21/24	136,675.17	8/28
225,000	1,891.93	456,077.65	945.97	21/24	153,752.27	8/28
250,000	2,102.14	506,761.04	1,051.07	21/24	170,833.74	8/28
275,000	2,312.35	557,443.82	1,156.18	21/24	187,927.73	8/28
300,000	2,522.57	608,110.32	1,261.29	21/24	205,005.27	8/28
350,000	2,942.99	709,476.07	1,471.50	21/24	239,180.74	8/28
400,000	3,363.42	810,824.66	1,681.71	21/24	273,338.35	8/28
450,000	3,783.85	912,174.03	1,891.93	21/24	307,509.98	8/28
500,000	4,204.28	1,013,522.49	2,102.14	21/24	341,667.50	8/28
550,000	4,624.70	1,114,888.96	2,312.35	21/24	375,843.86	8/28

9.75% 9.75%

BI-WEEKLY PAYMENT TABLE

TYPICAL 30 YEAR LOAN COMPARED TO A BI-WEEKLY

LOAN AMOUNT	MONTHLY PAYMENT	TOTAL INTEREST	BI-WKLY PAYMENT	TERM YR/WK	INTEREST SAVED	YR/WK SAVED
50	0.43	104.04	0.22	19/38	41.26	10/14
100	0.86	207.89	0.43	21/08	71.80	8/44
200	1.72	415.52	0.86	21/08	142.87	8/44
300	2.58	623.45	1.29	21/08	214.66	8/44
400	3.44	831.52	1.72	21/08	286.48	8/44
500	4.30	1,038.70	2.15	21/08	357.57	8/44
600	5.16	1,247.36	2.58	21/08	429.77	8/44
700	6.02	1,454.89	3.01	21/08	501.25	8/44
800	6.88	1,662.32	3.44	21/08	571.95	8/44
900	7.74	1,870.15	3.87	21/08	643.93	8/44
1,000	8.60	2,078.00	4.30	21/08	715.53	8/44
2,000	17.19	4,173.47	8.60	21/08	1,448.38	8/44
3,000	25.78	6,268.53	12.89	21/10	2,168.20	8/42
4,000	34.37	8,365.39	17.19	21/10	2,902.72	8/42
5,000	42.96	10,461.11	21.48	21/12	3,622.68	8/40
6,000	51.55	12,555.97	25.78	21/10	4,355.82	8/42
7,000	60.15	14,633.92	30.08	21/10	5,071.16	8/42
8,000	68.74	16,729.87	34.37	21/12	5,791.70	8/40
9,000	77.33	18,826.39	38.67	21/10	6,525.63	8/42
10,000	85.92	20,921.55	42.96	21/12	7,245.75	8/40
15,000	128.88	31,382.19	64.44	21/12	10,867.93	8/40
20,000	171.84	41,842.89	85.92	21/12	14,491.07	8/40
25,000	214.79	52,321.72	107.40	21/12	18,131.89	8/40
30,000	257.75	62,781.73	128.88	21/12	21,754.02	8/40
35,000	300.71	73,242.56	150.36	21/12	25,376.14	8/40
45,000	386.62	94,182.28	193.31	21/12	32,628.03	8/40
55,000	472.54	115,104.12	236.27	21/12	39,873.48	8/40
65,000	558.46	136,024.97	279.23	21/12	47,118.66	8/40
75,000	644.37	156,964.85	322.19	21/12	54,382.16	8/40
85,000	730.29	177,885.61	365.15	21/12	61,626.68	8/40
100,000	859.16	209,285.17	429.58	21/12	72,499.75	8/40
120,000	1,030.99	251,146.44	515.50	21/12	87,008.98	8/40
140,000	1,202.82	293,006.45	601.41	21/12	101,504.45	8/40
160,000	1,374.65	334,868.15	687.33	21/12	116,014.10	8/40
180,000	1,546.48	376,728.29	773.24	21/12	130,509.66	8/40
200,000	1,718.31	418,589.52	859.16	21/12	145,018.48	8/40
225,000	1,933.10	470,910.12	966.55	21/12	163,136.57	8/40
250,000	2,147.89	523,232.18	1,073.95	21/12	181,268.68	8/40
275,000	2,362.68	575,553.62	1,181.34	21/12	199,387.17	8/40
300,000	2,577.47	627,875.18	1,288.74	21/12	217,519.06	8/40
350,000	3,007.05	732,517.62	1,503.53	21/12	253,769.48	8/40
400,000	3,436.62	837,178.19	1,718.31	21/12	290,024.28	8/40
450,000	3,866.20	941,820.73	1,933.10	21/12	326,274.06	8/40
500,000	4,295.78	1,046,463.64	2,147.89	21/12	362,523.98	8/40
550,000	4,725.35	1,151,124.00	2,362.68	21/12	398,791.67	8/40

10.00% 10.00%

BI-WEEKLY PAYMENT TABLE

TYPICAL 30 YEAR LOAN COMPARED TO A BI-WEEKLY

LOAN AMOUNT	MONTHLY PAYMENT	TOTAL INTEREST	BI-WKLY PAYMENT	TERM YR/WK	INTEREST SAVED	YR/WK SAVED
50	0.44	106.15	0.22	20/44	37.04	9/08
100	0.88	211.51	0.44	20/40	74.11	9/12
200	1.76	423.11	0.88	20/40	147.86	9/12
300	2.64	634.34	1.32	20/40	221.71	9/12
400	3.52	845.98	1.76	20/40	295.83	9/12
500	4.39	1,075.72	2.20	20/40	388.05	9/12
600	5.27	1,287.18	2.64	20/40	461.68	9/12
700	6.15	1,497.65	3.08	20/40	534.83	9/12
800	7.03	1,710.05	3.52	20/40	609.50	9/12
900	7.90	1,939.71	3.95	20/50	689.28	9/02
1,000	8.78	2,151.04	4.39	20/48	762.94	9/04
2,000	17.56	4,302.17	8.78	20/50	1,525.23	9/02
3,000	26.33	6,473.18	13.17	20/50	2,308.50	9/02
4,000	35.11	8,623.13	17.56	20/50	3,070.41	9/02
5,000	43.88	10,793.87	21.94	20/50	3,839.34	9/02
6,000	52.66	12,944.63	26.33	20/50	4,602.25	9/02
7,000	61.44	15,095.87	30.72	20/50	5,364.60	9/02
8,000	70.21	17,266.16	35.11	20/50	6,146.77	9/02
9,000	78.99	19,417.99	39.50	20/50	6,910.04	9/02
10,000	87.76	21,587.63	43.88	20/50	7,678.52	9/02
15,000	131.64	32,380.73	65.82	20/50	11,516.85	9/02
20,000	175.52	43,173.79	87.76	20/50	15,355.62	9/02
25,000	219.40	53,968.35	109.70	20/50	19,195.77	9/02
30,000	263.28	64,761.40	131.64	20/50	23,034.20	9/02
35,000	307.16	75,556.32	153.58	20/50	26,874.76	9/02
45,000	394.91	97,161.06	197.46	20/50	34,570.24	9/02
55,000	482.67	118,748.77	241.34	20/50	42,249.36	9/02
65,000	570.43	140,336.06	285.22	20/50	49,926.93	9/02
75,000	658.18	161,941.57	329.09	20/50	57,611.03	9/02
85,000	745.94	183,529.16	372.97	20/50	65,289.44	9/02
100,000	877.58	215,909.34	438.79	20/50	76,805.96	9/02
120,000	1,053.09	259,102.77	526.55	20/50	92,180.97	9/02
140,000	1,228.61	302,277.09	614.31	20/50	107,537.41	9/02
160,000	1,404.12	345,470.91	702.06	20/50	122,899.93	9/02
180,000	1,579.63	388,663.44	789.82	20/50	138,274.51	9/02
200,000	1,755.15	431,838.23	877.58	20/50	153,631.14	9/02
225,000	1,974.54	485,826.00	987.27	20/50	172,833.42	9/02
250,000	2,193.93	539,812.00	1,096.97	20/50	192,046.70	9/02
275,000	2,413.33	593,780.77	1,206.67	20/50	211,242.36	9/02
300,000	2,632.72	647,767.27	1,316.36	20/50	230,443.09	9/02
350,000	3,071.51	755,722.30	1,535.76	20/50	268,853.87	9/02
400,000	3,510.29	863,695.39	1,755.15	20/50	307,267.93	9/02
450,000	3,949.08	971,650.18	1,974.54	20/50	345,664.46	9/02
500,000	4,387.86	1,079,625.42	2,193.93	20/50	384,081.35	9/02
550,000	4,826.65	1,187,579.43	2,413.33	20/50	422,491.06	9/02

10.25% **10.25%**

BI-WEEKLY PAYMENT TABLE

TYPICAL 30 YEAR LOAN COMPARED TO A BI-WEEKLY

LOAN AMOUNT	MONTHLY PAYMENT	TOTAL INTEREST	BI-WKLY PAYMENT	TERM YR/WK	INTEREST SAVED	YR/WK SAVED
50	0.45	108.01	0.23	19/04	44.03	10/48
100	0.90	214.94	0.45	20/22	76.18	9/30
200	1.80	429.99	0.90	20/22	152.34	9/30
300	2.69	663.86	1.35	20/22	247.51	9/30
400	3.59	878.67	1.80	20/22	323.36	9/30
500	4.49	1,094.26	2.25	20/22	400.16	9/30
600	5.38	1,328.93	2.69	20/36	482.99	9/16
700	6.28	1,544.08	3.14	20/34	559.46	9/18
800	7.17	1,777.40	3.59	20/32	653.91	9/20
900	8.07	1,992.32	4.04	20/32	730.29	9/20
1,000	8.97	2,207.92	4.49	20/30	806.98	9/22
2,000	17.93	4,436.00	8.97	20/34	1,621.56	9/18
3,000	26.89	6,663.81	13.45	20/36	2,434.78	9/16
4,000	35.85	8,891.35	17.93	20/36	3,248.35	9/16
5,000	44.81	11,119.73	22.41	20/38	4,063.07	9/14
6,000	53.77	13,348.53	26.89	20/38	4,877.76	9/14
7,000	62.73	15,576.75	31.37	20/38	5,691.51	9/14
8,000	71.69	17,803.51	35.85	20/38	6,505.40	9/14
9,000	80.65	20,031.23	40.33	20/38	7,318.62	9/14
10,000	89.62	22,239.48	44.81	20/38	8,112.81	9/14
15,000	134.42	33,379.91	67.21	20/38	12,183.78	9/14
20,000	179.23	44,499.63	89.62	20/38	16,245.71	9/14
25,000	224.03	55,639.90	112.02	20/38	20,316.58	9/14
30,000	268.84	66,759.60	134.42	20/38	24,366.10	9/14
35,000	313.64	77,899.51	156.82	20/38	28,436.28	9/14
45,000	403.25	100,159.65	201.63	20/38	36,569.71	9/14
55,000	492.86	122,419.43	246.43	20/38	44,689.26	9/14
65,000	582.47	144,678.77	291.24	20/38	52,821.74	9/14
75,000	672.08	166,939.53	336.04	20/38	60,942.90	9/14
85,000	761.69	189,199.40	380.85	20/38	69,075.71	9/14
100,000	896.11	222,578.53	448.06	20/38	81,257.94	9/14
120,000	1,075.33	267,099.20	537.67	20/38	97,511.73	9/14
140,000	1,254.55	311,618.38	627.28	20/38	113,763.99	9/14
160,000	1,433.77	356,138.27	716.89	20/38	130,017.73	9/14
180,000	1,612.99	400,658.31	806.50	20/38	146,270.34	9/14
200,000	1,792.21	445,178.32	896.11	20/38	162,523.90	9/14
225,000	2,016.23	500,837.85	1,008.12	20/38	182,846.76	9/14
250,000	2,240.26	556,477.54	1,120.13	20/38	203,150.10	9/14
275,000	2,464.28	612,137.58	1,232.14	20/38	223,472.60	9/14
300,000	2,688.31	667,777.45	1,344.16	20/38	243,789.00	9/14
350,000	3,136.36	779,076.16	1,568.18	20/38	284,414.39	9/14
400,000	3,584.41	890,375.86	1,792.21	20/38	325,054.24	9/14
450,000	4,032.46	1,001,676.37	2,016.23	20/38	365,681.36	9/14
500,000	4,480.51	1,112,974.53	2,240.26	20/38	406,319.02	9/14
550,000	4,928.56	1,224,275.25	2,464.28	20/38	446,946.67	9/14

10.50% 10.50%

BI-WEEKLY PAYMENT TABLE

TYPICAL 30 YEAR LOAN COMPARED TO A BI-WEEKLY

LOAN AMOUNT	MONTHLY PAYMENT	TOTAL INTEREST	BI-WKLY PAYMENT	TERM YR/WK	INTEREST SAVED	YR/WK SAVED
50	0.46	110.06	0.23	20/08	39.64	9/44
100	0.92	218.74	0.46	20/22	78.78	9/30
200	1.83	457.76	0.92	20/06	177.51	9/46
300	2.75	675.78	1.38	20/04	255.58	9/48
400	3.66	914.70	1.83	20/24	341.56	9/28
500	4.58	1,133.27	2.29	20/20	420.12	9/32
600	5.49	1,372.92	2.75	20/18	519.80	9/34
700	6.41	1,590.54	3.21	20/16	597.40	9/36
800	7.32	1,830.69	3.66	20/24	684.18	9/28
900	8.24	2,048.31	4.12	20/22	762.10	9/30
1,000	9.15	2,287.48	4.58	20/20	861.20	9/32
2,000	18.30	4,575.06	9.15	20/24	1,709.32	9/28
3,000	27.45	6,862.06	13.73	20/24	2,570.34	9/28
4,000	36.59	9,171.98	18.30	20/24	3,440.27	9/28
5,000	45.74	11,458.08	22.87	20/26	4,287.01	9/26
6,000	54.89	13,746.17	27.45	20/24	5,149.18	9/28
7,000	64.04	16,034.33	32.02	20/26	5,997.53	9/26
8,000	73.18	18,341.91	36.59	20/26	6,865.24	9/26
9,000	82.33	20,631.07	41.17	20/26	7,728.39	9/26
10,000	91.48	22,917.58	45.74	20/26	8,575.60	9/26
15,000	137.22	34,376.44	68.61	20/26	12,863.50	9/26
20,000	182.95	45,857.04	91.48	20/26	17,172.75	9/26
25,000	228.69	57,315.57	114.35	20/26	21,460.42	9/26
30,000	274.43	68,775.18	137.22	20/26	25,749.14	9/26
35,000	320.16	80,254.94	160.08	20/26	30,044.61	9/26
45,000	411.64	103,171.52	205.82	20/26	38,619.25	9/26
55,000	503.11	126,111.12	251.56	20/26	47,216.73	9/26
65,000	594.59	149,027.81	297.30	20/26	55,790.72	9/26
75,000	686.06	171,967.91	343.03	20/26	64,375.76	9/26
85,000	777.53	194,907.17	388.77	20/26	72,972.78	9/26
100,000	914.74	229,304.00	457.37	20/26	85,843.08	9/26
120,000	1,097.69	275,161.87	548.85	20/26	103,017.52	9/26
140,000	1,280.64	321,017.83	640.32	20/26	120,175.68	9/26
160,000	1,463.59	366,873.62	731.80	20/26	137,347.81	9/26
180,000	1,646.54	412,730.84	823.27	20/26	154,507.01	9/26
200,000	1,829.48	458,609.12	914.74	20/26	171,687.67	9/26
225,000	2,058.17	515,926.00	1,029.09	20/26	193,149.29	9/26
250,000	2,286.85	573,261.71	1,143.43	20/26	214,616.40	9/26
275,000	2,515.54	630,577.27	1,257.77	20/26	236,063.94	9/26
300,000	2,744.22	687,913.21	1,372.11	20/26	257,530.77	9/26
350,000	3,201.59	802,566.73	1,600.80	20/26	300,461.05	9/26
400,000	3,658.96	917,218.65	1,829.48	20/26	343,376.13	9/26
450,000	4,116.33	1,031,869.96	2,058.17	20/26	386,303.85	9/26
500,000	4,573.70	1,146,522.82	2,286.85	20/26	429,219.80	9/26
550,000	5,031.07	1,261,175.64	2,515.54	20/26	472,148.01	9/26

10.75% 10.75%

BI-WEEKLY PAYMENT TABLE

TYPICAL 30 YEAR LOAN COMPARED TO A BI-WEEKLY

LOAN AMOUNT	MONTHLY PAYMENT	TOTAL INTEREST	BI-WKLY PAYMENT	TERM YR/WK	INTEREST SAVED	YR/WK SAVED
50	0.47	111.88	0.24	18/24	46.76	11/28
100	0.94	222.28	0.47	19/40	80.94	10/12
200	1.87	465.36	0.94	19/40	182.76	10/12
300	2.81	687.37	1.41	19/40	263.53	10/12
400	3.74	930.09	1.87	20/06	352.08	9/46
500	4.67	1,174.28	2.34	20/04	455.03	9/48
600	5.61	1,396.19	2.81	20/00	535.92	10/00
700	6.54	1,640.21	3.27	20/10	625.59	9/42
800	7.47	1,883.07	3.74	20/06	727.34	9/46
900	8.41	2,104.96	4.21	20/04	808.12	9/48
1,000	9.34	2,348.55	4.67	20/10	897.09	9/42
2,000	18.67	4,719.41	9.34	20/10	1,816.48	9/42
3,000	28.01	7,068.51	14.01	20/10	2,714.47	9/42
4,000	37.34	9,441.17	18.67	20/12	3,621.54	9/40
5,000	46.68	11,788.62	23.34	20/12	4,517.84	9/40
6,000	56.01	14,160.86	28.01	20/12	5,438.88	9/40
7,000	65.35	16,509.76	32.68	20/12	6,336.51	9/40
8,000	74.68	18,881.22	37.34	20/12	7,242.62	9/40
9,000	84.02	21,228.68	42.01	20/12	8,138.84	9/40
10,000	93.35	23,600.35	46.68	20/12	9,059.00	9/40
15,000	140.03	35,390.08	70.02	20/12	13,578.13	9/40
20,000	186.70	47,202.61	93.35	20/12	18,105.94	9/40
25,000	233.38	58,991.65	116.69	20/12	22,624.81	9/40
30,000	280.05	70,802.58	140.03	20/12	27,164.27	9/40
35,000	326.72	82,614.45	163.36	20/12	31,692.21	9/40
45,000	420.07	106,216.43	210.04	20/12	40,752.94	9/40
55,000	513.42	129,816.55	256.71	20/12	49,797.72	9/40
65,000	606.77	153,418.98	303.39	20/12	58,858.46	9/40
75,000	700.12	177,018.74	350.06	20/12	67,903.58	9/40
85,000	793.46	200,643.30	396.73	20/12	76,972.89	9/40
100,000	933.49	236,033.87	466.75	20/12	90,551.25	9/40
120,000	1,120.18	283,258.84	560.09	20/12	108,666.83	9/40
140,000	1,306.88	330,461.41	653.44	20/12	126,772.46	9/40
160,000	1,493.58	377,662.36	746.79	20/12	144,877.32	9/40
180,000	1,680.27	424,887.88	840.14	20/12	163,006.23	9/40
200,000	1,866.97	472,089.23	933.49	20/12	181,110.97	9/40
225,000	2,100.34	531,105.20	1,050.17	20/12	203,746.16	9/40
250,000	2,333.71	590,117.51	1,166.86	20/12	226,391.92	9/40
275,000	2,567.08	649,131.62	1,283.54	20/12	249,024.80	9/40
300,000	2,800.45	708,146.86	1,400.23	20/12	271,673.04	9/40
350,000	3,267.19	826,173.97	1,633.60	20/12	316,952.28	9/40
400,000	3,733.93	944,203.67	1,866.97	20/12	362,233.96	9/40
450,000	4,200.67	1,062,230.36	2,100.34	20/12	407,512.75	9/40
500,000	4,667.41	1,180,258.58	2,333.71	20/12	452,793.16	9/40
550,000	5,134.15	1,298,288.01	2,567.08	20/12	498,074.80	9/40

11.00% 11.00%

BI-WEEKLY PAYMENT TABLE

TYPICAL 30 YEAR LOAN COMPARED TO A BI-WEEKLY

LOAN AMOUNT	MONTHLY PAYMENT	TOTAL INTEREST	BI-WKLY PAYMENT	TERM YR/WK	INTEREST SAVED	YR/WK SAVED
50	0.48	113.97	0.24	19/26	42.33	10/26
100	0.96	226.13	0.48	19/24	83.71	10/28
200	1.91	473.00	0.96	19/32	188.08	10/20
300	2.86	721.40	1.43	19/48	281.20	10/04
400	3.81	969.85	1.91	19/42	387.26	10/10
500	4.77	1,194.19	2.39	19/38	469.48	10/14
600	5.72	1,442.52	2.86	19/48	562.10	10/04
700	6.67	1,689.86	3.34	19/44	667.03	10/08
800	7.62	1,939.41	3.81	20/00	760.88	10/00
900	8.58	2,163.12	4.29	19/48	842.42	10/04
1,000	9.53	2,411.88	4.77	19/46	948.81	10/06
2,000	19.05	4,849.15	9.53	19/50	1,909.49	10/02
3,000	28.57	7,284.72	14.29	19/50	2,868.94	10/02
4,000	38.10	9,697.12	19.05	20/00	3,804.04	10/00
5,000	47.62	12,133.11	23.81	20/00	4,763.92	10/00
6,000	57.14	14,568.47	28.57	20/00	5,723.20	10/00
7,000	66.67	16,980.77	33.34	20/00	6,672.22	10/00
8,000	76.19	19,415.82	38.10	20/00	7,630.64	10/00
9,000	85.71	21,853.36	42.86	20/00	8,591.41	10/00
10,000	95.24	24,264.89	47.62	20/00	9,526.23	10/00
15,000	142.85	36,421.94	71.43	20/00	14,314.16	10/00
20,000	190.47	48,554.57	95.24	20/00	19,077.98	10/00
25,000	238.09	60,686.30	119.05	20/00	23,840.30	10/00
30,000	285.70	72,842.94	142.85	20/00	28,614.18	10/00
35,000	333.32	84,975.42	166.66	20/00	33,377.18	10/00
45,000	428.55	109,265.48	214.28	20/00	42,929.09	10/00
55,000	523.78	133,555.45	261.89	20/00	52,467.26	10/00
65,000	619.02	157,819.37	309.51	20/00	61,993.22	10/00
75,000	714.25	182,109.18	357.13	20/00	71,544.22	10/00
85,000	809.48	206,398.76	404.74	20/00	81,081.51	10/00
100,000	952.33	242,821.17	476.17	20/00	95,396.46	10/00
120,000	1,142.79	291,398.74	571.40	20/00	114,483.45	10/00
140,000	1,333.26	339,952.63	666.63	20/00	133,547.16	10/00
160,000	1,523.72	388,530.55	761.86	20/00	152,634.41	10/00
180,000	1,714.19	437,086.11	857.10	20/00	171,713.04	10/00
200,000	1,904.65	485,665.03	952.33	20/00	190,801.70	10/00
225,000	2,142.73	546,376.32	1,071.37	20/00	214,652.97	10/00
250,000	2,380.81	607,087.35	1,190.41	20/00	238,505.40	10/00
275,000	2,618.89	667,798.93	1,309.45	20/00	262,356.95	10/00
300,000	2,856.98	728,485.10	1,428.49	20/00	286,183.63	10/00
350,000	3,333.14	849,907.86	1,666.57	20/00	333,887.42	10/00
400,000	3,809.30	971,331.01	1,904.65	20/00	381,591.29	10/00
450,000	4,285.46	1,092,753.12	2,142.73	20/00	429,294.38	10/00
500,000	4,761.62	1,214,174.89	2,380.81	20/00	476,996.90	10/00
550,000	5,237.78	1,335,597.38	2,618.89	20/00	524,699.94	10/00

11.25% 11.25%

BI-WEEKLY PAYMENT TABLE

TYPICAL 30 YEAR LOAN COMPARED TO A BI-WEEKLY

LOAN AMOUNT	MONTHLY PAYMENT	TOTAL INTEREST	BI-WKLY PAYMENT	TERM YR/WK	INTEREST SAVED	YR/WK SAVED
50	0.49	115.71	0.25	17/48	49.43	12/04
100	0.98	230.03	0.49	19/08	86.44	10/44
200	1.95	480.89	0.98	19/06	193.84	10/46
300	2.92	733.54	1.46	19/32	289.75	10/20
400	3.89	985.77	1.95	19/26	398.64	10/26
500	4.86	1,239.33	2.43	18/42	495.54	11/10
600	5.83	1,491.86	2.92	19/32	604.82	10/20
700	6.80	1,743.83	3.40	19/40	699.45	10/12
800	7.78	1,972.32	3.89	19/34	784.75	10/18
900	8.75	2,224.85	4.38	19/32	894.10	10/20
1,000	9.72	2,477.49	4.86	19/36	989.50	10/16
2,000	19.43	4,981.47	9.72	19/36	2,005.78	10/16
3,000	29.14	7,484.91	14.57	19/40	3,007.88	10/12
4,000	38.86	9,961.46	19.43	19/38	3,996.35	10/14
5,000	48.57	12,464.68	24.29	19/38	5,012.64	10/14
6,000	58.28	14,967.24	29.14	19/40	6,013.49	10/12
7,000	67.99	17,470.96	34.00	19/38	7,029.09	10/14
8,000	77.71	19,947.50	38.86	19/38	8,017.78	10/14
9,000	87.42	22,452.73	43.71	19/40	9,021.42	10/12
10,000	97.13	24,955.53	48.57	19/40	10,036.32	10/12
15,000	145.69	37,445.40	72.85	19/40	15,059.87	10/12
20,000	194.26	49,910.99	97.13	19/40	20,059.07	10/12
25,000	242.82	62,402.00	121.41	19/40	25,083.96	10/12
30,000	291.38	74,893.04	145.69	19/40	30,108.14	10/12
35,000	339.95	87,356.24	169.98	19/40	35,119.05	10/12
45,000	437.07	112,338.61	218.54	19/40	45,168.44	10/12
55,000	534.20	137,293.33	267.10	19/40	55,190.56	10/12
65,000	631.32	162,274.50	315.66	19/40	65,238.71	10/12
75,000	728.45	187,229.85	364.23	19/40	75,275.52	10/12
85,000	825.58	212,184.94	412.79	19/40	85,297.38	10/12
100,000	971.27	249,632.97	485.64	19/40	100,359.62	10/12
120,000	1,165.52	299,568.41	582.76	19/40	120,429.71	10/12
140,000	1,359.77	349,505.45	679.89	19/40	140,514.78	10/12
160,000	1,554.02	399,441.73	777.01	19/40	160,586.00	10/12
180,000	1,748.28	449,352.98	874.14	19/40	180,644.83	10/12
200,000	1,942.53	499,289.30	971.27	19/40	200,729.96	10/12
225,000	2,185.34	561,716.42	1,092.67	19/40	225,824.79	10/12
250,000	2,428.16	624,118.25	1,214.08	19/40	250,907.97	10/12
275,000	2,670.97	686,545.06	1,335.49	19/40	276,016.62	10/12
300,000	2,913.79	748,946.91	1,456.90	19/40	301,100.39	10/12
350,000	3,399.42	873,777.01	1,699.71	19/40	351,280.11	10/12
400,000	3,885.05	998,604.81	1,942.53	19/40	401,471.53	10/12
450,000	4,370.68	1,123,433.65	2,185.34	19/40	451,649.62	10/12
500,000	4,856.31	1,248,263.00	2,428.16	19/40	501,842.26	10/12
550,000	5,341.94	1,373,092.34	2,670.97	19/40	552,021.68	10/12

11.50% 11.50%

BI-WEEKLY PAYMENT TABLE

TYPICAL 30 YEAR LOAN COMPARED TO A BI-WEEKLY

LOAN AMOUNT	MONTHLY PAYMENT	TOTAL INTEREST	BI-WKLY PAYMENT	TERM YR/WK	INTEREST SAVED	YR/WK SAVED
50	0.50	117.50	0.25	18/48	44.69	11/04
100	1.00	233.61	0.50	18/44	88.78	11/08
200	1.99	488.88	1.00	18/44	199.72	11/08
300	2.98	745.25	1.49	19/16	298.24	10/36
400	3.97	1,002.68	1.99	19/10	411.31	10/42
500	4.96	1,259.57	2.48	19/20	510.06	10/32
600	5.95	1,517.00	2.98	19/16	622.96	10/36
700	6.94	1,773.61	3.47	19/22	721.53	10/30
800	7.93	2,031.40	3.97	19/18	835.45	10/34
900	8.92	2,288.62	4.46	19/24	934.47	10/28
1,000	9.91	2,545.28	4.96	19/20	1,046.36	10/32
2,000	19.81	5,118.32	9.91	19/24	2,106.94	10/28
3,000	29.71	7,690.79	14.86	19/26	3,167.02	10/26
4,000	39.62	10,237.58	19.81	19/26	4,201.40	10/26
5,000	49.52	12,810.02	24.76	19/26	5,261.45	10/26
6,000	59.42	15,383.08	29.71	19/26	6,322.00	10/26
7,000	69.33	17,928.93	34.67	19/26	7,368.86	10/26
8,000	79.23	20,502.97	39.62	19/26	8,430.96	10/26
9,000	89.13	23,074.35	44.57	19/26	9,489.40	10/26
10,000	99.03	25,646.99	49.52	19/26	10,549.48	10/26
15,000	148.55	38,459.30	74.28	19/26	15,813.53	10/26
20,000	198.06	51,296.80	99.03	19/26	21,088.60	10/26
25,000	247.58	64,106.22	123.79	19/26	26,350.00	10/26
30,000	297.09	76,944.38	148.55	19/26	31,639.21	10/26
35,000	346.61	89,754.80	173.31	19/26	36,901.00	10/26
45,000	445.64	115,403.81	222.82	19/26	47,438.93	10/26
55,000	544.67	141,051.11	272.34	19/26	57,989.49	10/26
65,000	643.69	166,726.06	321.85	19/26	68,553.46	10/26
75,000	742.72	192,373.98	371.36	19/28	79,090.16	10/24
85,000	841.75	218,023.07	420.88	19/26	89,642.65	10/26
100,000	990.30	256,482.10	495.15	19/26	105,442.16	10/26
120,000	1,188.35	307,804.62	594.18	19/26	126,556.37	10/26
140,000	1,386.41	359,102.56	693.21	19/26	147,645.61	10/26
160,000	1,584.47	410,397.04	792.24	19/26	168,732.07	10/26
180,000	1,782.53	461,694.20	891.27	19/26	189,821.67	10/26
200,000	1,980.59	512,989.85	990.30	19/26	210,909.40	10/26
225,000	2,228.16	577,124.15	1,114.08	19/28	237,273.42	10/24
250,000	2,475.73	641,258.51	1,237.87	19/28	263,650.81	10/24
275,000	2,723.31	705,364.43	1,361.66	19/28	290,000.48	10/24
300,000	2,970.88	769,498.06	1,485.44	19/28	316,363.21	10/24
350,000	3,466.03	897,739.87	1,733.02	19/28	369,091.62	10/24
400,000	3,961.17	1,026,007.90	1,980.59	19/28	421,832.84	10/24
450,000	4,456.32	1,154,248.10	2,228.16	19/28	474,545.91	10/24
500,000	4,951.46	1,282,516.70	2,475.73	19/28	527,286.76	10/24
550,000	5,446.61	1,410,757.02	2,723.31	19/28	580,014.15	10/24

11.75% 11.75%

BI-WEEKLY PAYMENT TABLE

TYPICAL 30 YEAR LOAN COMPARED TO A BI-WEEKLY

LOAN AMOUNT	MONTHLY PAYMENT	TOTAL INTEREST	BI-WKLY PAYMENT	TERM YR/WK	INTEREST SAVED	YR/WK SAVED
50	0.51	119.32	0.26	17/20	52.05	12/32
100	1.01	262.58	0.51	18/30	116.73	11/22
200	2.02	523.44	1.01	19/12	218.93	10/40
300	3.03	785.30	1.52	19/00	335.03	11/00
400	4.04	1,046.62	2.02	19/12	437.29	10/40
500	5.05	1,308.47	2.53	19/04	553.73	10/48
600	6.06	1,569.13	3.03	19/12	655.10	10/40
700	7.07	1,831.50	3.54	19/06	772.55	10/46
800	8.08	2,093.78	4.04	19/12	874.98	10/40
900	9.09	2,355.22	4.55	19/08	991.46	10/44
1,000	10.10	2,616.93	5.05	19/12	1,093.94	10/40
2,000	20.19	5,262.10	10.10	19/12	2,216.05	10/40
3,000	30.29	7,880.15	15.15	19/12	3,310.54	10/40
4,000	40.38	10,525.98	20.19	19/14	4,419.43	10/38
5,000	50.48	13,141.18	25.24	19/14	5,511.50	10/38
6,000	60.57	15,786.65	30.29	19/14	6,633.79	10/38
7,000	70.66	18,433.30	35.33	19/14	7,744.40	10/38
8,000	80.76	21,049.50	40.38	19/14	8,836.24	10/38
9,000	90.85	23,696.85	45.43	19/14	9,961.18	10/38
10,000	100.95	26,313.33	50.48	19/14	11,055.20	10/38
15,000	151.42	39,482.33	75.71	19/14	16,580.54	10/38
20,000	201.89	52,653.56	100.95	19/14	22,122.18	10/38
25,000	252.36	65,824.42	126.18	19/14	27,649.90	10/38
30,000	302.83	78,995.49	151.42	19/14	33,190.88	10/38
35,000	353.30	92,165.48	176.65	19/14	38,717.59	10/38
45,000	454.24	118,507.70	227.12	19/14	49,788.03	10/38
55,000	555.18	144,848.31	277.59	19/14	60,854.92	10/38
65,000	656.12	171,191.81	328.06	19/14	71,926.60	10/38
75,000	757.06	197,532.74	378.53	19/14	82,994.74	10/38
85,000	858.00	223,874.00	429.00	19/14	94,062.97	10/38
100,000	1,009.41	263,387.05	504.71	19/14	110,674.37	10/38
120,000	1,211.30	316,040.10	605.65	19/14	132,781.33	10/38
140,000	1,413.18	368,723.74	706.59	19/14	154,919.87	10/38
160,000	1,615.06	421,406.20	807.53	19/14	177,057.42	10/38
180,000	1,816.94	474,090.92	908.47	19/14	199,196.83	10/38
200,000	2,018.82	526,772.80	1,009.41	19/14	221,332.73	10/38
225,000	2,271.18	592,597.52	1,135.59	19/14	248,982.93	10/38
250,000	2,523.53	658,452.73	1,261.77	19/14	276,663.37	10/38
275,000	2,775.88	724,306.32	1,387.94	19/14	304,328.91	10/38
300,000	3,028.23	790,159.98	1,514.12	19/14	332,007.66	10/38
350,000	3,532.94	921,838.94	1,766.47	19/14	387,322.74	10/38
400,000	4,037.64	1,053,547.93	2,018.82	19/14	442,668.64	10/38
450,000	4,542.35	1,185,225.33	2,271.18	19/14	497,996.08	10/38
500,000	5,047.05	1,316,933.23	2,523.53	19/14	553,340.74	10/38
550,000	5,551.76	1,448,612.23	2,775.88	19/14	608,656.33	10/38

12.00% 12.00%

BI-WEEKLY PAYMENT TABLE

TYPICAL 30 YEAR LOAN COMPARED TO A BI-WEEKLY

LOAN AMOUNT	MONTHLY PAYMENT	TOTAL INTEREST	BI-WKLY PAYMENT	TERM YR/WK	INTEREST SAVED	YR/WK SAVED
50	0.52	121.26	0.26	18/18	47.41	11/34
100	1.03	266.74	0.52	18/14	119.77	11/38
200	2.06	532.41	1.03	18/48	225.73	11/04
300	3.09	798.43	1.55	18/36	345.40	11/16
400	4.12	1,064.60	2.06	18/48	451.08	11/04
500	5.15	1,331.04	2.58	18/42	571.19	11/10
600	6.18	1,596.48	3.09	18/48	676.34	11/04
700	7.21	1,862.41	3.61	18/44	795.99	11/08
800	8.23	2,159.94	4.12	18/48	933.10	11/04
900	9.26	2,424.91	4.63	19/00	1,037.97	11/00
1,000	10.29	2,690.94	5.15	18/48	1,157.49	11/04
2,000	20.58	5,382.63	10.29	19/00	2,301.69	11/00
3,000	30.86	8,104.25	15.43	19/00	3,476.42	11/00
4,000	41.15	10,794.28	20.58	19/02	4,633.23	10/50
5,000	51.44	13,485.87	25.72	19/02	5,777.21	10/50
6,000	61.72	16,207.24	30.86	19/02	6,950.75	10/50
7,000	72.01	18,900.22	36.01	19/02	8,110.52	10/50
8,000	82.29	21,620.12	41.15	19/02	9,283.70	10/50
9,000	92.58	24,310.27	46.29	19/02	10,426.55	10/50
10,000	102.87	27,001.48	51.44	19/02	11,583.47	10/50
15,000	154.30	40,520.16	77.15	19/02	17,378.99	10/50
20,000	205.73	54,036.51	102.87	19/02	23,187.18	10/50
25,000	257.16	67,554.72	128.58	19/02	28,982.42	10/50
30,000	308.59	81,070.67	154.30	19/02	34,789.74	10/50
35,000	360.02	94,588.66	180.01	19/02	40,584.44	10/50
45,000	462.88	121,621.03	231.44	19/02	52,184.84	10/50
55,000	565.74	148,654.67	282.87	19/02	63,786.91	10/50
65,000	668.60	175,689.63	334.30	19/02	75,390.15	10/50
75,000	771.46	202,724.53	385.73	19/02	86,993.17	10/50
65,000	668.60	175,689.63	334.30	19/02	75,390.15	10/50
100,000	1,028.62	270,278.95	514.31	19/02	115,975.18	10/50
120,000	1,234.34	324,345.38	617.17	19/02	139,177.84	10/50
140,000	1,440.06	378,413.72	720.03	19/02	162,382.52	10/50
160,000	1,645.79	432,449.86	822.90	19/02	185,569.57	10/50
180,000	1,851.51	486,517.34	925.76	19/02	208,773.00	10/50
200,000	2,057.23	540,586.45	1,028.62	19/02	231,978.58	10/50
225,000	2,314.38	608,172.52	1,157.19	19/02	260,978.64	10/50
250,000	2,571.54	675,724.55	1,285.77	19/02	289,958.01	10/50
275,000	2,828.69	743,309.15	1,414.35	19/02	318,969.78	10/50
300,000	3,085.84	810,895.11	1,542.92	19/02	347,969.07	10/50
350,000	3,600.15	946,034.07	1,800.08	19/02	405,963.60	10/50
400,000	4,114.46	1,081,172.30	2,057.23	19/02	463,942.53	10/50
450,000	4,628.76	1,216,341.43	2,314.38	19/02	521,952.35	10/50
500,000	5,143.07	1,351,480.54	2,571.54	19/02	579,946.86	10/50
550,000	5,657.37	1,486,651.36	2,828.69	19/02	637,959.12	10/50

BI-WEEKLY PAYMENT TABLE

TYPICAL 30 YEAR LOAN COMPARED TO A BI-WEEKLY

LOAN AMOUNT	MONTHLY PAYMENT	TOTAL INTEREST	BI-WKLY PAYMENT	TERM YR/WK	INTEREST SAVED	YR/WK SAVED
50	0.53	123.05	0.27	16/46	54.78	13/06
100	1.05	271.37	0.53	18/00	123.37	12/00
200	2.10	541.33	1.05	18/34	232.53	11/18
300	3.15	811.87	1.58	18/22	355.62	11/30
400	4.20	1,081.42	2.10	18/34	464.19	11/18
500	5.24	1,383.77	2.62	18/42	605.00	11/10
600	6.29	1,654.28	3.15	18/34	728.15	11/18
700	7.34	1,924.66	3.67	18/40	837.22	11/12
800	8.39	2,195.51	4.20	18/34	960.69	11/18
900	9.44	2,464.93	4.72	18/38	1,069.00	11/14
1,000	10.48	2,768.93	5.24	18/42	1,211.27	11/10
2,000	20.96	5,538.36	10.48	18/42	2,423.43	11/10
3,000	31.44	8,307.29	15.72	18/42	3,634.48	11/10
4,000	41.92	11,076.10	20.96	18/42	4,846.40	11/10
5,000	52.40	13,844.78	26.20	18/42	6,057.44	11/10
6,000	62.88	16,613.67	31.44	18/42	7,269.15	11/10
7,000	73.36	19,384.27	36.68	18/42	8,481.76	11/10
8,000	83.84	22,150.80	41.92	18/42	9,691.25	11/10
9,000	94.32	24,920.96	47.16	18/42	10,904.59	11/10
10,000	104.79	27,723.66	52.40	18/42	12,149.53	11/10
15,000	157.19	41,568.04	78.60	18/42	18,206.69	11/10
20,000	209.58	55,446.60	104.79	18/42	24,283.85	11/10
25,000	261.98	69,291.17	130.99	18/42	30,341.74	11/10
30,000	314.37	83,169.03	157.19	18/42	36,431.85	11/10
35,000	366.77	97,015.41	183.39	18/42	42,491.39	11/10
45,000	471.56	124,736.55	235.78	18/42	54,624.19	11/10
55,000	576.35	152,460.34	288.18	18/42	66,773.33	11/10
65,000	681.14	180,181.87	340.57	18/42	78,906.81	11/10
75,000	785.93	207,907.14	392.97	18/42	91,057.78	11/10
85,000	890.72	235,630.56	445.36	18/42	103,192.24	11/10
100,000	1,047.90	277,229.93	523.95	18/42	121,416.64	11/10
120,000	1,257.48	332,677.74	628.74	18/42	145,701.06	11/10
140,000	1,467.06	388,122.92	733.53	18/42	169,984.12	11/10
160,000	1,676.64	443,569.04	838.32	18/42	194,267.26	11/10
180,000	1,886.22	499,015.77	943.11	18/42	218,552.48	11/10
200,000	2,095.80	554,462.37	1,047.90	18/42	242,835.54	11/10
225,000	2,357.77	623,786.76	1,178.89	18/42	273,210.26	11/10
250,000	2,619.75	693,076.63	1,309.88	18/42	303,550.11	11/10
275,000	2,881.72	762,402.23	1,440.86	18/42	333,911.67	11/10
300,000	3,143.69	831,724.89	1,571.85	18/42	364,284.16	11/10
350,000	3,667.64	970,340.62	1,833.82	18/42	424,985.98	11/10
400,000	4,191.59	1,108,956.72	2,095.80	18/42	485,703.16	11/10
450,000	4,715.54	1,247,571.72	2,357.77	18/42	546,403.78	11/10
500,000	5,239.49	1,386,188.78	2,619.75	18/42	607,121.90	11/10
550,000	5,763.44	1,524,802.51	2,881.72	18/42	667,821.87	11/10

12.50% 12.50%

BI-WEEKLY PAYMENT TABLE

TYPICAL 30 YEAR LOAN COMPARED TO A BI-WEEKLY

LOAN AMOUNT	MONTHLY PAYMENT	TOTAL INTEREST	BI-WKLY PAYMENT	TERM YR/WK	INTEREST SAVED	YR/WK SAVED
50	0.54	124.94	0.27	17/42	49.99	12/10
100	1.07	275.48	0.54	17/40	126.37	12/12
200	2.14	550.31	1.07	18/20	239.57	11/32
300	3.21	825.42	1.61	18/08	366.13	11/44
400	4.27	1,133.83	2.14	18/20	512.58	11/32
500	5.34	1,408.06	2.67	18/26	624.38	11/26
600	6.41	1,684.04	3.21	18/20	751.94	11/32
700	7.48	1,958.28	3.74	18/24	864.19	11/28
800	8.54	2,267.33	4.27	18/28	1,010.61	11/24
900	9.61	2,541.30	4.81	18/24	1,136.58	11/28
1,000	10.68	2,815.79	5.34	18/26	1,248.56	11/26
2,000	21.35	5,666.28	10.68	18/26	2,531.94	11/26
3,000	32.02	8,517.82	16.01	18/28	3,802.72	11/24
4,000	42.70	11,335.73	21.35	18/28	5,052.93	11/24
5,000	53.37	14,185.09	26.69	18/28	6,335.19	11/24
6,000	64.04	17,035.73	32.02	18/28	7,603.93	11/24
7,000	74.71	19,889.19	37.36	18/28	8,890.41	11/24
8,000	85.39	22,704.08	42.70	18/28	10,138.04	11/24
9,000	96.06	25,555.92	48.03	18/28	11,409.07	11/24
10,000	106.73	28,407.34	53.37	18/28	12,692.98	11/24
15,000	160.09	42,627.54	80.05	18/28	19,049.00	11/24
20,000	213.46	56,812.97	106.73	18/28	25,370.60	11/24
25,000	266.82	71,033.49	133.41	18/30	31,726.94	11/22
30,000	320.18	85,254.96	160.09	18/30	38,083.73	11/22
35,000	373.55	99,440.92	186.78	18/28	44,419.45	11/24
45,000	480.27	127,880.75	240.14	18/30	57,130.63	11/22
55,000	587.00	156,288.52	293.50	18/30	69,810.65	11/22
65,000	693.72	184,730.20	346.86	18/30	82,523.90	11/22
75,000	800.45	213,135.88	400.23	18/30	95,215.92	11/22
85,000	907.17	241,577.78	453.59	18/30	107,928.21	11/22
100,000	1,067.26	284,204.08	533.63	18/30	126,961.83	11/22
120,000	1,280.71	341,052.71	640.36	18/30	152,369.01	11/22
140,000	1,494.17	397,866.02	747.09	18/30	177,739.13	11/22
160,000	1,707.62	454,713.02	853.81	18/30	203,128.98	11/22
180,000	1,921.07	511,562.22	960.54	18/30	228,535.64	11/22
200,000	2,134.52	568,409.80	1,067.26	18/30	253,926.56	11/22
225,000	2,401.33	639,479.42	1,200.67	18/30	285,689.35	11/22
250,000	2,668.15	710,513.18	1,334.08	18/30	317,416.44	11/22
275,000	2,934.96	781,579.86	1,467.48	18/30	349,162.32	11/22
300,000	3,201.78	852,613.72	1,600.89	18/30	380,888.89	11/22
350,000	3,735.41	994,715.94	1,867.71	18/30	444,377.89	11/22
400,000	4,269.04	1,136,818.99	2,134.52	18/30	507,852.90	11/22
450,000	4,802.66	1,278,957.30	2,401.33	18/30	571,363.50	11/22
500,000	5,336.29	1,421,057.64	2,668.15	18/30	634,849.70	11/22
550,000	5,869.92	1,563,162.01	2,934.96	18/30	698,326.18	11/22

12.75% **12.75%**

BI-WEEKLY PAYMENT TABLE

TYPICAL 30 YEAR LOAN COMPARED TO A BI-WEEKLY

LOAN AMOUNT	MONTHLY PAYMENT	TOTAL INTEREST	BI-WKLY PAYMENT	TERM YR/WK	INTEREST SAVED	YR/WK SAVED
50	0.55	126.72	0.28	16/20	57.56	13/32
100	1.09	279.79	0.55	17/26	129.75	12/26
200	2.18	558.55	1.09	18/06	245.80	11/46
300	3.27	838.59	1.64	17/46	376.38	12/06
400	4.35	1,153.22	2.18	18/06	527.90	11/46
500	5.44	1,432.26	2.72	18/12	643.70	11/40
600	6.53	1,710.48	3.27	18/06	772.52	11/46
700	7.61	2,026.23	3.81	18/10	925.27	11/42
800	8.70	2,305.14	4.35	18/14	1,040.85	11/38
900	9.79	2,584.78	4.90	18/10	1,171.41	11/42
1,000	10.87	2,900.64	5.44	18/12	1,323.63	11/40
2,000	21.74	5,800.17	10.87	18/16	2,632.64	11/36
3,000	32.61	8,701.56	16.31	18/14	3,957.03	11/38
4,000	43.47	11,640.28	21.74	18/16	5,305.20	11/36
5,000	54.34	14,542.00	27.17	18/16	6,616.46	11/36
6,000	65.21	17,441.74	32.61	18/16	7,938.78	11/36
7,000	76.07	20,378.96	38.04	18/16	9,286.05	11/36
8,000	86.94	23,279.50	43.47	18/16	10,595.60	11/36
9,000	97.81	26,178.59	48.91	18/16	11,917.70	11/36
10,000	108.67	29,117.99	54.34	18/16	13,265.89	11/36
15,000	163.01	43,658.76	81.51	18/16	19,880.92	11/36
20,000	217.34	58,236.13	108.67	18/16	26,518.24	11/36
25,000	271.68	72,777.62	135.84	18/16	33,133.55	11/36
30,000	326.01	87,354.45	163.01	18/16	39,785.40	11/36
35,000	380.35	101,895.32	190.18	18/16	46,399.66	11/36
45,000	489.02	131,013.68	244.51	18/16	59,652.02	11/36
55,000	597.69	160,131.69	298.85	18/16	72,918.29	11/36
65,000	706.36	189,252.95	353.18	18/16	86,173.64	11/36
75,000	815.02	218,406.42	407.51	18/16	99,460.97	11/36
85,000	923.69	247,525.07	461.85	18/16	112,727.65	11/36
100,000	1,086.70	291,184.52	543.35	18/16	132,595.53	11/36
120,000	1,304.04	349,419.52	652.02	18/16	159,112.29	11/36
140,000	1,521.38	407,658.82	760.69	18/16	185,633.88	11/36
160,000	1,738.71	465,933.23	869.36	18/16	212,190.74	11/36
180,000	1,956.05	524,172.01	978.03	18/16	238,711.66	11/36
200,000	2,173.39	582,405.82	1,086.70	18/16	265,228.01	11/36
225,000	2,445.06	655,220.80	1,222.53	18/16	298,385.22	11/36
250,000	2,716.74	727,996.93	1,358.37	18/16	331,517.31	11/36
275,000	2,988.41	800,812.29	1,494.21	18/16	364,688.65	11/36
300,000	3,260.08	873,628.67	1,630.04	18/16	397,847.54	11/36
350,000	3,803.43	1,019,218.50	1,901.72	18/16	464,149.77	11/36
400,000	4,346.78	1,164,810.86	2,173.39	18/16	530,440.01	11/36
450,000	4,890.12	1,310,441.00	2,445.06	18/16	596,769.31	11/36
500,000	5,433.47	1,456,032.77	2,716.74	18/16	663,073.73	11/36
550,000	5,976.82	1,601,626.33	2,988.41	18/16	729,365.08	11/36

BI-WEEKLY PAYMENT TABLE

TYPICAL 30 YEAR LOAN COMPARED TO A BI-WEEKLY

LOAN AMOUNT	MONTHLY PAYMENT	TOTAL INTEREST	BI-WKLY PAYMENT	TERM YR/WK	INTEREST SAVED	YR/WK SAVED
50	0.56	128.40	0.28	17/16	52.49	12/36
100	1.11	284.16	0.56	17/14	133.12	12/38
200	2.22	568.12	1.11	17/44	253.55	12/08
300	3.32	889.49	1.66	18/04	410.68	11/48
400	4.43	1,172.62	2.22	17/44	543.67	12/08
500	5.54	1,456.91	2.77	18/04	663.87	11/48
600	6.64	1,778.71	3.32	18/04	821.33	11/48
700	7.75	2,060.31	3.88	17/48	953.04	12/04
800	8.85	2,384.07	4.43	18/00	1,112.14	12/00
900	9.96	2,667.76	4.98	18/04	1,231.55	11/48
1,000	11.07	2,950.78	5.54	17/50	1,364.80	12/02
2,000	22.13	5,941.21	11.07	18/02	2,755.30	11/50
3,000	33.19	8,931.48	16.60	18/04	4,145.11	11/48
4,000	44.25	11,920.03	22.13	18/04	5,533.60	11/48
5,000	55.31	14,911.29	27.66	18/04	6,924.66	11/48
6,000	66.38	17,861.67	33.19	18/04	8,274.80	11/48
7,000	77.44	20,852.60	38.72	18/04	9,665.64	11/48
8,000	88.50	23,843.60	44.25	18/04	11,057.00	11/48
9,000	99.56	26,831.50	49.78	18/04	12,444.46	11/48
10,000	110.62	29,822.21	55.31	18/04	13,835.24	11/48
15,000	165.93	44,734.85	82.97	18/04	20,761.50	11/48
20,000	221.24	59,646.91	110.62	18/04	27,672.59	11/48
25,000	276.55	74,556.63	138.28	18/04	34,595.73	11/48
30,000	331.86	89,468.41	165.93	18/04	41,507.26	11/48
35,000	387.17	104,379.43	193.59	18/04	48,431.93	11/48
45,000	497.79	134,203.85	248.90	18/04	62,269.73	11/48
55,000	608.41	164,026.76	304.21	18/04	76,104.92	11/48
65,000	719.03	193,850.07	359.52	18/04	89,940.94	11/48
75,000	829.65	223,672.01	414.83	18/04	103,776.48	11/48
85,000	940.27	253,495.50	470.14	18/04	117,612.30	11/48
100,000	1,106.20	298,231.37	553.10	18/04	138,360.14	11/48
120,000	1,327.44	357,877.38	663.72	18/04	166,032.75	11/48
140,000	1,548.68	417,521.13	774.34	18/04	193,702.47	11/48
160,000	1,769.92	477,166.47	884.96	18/04	221,373.71	11/48
180,000	1,991.16	536,812.67	995.58	18/04	249,045.72	11/48
200,000	2,212.40	596,458.52	1,106.20	18/04	276,717.59	11/48
225,000	2,488.95	671,017.87	1,244.48	18/04	311,316.66	11/48
250,000	2,765.50	745,576.52	1,382.75	18/04	345,900.54	11/48
275,000	3,042.05	820,134.02	1,521.03	18/04	380,497.48	11/48
300,000	3,318.60	894,691.90	1,659.30	18/04	415,080.30	11/48
350,000	3,871.70	1,043,805.07	1,935.85	18/04	484,258.58	11/48
400,000	4,424.80	1,192,919.64	2,212.40	18/04	553,438.49	11/48
450,000	4,977.90	1,342,034.48	2,488.95	18/04	622,617.72	11/48
500,000	5,531.00	1,491,148.32	2,765.50	18/04	691,796.27	11/48
550,000	6,084.10	1,640,264.77	3,042.05	18/04	760,977.68	11/48

13.25% 13.25%

BI-WEEKLY PAYMENT TABLE

TYPICAL 30 YEAR LOAN COMPARED TO A BI-WEEKLY

LOAN AMOUNT	MONTHLY PAYMENT	TOTAL INTEREST	BI-WKLY PAYMENT	TERM YR/WK	INTEREST SAVED	YR/WK SAVED
50	0.57	130.30	0.29	15/50	60.16	14/02
100	1.13	288.33	0.57	17/02	136.38	12/50
200	2.26	578.33	1.13	17/32	261.82	12/20
300	3.38	904.78	1.69	17/42	423.43	12/10
400	4.51	1,192.85	2.26	17/30	560.14	12/22
500	5.63	1,521.06	2.82	17/40	723.46	12/12
600	6.76	1,809.79	3.38	17/42	847.07	12/10
700	7.89	2,097.81	3.95	17/36	984.15	12/16
800	9.01	2,426.16	4.51	17/38	1,147.05	12/14
900	10.14	2,714.59	5.07	17/42	1,270.94	12/10
1,000	11.26	3,043.48	5.63	17/44	1,434.08	12/08
2,000	22.52	6,087.17	11.26	17/44	2,869.29	12/08
3,000	33.78	9,130.54	16.89	17/44	4,302.76	12/08
4,000	45.04	12,174.10	22.52	17/44	5,737.30	12/08
5,000	56.29	15,259.42	28.15	17/44	7,213.79	12/08
6,000	67.55	18,302.02	33.78	17/44	8,647.88	12/08
7,000	78.81	21,345.07	39.41	17/44	10,080.70	12/08
8,000	90.07	24,386.15	45.04	17/44	11,512.40	12/08
9,000	101.32	27,474.26	50.66	17/44	12,977.61	12/08
10,000	112.58	30,515.32	56.29	17/44	14,409.70	12/08
15,000	168.87	45,776.28	84.44	17/44	21,624.67	12/08
20,000	225.16	61,034.54	112.58	17/44	28,822.88	12/08
25,000	281.45	76,290.39	140.73	17/44	36,032.70	12/08
30,000	337.74	91,551.01	168.87	17/44	43,233.80	12/08
35,000	394.03	106,806.29	197.02	17/44	50,443.42	12/08
45,000	506.60	137,367.51	253.30	17/44	64,884.56	12/08
55,000	619.18	167,883.63	309.59	17/44	79,294.58	12/08
65,000	731.76	198,400.61	365.88	17/44	93,705.32	12/08
75,000	844.34	228,918.21	422.17	17/44	108,117.87	12/08
85,000	956.91	259,474.06	478.46	17/44	122,568.45	12/08
100,000	1,125.78	305,249.63	562.89	17/44	144,178.06	12/08
120,000	1,350.93	366,325.73	675.47	17/44	173,041.83	12/08
140,000	1,576.09	427,360.79	788.05	17/44	201,865.74	12/08
160,000	1,801.24	488,433.88	900.62	17/44	230,713.21	12/08
180,000	2,026.40	549,468.77	1,013.20	17/44	259,536.15	12/08
200,000	2,251.55	610,543.16	1,125.78	17/44	288,399.18	12/08
225,000	2,533.00	686,837.01	1,266.50	17/44	324,421.64	12/08
250,000	2,814.44	763,170.17	1,407.22	17/44	360,482.84	12/08
275,000	3,095.88	839,503.81	1,547.94	17/44	396,544.80	12/08
300,000	3,377.33	915,796.07	1,688.67	17/44	432,581.02	12/08
350,000	3,940.21	1,068,462.70	1,970.11	17/44	504,703.70	12/08
400,000	4,503.10	1,221,088.37	2,251.55	17/44	576,785.90	12/08
450,000	5,065.99	1,373,715.20	2,533.00	17/44	648,883.92	12/08
500,000	5,628.87	1,526,381.99	2,814.44	17/44	721,007.84	12/08
550,000	6,191.76	1,679,007.53	3,095.88	17/44	793,090.59	12/08

13.50% 13.50%

BI-WEEKLY PAYMENT TABLE

TYPICAL 30 YEAR LOAN COMPARED TO A BI-WEEKLY

LOAN AMOUNT	MONTHLY PAYMENT	TOTAL INTEREST	BI-WKLY PAYMENT	TERM YR/WK	INTEREST SAVED	YR/WK SAVED
50	0.58	132.18	0.29	16/44	55.40	13/08
100	1.15	293.37	0.58	16/40	140.49	13/12
200	2.30	587.37	1.15	17/18	269.19	12/34
300	3.44	919.90	1.72	17/28	435.79	12/24
400	4.59	1,213.22	2.30	17/18	577.01	12/34
500	5.73	1,549.13	2.87	17/24	746.97	12/28
600	6.88	1,840.77	3.44	17/28	872.60	12/24
700	8.02	2,176.83	4.01	17/32	1,042.80	12/20
800	9.17	2,469.37	4.59	17/26	1,183.35	12/26
900	10.31	2,805.08	5.16	17/28	1,352.86	12/24
1,000	11.46	3,097.86	5.73	17/30	1,479.83	12/22
2,000	22.91	6,239.16	11.46	17/30	3,003.29	12/22
3,000	34.37	9,334.05	17.19	17/30	4,480.02	12/22
4,000	45.82	12,477.77	22.91	17/32	5,991.47	12/20
5,000	57.28	15,575.52	28.64	17/32	7,471.30	12/20
6,000	68.73	18,717.19	34.37	17/32	8,995.56	12/20
7,000	80.18	21,858.26	40.09	17/32	10,504.01	12/20
8,000	91.64	24,956.95	45.82	17/32	11,984.60	12/20
9,000	103.09	28,098.58	51.55	17/32	13,508.69	12/20
10,000	114.55	31,193.31	57.28	17/32	14,985.07	12/20
15,000	171.82	46,816.32	85.91	17/32	22,489.44	12/20
20,000	229.09	62,434.77	114.55	17/32	30,004.23	12/20
25,000	286.36	78,057.79	143.18	17/32	37,509.10	12/20
30,000	343.63	93,675.44	171.82	17/32	45,022.63	12/20
35,000	400.90	109,294.68	200.45	17/32	52,523.70	12/20
45,000	515.44	140,537.23	257.72	17/32	67,544.25	12/20
55,000	629.98	171,778.38	314.99	17/32	82,562.54	12/20
65,000	744.52	203,016.01	372.26	17/32	97,577.96	12/20
75,000	859.06	234,256.85	429.53	17/32	112,596.78	12/20
85,000	973.61	265,452.69	486.81	17/32	127,584.51	12/20
100,000	1,145.42	312,311.62	572.71	17/32	150,103.56	12/20
120,000	1,374.50	374,793.05	687.25	17/32	180,139.83	12/20
140,000	1,603.58	437,274.52	801.79	17/32	210,177.10	12/20
160,000	1,832.66	499,753.96	916.33	17/32	240,211.37	12/20
180,000	2,061.75	562,191.95	1,030.88	17/32	270,219.05	12/20
200,000	2,290.83	624,670.81	1,145.42	17/32	300,253.38	12/20
225,000	2,577.18	702,770.62	1,288.59	17/32	337,790.23	12/20
250,000	2,863.54	780,827.49	1,431.77	17/32	375,299.01	12/20
275,000	3,149.89	858,927.47	1,574.95	17/32	412,850.15	12/20
300,000	3,436.24	937,030.36	1,718.12	17/32	450,389.97	12/20
350,000	4,008.95	1,093,184.69	2,004.48	17/32	525,446.48	12/20
400,000	4,581.65	1,249,388.02	2,290.83	17/32	600,539.77	12/20
450,000	5,154.36	1,405,545.72	2,577.18	17/32	675,585.16	12/20
500,000	5,727.07	1,561,700.45	2,863.54	17/32	750,642.51	12/20
550,000	6,299.77	1,717,901.51	3,149.89	17/32	825,732.39	12/20

13.75% **13.75%**

BI-WEEKLY PAYMENT TABLE

TYPICAL 30 YEAR LOAN COMPARED TO A BI-WEEKLY

LOAN AMOUNT	MONTHLY PAYMENT	TOTAL INTEREST	BI-WKLY PAYMENT	TERM YR/WK	INTEREST SAVED	YR/WK SAVED
50	0.59	133.72	0.30	15/28	62.56	14/24
100	1.17	298.33	0.59	16/30	144.48	13/22
200	2.34	597.06	1.17	17/06	277.12	12/46
300	3.50	936.88	1.75	17/16	450.30	12/36
400	4.67	1,234.09	2.34	17/12	594.11	12/40
500	5.83	1,576.40	2.92	17/12	769.85	12/40
600	7.00	1,873.45	3.50	17/16	900.22	12/36
700	8.16	2,216.73	4.08	17/20	1,076.60	12/32
800	9.33	2,512.05	4.67	17/14	1,219.10	12/38
900	10.49	2,855.18	5.25	17/16	1,395.35	12/36
1,000	11.66	3,152.54	5.83	17/18	1,525.64	12/34
2,000	23.31	6,351.46	11.66	17/18	3,098.38	12/34
3,000	34.96	9,552.13	17.48	17/20	4,657.66	12/32
4,000	46.61	12,752.54	23.31	17/20	6,231.95	12/32
5,000	58.26	15,950.66	29.13	17/20	7,789.49	12/32
6,000	69.91	19,150.29	34.96	17/20	9,362.14	12/32
7,000	81.56	22,349.85	40.78	17/20	10,921.57	12/32
8,000	93.21	25,549.84	46.61	17/20	12,495.09	12/32
9,000	104.87	28,702.01	52.44	17/20	14,020.39	12/32
10,000	116.52	31,902.85	58.26	17/20	15,580.26	12/32
15,000	174.77	47,902.27	87.39	17/20	23,418.67	12/32
20,000	233.03	63,852.35	116.52	17/20	31,207.64	12/32
25,000	291.28	79,852.16	145.64	17/20	39,032.14	12/32
30,000	349.54	95,801.22	174.77	17/20	46,819.77	12/32
35,000	407.79	111,800.77	203.90	17/20	54,658.06	12/32
45,000	524.31	143,703.05	262.16	17/20	70,238.12	12/32
55,000	640.82	175,652.84	320.41	17/20	85,850.85	12/32
65,000	757.33	207,604.22	378.67	17/20	101,479.84	12/32
75,000	873.84	239,552.31	436.92	17/20	117,090.96	12/32
85,000	990.35	271,504.62	495.18	17/20	132,721.52	12/32
100,000	1,165.12	319,404.69	582.56	17/20	156,122.69	12/32
120,000	1,398.14	383,303.63	699.07	17/20	187,362.96	12/32
140,000	1,631.16	447,205.61	815.58	17/20	218,606.16	12/32
160,000	1,864.19	511,055.70	932.10	17/20	249,811.42	12/32
180,000	2,097.21	574,956.84	1,048.61	17/20	281,053.16	12/32
200,000	2,330.23	638,858.43	1,165.12	17/20	312,296.20	12/32
225,000	2,621.51	718,708.18	1,310.76	17/20	351,325.34	12/32
250,000	2,912.79	798,558.56	1,456.40	17/20	390,355.33	12/32
275,000	3,204.06	878,457.70	1,602.03	17/20	429,419.62	12/32
300,000	3,495.34	958,310.31	1,747.67	17/20	468,452.73	12/32
350,000	4,077.90	1,118,012.80	2,038.95	17/20	546,514.27	12/32
400,000	4,660.46	1,277,713.86	2,330.23	17/20	624,574.18	12/32
450,000	5,243.01	1,437,464.68	2,621.51	17/20	702,684.82	12/32
500,000	5,825.57	1,597,168.41	2,912.79	17/20	780,747.39	12/32
550,000	6,408.12	1,756,919.81	3,204.06	17/20	858,844.62	12/32

14.00% 14.00%

BI-WEEKLY PAYMENT TABLE

TYPICAL 30 YEAR LOAN COMPARED TO A BI-WEEKLY

LOAN AMOUNT	MONTHLY PAYMENT	TOTAL INTEREST	BI-WKLY PAYMENT	TERM YR/WK	INTEREST SAVED	YR/WK SAVED
50	0.60	135.41	0.30	16/20	57.68	13/32
100	1.19	304.48	0.60	16/18	149.90	13/34
200	2.37	651.85	1.19	16/46	330.18	13/06
300	3.56	954.40	1.78	17/04	465.25	12/48
400	4.74	1,303.66	2.37	17/08	646.89	12/44
500	5.93	1,604.55	2.97	17/00	794.22	13/00
600	7.11	1,955.14	3.56	17/04	976.81	12/48
700	8.30	2,256.94	4.15	17/06	1,110.78	12/46
800	9.48	2,606.28	4.74	17/08	1,292.52	12/44
900	10.67	2,907.39	5.34	17/04	1,440.13	12/48
1,000	11.85	3,258.12	5.93	17/06	1,622.98	12/46
2,000	23.70	6,515.65	11.85	17/08	3,231.51	12/44
3,000	35.55	9,775.75	17.78	17/08	4,856.28	12/44
4,000	47.40	13,037.02	23.70	17/08	6,468.50	12/44
5,000	59.25	16,293.84	29.63	17/08	8,090.87	12/44
6,000	71.10	19,552.91	35.55	17/08	9,700.35	12/44
7,000	82.95	22,813.67	41.48	17/08	11,326.95	12/44
8,000	94.79	26,123.63	47.40	17/08	12,987.16	12/44
9,000	106.64	29,381.53	53.32	17/08	14,596.44	12/44
10,000	118.49	32,642.39	59.25	17/08	16,221.58	12/44
15,000	177.74	48,934.67	88.87	17/10	24,296.80	12/42
20,000	236.98	65,282.40	118.49	17/10	32,426.55	12/42
25,000	296.22	81,627.44	148.11	17/10	40,554.77	12/42
30,000	355.47	97,921.61	177.74	17/10	48,645.32	12/42
35,000	414.71	114,269.05	207.36	17/10	56,775.34	12/42
45,000	533.20	146,909.46	266.60	17/10	72,981.26	12/42
55,000	651.68	179,602.02	325.84	17/10	89,238.76	12/42
65,000	770.17	212,242.33	385.09	17/10	105,458.16	12/42
75,000	888.66	244,884.28	444.33	17/10	121,665.58	12/42
85,000	1,007.15	277,525.40	503.58	17/10	137,886.30	12/42
100,000	1,184.88	326,512.75	592.44	17/10	162,221.73	12/42
120,000	1,421.85	391,847.18	710.93	17/10	194,700.21	12/42
140,000	1,658.83	457,127.27	829.42	17/10	227,125.06	12/42
160,000	1,895.80	522,460.42	947.90	17/10	259,588.85	12/42
180,000	2,132.77	587,792.76	1,066.39	17/10	292,066.14	12/42
200,000	2,369.75	653,073.01	1,184.88	17/10	324,490.90	12/42
225,000	2,665.97	734,701.31	1,332.99	17/10	365,045.92	12/42
250,000	2,962.18	816,383.33	1,481.09	17/10	405,641.63	12/42
275,000	3,258.40	898,009.49	1,629.20	17/10	446,194.40	12/42
300,000	3,554.62	979,636.90	1,777.31	17/10	486,749.41	12/42
350,000	4,147.06	1,142,894.90	2,073.53	17/10	567,861.47	12/42
400,000	4,739.49	1,306,200.41	2,369.75	17/10	649,022.30	12/42
450,000	5,331.93	1,469,455.15	2,665.97	17/10	730,130.83	12/42
500,000	5,924.36	1,632,760.00	2,962.18	17/10	811,276.50	12/42
550,000	6,516.80	1,796,018.38	3,258.40	17/10	892,389.22	12/42

BI-WEEKLY PAYMENT TABLE

TYPICAL 30 YEAR LOAN COMPARED TO A BI-WEEKLY

LOAN AMOUNT	MONTHLY PAYMENT	TOTAL INTEREST	BI-WKLY PAYMENT	TERM YR/WK	INTEREST SAVED	YR/WK SAVED
50	0.61	137.23	0.31	15/08	65.12	14/44
100	1.21	309.24	0.61	16/06	153.80	13/46
200	2.41	664.00	1.21	16/34	340.71	13/18
300	3.62	970.57	1.81	16/44	479.06	13/08
400	4.82	1,328.57	2.41	16/48	668.68	13/04
500	6.03	1,634.59	3.02	16/40	819.82	13/12
600	7.23	1,992.53	3.62	16/44	1,009.46	13/08
700	8.44	2,296.85	4.22	16/46	1,145.22	13/06
800	9.64	2,657.08	4.82	16/48	1,336.79	13/04
900	10.85	2,962.14	5.43	16/44	1,487.56	13/08
1,000	12.05	3,320.69	6.03	16/46	1,677.51	13/06
2,000	24.10	6,641.08	12.05	16/48	3,340.27	13/04
3,000	36.15	9,961.92	18.08	16/48	5,018.02	13/04
4,000	48.19	13,335.23	24.10	16/48	6,734.32	13/04
5,000	60.24	16,652.00	30.12	16/50	8,393.94	13/02
6,000	72.29	19,972.79	36.15	16/48	10,070.95	13/04
7,000	84.33	23,346.71	42.17	16/50	11,787.69	13/02
8,000	96.38	26,666.45	48.19	16/50	13,450.41	13/02
9,000	108.43	29,989.50	54.22	16/50	15,129.88	13/02
10,000	120.47	33,361.78	60.24	16/50	16,844.75	13/02
15,000	180.71	50,015.04	90.36	16/50	25,239.98	13/02
20,000	240.94	66,724.32	120.47	16/50	33,675.96	13/02
25,000	301.18	83,378.34	150.59	16/50	42,072.10	13/02
30,000	361.41	100,085.41	180.71	16/50	50,521.39	13/02
35,000	421.65	116,738.30	210.83	16/50	58,915.51	13/02
45,000	542.11	150,157.06	271.06	16/50	75,803.47	13/02
55,000	662.58	183,518.92	331.29	16/50	92,634.26	13/02
65,000	783.05	216,879.80	391.53	16/50	109,477.87	13/02
75,000	903.52	250,240.24	451.76	16/50	126,306.99	13/02
85,000	1,023.99	283,603.07	512.00	16/50	143,153.09	13/02
100,000	1,204.69	333,671.78	602.35	16/50	168,432.87	13/02
120,000	1,445.63	400,395.73	722.82	16/50	202,108.62	13/02
140,000	1,686.57	467,117.74	843.29	16/50	235,783.45	13/02
160,000	1,927.50	533,897.13	963.75	16/50	269,500.81	13/02
180,000	2,168.44	600,618.85	1,084.22	16/50	303,174.68	13/02
200,000	2,409.38	667,343.29	1,204.69	16/50	336,851.34	13/02
225,000	2,710.55	750,774.23	1,355.28	16/50	378,975.74	13/02
250,000	3,011.72	834,207.05	1,505.86	16/50	421,088.59	13/02
275,000	3,312.89	917,638.53	1,656.45	16/50	463,214.14	13/02
300,000	3,614.07	1,001,016.22	1,807.04	16/50	505,285.27	13/02
350,000	4,216.41	1,167,877.70	2,108.21	16/50	589,520.81	13/02
400,000	4,818.75	1,334,739.12	2,409.38	16/50	673,754.80	13/02
450,000	5,421.10	1,501,548.90	2,710.55	16/50	757,938.33	13/02
500,000	6,023.44	1,668,411.44	3,011.72	16/50	842,174.42	13/02
550,000	6,625.78	1,835,275.14	3,312.89	16/50	926,411.61	13/0

14.50% **14.50%**

BI-WEEKLY PAYMENT TABLE

TYPICAL 30 YEAR LOAN COMPARED TO A BI-WEEKLY

LOAN AMOUNT	MONTHLY PAYMENT	TOTAL INTEREST	BI-WKLY PAYMENT	TERM YR/WK	INTEREST SAVED	YR/WK SAVED
50	0.62	138.84	0.31	15/50	60.42	14/02
100	1.23	315.26	0.62	15/48	158.83	14/04
200	2.45	677.24	1.23	16/22	352.27	13/30
300	3.68	987.51	1.84	16/32	493.47	13/20
400	4.90	1,352.82	2.45	16/38	689.35	13/14
500	6.13	1,665.39	3.07	16/28	846.42	13/24
600	7.35	2,030.37	3.68	16/32	1,042.32	13/20
700	8.58	2,340.27	4.29	16/34	1,182.87	13/18
800	9.80	2,706.70	4.90	16/38	1,380.03	13/14
900	11.03	3,018.32	5.52	16/32	1,536.36	13/20
1,000	12.25	3,383.68	6.13	16/34	1,732.27	13/18
2,000	24.50	6,765.22	12.25	16/38	3,448.51	13/14
3,000	36.74	10,205.44	18.37	16/38	5,223.34	13/14
4,000	48.99	13,585.47	24.50	16/38	6,952.25	13/14
5,000	61.23	17,032.20	30.62	16/38	8,733.27	13/14
6,000	73.48	20,411.94	36.74	16/38	10,448.01	13/14
7,000	85.72	23,853.65	42.86	16/38	12,224.59	13/14
8,000	97.97	27,235.71	48.99	16/38	13,955.18	13/14
9,000	110.22	30,617.39	55.11	16/38	15,671.96	13/14
10,000	122.46	34,057.83	61.23	16/38	17,446.58	13/14
15,000	183.69	51,085.86	91.85	16/38	26,176.11	13/14
20,000	244.92	68,119.50	122.46	16/38	34,897.30	13/14
25,000	306.14	85,201.58	153.07	16/38	43,666.96	13/14
30,000	367.37	102,233.04	183.69	16/38	52,399.64	13/14
35,000	428.60	119,263.03	214.30	16/38	61,117.33	13/14
45,000	551.06	153,320.15	275.53	16/38	78,562.69	13/14
55,000	673.51	187,436.24	336.76	16/38	96,067.96	13/14
65,000	795.97	221,494.96	397.99	16/38	113,515.58	13/14
75,000	918.42	255,611.31	459.21	16/38	131,007.12	13/14
85,000	1,040.88	289,670.03	520.44	16/38	148,454.13	13/14
100,000	1,224.56	340,817.73	612.28	16/38	174,678.49	13/14
120,000	1,469.47	408,991.81	734.74	16/38	209,630.27	13/14
140,000	1,714.38	477,166.71	857.19	16/38	244,568.35	13/14
160,000	1,959.29	545,340.87	979.65	16/38	279,520.43	13/14
180,000	2,204.21	613,457.78	1,102.11	16/38	314,414.93	13/14
200,000	2,449.12	681,633.14	1,224.56	16/38	349,353.53	13/14
225,000	2,755.26	766,836.76	1,377.63	16/38	393,023.02	13/14
250,000	3,061.39	852,100.45	1,530.70	16/38	436,751.80	13/14
275,000	3,367.53	937,302.46	1,683.77	16/38	480,418.81	13/14
300,000	3,673.67	1,022,506.00	1,836.84	16/38	524,086.88	13/14
350,000	4,285.95	1,192,916.02	2,142.98	16/38	611,427.69	13/14
400,000	4,898.23	1,363,324.35	2,449.12	16/38	698,766.63	13/14
450,000	5,510.51	1,533,732.14	2,755.26	16/38	786,104.10	13/14
500,000	6,122.78	1,704,198.28	3,061.39	16/38	873,486.80	13/14
550,000	6,735.06	1,874,605.29	3,367.53	16/38	960,823.81	13/14

14.75% 14.75%

BI-WEEKLY PAYMENT TABLE

TYPICAL 30 YEAR LOAN COMPARED TO A BI-WEEKLY

LOAN AMOUNT	MONTHLY PAYMENT	TOTAL INTEREST	BI-WKLY PAYMENT	TERM YR/WK	INTEREST SAVED	YR/WK SAVED
50	0.63	140.61	0.32	14/42	67.51	15/10
100	1.25	320.78	0.63	15/38	163.72	14/14
200	2.49	691.49	1.25	16/12	365.16	13/40
300	3.74	1,006.56	1.87	16/22	509.92	13/30
400	4.98	1,379.72	2.49	16/26	713.16	13/26
500	6.23	1,694.15	3.12	16/16	871.34	13/36
600	7.47	2,068.02	3.74	16/20	1,075.42	13/32
700	8.72	2,383.80	4.36	16/26	1,220.68	13/26
800	9.96	2,760.14	4.98	16/26	1,427.48	13/26
900	11.21	3,072.73	5.61	16/20	1,583.31	13/32
1,000	12.45	3,449.32	6.23	16/22	1,790.40	13/30
2,000	24.89	6,955.02	12.45	16/26	3,622.81	13/26
3,000	37.34	10,402.93	18.67	16/26	5,398.14	13/26
4,000	49.78	13,916.15	24.89	16/28	7,237.28	13/24
5,000	62.23	17,362.75	31.12	16/26	9,025.15	13/26
6,000	74.67	20,871.95	37.34	16/26	10,861.24	13/26
7,000	87.12	24,318.62	43.56	16/26	12,634.19	13/26
8,000	99.56	27,829.05	49.78	16/28	14,471.95	13/24
9,000	112.01	31,278.62	56.01	16/26	16,261.64	13/26
10,000	124.45	34,788.12	62.23	16/26	18,098.42	13/26
15,000	186.68	52,149.41	93.34	16/26	27,107.70	13/26
20,000	248.90	69,573.46	124.45	16/28	36,180.23	13/24
25,000	311.12	86,996.24	155.56	16/28	45,250.93	13/24
30,000	373.35	104,359.08	186.68	16/26	54,276.55	13/26
35,000	435.57	121,780.93	217.79	16/28	63,346.29	13/24
45,000	560.02	156,568.02	280.01	16/28	81,429.66	13/24
55,000	684.47	191,354.12	342.24	16/28	99,526.30	13/24
65,000	808.91	226,204.34	404.46	16/28	117,672.74	13/24
75,000	933.36	260,990.39	466.68	16/28	135,755.40	13/24
85,000	1,057.81	295,775.66	528.91	16/28	153,851.32	13/24
100,000	1,244.48	347,985.85	622.24	16/28	181,005.91	13/24
120,000	1,493.38	417,557.92	746.69	16/28	217,185.07	13/24
140,000	1,742.27	487,189.72	871.14	16/28	253,423.56	13/24
160,000	1,991.17	556,764.30	995.59	16/28	289,605.11	13/24
180,000	2,240.06	626,397.67	1,120.03	16/28	325,831.07	13/24
200,000	2,488.96	695,968.33	1,244.48	16/28	362,008.79	13/24
225,000	2,800.08	782,965.80	1,400.04	16/28	407,261.00	13/24
250,000	3,111.19	870,023.69	1,555.60	16/28	452,573.44	13/24
275,000	3,422.31	957,021.90	1,711.16	16/28	497,827.56	13/24
300,000	3,733.43	1,044,016.06	1,866.72	16/28	543,076.44	13/24
350,000	4,355.67	1,218,009.11	2,177.84	16/28	633,580.28	13/24
400,000	4,977.91	1,392,002.86	2,488.96	16/28	724,083.85	13/24
450,000	5,600.15	1,565,995.05	2,800.08	16/28	814,587.30	13/24
500,000	6,222.38	1,740,048.49	3,111.19	16/28	905,136.23	13/24
550,000	6,844.62	1,914,039.18	3,422.31	16/28	995,636.26	13/24

10.000% TO 10.975% **10.000% TO 10.975%**

MORTGAGE FACTORS TABLE

INTEREST RATE %	TERM OF LOAN IN YEARS					
	10	12.5	15	20	25	30
10.000	1321.51	1170.40	1074.61	965.03	908.71	877.58
10.025	1322.90	1171.86	1076.14	966.68	910.47	879.42
10.050	1324.28	1173.32	1077.67	968.34	912.23	881.27
10.075	1325.67	1174.79	1079.20	970.00	914.00	883.12
10.100	1327.06	1176.25	1080.74	971.66	915.76	884.98
10.125	1328.44	1177.71	1082.27	973.32	917.53	886.83
10.150	1329.83	1179.17	1083.81	974.99	919.30	888.68
10.175	1331.22	1180.64	1085.34	976.65	921.07	890.54
10.200	1332.61	1182.10	1086.88	978.31	922.84	892.39
10.225	1334.00	1183.57	1088.42	979.98	924.61	894.25
10.250	1335.40	1185.04	1089.96	981.65	926.39	896.11
10.275	1336.79	1186.51	1091.50	983.32	928.16	897.97
10.300	1338.18	1187.98	1093.04	984.99	929.94	899.83
10.325	1339.57	1189.45	1094.58	986.66	931.72	901.69
10.350	1340.97	1190.92	1096.12	988.33	933.49	903.55
10.375	1342.37	1192.39	1097.67	990.00	935.27	905.41
10.400	1343.76	1193.86	1099.21	991.68	937.05	907.28
10.425	1345.16	1195.34	1100.76	993.35	938.84	909.14
10.450	1346.56	1196.81	1102.31	995.03	940.62	911.01
10.475	1347.96	1198.29	1103.85	996.71	942.40	912.88
10.500	1349.35	1199.76	1105.40	998.38	944.19	914.74
10.525	1350.76	1201.24	1106.95	1000.06	945.97	916.61
10.550	1352.16	1202.72	1108.51	1001.75	947.76	918.48
10.575	1353.56	1204.20	1110.06	1003.43	949.55	920.36
10.600	1354.96	1205.68	1111.61	1005.11	951.34	922.23
10.625	1356.36	1207.16	1113.17	1006.80	953.13	924.10
10.650	1357.77	1208.64	1114.72	1008.48	954.92	925.98
10.675	1359.17	1210.13	1116.28	1010.17	956.71	927.85
10.700	1360.58	1211.61	1117.84	1011.86	958.51	929.73
10.725	1361.98	1213.10	1119.39	1013.54	960.30	931.61
10.750	1363.39	1214.58	1120.95	1015.23	962.10	933.49
10.775	1364.80	1216.07	1122.51	1016.92	963.89	935.37
10.800	1366.21	1217.55	1124.07	1018.62	965.69	937.25
10.825	1367.62	1219.04	1125.64	1020.31	967.49	939.13
10.850	1369.03	1220.53	1127.20	1022.00	969.29	941.01
10.875	1370.44	1222.02	1128.77	1023.70	971.09	942.90
10.900	1371.85	1223.51	1130.33	1025.40	972.90	944.78
10.925	1373.26	1225.01	1131.90	1027.09	974.70	946.67
10.950	1374.68	1226.50	1133.46	1028.79	976.51	948.55
10.975	1376.09	1227.99	1135.03	1030.49	978.31	950.44

$$\text{Your Monthly Payment} = \frac{\text{(Your Loan Amount) X (The Above Figure)}}{100{,}000}$$

MORTGAGE FACTOR TABLES

INSTRUCTIONS

The Mortgage Factor Tables were designed to make it easy for you to calculate the monthly payment required to amortize any loan at any listed interest rate.

Here's how to proceed: Let's say you want to borrow $75,867 at 10.25% for 30 years, and you want the loan to be retired by its maturity date.

- Turn to the 10.000% to 10.975% Tables. You'll note that the table on the left hand page runs through 7.5 years, while the right hand table begins with 10 years and runs through 30. We need the table that goes to 30 years, which is reproduced on the preceding page for your convenience.
- Look down the left hand *(Interest Rate)* column until you come to 10.250%.
- Read across to the right, until you are under the *30 Year* column.
- Write down the *Mortgage Factor* (which in this case is 896.11). This is the monthly payment required to amortize a $100,000 loan in 30 years.
- Now multiply the *Loan Amount* ($75,867) by the *Mortgage Factor* ($896.11). Divide that result by 100,000. Round off to the nearest penny. The result is the *Monthly Payment* required to pay off the loan by the end of its 30 year term ($679.85 in this case)

Add whatever few dollars you can each month to your required payment, and watch your savings mount up quickly!

MORTGAGE FACTORS TABLE

INTEREST RATE %	TERM OF LOAN IN YEARS					
	1	2	3	4	5	7.5
7.000	8652.68	4477.26	3087.71	2394.63	1980.12	1431.35
7.025	8653.83	4478.40	3088.86	2395.79	1981.30	1432.58
7.050	8654.98	4479.53	3090.00	2396.95	1982.48	1433.82
7.075	8656.14	4480.66	3091.14	2398.11	1983.67	1435.05
7.100	8657.29	4481.80	3092.29	2399.27	1984.85	1436.29
7.125	8658.44	4482.93	3093.43	2400.43	1986.03	1437.52
7.150	8659.60	4484.07	3094.58	2401.59	1987.21	1438.76
7.175	8660.75	4485.20	3095.72	2402.76	1988.39	1440.00
7.200	8661.90	4486.34	3096.87	2403.92	1989.57	1441.24
7.225	8663.06	4487.47	3098.01	2405.08	1990.76	1442.47
7.250	8664.21	4488.61	3099.16	2406.25	1991.94	1443.71
7.275	8665.36	4489.74	3100.30	2407.41	1993.13	1444.95
7.300	8666.52	4490.88	3101.45	2408.57	1994.31	1446.19
7.325	8667.67	4492.01	3102.60	2409.74	1995.49	1447.43
7.350	8668.82	4493.15	3103.74	2410.90	1996.68	1448.68
7.375	8669.98	4494.28	3104.89	2412.07	1997.87	1449.92
7.400	8671.13	4495.42	3106.04	2413.23	1999.05	1451.16
7.425	8672.28	4496.55	3107.18	2414.40	2000.24	1452.40
7.450	8673.44	4497.69	3108.33	2415.56	2001.42	1453.65
7.475	8674.59	4498.83	3109.48	2416.73	2002.61	1454.89
7.500	8675.75	4499.96	3110.63	2417.90	2003.80	1456.14
7.525	8676.90	4501.10	3111.78	2419.06	2004.99	1457.38
7.550	8678.06	4502.24	3112.92	2420.23	2006.18	1458.63
7.575	8679.21	4503.38	3114.07	2421.40	2007.37	1459.88
7.600	8680.36	4504.51	3115.22	2422.56	2008.56	1461.13
7.625	8681.52	4505.65	3116.37	2423.73	2009.75	1462.37
7.650	8682.67	4506.79	3117.52	2424.90	2010.94	1463.62
7.675	8683.83	4507.93	3118.67	2426.07	2012.13	1464.87
7.700	8684.98	4509.06	3119.82	2427.24	2013.32	1466.12
7.725	8686.14	4510.20	3120.97	2428.41	2014.51	1467.37
7.750	8687.29	4511.34	3122.12	2429.58	2015.70	1468.63
7.775	8688.45	4512.48	3123.27	2430.75	2016.89	1469.88
7.800	8689.60	4513.62	3124.42	2431.92	2018.09	1471.13
7.825	8690.76	4514.76	3125.57	2433.09	2019.28	1472.38
7.850	8691.91	4515.90	3126.73	2434.26	2020.47	1473.64
7.875	8693.07	4517.04	3127.88	2435.43	2021.67	1474.89
7.900	8694.22	4518.17	3129.03	2436.61	2022.86	1476.15
7.925	8695.38	4519.31	3130.18	2437.78	2024.06	1477.40
7.950	8696.54	4520.45	3131.34	2438.95	2025.25	1478.66
7.975	8697.69	4521.59	3132.49	2440.12	2026.45	1479.92

$$\text{Your Monthly Payment} = \frac{\text{(Your Loan Amount) X (The Above Figure)}}{100{,}000}$$

7.000% TO 7.975% **7.000% TO 7.975%**

MORTGAGE FACTORS TABLE

INTEREST RATE %	TERM OF LOAN IN YEARS					
	10	12.5	15	20	25	30
7.000	1161.09	1002.16	898.83	775.30	706.78	665.31
7.025	1162.38	1003.51	900.23	776.81	708.38	666.99
7.050	1163.67	1004.85	901.63	778.31	709.98	668.67
7.075	1164.96	1006.20	903.03	779.81	711.58	670.35
7.100	1166.25	1007.55	904.43	781.32	713.18	672.04
7.125	1167.54	1008.89	905.84	782.82	714.78	673.72
7.150	1168.84	1010.24	907.24	784.33	716.38	675.41
7.175	1170.13	1011.59	908.65	785.84	717.99	677.10
7.200	1171.42	1012.94	910.05	787.35	719.59	678.79
7.225	1172.72	1014.30	911.46	788.87	721.20	680.49
7.250	1174.02	1015.65	912.87	790.38	722.81	682.18
7.275	1175.31	1017.00	914.28	791.90	724.42	683.88
7.300	1176.61	1018.36	915.69	793.41	726.04	685.58
7.325	1177.91	1019.71	917.10	794.93	727.65	687.28
7.350	1179.21	1021.07	918.51	796.45	729.27	688.98
7.375	1180.51	1022.43	919.93	797.97	730.88	690.68
7.400	1181.81	1023.79	921.34	799.49	732.50	692.38
7.425	1183.11	1025.15	922.76	801.02	734.12	694.09
7.450	1184.41	1026.51	924.18	802.54	735.75	695.80
7.475	1185.72	1027.87	925.60	804.07	737.37	697.51
7.500	1187.02	1029.23	927.02	805.60	739.00	699.22
7.525	1188.33	1030.60	928.44	807.13	740.62	700.93
7.550	1189.63	1031.96	929.86	808.66	742.25	702.65
7.575	1190.94	1033.33	931.28	810.19	743.88	704.36
7.600	1192.25	1034.70	932.71	811.72	745.51	706.08
7.625	1193.56	1036.06	934.13	813.26	747.15	707.80
7.650	1194.87	1037.43	935.56	814.79	748.78	709.52
7.675	1196.18	1038.80	936.99	816.33	750.42	711.24
7.700	1197.49	1040.17	938.42	817.87	752.05	712.97
7.725	1198.80	1041.55	939.85	819.41	753.69	714.69
7.750	1200.11	1042.92	941.28	820.95	755.33	716.42
7.775	1201.42	1044.29	942.71	822.50	756.98	718.15
7.800	1202.74	1045.67	944.15	824.04	758.62	719.88
7.825	1204.05	1047.04	945.58	825.59	760.26	721.61
7.850	1205.37	1048.42	947.02	827.13	761.91	723.34
7.875	1206.69	1049.80	948.45	828.68	763.56	725.07
7.900	1208.00	1051.18	949.89	830.23	765.21	726.81
7.925	1209.32	1052.56	951.33	831.78	766.86	728.55
7.950	1210.64	1053.94	952.77	833.34	768.51	730.29
7.975	1211.96	1055.32	954.21	834.89	770.17	732.03

$$\text{Your Monthly Payment} = \frac{\text{(Your Loan Amount) X (The Above Figure)}}{100{,}000}$$

MORTGAGE FACTORS TABLE

INTEREST RATE %	TERM OF LOAN IN YEARS					
	1	2	3	4	5	7.5
8.000	8698.85	4522.73	3133.64	2441.30	2027.64	1481.18
8.025	8700.00	4523.87	3134.79	2442.47	2028.84	1482.43
8.050	8701.16	4525.01	3135.95	2443.64	2030.04	1483.69
8.075	8702.32	4526.16	3137.10	2444.82	2031.24	1484.95
8.100	8703.47	4527.30	3138.26	2445.99	2032.43	1486.21
8.125	8704.63	4528.44	3139.41	2447.17	2033.63	1487.47
8.150	8705.78	4529.58	3140.57	2448.34	2034.83	1488.74
8.175	8706.94	4530.72	3141.72	2449.52	2036.03	1490.00
8.200	8708.10	4531.86	3142.88	2450.70	2037.23	1491.26
8.225	8709.25	4533.00	3144.03	2451.87	2038.43	1492.52
8.250	8710.41	4534.14	3145.19	2453.05	2039.63	1493.79
8.275	8711.57	4535.29	3146.34	2454.23	2040.83	1495.05
8.300	8712.73	4536.43	3147.50	2455.40	2042.03	1496.32
8.325	8713.88	4537.57	3148.66	2456.58	2043.23	1497.58
8.350	8715.04	4538.71	3149.81	2457.76	2044.44	1498.85
8.375	8716.20	4539.86	3150.97	2458.94	2045.64	1500.12
8.400	8717.35	4541.00	3152.13	2460.12	2046.84	1501.38
8.425	8718.51	4542.14	3153.28	2461.30	2048.05	1502.65
8.450	8719.67	4543.29	3154.44	2462.48	2049.25	1503.92
8.475	8720.83	4544.43	3155.60	2463.66	2050.45	1505.19
8.500	8721.98	4545.57	3156.76	2464.84	2051.66	1506.46
8.525	8723.14	4546.72	3157.92	2466.02	2052.86	1507.73
8.550	8724.30	4547.86	3159.08	2467.20	2054.07	1509.00
8.575	8725.46	4549.00	3160.24	2468.38	2055.27	1510.28
8.600	8726.61	4550.15	3161.39	2469.56	2056.48	1511.55
8.625	8727.77	4551.29	3162.55	2470.74	2057.69	1512.82
8.650	8728.93	4552.44	3163.71	2471.92	2058.90	1514.10
8.675	8730.09	4553.58	3164.87	2473.11	2060.10	1515.37
8.700	8731.25	4554.73	3166.03	2474.29	2061.31	1516.64
8.725	8732.41	4555.87	3167.19	2475.47	2062.52	1517.92
8.750	8733.56	4557.02	3168.36	2476.66	2063.73	1519.20
8.775	8734.72	4558.16	3169.52	2477.84	2064.94	1520.47
8.800	8735.88	4559.31	3170.68	2479.02	2066.15	1521.75
8.825	8737.04	4560.45	3171.84	2480.21	2067.36	1523.03
8.850	8738.20	4561.60	3173.00	2481.39	2068.57	1524.31
8.875	8739.36	4562.75	3174.16	2482.58	2069.78	1525.59
8.900	8740.52	4563.89	3175.33	2483.76	2070.99	1526.87
8.925	8741.68	4565.04	3176.49	2484.95	2072.20	1528.15
8.950	8742.83	4566.19	3177.65	2486.14	2073.41	1529.43
8.975	8743.99	4567.33	3178.81	2487.32	2074.63	1530.71

$$\text{Your Monthly Payment} = \frac{\text{(Your Loan Amount) X (The Above Figure)}}{100{,}000}$$

8.000% TO 8.975% 8.000% TO 8.975%

MORTGAGE FACTORS TABLE

INTEREST RATE %	TERM OF LOAN IN YEARS					
	10	12.5	15	20	25	30
8.000	1213.28	1056.70	955.66	836.45	771.82	733.77
8.025	1214.60	1058.08	957.10	838.00	773.48	735.51
8.050	1215.92	1059.47	958.55	839.56	775.14	737.26
8.075	1217.25	1060.85	959.99	841.12	776.80	739.00
8.100	1218.57	1062.24	961.44	842.68	778.46	740.75
8.125	1219.90	1063.63	962.89	844.24	780.12	742.50
8.150	1221.22	1065.02	964.34	845.80	781.78	744.25
8.175	1222.55	1066.41	965.79	847.37	783.45	746.01
8.200	1223.87	1067.80	967.24	848.93	785.12	747.76
8.225	1225.20	1069.19	968.69	850.50	786.79	749.51
8.250	1226.53	1070.58	970.15	852.07	788.46	751.27
8.275	1227.86	1071.97	971.60	853.64	790.13	753.03
8.300	1229.19	1073.37	973.06	855.21	791.80	754.79
8.325	1230.52	1074.76	974.51	856.78	793.47	756.55
8.350	1231.85	1076.16	975.97	858.36	795.15	758.31
8.375	1233.19	1077.56	977.43	859.93	796.83	760.08
8.400	1234.52	1078.95	978.89	861.51	798.50	761.84
8.425	1235.85	1080.35	980.35	863.09	800.18	763.61
8.450	1237.19	1081.75	981.82	864.67	801.87	765.38
8.475	1238.53	1083.15	983.28	866.25	803.55	767.15
8.500	1239.86	1084.56	984.74	867.83	805.23	768.92
8.525	1241.20	1085.96	986.21	869.41	806.92	770.69
8.550	1242.54	1087.36	987.68	871.00	808.60	772.46
8.575	1243.88	1088.77	989.15	872.58	810.29	774.24
8.600	1245.22	1090.17	990.62	874.17	811.98	776.02
8.625	1246.56	1091.58	992.09	875.76	813.67	777.79
8.650	1247.90	1092.99	993.56	877.35	815.37	779.57
8.675	1249.24	1094.40	995.03	878.94	817.06	781.35
8.700	1250.58	1095.81	996.50	880.53	818.75	783.14
8.725	1251.93	1097.22	997.98	882.12	820.45	784.92
8.750	1253.27	1098.63	999.45	883.72	822.15	786.71
8.775	1254.62	1100.04	1000.93	885.31	823.85	788.49
8.800	1255.96	1101.45	1002.41	886.91	825.55	790.28
8.825	1257.31	1102.87	1003.89	888.51	827.25	792.07
8.850	1258.66	1104.28	1005.37	890.11	828.95	793.86
8.875	1260.01	1105.70	1006.85	891.71	830.66	795.65
8.900	1261.36	1107.12	1008.33	893.31	832.36	797.44
8.925	1262.71	1108.53	1009.81	894.91	834.07	799.24
8.950	1264.06	1109.95	1011.30	896.52	835.78	801.03
8.975	1265.41	1111.37	1012.78	898.12	837.49	802.83

$$\text{Your Monthly Payment} = \frac{\text{(Your Loan Amount) X (The Above Figure)}}{100{,}000}$$

MORTGAGE FACTORS TABLE

INTEREST RATE %	TERM OF LOAN IN YEARS					
	1	2	3	4	5	7.5
9.000	8745.15	4568.48	3179.98	2488.51	2075.84	1531.99
9.025	8746.31	4569.63	3181.14	2489.70	2077.05	1533.28
9.050	8747.47	4570.77	3182.31	2490.88	2078.27	1534.56
9.075	8748.63	4571.92	3183.47	2492.07	2079.48	1535.85
9.100	8749.79	4573.07	3184.63	2493.26	2080.70	1537.13
9.125	8750.95	4574.22	3185.80	2494.45	2081.91	1538.42
9.150	8752.11	4575.36	3186.96	2495.64	2083.13	1539.70
9.175	8753.27	4576.51	3188.13	2496.83	2084.34	1540.99
9.200	8754.43	4577.66	3189.29	2498.02	2085.56	1542.28
9.225	8755.59	4578.81	3190.46	2499.21	2086.78	1543.56
9.250	8756.75	4579.96	3191.63	2500.40	2087.99	1544.85
9.275	8757.91	4581.11	3192.79	2501.59	2089.21	1546.14
9.300	8759.07	4582.26	3193.96	2502.78	2090.43	1547.43
9.325	8760.23	4583.41	3195.13	2503.97	2091.65	1548.72
9.350	8761.39	4584.55	3196.29	2505.16	2092.87	1550.01
9.375	8762.55	4585.70	3197.46	2506.35	2094.09	1551.31
9.400	8763.71	4586.85	3198.63	2507.55	2095.31	1552.60
9.425	8764.87	4588.00	3199.80	2508.74	2096.53	1553.89
9.450	8766.03	4589.15	3200.96	2509.93	2097.75	1555.18
9.475	8767.20	4590.30	3202.13	2511.12	2098.97	1556.48
9.500	8768.36	4591.45	3203.30	2512.32	2100.19	1557.77
9.525	8769.52	4592.60	3204.47	2513.51	2101.41	1559.07
9.550	8770.68	4593.76	3205.64	2514.71	2102.64	1560.36
9.575	8771.84	4594.91	3206.81	2515.90	2103.86	1561.66
9.600	8773.00	4596.06	3207.98	2517.10	2105.08	1562.96
9.625	8774.16	4597.21	3209.15	2518.29	2106.31	1564.26
9.650	8775.32	4598.36	3210.32	2519.49	2107.53	1565.56
9.675	8776.49	4599.51	3211.49	2520.68	2108.75	1566.85
9.700	8777.65	4600.66	3212.66	2521.88	2109.98	1568.15
9.725	8778.81	4601.82	3213.83	2523.08	2111.20	1569.45
9.750	8779.97	4602.97	3215.00	2524.27	2112.43	1570.76
9.775	8781.13	4604.12	3216.17	2525.47	2113.66	1572.06
9.800	8782.29	4605.27	3217.34	2526.67	2114.88	1573.36
9.825	8783.46	4606.42	3218.51	2527.87	2116.11	1574.66
9.850	8784.62	4607.58	3219.69	2529.07	2117.34	1575.96
9.875	8785.78	4608.73	3220.86	2530.26	2118.56	1577.27
9.900	8786.94	4609.88	3222.03	2531.46	2119.79	1578.57
9.925	8788.11	4611.04	3223.20	2532.66	2121.02	1579.88
9.950	8789.27	4612.19	3224.38	2533.86	2122.25	1581.18
9.975	8790.43	4613.34	3225.55	2535.06	2123.48	1582.49

$$\text{Your Monthly Payment} = \frac{\text{(Your Loan Amount) X (The Above Figure)}}{100{,}000}$$

9.000% TO 9.975%

MORTGAGE FACTORS TABLE

INTEREST RATE %	TERM OF LOAN IN YEARS					
	10	12.5	15	20	25	30
9.000	1266.76	1112.79	1014.27	899.73	839.20	804.63
9.025	1268.12	1114.22	1015.76	901.34	840.91	806.43
9.050	1269.47	1115.64	1017.25	902.95	842.63	808.23
9.075	1270.83	1117.06	1018.74	904.56	844.34	810.03
9.100	1272.18	1118.49	1020.23	906.17	846.06	811.83
9.125	1273.54	1119.91	1021.72	907.79	847.78	813.64
9.150	1274.89	1121.34	1023.21	909.40	849.50	815.44
9.175	1276.25	1122.77	1024.71	911.02	851.22	817.25
9.200	1277.61	1124.20	1026.20	912.63	852.94	819.06
9.225	1278.97	1125.63	1027.70	914.25	854.66	820.87
9.250	1280.33	1127.06	1029.20	915.87	856.39	822.68
9.275	1281.69	1128.49	1030.70	917.49	858.11	824.49
9.300	1283.06	1129.92	1032.20	919.11	859.84	826.31
9.325	1284.42	1131.35	1033.70	920.74	861.57	828.12
9.350	1285.78	1132.79	1035.20	922.36	863.30	829.94
9.375	1287.15	1134.22	1036.70	923.99	865.03	831.75
9.400	1288.51	1135.66	1038.20	925.62	866.76	833.57
9.425	1289.88	1137.10	1039.71	927.24	868.49	835.39
9.450	1291.24	1138.53	1041.21	928.87	870.23	837.21
9.475	1292.61	1139.97	1042.72	930.50	871.96	839.04
9.500	1293.98	1141.41	1044.23	932.14	873.70	840.86
9.525	1295.35	1142.85	1045.74	933.77	875.44	842.68
9.550	1296.72	1144.30	1047.25	935.40	877.18	844.51
9.575	1298.09	1145.74	1048.76	937.04	878.92	846.34
9.600	1299.46	1147.18	1050.27	938.68	880.66	848.16
9.625	1300.83	1148.63	1051.79	940.31	882.41	849.99
9.650	1302.21	1150.07	1053.30	941.95	884.15	851.83
9.675	1303.58	1151.52	1054.82	943.59	885.90	853.66
9.700	1304.96	1152.97	1056.33	945.24	887.64	855.49
9.725	1306.33	1154.41	1057.85	946.88	889.39	857.32
9.750	1307.71	1155.86	1059.37	948.52	891.14	859.16
9.775	1309.08	1157.31	1060.89	950.17	892.89	861.00
9.800	1310.46	1158.76	1062.41	951.81	894.65	862.83
9.825	1311.84	1160.22	1063.93	953.46	896.40	864.67
9.850	1313.22	1161.67	1065.45	955.11	898.15	866.51
9.875	1314.60	1163.12	1066.98	956.76	899.91	868.35
9.900	1315.98	1164.58	1068.50	958.41	901.67	870.20
9.925	1317.36	1166.03	1070.03	960.06	903.42	872.04
9.950	1318.75	1167.49	1071.55	961.72	905.18	873.88
9.975	1320.13	1168.95	1073.08	963.37	906.94	875.73

$$\text{Your Monthly Payment} = \frac{\text{(Your Loan Amount) X (The Above Figure)}}{100{,}000}$$

10.000% TO 10.975% **10.000% TO 10.975%**

MORTGAGE FACTORS TABLE

INTEREST RATE %	TERM OF LOAN IN YEARS					
	1	2	3	4	5	7.5
10.000	8791.59	4614.50	3226.72	2536.26	2124.71	1583.80
10.025	8792.76	4615.65	3227.90	2537.46	2125.94	1585.11
10.050	8793.92	4616.81	3229.07	2538.67	2127.17	1586.41
10.075	8795.08	4617.96	3230.25	2539.87	2128.40	1587.72
10.100	8796.25	4619.11	3231.42	2541.07	2129.63	1589.03
10.125	8797.41	4620.27	3232.60	2542.27	2130.87	1590.34
10.150	8798.57	4621.42	3233.77	2543.47	2132.10	1591.65
10.175	8799.73	4622.58	3234.95	2544.68	2133.33	1592.96
10.200	8800.90	4623.73	3236.12	2545.88	2134.56	1594.28
10.225	8802.06	4624.89	3237.30	2547.08	2135.80	1595.59
10.250	8803.23	4626.04	3238.47	2548.29	2137.03	1596.90
10.275	8804.39	4627.20	3239.65	2549.49	2138.27	1598.21
10.300	8805.55	4628.36	3240.83	2550.69	2139.50	1599.53
10.325	8806.72	4629.51	3242.00	2551.90	2140.74	1600.84
10.350	8807.88	4630.67	3243.18	2553.10	2141.97	1602.16
10.375	8809.04	4631.82	3244.36	2554.31	2143.21	1603.48
10.400	8810.21	4632.98	3245.54	2555.52	2144.44	1604.79
10.425	8811.37	4634.14	3246.71	2556.72	2145.68	1606.11
10.450	8812.54	4635.29	3247.89	2557.93	2146.92	1607.43
10.475	8813.70	4636.45	3249.07	2559.14	2148.16	1608.75
10.500	8814.87	4637.61	3250.25	2560.34	2149.40	1610.06
10.525	8816.03	4638.77	3251.43	2561.55	2150.63	1611.38
10.550	8817.19	4639.92	3252.61	2562.76	2151.87	1612.70
10.575	8818.36	4641.08	3253.79	2563.97	2153.11	1614.03
10.600	8819.52	4642.24	3254.97	2565.18	2154.35	1615.35
10.625	8820.69	4643.40	3256.15	2566.38	2155.59	1616.67
10.650	8821.85	4644.56	3257.33	2567.59	2156.83	1617.99
10.675	8823.02	4645.71	3258.51	2568.80	2158.07	1619.32
10.700	8824.18	4646.87	3259.69	2570.01	2159.32	1620.64
10.725	8825.35	4648.03	3260.87	2571.22	2160.56	1621.96
10.750	8826.51	4649.19	3262.05	2572.43	2161.80	1623.29
10.775	8827.68	4650.35	3263.23	2573.64	2163.04	1624.62
10.800	8828.84	4651.51	3264.41	2574.86	2164.29	1625.94
10.825	8830.01	4652.67	3265.60	2576.07	2165.53	1627.27
10.850	8831.18	4653.83	3266.78	2577.28	2166.77	1628.60
10.875	8832.34	4654.99	3267.96	2578.49	2168.02	1629.92
10.900	8833.51	4656.15	3269.14	2579.70	2169.26	1631.25
10.925	8834.67	4657.31	3270.33	2580.92	2170.51	1632.58
10.950	8835.84	4658.47	3271.51	2582.13	2171.75	1633.91
10.975	8837.00	4659.63	3272.69	2583.34	2173.00	1635.24

$$\text{Your Monthly Payment} = \frac{\text{(Your Loan Amount) X (The Above Figure)}}{100{,}000}$$

 10.000% TO 10.975%

MORTGAGE FACTORS TABLE

INTEREST RATE %	TERM OF LOAN IN YEARS					
	10	12.5	15	20	25	30
10.000	1321.51	1170.40	1074.61	965.03	908.71	877.58
10.025	1322.90	1171.86	1076.14	966.68	910.47	879.42
10.050	1324.28	1173.32	1077.67	968.34	912.23	881.27
10.075	1325.67	1174.79	1079.20	970.00	914.00	883.12
10.100	1327.06	1176.25	1080.74	971.66	915.76	884.98
10.125	1328.44	1177.71	1082.27	973.32	917.53	886.83
10.150	1329.83	1179.17	1083.81	974.99	919.30	888.68
10.175	1331.22	1180.64	1085.34	976.65	921.07	890.54
10.200	1332.61	1182.10	1086.88	978.31	922.84	892.39
10.225	1334.00	1183.57	1088.42	979.98	924.61	894.25
10.250	1335.40	1185.04	1089.96	981.65	926.39	896.11
10.275	1336.79	1186.51	1091.50	983.32	928.16	897.97
10.300	1338.18	1187.98	1093.04	984.99	929.94	899.83
10.325	1339.57	1189.45	1094.58	986.66	931.72	901.69
10.350	1340.97	1190.92	1096.12	988.33	933.49	903.55
10.375	1342.37	1192.39	1097.67	990.00	935.27	905.41
10.400	1343.76	1193.86	1099.21	991.68	937.05	907.28
10.425	1345.16	1195.34	1100.76	993.35	938.84	909.14
10.450	1346.56	1196.81	1102.31	995.03	940.62	911.01
10.475	1347.96	1198.29	1103.85	996.71	942.40	912.88
10.500	1349.35	1199.76	1105.40	998.38	944.19	914.74
10.525	1350.76	1201.24	1106.95	1000.06	945.97	916.61
10.550	1352.16	1202.72	1108.51	1001.75	947.76	918.48
10.575	1353.56	1204.20	1110.06	1003.43	949.55	920.36
10.600	1354.96	1205.68	1111.61	1005.11	951.34	922.23
10.625	1356.36	1207.16	1113.17	1006.80	953.13	924.10
10.650	1357.77	1208.64	1114.72	1008.48	954.92	925.98
10.675	1359.17	1210.13	1116.28	1010.17	956.71	927.85
10.700	1360.58	1211.61	1117.84	1011.86	958.51	929.73
10.725	1361.98	1213.10	1119.39	1013.54	960.30	931.61
10.750	1363.39	1214.58	1120.95	1015.23	962.10	933.49
10.775	1364.80	1216.07	1122.51	1016.92	963.89	935.37
10.800	1366.21	1217.55	1124.07	1018.62	965.69	937.25
10.825	1367.62	1219.04	1125.64	1020.31	967.49	939.13
10.850	1369.03	1220.53	1127.20	1022.00	969.29	941.01
10.875	1370.44	1222.02	1128.77	1023.70	971.09	942.90
10.900	1371.85	1223.51	1130.33	1025.40	972.90	944.78
10.925	1373.26	1225.01	1131.90	1027.09	974.70	946.67
10.950	1374.68	1226.50	1133.46	1028.79	976.51	948.55
10.975	1376.09	1227.99	1135.03	1030.49	978.31	950.44

$$\text{Your Monthly Payment} = \frac{\text{(Your Loan Amount) X (The Above Figure)}}{100{,}000}$$

MORTGAGE FACTORS TABLE

INTEREST RATE %	TERM OF LOAN IN YEARS					
	1	2	3	4	5	7.5
11.000	8838.17	4660.79	3273.88	2584.56	2174.25	1636.57
11.025	8839.34	4661.95	3275.06	2585.77	2175.49	1637.91
11.050	8840.50	4663.11	3276.25	2586.99	2176.74	1639.24
11.075	8841.67	4664.27	3277.43	2588.20	2177.99	1640.57
11.100	8842.84	4665.43	3278.61	2589.42	2179.24	1641.90
11.125	8844.00	4666.59	3279.80	2590.63	2180.49	1643.24
11.150	8845.17	4667.76	3280.98	2591.85	2181.74	1644.57
11.175	8846.34	4668.92	3282.17	2593.06	2182.98	1645.91
11.200	8847.50	4670.08	3283.36	2594.28	2184.23	1647.24
11.225	8848.67	4671.24	3284.54	2595.50	2185.49	1648.58
11.250	8849.84	4672.40	3285.73	2596.71	2186.74	1649.92
11.275	8851.00	4673.57	3286.92	2597.93	2187.99	1651.26
11.300	8852.17	4674.73	3288.10	2599.15	2189.24	1652.59
11.325	8853.34	4675.89	3289.29	2600.37	2190.49	1653.93
11.350	8854.50	4677.06	3290.48	2601.59	2191.74	1655.27
11.375	8855.67	4678.22	3291.66	2602.81	2193.00	1656.61
11.400	8856.84	4679.38	3292.85	2604.03	2194.25	1657.95
11.425	8858.01	4680.55	3294.04	2605.25	2195.50	1659.30
11.450	8859.17	4681.71	3295.23	2606.46	2196.76	1660.64
11.475	8860.34	4682.87	3296.42	2607.69	2198.01	1661.98
11.500	8861.51	4684.04	3297.61	2608.91	2199.27	1663.32
11.525	8862.68	4685.20	3298.79	2610.13	2200.52	1664.67
11.550	8863.85	4686.37	3299.98	2611.35	2201.78	1666.01
11.575	8865.01	4687.53	3301.17	2612.57	2203.03	1667.36
11.600	8866.18	4688.69	3302.36	2613.79	2204.29	1668.70
11.625	8867.35	4689.86	3303.55	2615.01	2205.55	1670.05
11.650	8868.52	4691.02	3304.74	2616.24	2206.80	1671.39
11.675	8869.69	4692.19	3305.93	2617.46	2208.06	1672.74
11.700	8870.86	4693.35	3307.13	2618.68	2209.32	1674.09
11.725	8872.02	4694.52	3308.32	2619.91	2210.58	1675.44
11.750	8873.19	4695.69	3309.51	2621.13	2211.84	1676.79
11.775	8874.36	4696.85	3310.70	2622.35	2213.10	1678.14
11.800	8875.53	4698.02	3311.89	2623.58	2214.36	1679.49
11.825	8876.70	4699.18	3313.08	2624.80	2215.62	1680.84
11.850	8877.87	4700.35	3314.28	2626.03	2216.88	1682.19
11.875	8879.04	4701.52	3315.47	2627.26	2218.14	1683.54
11.900	8880.21	4702.68	3316.66	2628.48	2219.40	1684.89
11.925	8881.38	4703.85	3317.85	2629.71	2220.66	1686.25
11.950	8882.54	4705.02	3319.05	2630.93	2221.92	1687.60
11.975	8883.71	4706.18	3320.24	2632.16	2223.19	1688.96

$$\text{Your Monthly Payment} = \frac{\text{(Your Loan Amount) X (The Above Figure)}}{100{,}000}$$

MORTGAGE FACTORS TABLE

INTEREST RATE %	TERM OF LOAN IN YEARS					
	10	12.5	15	20	25	30
11.000	1377.51	1229.49	1136.60	1032.19	980.12	952.33
11.025	1378.92	1230.98	1138.17	1033.90	981.93	954.22
11.050	1380.34	1232.48	1139.74	1035.60	983.73	956.11
11.075	1381.75	1233.98	1141.32	1037.30	985.55	958.00
11.100	1383.17	1235.47	1142.89	1039.01	987.36	959.89
11.125	1384.59	1236.97	1144.46	1040.71	989.17	961.79
11.150	1386.01	1238.47	1146.04	1042.42	990.98	963.68
11.175	1387.43	1239.97	1147.62	1044.13	992.80	965.58
11.200	1388.85	1241.48	1149.19	1045.84	994.61	967.47
11.225	1390.27	1242.98	1150.77	1047.55	996.43	969.37
11.250	1391.69	1244.48	1152.35	1049.26	998.24	971.27
11.275	1393.12	1245.99	1153.93	1050.97	1000.06	973.17
11.300	1394.54	1247.49	1155.51	1052.69	1001.88	975.07
11.325	1395.97	1249.00	1157.09	1054.40	1003.70	976.97
11.350	1397.39	1250.50	1158.68	1056.12	1005.52	978.87
11.375	1398.82	1252.01	1160.26	1057.83	1007.35	980.77
11.400	1400.24	1253.52	1161.85	1059.55	1009.17	982.67
11.425	1401.67	1255.03	1163.43	1061.27	1010.99	984.58
11.450	1403.10	1256.54	1165.02	1062.99	1012.82	986.48
11.475	1404.53	1258.05	1166.61	1064.71	1014.65	988.39
11.500	1405.96	1259.56	1168.19	1066.43	1016.47	990.30
11.525	1407.39	1261.08	1169.78	1068.16	1018.30	992.20
11.550	1408.82	1262.59	1171.38	1069.88	1020.13	994.11
11.575	1410.25	1264.11	1172.97	1071.61	1021.96	996.02
11.600	1411.69	1265.62	1174.56	1073.33	1023.79	997.93
11.625	1413.12	1267.14	1176.15	1075.06	1025.63	999.84
11.650	1414.55	1268.66	1177.75	1076.79	1027.46	1001.76
11.675	1415.99	1270.17	1179.34	1078.52	1029.29	1003.67
11.700	1417.43	1271.69	1180.94	1080.25	1031.13	1005.58
11.725	1418.86	1273.21	1182.54	1081.98	1032.97	1007.50
11.750	1420.30	1274.74	1184.14	1083.71	1034.80	1009.41
11.775	1421.74	1276.26	1185.74	1085.45	1036.64	1011.33
11.800	1423.18	1277.78	1187.34	1087.18	1038.48	1013.25
11.825	1424.62	1279.30	1188.94	1088.92	1040.32	1015.17
11.850	1426.06	1280.83	1190.54	1090.65	1042.16	1017.09
11.875	1427.50	1282.35	1192.14	1092.39	1044.00	1019.01
11.900	1428.94	1283.88	1193.75	1094.13	1045.85	1020.93
11.925	1430.38	1285.41	1195.35	1095.87	1047.69	1022.85
11.950	1431.83	1286.93	1196.96	1097.61	1049.54	1024.77
11.975	1433.27	1288.46	1198.57	1099.35	1051.38	1026.69

Your Monthly Payment = (Your Loan Amount) X (The Above Figure) / 100,000

MORTGAGE FACTORS TABLE

INTEREST RATE %	TERM OF LOAN IN YEARS					
	1	2	3	4	5	7.5
12.000	8884.88	4707.35	3321.44	2633.39	2224.45	1690.31
12.025	8886.05	4708.52	3322.63	2634.62	2225.71	1691.67
12.050	8887.22	4709.69	3323.82	2635.84	2226.98	1693.02
12.075	8888.39	4710.86	3325.02	2637.07	2228.24	1694.38
12.100	8889.56	4712.02	3326.21	2638.30	2229.51	1695.74
12.125	8890.73	4713.19	3327.41	2639.53	2230.77	1697.10
12.150	8891.90	4714.36	3328.60	2640.76	2232.04	1698.45
12.175	8893.07	4715.53	3329.80	2641.99	2233.30	1699.81
12.200	8894.24	4716.70	3331.00	2643.22	2234.57	1701.17
12.225	8895.41	4717.87	3332.19	2644.45	2235.84	1702.53
12.250	8896.58	4719.04	3333.39	2645.68	2237.10	1703.89
12.275	8897.75	4720.20	3334.59	2646.91	2238.37	1705.26
12.300	8898.92	4721.37	3335.78	2648.14	2239.64	1706.62
12.325	8900.09	4722.54	3336.98	2649.37	2240.91	1707.98
12.350	8901.27	4723.71	3338.18	2650.61	2242.18	1709.34
12.375	8902.44	4724.88	3339.38	2651.84	2243.45	1710.71
12.400	8903.61	4726.05	3340.57	2653.07	2244.72	1712.07
12.425	8904.78	4727.22	3341.77	2654.30	2245.99	1713.44
12.450	8905.95	4728.39	3342.97	2655.54	2247.26	1714.80
12.475	8907.12	4729.57	3344.17	2656.77	2248.53	1716.17
12.500	8908.29	4730.74	3345.37	2658.00	2249.80	1717.54
12.525	8909.46	4731.91	3346.57	2659.24	2251.07	1718.90
12.550	8910.63	4733.08	3347.77	2660.47	2252.34	1720.27
12.575	8911.81	4734.25	3348.97	2661.71	2253.62	1721.64
12.600	8912.98	4735.42	3350.17	2662.94	2254.89	1723.01
12.625	8914.15	4736.59	3351.37	2664.18	2256.16	1724.38
12.650	8915.32	4737.76	3352.57	2665.42	2257.44	1725.75
12.675	8916.49	4738.94	3353.77	2666.65	2258.71	1727.12
12.700	8917.66	4740.11	3354.97	2667.89	2259.98	1728.49
12.725	8918.84	4741.28	3356.17	2669.13	2261.26	1729.86
12.750	8920.01	4742.45	3357.37	2670.36	2262.54	1731.24
12.775	8921.18	4743.63	3358.57	2671.60	2263.81	1732.61
12.800	8922.35	4744.80	3359.78	2672.84	2265.09	1733.98
12.825	8923.52	4745.97	3360.98	2674.08	2266.36	1735.36
12.850	8924.70	4747.14	3362.18	2675.32	2267.64	1736.73
12.875	8925.87	4748.32	3363.38	2676.55	2268.92	1738.11
12.900	8927.04	4749.49	3364.59	2677.79	2270.20	1739.49
12.925	8928.21	4750.67	3365.79	2679.03	2271.47	1740.86
12.950	8929.39	4751.84	3366.99	2680.27	2272.75	1742.24
12.975	8930.56	4753.01	3368.20	2681.51	2274.03	1743.62

$$\text{Your Monthly Payment} = \frac{\text{(Your Loan Amount) X (The Above Figure)}}{100{,}000}$$

 12.000% TO 12.975%

MORTGAGE FACTORS TABLE

INTEREST RATE %	TERM OF LOAN IN YEARS					
	10	12.5	15	20	25	30
12.000	1434.71	1289.99	1200.17	1101.09	1053.23	1028.62
12.025	1436.16	1291.52	1201.78	1102.83	1055.08	1030.54
12.050	1437.61	1293.05	1203.39	1104.58	1056.93	1032.47
12.075	1439.05	1294.59	1205.00	1106.32	1058.78	1034.39
12.100	1440.50	1296.12	1206.61	1108.07	1060.63	1036.32
12.125	1441.95	1297.65	1208.23	1109.82	1062.48	1038.25
12.150	1443.40	1299.19	1209.84	1111.57	1064.33	1040.18
12.175	1444.85	1300.72	1211.45	1113.32	1066.18	1042.11
12.200	1446.30	1302.26	1213.07	1115.07	1068.04	1044.04
12.225	1447.75	1303.80	1214.69	1116.82	1069.89	1045.97
12.250	1449.20	1305.34	1216.30	1118.57	1071.75	1047.90
12.275	1450.66	1306.87	1217.92	1120.32	1073.61	1049.83
12.300	1452.11	1308.41	1219.54	1122.08	1075.46	1051.77
12.325	1453.56	1309.96	1221.16	1123.83	1077.32	1053.70
12.350	1455.02	1311.50	1222.78	1125.59	1079.18	1055.64
12.375	1456.48	1313.04	1224.40	1127.35	1081.04	1057.57
12.400	1457.93	1314.58	1226.03	1129.10	1082.90	1059.51
12.425	1459.39	1316.13	1227.65	1130.86	1084.77	1061.45
12.450	1460.85	1317.67	1229.28	1132.62	1086.63	1063.38
12.475	1462.31	1319.22	1230.90	1134.38	1088.49	1065.32
12.500	1463.77	1320.76	1232.53	1136.15	1090.36	1067.26
12.525	1465.23	1322.31	1234.15	1137.91	1092.23	1069.20
12.550	1466.69	1323.86	1235.78	1139.67	1094.09	1071.14
12.575	1468.15	1325.41	1237.41	1141.44	1095.96	1073.09
12.600	1469.61	1326.96	1239.04	1143.20	1097.83	1075.03
12.625	1471.08	1328.51	1240.67	1144.97	1099.70	1076.97
12.650	1472.54	1330.06	1242.31	1146.74	1101.57	1078.92
12.675	1474.00	1331.61	1243.94	1148.51	1103.44	1080.86
12.700	1475.47	1333.17	1245.57	1150.27	1105.31	1082.81
12.725	1476.94	1334.72	1247.21	1152.05	1107.18	1084.75
12.750	1478.40	1336.28	1248.84	1153.82	1109.06	1086.70
12.775	1479.87	1337.83	1250.48	1155.59	1110.93	1088.65
12.800	1481.34	1339.39	1252.12	1157.36	1112.81	1090.59
12.825	1482.81	1340.95	1253.75	1159.14	1114.68	1092.54
12.850	1484.28	1342.51	1255.39	1160.91	1116.56	1094.49
12.875	1485.75	1344.06	1257.03	1162.69	1118.44	1096.44
12.900	1487.22	1345.63	1258.67	1164.46	1120.32	1098.39
12.925	1488.69	1347.19	1260.32	1166.24	1122.20	1100.35
12.950	1490.16	1348.75	1261.96	1168.02	1124.08	1102.30
12.975	1491.64	1350.31	1263.60	1169.80	1125.96	1104.25

$$\text{Your Monthly Payment} = \frac{\text{(Your Loan Amount) X (The Above Figure)}}{100{,}000}$$

MORTGAGE FACTORS TABLE

INTEREST RATE %	TERM OF LOAN IN YEARS					
	1	2	3	4	5	7.5
13.000	8931.73	4754.19	3369.40	2682.75	2275.31	1745.00
13.025	8932.91	4755.36	3370.60	2684.00	2276.59	1746.37
13.050	8934.08	4756.54	3371.81	2685.24	2277.87	1747.75
13.075	8935.25	4757.71	3373.01	2686.48	2279.15	1749.13
13.100	8936.42	4758.89	3374.22	2687.72	2280.43	1750.52
13.125	8937.60	4760.06	3375.42	2688.96	2281.72	1751.90
13.150	8938.77	4761.24	3376.63	2690.21	2283.00	1753.28
13.175	8939.95	4762.41	3377.84	2691.45	2284.28	1754.66
13.200	8941.12	4763.59	3379.04	2692.69	2285.56	1756.05
13.225	8942.29	4764.76	3380.25	2693.94	2286.85	1757.43
13.250	8943.47	4765.94	3381.45	2695.18	2288.13	1758.81
13.275	8944.64	4767.11	3382.66	2696.42	2289.41	1760.20
13.300	8945.81	4768.29	3383.87	2697.67	2290.70	1761.58
13.325	8946.99	4769.47	3385.08	2698.91	2291.98	1762.97
13.350	8948.16	4770.64	3386.28	2700.16	2293.27	1764.36
13.375	8949.34	4771.82	3387.49	2701.40	2294.55	1765.74
13.400	8950.51	4773.00	3388.70	2702.65	2295.84	1767.13
13.425	8951.68	4774.17	3389.91	2703.90	2297.13	1768.52
13.450	8952.86	4775.35	3391.12	2705.14	2298.41	1769.91
13.475	8954.03	4776.53	3392.32	2706.39	2299.70	1771.30
13.500	8955.21	4777.71	3393.53	2707.64	2300.99	1772.69
13.525	8956.38	4778.88	3394.74	2708.88	2302.28	1774.08
13.550	8957.56	4780.06	3395.95	2710.13	2303.57	1775.47
13.575	8958.73	4781.24	3397.16	2711.38	2304.86	1776.86
13.600	8959.91	4782.42	3398.37	2712.63	2306.14	1778.26
13.625	8961.08	4783.60	3399.58	2713.88	2307.43	1779.65
13.650	8962.26	4784.78	3400.79	2715.13	2308.72	1781.04
13.675	8963.43	4785.95	3402.00	2716.38	2310.02	1782.44
13.700	8964.61	4787.13	3403.22	2717.63	2311.31	1783.83
13.725	8965.78	4788.31	3404.43	2718.88	2312.60	1785.23
13.750	8966.96	4789.49	3405.64	2720.13	2313.89	1786.62
13.775	8968.13	4790.67	3406.85	2721.38	2315.18	1788.02
13.800	8969.31	4791.85	3408.06	2722.63	2316.47	1789.42
13.825	8970.48	4793.03	3409.27	2723.88	2317.77	1790.81
13.850	8971.66	4794.21	3410.49	2725.13	2319.06	1792.21
13.875	8972.84	4795.39	3411.70	2726.39	2320.35	1793.61
13.900	8974.01	4796.57	3412.91	2727.64	2321.65	1795.01
13.925	8975.19	4797.75	3414.13	2728.89	2322.94	1796.41
13.950	8976.36	4798.93	3415.34	2730.15	2324.24	1797.81
13.975	8977.54	4800.11	3416.55	2731.40	2325.53	1799.21

$$\text{Your Monthly Payment} = \frac{\text{(Your Loan Amount) X (The Above Figure)}}{100{,}000}$$

MORTGAGE FACTORS TABLE

INTEREST RATE %	TERM OF LOAN IN YEARS					
	10	12.5	15	20	25	30
13.000	1493.11	1351.87	1265.25	1171.58	1127.84	1106.20
13.025	1494.59	1353.44	1266.89	1173.36	1129.72	1108.16
13.050	1496.06	1355.00	1268.54	1175.14	1131.61	1110.11
13.075	1497.54	1356.57	1270.19	1176.93	1133.49	1112.07
13.100	1499.02	1358.14	1271.83	1178.71	1135.38	1114.03
13.125	1500.49	1359.70	1273.48	1180.50	1137.26	1115.98
13.150	1501.97	1361.27	1275.13	1182.28	1139.15	1117.94
13.175	1503.45	1362.84	1276.78	1184.07	1141.04	1119.90
13.200	1504.93	1364.41	1278.44	1185.86	1142.93	1121.86
13.225	1506.41	1365.98	1280.09	1187.65	1144.82	1123.82
13.250	1507.89	1367.55	1281.74	1189.44	1146.71	1125.78
13.275	1509.38	1369.13	1283.40	1191.23	1148.60	1127.74
13.300	1510.86	1370.70	1285.05	1193.02	1150.49	1129.70
13.325	1512.34	1372.27	1286.71	1194.81	1152.38	1131.66
13.350	1513.83	1373.85	1288.36	1196.60	1154.27	1133.63
13.375	1515.31	1375.42	1290.02	1198.40	1156.17	1135.59
13.400	1516.80	1377.00	1291.68	1200.19	1158.06	1137.55
13.425	1518.28	1378.58	1293.34	1201.99	1159.96	1139.52
13.450	1519.77	1380.15	1295.00	1203.78	1161.85	1141.48
13.475	1521.26	1381.73	1296.66	1205.58	1163.75	1143.45
13.500	1522.75	1383.31	1298.32	1207.38	1165.65	1145.42
13.525	1524.24	1384.89	1299.99	1209.18	1167.55	1147.38
13.550	1525.73	1386.48	1301.65	1210.98	1169.45	1149.35
13.575	1527.22	1388.06	1303.32	1212.78	1171.35	1151.32
13.600	1528.71	1389.64	1304.98	1214.58	1173.25	1153.29
13.625	1530.20	1391.22	1306.65	1216.38	1175.15	1155.26
13.650	1531.69	1392.81	1308.31	1218.19	1177.05	1157.23
13.675	1533.19	1394.39	1309.98	1219.99	1178.96	1159.20
13.700	1534.68	1395.98	1311.65	1221.80	1180.86	1161.17
13.725	1536.18	1397.57	1313.32	1223.60	1182.77	1163.14
13.750	1537.67	1399.16	1314.99	1225.41	1184.67	1165.12
13.775	1539.17	1400.74	1316.66	1227.22	1186.58	1167.09
13.800	1540.67	1402.33	1318.34	1229.03	1188.48	1169.06
13.825	1542.16	1403.92	1320.01	1230.84	1190.39	1171.04
13.850	1543.66	1405.52	1321.68	1232.65	1192.30	1173.01
13.875	1545.16	1407.11	1323.36	1234.46	1194.21	1174.99
13.900	1546.66	1408.70	1325.03	1236.27	1196.12	1176.97
13.925	1548.16	1410.29	1326.71	1238.08	1198.03	1178.94
13.950	1549.66	1411.89	1328.39	1239.90	1199.94	1180.92
13.975	1551.17	1413.48	1330.07	1241.71	1201.85	1182.90

$$\text{Your Monthly Payment} = \frac{\text{(Your Loan Amount) X (The Above Figure)}}{100{,}000}$$

MORTGAGE FACTORS TABLE

INTEREST RATE %	TERM OF LOAN IN YEARS					
	1	2	3	4	5	7.5
14.000	8978.72	4801.29	3417.77	2732.65	2326.83	1800.61
14.025	8979.89	4802.47	3418.98	2733.91	2328.13	1802.02
14.050	8981.07	4803.66	3420.20	2735.16	2329.42	1803.42
14.075	8982.25	4804.84	3421.41	2736.42	2330.72	1804.82
14.100	8983.42	4806.02	3422.63	2737.67	2332.02	1806.23
14.125	8984.60	4807.20	3423.84	2738.93	2333.32	1807.63
14.150	8985.78	4808.38	3425.06	2740.18	2334.61	1809.04
14.175	8986.95	4809.56	3426.27	2741.44	2335.91	1810.44
14.200	8988.13	4810.75	3427.49	2742.70	2337.21	1811.85
14.225	8989.31	4811.93	3428.71	2743.95	2338.51	1813.26
14.250	8990.48	4813.11	3429.92	2745.21	2339.81	1814.66
14.275	8991.66	4814.29	3431.14	2746.47	2341.11	1816.07
14.300	8992.84	4815.48	3432.36	2747.73	2342.41	1817.48
14.325	8994.02	4816.66	3433.57	2748.98	2343.71	1818.89
14.350	8995.19	4817.84	3434.79	2750.24	2345.02	1820.30
14.375	8996.37	4819.03	3436.01	2751.50	2346.32	1821.71
14.400	8997.55	4820.21	3437.23	2752.76	2347.62	1823.12
14.425	8998.73	4821.40	3438.45	2754.02	2348.92	1824.53
14.450	8999.90	4822.58	3439.66	2755.28	2350.23	1825.94
14.475	9001.08	4823.76	3440.88	2756.54	2351.53	1827.36
14.500	9002.26	4824.95	3442.10	2757.80	2352.83	1828.77
14.525	9003.44	4826.13	3443.32	2759.06	2354.14	1830.18
14.550	9004.62	4827.32	3444.54	2760.32	2355.44	1831.60
14.575	9005.79	4828.50	3445.76	2761.58	2356.75	1833.01
14.600	9006.97	4829.69	3446.98	2762.85	2358.05	1834.43
14.625	9008.15	4830.87	3448.20	2764.11	2359.36	1835.84
14.650	9009.33	4832.06	3449.42	2765.37	2360.67	1837.26
14.675	9010.51	4833.24	3450.64	2766.63	2361.97	1838.68
14.700	9011.69	4834.43	3451.86	2767.90	2363.28	1840.09
14.725	9012.86	4835.61	3453.09	2769.16	2364.59	1841.51
14.750	9014.04	4836.80	3454.31	2770.42	2365.90	1842.93
14.775	9015.22	4837.99	3455.53	2771.69	2367.20	1844.35
14.800	9016.40	4839.17	3456.75	2772.95	2368.51	1845.77
14.825	9017.58	4840.36	3457.97	2774.22	2369.82	1847.19
14.850	9018.76	4841.55	3459.20	2775.48	2371.13	1848.61
14.875	9019.94	4842.73	3460.42	2776.75	2372.44	1850.03
14.900	9021.12	4843.92	3461.64	2778.01	2373.75	1851.46
14.925	9022.30	4845.11	3462.87	2779.28	2375.06	1852.88
14.950	9023.48	4846.29	3464.09	2780.55	2376.37	1854.30
14.975	9024.66	4847.48	3465.31	2781.81	2377.69	1855.73

$$\text{Your Monthly Payment} = \frac{\text{(Your Loan Amount) X (The Above Figure)}}{100{,}000}$$

MORTGAGE FACTORS TABLE

INTEREST RATE %	TERM OF LOAN IN YEARS					
	10	12.5	15	20	25	30
14.000	1552.67	1415.08	1331.75	1243.53	1203.77	1184.88
14.025	1554.17	1416.67	1333.43	1245.34	1205.68	1186.86
14.050	1555.68	1418.27	1335.11	1247.16	1207.59	1188.84
14.075	1557.18	1419.87	1336.79	1248.98	1209.51	1190.82
14.100	1558.69	1421.47	1338.47	1250.80	1211.42	1192.80
14.125	1560.19	1423.07	1340.16	1252.61	1213.34	1194.78
14.150	1561.70	1424.67	1341.84	1254.43	1215.26	1196.76
14.175	1563.21	1426.27	1343.52	1256.26	1217.18	1198.74
14.200	1564.72	1427.87	1345.21	1258.08	1219.09	1200.72
14.225	1566.23	1429.48	1346.90	1259.90	1221.01	1202.71
14.250	1567.74	1431.08	1348.58	1261.72	1222.93	1204.69
14.275	1569.25	1432.68	1350.27	1263.55	1224.85	1206.68
14.300	1570.76	1434.29	1351.96	1265.37	1226.77	1208.66
14.325	1572.27	1435.90	1353.65	1267.20	1228.70	1210.65
14.350	1573.78	1437.50	1355.34	1269.03	1230.62	1212.63
14.375	1575.30	1439.11	1357.03	1270.85	1232.54	1214.62
14.400	1576.81	1440.72	1358.73	1272.68	1234.47	1216.61
14.425	1578.32	1442.33	1360.42	1274.51	1236.39	1218.59
14.450	1579.84	1443.94	1362.12	1276.34	1238.32	1220.58
14.475	1581.36	1445.55	1363.81	1278.17	1240.24	1222.57
14.500	1582.87	1447.16	1365.51	1280.00	1242.17	1224.56
14.525	1584.39	1448.77	1367.20	1281.84	1244.10	1226.55
14.550	1585.91	1450.39	1368.90	1283.67	1246.02	1228.54
14.575	1587.43	1452.00	1370.60	1285.50	1247.95	1230.53
14.600	1588.95	1453.61	1372.30	1287.34	1249.88	1232.52
14.625	1590.47	1455.23	1374.00	1289.17	1251.81	1234.51
14.650	1591.99	1456.85	1375.70	1291.01	1253.74	1236.51
14.675	1593.51	1458.46	1377.40	1292.84	1255.67	1238.50
14.700	1595.03	1460.08	1379.10	1294.68	1257.60	1240.49
14.725	1596.56	1461.70	1380.80	1296.52	1259.54	1242.49
14.750	1598.08	1463.32	1382.51	1298.36	1261.47	1244.48
14.775	1599.60	1464.94	1384.21	1300.20	1263.40	1246.48
14.800	1601.13	1466.56	1385.92	1302.04	1265.34	1248.47
14.825	1602.65	1468.18	1387.63	1303.88	1267.27	1250.47
14.850	1604.18	1469.80	1389.33	1305.72	1269.21	1252.46
14.875	1605.71	1471.43	1391.04	1307.57	1271.14	1254.46
14.900	1607.24	1473.05	1392.75	1309.41	1273.08	1256.46
14.925	1608.76	1474.67	1394.46	1311.26	1275.02	1258.45
14.950	1610.29	1476.30	1396.17	1313.10	1276.96	1260.45
14.975	1611.82	1477.93	1397.88	1314.95	1278.90	1262.45

$$\text{Your Monthly Payment} = \frac{\text{(Your Loan Amount) X (The Above Figure)}}{100{,}000}$$

PART FOUR: APPENDICES

APPENDIX #1: GLOSSARY

Adjustable Rate Mortgage (ARM): A mortgage where the interest rate and therefore the monthly loan payment, can change either up or down from time to time.

Amortize: To pay back a loan by making periodic payments. In general, mortgages *self-amortize.* That is, they are completely paid back by the end of their term. An *unamortized* loan is one where only *interest* payments are made. At the due date, the entire *principal* borrowed must still be repaid. A *partially amortized* loan is partly paid back over its term, but a balance (called a *balloon*) will remain. That balance will have to be repaid in a lump sum, possibly requiring refinancing of the property.

Amortization Schedule: See *Pre-Payment Schedule.*

Balance of Loan: The amount of *principal* remaining to be paid after each monthly mortgage payment.

Balloon: The *principal* amount still due when a loan's term ends prior to the complete repayment of the loan (see *Amortize*).

Banker's Secret Pre-Payment System: A method of accumulating very large savings by making relatively small advance payments on home mortgages and other loans. The payments and resulting savings are tracked on *pre-payment schedules* designed for easy record keeping.

Bi-Weekly Mortgage: Mortgages that are repaid at the rate of 1/2 of a typical loan's monthly payment every 2 weeks (26 times a year). This effectively designs in a pre-payment equal to 1 monthly payment per year, which speeds up the loan's retirement, and therefore reduces the loan's overall cost.

Default: Failure to live up to the agreements of a contract. For example, by missing mortgage payments.

Equity: That portion of a property's worth which represents the fair market value, less the outstanding balance of all mortgages and other *liens*. Also see *Second Mortgage*.

Fixed Interest: The rate of interest remains constant for the life of the loan.

Foreclosure: The procedure used by a *mortgagee* (bank) to force the sale of mortgaged property on which the owner has *defaulted*. The proceeds from the auction are used to repay the debt.

Graduated Payment Mortgage (GPM) : Monthly payments increase at a set rate for the first 5 to 10 years of the loan, then level off. They are intended to keep payments in line with the homeowner's projected income increases, and can involve *negative amortization* in the early years

Home Equity Loan: See *Second Mortgage*.

Interest: A fee paid to a lender for the privilege of borrowing money, usually expressed as an annual percentage rate (e.g., 10%).

Irregular Pre-Payment: An additional sum sent in with any mortgage payment. *A Banker's Secret* describes *Irregular Pre-Payments* as a method whereby homeowners can track their savings by varying the amount of their pre-payments every month to match the principal payments shown on their pre-payment schedule.

Lien: A claim against property. As part of the process of obtaining a mortgage, the borrower gives the lender a *lien* on the property being financed. Should the homeowner *default*, the *lien* holder can *foreclose*.

Mortgage: Actually, a pledge of property as security for repayment of a loan. This term is commonly used to refer to the loan itself.

Mortgagee: The person or bank who lends the mortgage money.

Mortgagor: The person who borrows the mortgage money.

Negative Amortization: When the monthly payment is so low that it does not cover all the interest due that month, the balance of the interest due will be added to the *principal.* In this type of loan, the amount owed actually increases month after month.

Pre-Payment: A payment in advance of its due date. Frequently used to mean payment of principal in full. In *A Banker's Secret,* the term *Pre-Payment* implies small advance payments applied toward the outstanding balance, at either *Regular* or *Irregular* intervals, during the loan's term.

Pre-Payment Schedule: A chart showing each loan payment broken down into its interest and principal components. The balance due, after crediting the principal portion of the payment is also normally shown. The *Banker's Secret Pre-Payment Schedules* are designed for easy record keeping and for tracking savings to the penny.

Principal: The sum of money that was borrowed and/or remains due. The outstanding debt against which interest is being charged is referred to as the *principal.* On *pre-payment schedules*, the word *principal* is used to mean the component of that month's payment which is applied towards the *equity* of the loan. The word *balance* is used to mean the amount of *principal* still due to be repaid.

Refinance: To replace one loan with another (usually at a lower interest rate).

Regular Pre-Payment: A set amount sent in every month along with the monthly mortgage payment. For example, $25 a month.

Secondary Mortgage Market: When banks write mortgages, they frequently turn around and sell them on the *Secondary Mortgage Market* to other investors.

Second Mortgage: Available for some portion of the difference between the property's market value and the balance due on the first mortgage. Recently, *home equity* lines of credit have taken the place of second mortgages. With a home equity line of credit, you generally have the right to borrow, as needed, up to a specified limit. But remember: *second mortgages*, like *home equity* loans, place a lien on your home. If not paid back in accordance with your agreement, your property may be *foreclosed.*

APPENDIX #2: THE BASIC MATH

Between our various Pre-Payment Tables and our Software, no one should ever *have* to do hand calculations. But, if you'd like to work up some figures, you'll be happy to know that pre-payment math is really quite simple.

PREPARING YOUR OWN PRE-PAYMENT SCHEDULE

If you want to make your own pre-payment schedule, here is the procedure to follow for a self-amortizing loan. The numbers refer to the example we've used throughout this book. Substitute the numbers from your loan.

First, write down the figures for your loan:

Let A = Loan Amount
Ours = $75,000 Yours = ______________
i = Annual Interest Rate, expressed in decimal form
Ours = 0.10 Yours = ______________
$i \div 12$ = Monthly Interest Rate
Ours = 0.10 divided by 12 Yours = ______________
M = Monthly Payment, less insurance and taxes.
Ours = $658.18 Yours = ______________

We'll be trying to find these amounts:

I_1 = The 1st interest payment (I_2, the 2nd; I_3, the 3rd; etc.)
P_1 = The 1st principal payment (P_2, the 2nd; P_3, the 3rd ...)
B_1 = The principal balance after making payment #1 (B_2, after making payment #2; B_3, after making payment #3; etc.)

Below are the formulas we'll be using:

FORMULAS

$$I_1 = (i \div 12) \times A$$
$$P_1 = M - I_1$$
$$B_1 = A - P_1$$

Follow our example and then do the calculations for your mortgage or loan:

OUR EXAMPLE

$$I_1 = (0.10 \div 12) \times (75{,}000.00) = 625.00$$
$$P_1 = (658.18) - (625.00) = 33.18$$
$$B_1 = (75{,}000.00) - (33.18) = 74{,}966.82$$

These are the numbers which appear on our sample pre-payment schedule for payment #1:

Interest Payment	=	625.00
Principal Payment	=	33.18
Balance Due	=	74,966.82

Look at Figure #2, both to confirm the numbers and to see a good way to set up the schedule for yourself.

The calculations for payment #2 would be as follows:

FORMULAS

$$I_2 = (i \div 12) \times B_1$$
$$P_2 = M - I_2$$
$$B_2 = B_1 - P_2$$

OUR EXAMPLE

$$I_2 = (0.10 \div 12) \times (74{,}966.82) = 624.72$$
$$P_2 = (658.18) - (624.72) = 33.46$$
$$B_2 = (74{,}966.82) - (33.46) = 74{,}933.36$$

These are the numbers which appear on the pre-payment schedule for payment #2:

Interest Payment	=	624.72
Principal Payment	=	33.46
Balance Due	=	74,933.36

Each of the subsequent payments would be calculated in exactly the same way -- payment by payment, line by line. If you have the patience to make these calculations, go to it! Otherwise, obtain a pre-payment schedule, our *Banker's Secret Software*, or just send in whatever extra money you have each month, and let the bank's computer do the calculations and record keeping.

CALCULATING TOTAL INTEREST COSTS

As you probably noticed, the actual interest costs for a wide selection of 30 year monthly loans can be read directly from the third column of the appropriate Bi-Weekly Payment Table in PART THREE. However, it's easy enough to make a quick, rough calculation by hand.

Let's go back to our example for a moment. The bank expects a check in the amount of $658.18 every month for 30 years (or 360 months). Even though you only borrowed $75,000, you will eventually repay ($658.18 x 360 months =) $236,944.80. Of the $236,944.80, roughly $161,944.80 would be interest ($236,944.80 - $75,000 = $161,944.80).

Note: Because the last payment is typically smaller than the rest, the total repayment and interest figures will generally be somewhat less than these "quick" calculations.

CALCULATING PRE-PAYMENT SAVINGS

Let's say you wanted to convert our sample $75,000 loan from 30 years to 20 years. You could calculate the monthly payment using the formula we'll give you below. Or far easier, you could just look up the monthly payment for the 20 year loan on the appropriate Monthly Loan Payment Table.

However you come up with it, you would find that $723.77 a month will amortize this loan in 20 years (or 240 months). Compared to a 30 year payback, that represents a pre-payment of $65.59 each month ($723.77 - $658.18 = $65.59). By prepaying $65.59, on a *Regular* basis for 20 years, you would pay off your loan at a total cost of $173,704.80 ($723.77 x 240 months).

As you'll recall from an earlier calculation, the total payback for the 30 year loan would have been (approximately) $236,944.80. Therefore, converting to the 20 year term will save you some $63,240 in interest costs ($236,944.80 - $173,704.80).

Of course, you could also turn directly to our Debt Reduction Tables, where you would find that a *Regular* monthly prepayment of $65.59 would pay this loan off in 20 years, while saving $63,239.

CALCULATING THE MONTHLY PAYMENT

You would have to love math to want to calculate your loan's monthly payment. And, if you do, you'll need M's complicated formula:

$$M = A\left[\frac{\frac{i}{12}\left(1+\frac{i}{12}\right)^{12n}}{\left(1+\frac{i}{12}\right)^{12n}-1}\right]$$

Where n = the term of the loan in years

By the way, if yours is a bi-weekly loan, you'll need to replace all of the "12's" with "26's." And, remember that "n" will not be 30 years, but will be shorter (in the range of 18 to 22 years ... with the weeks converted to decimals).

The bottom line is that pre-paying -- however you calculate the numbers -- will save you a fortune. Happy savings!

GOOD ADVICE PRESS

Box 78 **Elizaville, NY 12523** **914-758-1400**

ORDERING INFORMATION

1. **A Banker's Secret** **$9.95**

We hope this copy of *A Banker's Secret* has put you on the track to early retirement from debt. Please consider ordering gift copies for your homeowning friends, colleagues, clients, and relatives. We'll happily enclose a gift card signed in accordance with your instructions.

2. **The Banker's Secret Software** **$29.95**

Our user friendly IBM® compatible software computes pre-payment schedules for adjustable, fixed rate, and bi-weekly loans. Each schedule lets you accurately track your interest savings -- while you verify that your bank's records are correct.

This software answers important "What If?" questions -- for example, *how much will I save with a $25 pre-payment? How about $50?* You'll find it invaluable when shopping for a loan or considering refinancing -- *if I can afford $650 a month, how much can I borrow at 10% for 30 years? For 15 years?*

Whether you have one loan or many, and whatever your personal finances, our software allows you unlimited flexibility when pre-paying. We will ship a 5.25 inch diskette unless you request a 3.5 inch one (available at no extra charge).

UPGRADE: If you already have *A Banker's Secret* and don't want another copy, let us know you have the book and deduct $9.95 from the software price.

3. **Personalized Pre-Payment Schedule** **$12.95**

Pre-Payment Schedules are indispensable for accurately tracking your savings. If you don't have access to an IBM® compatible computer, we can run a personalized schedule for you. Just fill in the DATA SHEET on the following page, and return it with the Order Form. Your personalized schedule will be computed, printed, and back on its way to you, generally, within 24 hours of our receipt of your order.

★ DATA SHEET ★

We suggest that you read *A Banker's Secret* before ordering your personalized Pre-Payment Schedule. Please make sure to provide us with exact, current figures. If you are unsure, please verify your loan's details with your lender. Your personalized schedule can only be as accurate as the information you provide.

To obtain your schedule, just fill in these blanks and mail us a copy of this Data Sheet along with your payment:

1. **ORIGINAL LOAN AMOUNT:** $______________

2. **CURRENT LOAN BALANCE:** $______________

3. **CURRENT INTEREST RATE:** ______________%

4. **ORIGINAL TERM OF LOAN:** __________**YEARS**

5. **PAYMENTS ARE MADE: [ ] MONTHLY [ ] BI-WEEKLY**
(If neither is checked, we will assume yours is a monthly loan).

6. **CURRENT PAYMENT AMOUNT:** $______________
(Principal plus Interest, <u>only</u>. Do *not* include taxes or insurance, even if you include these payments in your mortgage check.)

7. **CHOOSE ONE OF THE FOLLOWING SCHEDULES:**
(If none is selected, we will run an *Irregular* Schedule for you.)

[ ] **A. IRREGULAR**. I want the most flexibility.

[ ] **B. REGULAR**. I will add the following amount to each loan payment (e.g., $25): $______________

[ ] **C. REFINANCER'S SPECIAL**. Before refinancing, my payments were: $______________

[ ] **D. DEBT REDUCTION**. I want to pay off my loan in: ______Years and _______ Months from now.

WE'RE HERE TO HELP. If, after reading *A Banker's Secret* and calling your lender, you are still unsure of your numbers, just fill in the Data Sheet as best you can. Enclose copies of both your loan agreement and your current statement along with the Data Sheet and Order Form.

FEEL FREE TO PHOTOCOPY THIS PAGE

FEEL FREE TO PHOTOCOPY THIS ORDER FORM

QTY	DESCRIPTION	COST	TOTAL
	1. A BANKER'S SECRET	**$ 9.95**	
	2. THE SOFTWARE [ ] Check here for a 3.5" disk	**29.95**	
	3. PRE-PAYMENT SCHEDULE (Complete DATA SHEET)	**12.95**	
	4. GIFT ORDER(S) (Please list on a separate sheet)		

CREDIT CARD ORDERS CALL 914-758-1400 Please have your Visa, MC or AMEX ready.	**POSTAGE AND HANDLING**	**$ 2.00**
	SUB-TOTAL	
	SALES TAX (New York State residents only)	
	TOTAL	

[ ] Enclosed is my check to: **GOOD ADVICE PRESS**

[ ] Please charge my: [ ] **VISA** [ ] **MC** [ ] **AMEX**

Account #: ______________________________ Expires: _______

Signature: ____________________________________
(Credit card orders must be signed)

PLEASE PRINT

Name____

Address______________________________________

City__________________ **State**______ **Zip**_________

PLEASE MAIL THIS ORDER FORM TO:

GOOD ADVICE PRESS
BOX 78
ELIZAVILLE, NEW YORK 12523

GOOD ADVICE PRESS

Box 78 **Elizaville, NY 12523** **914-758-1400**

Dear Reader,

I hope *A Banker's Secret* has convinced you to pre-pay your mortgage. All it takes is a little will power, and your pocket change ... money that none of us would ever notice, miss, or otherwise invest. The benefits to your family ... both financial and emotional ... will be tremendous!

All of us at *Good Advice Press* believe in debt-free living and want to make it as easy as possible for everyone to achieve that goal. You can help us. I'd very much appreciate getting your reactions to *A Banker's Secret.* What did we do well? What could we have done better?

It was nearly 25 years ago that my brother Sam taught me how to profit from making small mortgage pre-payments. Since then, we've started untold thousands of families on their way to extraordinary interest savings. But, there are still millions of families who needlessly pay too much in interest. Please share our "secret" with your friends and relatives.

And remember, the sooner you begin your personalized pre-payment program, the faster your net worth will grow. I guarantee it!

Happy Savings,

Marc Eisenson